Abigail F. Van Tassel

AUTISM

Identification, Education, and Treatment

AUTISM

Identification, Education, and Treatment

Edited by
Dianne E. Berkell
Long Island University

1992
LAWRENCE ERLBAUM ASSOCIATES, PUBLISHERS
Hillsdale, New Jersey Hove and London

Lawrence Erlbaum Associates, Inc., Publishers
365 Broadway
Hillsdale, New Jersey 07642

Library of Congress Cataloging in Publication Data

Autism : identification, education, and treatment / edited by Dianne E. Berkell.
p. cm.
Includes bibliographical references and index.
1. Autism. I. Berkell, Dianne E.
RJ506.A9A9223 1992
618.92'8982—dc20 91-24893
CIP

Printed in the United States of America
10 9 8 7 6 5 4 3

To the parents of children and adults with autism, who have had to fight innumerable battles for the rights of their children over the years. May the next decade bring increased understanding and awareness of their needs and those of their children.

Contents

Preface

Autism has been the focus of extensive study and controversial debate. Issues pertaining to its etiology, identification, treatment, and education continue to intrigue those who come into contact with this extreme form of psychopathology. This volume has been designed to provide both an understanding of the autistic syndrome and information regarding effective diagnostic and treatment approaches. The book is comprised of three major sections dealing with topics related to the characteristics and needs of children and adults with autism.

Part I introduces the reader to the field of autism. The autistic syndrome is defined, and an overview of past and current philosophies and practices in this field are presented. Research and development in related disciplines, such as genetics, biochemistry, and psychology are examined for relevance to treatment.

Part II deals with intervention practices and strategies. Approaches to assessment and instruction are discussed, relating instructional planning to student behavior and learning characteristics. A model for multielement treatment planning provides information on current behavior management practices. Also highlighted are language and communication assessment and intervention guidelines.

Part III concerns itself with emerging trends in autism. Chapters in this section deal with the critical issues of early intervention, family involvement and services, community integration, and supported employment. In closing, a discussion of new directions in educational programming and policy is provided.

Each of the 12 chapters in this volume has been prepared by leading experts in the area of autism. The contributing authors have filled the pages of this text with innovative and practical state-of-the-art information to facilitate improved programming and a higher quality of life for persons with autism. Their contributions to this text as well as to their respective disciplines are acknowledged and appreciated.

Dianne E. Berkell

I AUTISM: A PERSPECTIVE

1 Autism: Historical Overview, Definition, and Characteristics

J. Gregory Olley
University of North Carolina at Chapel Hill

Mark is a 10-year-old boy who avoids looking directly at others, resists being held by his parents, does not speak, and plays with only one toy, which he spins over and over. Sarah is a 24-year-old woman who has a steady job, lives in an apartment, and enjoys activities at the recreation center. Sarah and Mark have autism. Their similarities and their differences are better understood now than in 1943 when Dr. Leo Kanner introduced the term *early childhood autism*. Yet many puzzles remain in this most puzzling of developmental disabilities.

To introduce our examination of autism, this chapter reviews the viewpoints and findings that have shaped our understanding of this disorder. The changing definitions, characteristics, and approaches to treatment are reviewed. This information is the context in which our current understanding of autism is described throughout this volume.

History

Today, the term *autism* is usually associated with the syndrome described by Kanner, but its use began much earlier in psychiatry. Bleuler (1911/1950) used the term to describe a withdrawal into fantasy in schizophrenia. Kanner's (1943) use of the word "autism" reflected his emphasis on the social deficits of the disorder, but it was unfortunate, because it confused the syndrome he described with schizophrenia. The 11 children whose lives Kanner recounted in 1943 showed characteristics that have since been shown to be quite different from schizophrenia.

The term *autism* was introduced in this century, but accounts of children with similar behavior have been present for many generations. Schopler (1983) gave the examples of Romulus and Remus, who legend says founded Rome, and the feral children Kamala and Amala found by the Reverend Singh in Midnapore, India in 1929. Many accounts of special education trace the beginnings of the field to the work of Itard and his student, Edward Seguin, in teaching Victor, the "Wild Boy of Aveyron" (Itard, 1894/1962). As Schopler pointed out, these early reports accepted uncritically the legends that the children had been raised by wolves. Such reports did little to clarify the origins of childhood psychopathology, but they did document that others observed children with very deviant social and language development long before Kanner did.

Current views of autism differ sharply with some of Kanner's observations, but many of his points remain essential to today's perspective. Kanner saw the social disorder as the cardinal sign and even chose the word "autism" to convey that emphasis. Characteristics, such as avoiding the gaze of others and showing no recognition of a parent's absence, continue to be viewed as classic symptoms of autism. Later writers described this social deficit as *withdrawal.* However, Kanner (1943) noted that unlike people with schizophrenia who withdraw from a distressing world, those with autism show "extreme aloneness from the very beginning of life." He gave the example of the "failure of the child to assume an anticipatory posture upon being picked up," and he described the children as "from the start anxiously and tensely impervious to people" (p. 249). Rather than withdrawing from a difficult world, Kanner saw people with autism living in "a world in which they have been total strangers from the beginning" (p. 249).

Kanner's (1943) original description also pointed out the isolated play, unusual language traits, insistence on ritual behavior, and resistance to change that continue to be cited as central traits. In addition to these insights, Kanner drew some conclusions that have not stood the test of time. For instance, he noted the absence of physical stigmata of the children in his sample. Recent research with larger samples has demonstrated that people with autism may also have other identifiable medical syndromes. Kanner's mistaken first impressions led him to conclude that the children had "intelligent physiognomies" and that their faces showed "serious-mindedness." He determined that children with autism had "good cognitive potentialities." This myth of the autistic child as latent genius has endured and caused great distress for family members and teachers who have nearly always failed to find the key to unlock the alleged genius. More recent research has consistently found about 80% of people with autism to function in the mentally retarded range of intellectual development (National Society for Autistic Children, 1978). The remaining 20% show social, language, and other learning problems that seriously impair their adaptive behavior. Kanner's optimism about the intellectual potential of people with autism was sadly unfounded.

Another misconception that Kanner began, and later writers such as Bruno Bettleheim perpetuated, was the view that parent behavior caused the autistic condition. Although noting that characteristics of autism were present "from the very beginning of life," Kanner also observed the parents in his sample to be from upper middle-class backgrounds and to have a cold manner in dealing with their autistic child. Bettleheim (1967) picked up this theme and built a theory of the nature of autism in which the emotional coldness of parents, particularly mothers, was the central cause.

Bettleheim had been a prisoner in a Nazi death camp, and this experience influenced his view of autism. Rimland (1989) summarized Bettleheim's view "that autistic children had been mistreated by their mothers in about the same way in which Nazi concentration camp prisoners had been mistreated by their guards, thus giving the children (or the prisoners) feelings of hopelessness, despair, and apathy, and leading them to withdraw from contact with reality" (p. xiii). Rimland and other writers of the 1960s played an important role in changing the prevailing psychoanalytic view of autism that had been popularized by Bettleheim.

In 1964, Rimland, influenced by his experience with his own autistic son, wrote the classic book *Early Infantile Autism: The Syndrome and Its Implications for a Neural Theory of Behavior*. Rimland found no evidence for the psychogenic or psychologically caused view of autism. Instead, he put forth a neurologically based approach, which opened the door for the burgeoning biomedical research of today. In addition to publicly removing the burden of guilt for causing autism from thousands of parents, Rimland organized parents to form what is now the Autism Society of America, a parents' organization with state and local chapters throughout the nation.

The departure of the psychoanalytic approach led to the rapid growth of research based on other viewpoints. Today, behavioral, cognitive-developmental, and medical research and treatment are changing the lives of thousands of people with autism.

Behavioral. Beginning in the 1960s, researchers applied psychological research from the laboratory to the learning of children with autism. Today the integration of basic behavioral research and treatment programs in many settings has led to substantial knowledge and improved services. Early studies on the effects of rewards and punishments have led to a much broader emphasis on teaching practical skills for community living throughout the life span (Horner, Dunlap, & Koegel, 1988; Smith, 1989; Strain, Jamieson, & Hoyson, 1986).

Cognitive–Developmental. The basic deficits in cognitive processing, such as language, social, and related learning, have been the basis for another contemporary approach to autism. Some writers, such as Rutter (1983), have identified cognitive deficits in language, abstraction, and sequencing as the primary deficit in autism. Others, such as Hobson (1989), have stressed problems in social relatedness and affect.

Dawson and Galpert (1986) described their model for the application of developmental theory to explain and treat the language, social, and other cognitive deficits of children with autism. A common thread connects these viewpoints by emphasizing deficits in understanding abstractions, particularly those governing social behavior.

Medical. Recent medical research has contributed in important ways to our knowledge of the organic basis of autism. The neuroanatomical, neurochemical, and genetic abnormalities present in autism, as well as medicines that can treat at least some autism symptoms are now far better understood than they were even a few years ago (Dawson, 1989). Recent studies of the autopsied brains of people with autism have found abnormalities in the limbic system and the cerebellum, areas known to be linked to memory and emotion (Bauman, 1990).

An example of the application of medical research is the discovery of Fragile X syndrome, an important genetic cause of mental retardation. The growth of research has been dramatic on this topic, although experts currently differ in their views about the link between Fragile X and autism (Einfeld, Molony, & Hall, 1989).

DEFINING AUTISM

The characteristics of autism as first described by Kanner have been revised and broadened in subsequent years (Schopler, 1983), although current definitions still reflect Kanner's important observations. Formal definitions and the rich clinical accounts of Kanner and others combine to give us a greater understanding of autism. The most commonly used current definition is that contained in the revised, third edition of the *Diagnostic and Statistical Manual of Mental Disorders* (*DSM-III-R;* American Psychiatric Association, 1987).

DSM-III-R

The classification system of the American Psychiatric Association places autism in a category called "developmental disorders." Disorders in this group have a "predominant disturbance . . . in the acquisition of cognitive, language, motor, or social skills" (p. 28). Developmental disorders are easily confused with *developmental disabilities*, a term defined in federal legislation to include autism, mental retardation, cerebral palsy, and other disorders of the developmental period that have long-term effects on learning, language, mobility, and self-care.

In the *DSM-III-R*, autism is classified as a "pervasive developmental disorder," which has replaced several earlier terms "including Atypical Development, Symbiotic Psychosis, Childhood Psychosis, Childhood Schizophrenia, and others" (p. 33). The *DSM-III-R* definition of autism has three primary characteristics, which must be present before the age of 3 years. They are:

1. qualitative impairment in reciprocal social interaction,
2. impairment in communication and imaginative activity, and
3. markedly restricted repertoire of activities and interests.

The *DSM-III-R* definition also notes that younger and more severely impaired children with autism often show "associated features" including mental retardation, uneven cognitive skill development, abnormal postures and motor behavior (e.g., stereotypies, such as arm flapping), unusual responses to sensory stimuli (e.g., ignoring pain or overreacting to certain sounds), abnormalities of eating, drinking, sleeping, or mood, and self-injury.

Other Definitions

Other current definitions have placed their emphasis in different ways, but nearly all definitions highlight the importance of social and language deficits. Rutter (1978) identified impairments in social relationships and language development and insistence on sameness as the key features. Other groups studying autism have produced similar definitions that are still in use (e.g., Creak, 1961; National Society for Autistic Children, 1978).

Clinical Applications of Definitions

In order to give these definitions more clinical usefulness, several scales have been developed for use in identifying children with autism and measuring progress in their treatment. Parks (1983) reviewed five of these instruments, and recently Barthelemy et al. (1990) introduced another.

The most recent version of one of these scales, the Childhood Autism Rating Scale (CARS; Schopler, Reichler, & Renner, 1988), contains a useful comparison of the current definitions of autism and their emphases upon different characteristics. It includes the following 15 traits: impairment in social relationships, impairment in imitation skills, disturbance in emotional response, peculiarities in use of body, inappropriate use of objects, difficulty in adapting to change, unusual visual responses, unusual auditory responses, unusual use of response to taste, smell, or touch, unusual fears, impairment of verbal communication, impairment of nonverbal communication, abnormal activity level, unevenness in intellectual functioning, and onset prior to 30 months.

CHARACTERISTICS

In addition to the information in formal definitions, several other aspects of autism are well-established and important for planning services.

Prevalence

As definitions of autism have changed, so have figures on prevalence of the disorder. Kanner's version of autism, sometimes called "Kanner syndrome," is very rare (Wing, 1981). Lotter's (1966) classic epidemiological study yielded a somewhat higher prevalence figure of 4 or 5 in 10,000. In England the Camberwell Study further clarified the relation of autism to other disorders of social impairment and cited a combined prevalence of 21 in 10,000 children (Wing & Gould, 1979).

Autism is similar to other disabilities in that it occurs more frequently in males than females, perhaps 3 to 4 times more frequently. Their relative rarity has discouraged study of females with autism, but recent research has consistently shown females as a group to have slightly lower IQ, as well as greater problems in other areas of cognition and language (Konstantareas, Homatidis, & Busch, 1989; Lord & Schopler, 1987). Lord, Goode, Rutter, and Schopler (1989) are continuing their research in this area in order to clarify the role of genetic vulnerability and polygenic patterns of inheritance in autism.

Relation to Other Developmental Disabilities

Recent evidence from several sources has contradicted Kanner's view that people with autism are latent geniuses. However, unusual or "savant" skills are found in rare cases of autism. Such skills were well displayed in the popular film, *Rainman*. People with autism or mental retardation and savant skills are very rare (Rimland, 1990), and such skills seldom help them to achieve anything close to normal adult adjustment.

The characteristics of autism may be found in people at virtually any level of intelligence; however, autism coexists with mental retardation in about 80% of cases (Wing & Gould, 1979). As one examines people of lower IQ, the likelihood of finding characteristics of autism becomes greater (Bartak

& Rutter, 1976; National Society for Autistic Children, 1978). However, at the level of profound mental retardation, some autistic behaviors that require motor or cognitive skill, such as elaborate rituals, are not seen (Wing & Gould, 1979). In this group, identification of autism becomes very difficult and probably not meaningful for planning services.

In addition to mental retardation, autism may coexist with several specific disorders. Wing and Gould's (1979) epidemiological study found cases of autism and related disorders associated with congenital rubella syndrome, encephalitis/meningitis, infantile spasms, epilepsy, severe perinatal asphyxia, phenylketonuria, tuberous sclerosis, and in very rare instances, Down syndrome.

Changes in Perspective on Autism

Changes in definition have been accompanied by research on several characteristics of autism that have clinical importance. These findings go beyond the characteristics needed to define autism and include aspects of learning and social behavior that are useful in understanding the nature of the disorder and individualizing services.

Social Deficits. Kanner's use of the term *autism* and his rich descriptions of the social deficits in childhood (1943) and adulthood (1971) continue to be essential contributions. Rutter (1978) described insistence on sameness and oddities of play as essential characteristics. Other researchers have taken the view that social inadequacies are the fundamental problem in autism. Fein, Pennington, Markowitz, Braverman, and Waterhouse (1986) described a neuropsychological model of autism in which the social deficits are the primary characteristics. More recently Walters, Barrett, and Feinstein (1990) reviewed studies on such diverse topics as attachment, recognition of emotions, play, social cognition, and neurochemistry, and concluded that Kanner was correct in his assertion "that social–affective deficits or deviations lie at the root of this disorder" (p. 320).

The inability to relate to others is a problem throughout life. It is one of the early characteristics that often leads to the identification of autism. In later years, it is a major obstacle to adult adjustment (Schopler & Mesibov, 1983). The social deficit in autism is pervasive and multifaceted. It is part of the cognitive (Rutter, 1983) and the language difficulties (Olley, 1985) of people with autism. Even among the few people who have overcome the major obstacles of autism to achieve productive adult lives, social interaction remains a daily challenge (Grandin & Scariano, 1986).

Language Deficits. The forms that language problems may take in autism are many and varied, but some type of language difficulty is virtually always present. Many people with autism, particularly those of lower intelligence, do not speak, or may make only unintelligible noises, or may speak only on rare occasions, such as during a temper outburst. Others may speak clearly but only repeat things that they have heard. This repetition, or echolalia, may be immediate or delayed. Earlier writers believed that echolalia was meaningless, but Prizant (1983) and others have identified many social functions served by it.

Communication takes many forms, including smiles, gestures, and postures (Watson, Lord, Schaffer, & Schopler, 1989). Communication may be an initiation, a response, or an imitation. It may serve to express emotion, make a request, or protest. The forms and functions are too extensive to list, but in autism virtually all aspects of language and communication can be impaired. The impact of this impairment touches all aspects of life.

Cognitive Skills. The impairment of intelligence in autism has been described often, but many other aspects of cognition and learning are also affected. Researchers who take the view that autism is primarily a disorder of cognition attribute the social and language problems to defects in logic, attention, planning, use of symbols, and related processes (Rumsey, 1985; Rutter, 1983). Dawson and Fernald (1987) pointed out difficulties in taking the perspective of others. In England, Baron-Cohen, Leslie, and Frith (1985) described the cognitive deficits in autism as a specific problem in "theory of mind." In their view, people with autism lack the ability to infer what other people feel or believe or understand, and, therefore, the behavior of others makes little sense to them.

Biological Basis. Despite these differing views of what is the primary deficit in autism, virtually all writers accept the view that autism and related disorders have a biological basis. Also, regardless of what trait is considered primary, all agree that biological, social, language, and cognitive traits coexist to form the syndrome of autism. Wing (1981) described the common coexistence of "abnormalities of social interaction, verbal and nonverbal communication, and imaginative activities" (p. 37). She referred to these as "the triad of social and language impairment" (p. 37).

Characteristics Related to Education and Treatment

In addition to research on the nature of autism, a large body of research exists on behavioral characteristics. All of these traits can be found in nonautistic people; hence, they are not essential traits for a definition. They are, nevertheless, important to take into consideration when planning a treatment program. No research exists on how to give people with autism a "theory of mind," but much is known about teaching practical skills.

Behavior Problems. Very serious or dangerous behavior problems are found in only a small minority of people with autism, but such problems interfere greatly with learning and independent living. Aggression, self-injury, and property destruction are the behaviors most likely to lead to placement in a more restrictive treatment setting. Milder problems, such as tantrums and noncompliance, are seen more often and are more amenable to change, particularly in younger children.

Frequently children and adults with autism show an unusual way of responding to sensory stimuli. They may overreact (e.g., to sounds or touch) or underreact (e.g., to pain) (Frith & Baron-Cohen, 1987). Another behavior, which is common enough to appear in some definitions of autism, is self-stimulation. Repetitive behaviors performed in a stereotyped manner can continue for very long periods to the exclusion of other activities. For this reason, some early research focused on eliminating self-stimulation as a prerequisite for learning functional skills (see review by Koegel & Koegel, 1989).

Much research on behavior problems has focused on eliminating the behaviors, and, unfortunately, punishment has been the most common treatment approach (LaVigna, 1987). The role of punishment remains a great controversy (National Institutes of Health, 1989). Increasingly, the approach of choice in dealing with behavior problems of all types is to teach other functional skills at an early age (Dunlap, Johnson, & Robbins, 1990). This emphasis on positive approaches has led to treatments that are more widely accepted by parents and advocates and has kept an important emphasis on the rights of people with disabilities.

Motivation. One of the most commonly heard comments about people with autism is that they are not motivated to engage in education or treatment programs. Rather than saying that they are not motivated, it may be more accurate to say that they are motivated by things that most people would find unusual or odd. Age-appropriate play with toys or exploration of materials may hold no interest, whereas isolated, repetitive manipulation of objects may be a high priority. The usual activities of childhood, especially social activities, seem to hold no attraction. Commonly used positive reinforcers, especially those with a social component, may not be motivating. Even parents and staff who work closely with people with autism find it difficult to identify reinforcers for them.

Systematic assessment of a wide variety of possibilities is needed to determine what is reinforcing (Green, Reid, White, Halford, Brittain, & Gardner, 1988). This assessment may reveal some surprising idiosyncratic motivators. For instance, access to self-stimulation or aberrant behavior may be reinforcing (Charlop, Kurtz, & Casey, 1990). In light of their well-known desire for sameness, it is surprising to find that people with autism often find variation in their activities to be reinforcing (Dunlap, 1984). The search for motivating factors sometimes reveals that people with autism are much like other people. They are motivated by being in control of their lives. Dyer, Dunlap, and Winterling (1990) found students to be more motivated by activities that they chose than by activities chosen for them. These studies draw us to the conclusion that people with autism are, indeed, motivated, but it requires creativity and determination to identify individual factors that can be used as effective motivators.

Generalization. Advances in the education of children with autism have been noteworthy in the past 20 years. Children and adults have learned important academic, social, leisure, and work skills. Yet people with autism have shown very little inclination to use their skills outside of the narrow circumstances in which they learned them. Students may learn to read in class but fail to check the sign on the door before going into a rest room. They may follow their teacher's verbal instructions reliably but ignore the instructions of others. They may function smoothly in McDonald's and appear totally confused in Burger King. Skills that are so difficult to gain are more difficult to generalize.

In recent years, the emphasis in instruction of students and adults with autism has shifted from classroom to community. Research and practice have shown that skills must be learned in the setting in which they will actually be used. In addition, techniques of teaching have been developed to help make generalization easier (Horner, Dunlap, & Koegel, 1988). As a result of these new efforts, people with autism are able to use their skills in more settings and with greater flexibility.

Attention and Distractibility. Like many other people with mental retardation and learning difficulties, people with autism usually have problems paying attention for long periods. Their attention wanders, and they are easily distracted by all sorts of things. Problems in attention are made more complex by a tendency to attend to only certain, preferred stimuli. This tendency is referred to as *stimulus overselectivity* (Dunlap, Koegel, & Burke, 1981).

This pattern of attending to some things and not others has made many parents of very young autistic children suspect a hearing impairment. It has also been a part of the children's social oddities. An appropriate response to something that we see or hear requires that we ignore many irrelevant stimuli and attend to the important details. Teachers are aware of stimulus overselectivity, and they present information to students with autism in a manner that makes the important part very clear and obvious.

Other Characteristics. People with autism share many traits with people with mental retardation. In their learning style, both groups tend to learn concrete tasks that they can see and manipulate more easily than they learn abstract tasks that require understanding of concepts or complex language. Teachers take all of these traits into account in planning an environment that makes learning practical skills clear and motivating.

TREATMENT

The search for knowledge about autism has led us to better description but, more importantly, to better treatment. Services to people with autism now begin earlier, continue longer, and apply to more aspects of their lives than ever before.

Early Identification

Unlike other severe handicaps that result in easily recognized physical features, autism is very difficult to identify in a child's early months and years. In retrospect, many parents can identify features that made them suspect that their infant's development was unusual. In infancy, however, these characteristics do not point to a clear diagnosis of autism. Freeman and Ritvo (1984) suggested several important traits in the areas of sensorimotor, speech/language, and relating to people, objects, and events that are recognizably different within the first few months of life. These included the extremes of quiet or fussy, overresponsive or not responsive to stimuli, and the absence of eye contact and social response. Individual variation in such traits is so great that clear identification of autism usually must wait until 18 to 24 months of age.

Most parents are aware of the expected milestones for social and language development in the second year of life. If their child is not speaking socially and is not socially responsive by this time, parents are likely to express their concern to their pediatrician. In her review of early development, Ungerer (1989) pointed to "symbolic play, vocal and gestural communication, imitation, and more abstract concepts of persons" (p. 85) as early deficits that characterize autism. A thorough developmental evaluation at this age can usually lead to a valid identification of autism. Because autistic traits are expressed in differing degrees, early descriptions may be tentative and may involve qualifying phrases, such as "autistic-like." Even with such a cautious diagnosis, it is important that treatment begin.

Education

Isolated attempts to provide early education and related services to children with autism began in the 1960s, but it was not until the 1980s that convincing research became available to show that such efforts were effective (Simeonsson, Olley, & Rosenthal, 1987). In 1984 Hoyson, Jamieson, and Strain described the impressive results of their program at the University of Pittsburgh. The combination of systematic behavioral teaching in groups, an emphasis on social skills, and intensive parent involvement led to an encouraging level of success for these children as they moved into elementary school.

Ivar Lovaas at UCLA has conducted the longest running study of early intervention involving the largest number of children (Lovaas, 1987). He reported that 9 of 19 children studied completed first grade successfully with no special assistance and achieved average scores on a variety of measures following intensive preschool instruction. The program used reinforcement and mild punishment to teach social and preacademic skills and compliance. Parent involvement and careful planning for school preparation were emphasized. Although Lovaas' work has been criticized on methodological grounds (Schopler, 1988), his research is continuing, and interest in early treatment is growing rapidly.

Services for school-age children with autism have expanded and improved since the mid-1970s due to the influence of a series of federal laws. Most recently, on October 30, 1990, President Bush signed Public Law 101-476. The Individuals with Disabilities Education Act (IDEA), specifically includes children with autism in its guarantees of equal access to an appropriate education in the least restrictive environment. Further, it emphasizes education that prepares students for adult living and requires a transition plan between school and adult services.

Medical Treatment

Children identified with autism today are quite heterogeneous in their medical characteristics. They may be healthy and attractive, such as those in Kanner's (1943) original sample, or they may have one or more other conditions requiring medical care (Wing, 1981). This greater awareness of the medical aspects of autism has led to expanding research in the neuroanatomical (Courchesne, 1989), neurochemical (Volkmar & Anderson, 1989), and genetic (Silliman, Campbell, & Mitchell, 1989) influences in autism. These findings add significantly to our understanding of the diverse underpinnings of autism, and they will eventually have great impact on treatment and prevention.

Medicines intended for the treatment of psychotic symptoms have been used and sometimes misused for people with autism. A recent conference entitled *Treatment of Destructive Behaviors in Persons With Developmental Disabilities* sponsored by the National Institutes of Health (1989) concluded that "the prevalence of drug treatment for persons with developmental disabilities is disturbingly high" (p. 6). The report noted that neuroleptic drugs "are rarely prescribed with the specific therapeutic intent of treating a psychiatric condition" (p. 7). Thus, medical research continues to bring advances in knowledge and treatment, as well as important cautions.

At this time medical treatment consists primarily of treating the medical problems that may accompany autism (e.g., seizures), administering medication to limit behavior problems, and preventing future cases through genetic counseling.

Life-Span Issues

Kanner's term, *early infantile autism*, highlights the emphasis that has been placed on young children with autism. That influence is still important, as evidenced by current interest in early treatment, but in addition, services must now cover the whole life span. Schopler and Mesibov (1983) pointed out the changing characteristics and the changing service requirements as children become adolescents and adults. Recognition of these changes has led to greater opportunities for adult employment, recreation, and community participation.

FAMILY ISSUES

The changes after a half century of research and service in autism are nowhere more dramatic than in our view of families. Parents still write with great emotion of their experiences in the 1950s and 1960s when they were blamed for their children's disabilities. But more frequently they now take new roles. They write to guide other parents through the difficult steps of obtaining services and dealing with the stresses of parenthood (Tommasone & Tommasone, 1989), and they teach parents to be advocates for their own children (Surratt, 1984).

Family Stresses

People with even casual experience with autism will not be surprised to find that this disorder places unusual stresses on parents. Hoppes and Harris

(1990) put forth the view that parents of children with autism experience more stress than parents of children with mental retardation because of the lack of interpersonal responsiveness associated with autism. The severity of symptoms is another obvious contributor to parent stress (Bebko, Konstantareas, & Springer, 1987). However, parent stress has been shown to be lower for families that use active coping strategies and have social support (Bristol, 1987).

The focus of treatment is now typically on the family rather than on the child alone. Parents contribute to evaluation of their child's progress, instruct their child at home and in the community, and give support to other parents to manage the stresses of life with autism.

Siblings

The brothers and sisters of children with autism experience their own stresses and make their own contributions to strengthen family life. McHale, Simeonsson, and Sloan (1984) reviewed the literature on siblings and concluded that they often bear more responsibilities and experience more stresses than children without a handicapped brother or sister. Nevertheless, they found that "children with handicapped siblings as a whole do not have more problems in adjustment than do other children" (p. 331).

Siblings have been the focus of research and service in several ways. For instance, Schriebman, O'Neill, and Koegel (1983) taught siblings behavioral methods for working with their autistic brother or sister, and these skills generalized to other settings. Siblings have also contributed to our knowledge and services by giving their personal perspective on the joys and sorrows of life with a disabled brother or sister (Fromberg, 1984)

CONCLUSION

If the past is a good predictor of the future, we can expect continued rapid change for people with autism. Studies of parent involvement and generalization of skills (Laski, Charlop, & Schreibman, 1988), teaching self-control of behavior problems (Koegel & Koegel, 1990), and students with autism helping other students (Krantz, Ramsland, & McClannahan, 1989) are only a few of the promising approaches that are likely to continue to change the face of autism in the future.

REFERENCES

American Psychiatric Association. (1987). *Diagnostic and statistical manual of mental disorders* (3rd ed., rev.). Washington, DC: Author.

Baron-Cohen, S., Leslie, A., & Frith, U. (1985). Does the autistic child have a "theory of mind?" *Cognition, 21,* 37–46.

Bartak, L., & Rutter, M. (1976). Differences between mentally retarded and normally intelligent autistic children. *Journal of Autism and Childhood Schizophrenia, 6,* 109–120.

Barthelemy, C., Adrien, J. L., Tanguay, P., Garreau, B., Fermanian, J., Roux, S., Sauvage, D., & LeLord, G. (1990). The Behavioral Summarized Evaluation: Validity and reliability of a scale for the assessment of autistic behaviors. *Journal of Autism and Developmental Disorders, 20,* 189–204.

Bauman, M. (1990). Autism: What do we know? *The Behavior Specialist, 1*(1), 3.

Bebko, J. M., Konstantareas, M. M., & Springer, J. (1987). Parent and professional evaluations of family stress associated with characteristics of autism. *Journal of Autism and Developmental Disorders, 17,* 565–576.

Bettelheim, B. (1967). *The empty fortress: Infantile autism and the birth of self.* New York: Free Press.

Bleuler, E. (1950). *Dementia praecox oder Gruppe der Schizophrenien* [Dementia praecox or a group within the schizophrenias] (J. Zinkin, Trans.). New York: International University Press. (Original work published 1911)

Bristol, M. M. (1987). Mothers of children with autism or communication disorders: Successful adaptations and the double ABCX model. *Journal of Autism and Developmental Disorders, 17,* 469–486.

Charlop, M. H., Kurtz, P. F., & Casey, F. G. (1990). Using aberrant behaviors as reinforcers for autistic children. *Journal of Applied Behavior Analysis, 23,* 163–181.

Courchesne, E. (1989). Neuroanatomical systems involved in infantile autism: The implications of cerebellar abnormalities. In G. Dawson (Ed.), *Autism: Nature, diagnosis, and treatment* (pp. 119–143). New York: Guilford.

Creak, M. (1961). Schizophrenia syndrome in childhood: Progress report of a working party. *Cerebral Palsy Bulletin, 3,* 501–504.

Dawson, G. (Ed.). (1989). *Autism: Nature, diagnosis, and treatment.* New York: Guilford.

Dawson, G., & Fernald, M. (1987). Perspective-taking ability and its relationship to the social behavior of autistic children. *Journal of Autism and Developmental Disorders, 17,* 487–498.

Dawson, G., & Galpert, L. (1986). A developmental model for facilitating the social behavior of autistic children. In E. Schopler & G. B. Mesibov (Eds.), *Social behavior in autism* (pp. 237–261). New York: Plenum.

Dunlap, G. (1984). The influence of task variation and maintenance tasks on the learning and affect of autistic children. *Journal of Experimental Child Psychology, 37,* 41–64.

Dunlap, G., Johnson, L. F., & Robbins, F. R. (1990). Preventing serious behavior problems through skill development and early intervention. In A. C. Repp & N. N. Singh (Eds.), *Perspectives on the use of nonaversive interventions for persons with developmental disabilities* (pp. 273–286). Sycamore, IL: Sycamore.

Dunlap, G., Koegel, R. L., & Burke, J. C. (1981). Educational implications of stimulus overselectivity in autistic children. *Exceptional Education Quarterly, 2*(3), 37–49.

Dyer, K., Dunlap, G., & Winterling, V. (1990). Effects of choice making on the serious problem behaviors of students with severe handicaps. *Journal of Applied Behavior Analysis, 23,* 515–524.

Einfeld, S., Molony, H., & Hall, W. (1989). Autism is not associated with the Fragile X syndrome. *American Journal of Medical Genetics, 34,* 187–193.

Fein, D., Pennington, B., Markowitz, M. D., Braverman, M., & Waterhouse, L. (1986). Toward a neuropsychological model of infantile autism: Are the social deficits primary? *Journal of the American Academy of Child Psychiatry, 25,* 198–212.

Freeman, B. J., & Ritvo, E. R. (1984). The syndrome of autism: Establishing the diagnosis and principles of management. *Pediatric Annals, 13,* 284–296.

Frith, U., & Baron-Cohen, S. (1987). Perception in autistic children. In D. J. Cohen, A. M. Donnellan, & R. Paul (Eds.), *Handbook of autism and pervasive developmental disorders* (pp. 85–102). New York: Wiley.

Fromberg, R. (1984). The sibling's changing roles. In E. Schopler & G. B. Mesibov (Eds.), *The effects of autism on the family* (pp. 343–353). New York: Plenum.

Grandin, T., & Scariano, M. M. (1986). *Emergence: Labeled autistic.* Novato, CA: Arena.

Green, C. W., Reid, D. H., White, L. K., Halford, R. C., Brittain, D. P., & Gardner, S. M. (1988). Identifying reinforcers for persons with profound handicaps: Staff opinion versus systematic assessment of preferences. *Journal of Applied Behavior Analysis, 21,* 31–43.

Hobson, R. P. (1989). Beyond cognition: A theory of autism. In G. Dawson (Ed.), *Autism: Nature, diagnosis, and treatment* (pp. 22–48). New York: Guilford.

Hoppes, K., & Harris, S. L. (1990). Perceptions of child attachment and maternal gratification in mothers of children with autism and Down syndrome. *Journal of Clinical Child Psychology, 4,* 365–370.

Horner, R. H., Dunlap, G., & Koegel, R. L. (1988). *Generalization and maintenance: Life-style changes in applied settings.* Baltimore: Paul H. Brookes.

Hoyson, M., Jamieson, B., & Strain, P. S. (1984). Individualized group instruction of normally developing and autistic-like children: The LEAP curriculum model. *Journal of the Division for Early Childhood, 8,* 157–172.

Itard, J. (1962). *The wild boy of Aveyron* (G. Humphrey & M. Humphrey, Trans.). New York: Appleton-Century-Crofts. (Original work published 1894)

Kanner, L. (1943). Autistic disturbances of affective contact. *The Nervous Child, 2,* 217–250.

Kanner, L. (1971). Follow-up study of 11 autistic children originally reported in 1943. *Journal of Autism and Childhood Schizophrenia, 1,* 119–145.

Koegel, R. L., & Koegel, L. K. (1989). Community-referenced research on self-stimulation. In E. Cipani (Ed.), *The treatment of severe behavior disorders: Behavior analysis approaches* (pp. 129–150). Washington, DC: American Association on Mental Retardation.

Koegel, R. L., & Koegel, L. K. (1990). Extended reductions in stereotypic behavior of students with autism through a self-management treatment package. *Journal of Applied Behavior Analysis, 23,* 119–127.

Konstantareas, M. M., Homatidis, S., & Busch, J. (1989). Cognitive, communication, and social differences between autistic boys and girls. *Journal of Applied Developmental Psychology, 10,* 411–424.

Krantz, P. J., Ramsland, S. E., & McClannahan, L. E. (1989). Conversational skills for autistic adolescents: An autistic peer as prompter. *Behavioral Residential Treatment, 4,* 171–189.

Laski, K. E., Charlop, M. H., & Schreibman, L. (1988). Training parents to use the natural language paradigm to increase their autistic children's speech. *Journal of Applied Behavior Analysis, 21,* 391–400.

LaVigna, G. W. (1987). Nonaversive strategies for managing behavior problems. In D. J. Cohen, A. M. Donnellan, & R. Paul (Eds.), *Handbook of autism and pervasive developmental disorders* (pp. 418–429). New York: Wiley.

Lord, C., Goode, S., Rutter, M., & Schopler, E. (1989). Sex differences in autism. *International Journal of Rehabilitation Research, 12,* 113–114.

Lord, C., & Schopler, E. (1987). Neurobiological implications of sex differences in autism. In E. Schopler & G. B. Mesibov (Eds.), *Neurobiological issues of autism* (pp. 191–211). New York: Plenum.

Lotter, V. (1966). Epidemiology of autistic conditions in young children. *Social Psychiatry, 1,* 124–137.

Lovaas, O. I. (1987). Behavioral treatment and normal educational and intellectual functioning in young autistic children. *Journal of Consulting and Clinical Psychology, 55,* 3–9.

McHale, S. M., Simeonsson, R. J., & Sloan, J. L. (1984). Children with handicapped brothers and sisters. In E. Schopler & G. B. Mesibov (Eds.), *The effects of autism on the family* (pp. 327–342). New York: Plenum.

National Institutes of Health. (1989). Treatment of destructive behaviors in persons with developmental disabilities. *National Institutes of Health Consensus Development Conference Statement, 1*(9), 1–14.

National Society for Autistic Children. (1978). National Society for Autistic Children definition of the syndrome of autism. *Journal of Autism and Childhood Schizophrenia, 8,* 162–167.

Olley, J. G. (1985). Social aspects of communication in children with autism. In E. Schopler & G. B. Mesibov (Eds.), *Communication problems in autism* (pp. 311–328). New York: Plenum.

Parks, S. L. (1983). The assessment of autistic children: A selective review of available instruments. *Journal of Autism and Developmental Disorders, 13,* 255–267.

Prizant, B. M. (1983). Echolalia in autism: Assessment and intervention. *Seminars in Speech and Language, 4,* 63–77.

Rimland, B. (1964). *Infantile autism: The syndrome and its implications for a neural theory of behavior.* New York: Appleton-Century-Crofts.

Rimland, B. (1989). Introduction. In M. D. Powers (Ed.), *Children with autism: A parents' guide* (pp. ix–xviii). Rockville, MD: Woodbine.

Rimland, B. (1990). Autistic crypto-savants. *Autistic Research Review International, 4*(1), 3.

Rumsey, J. (1985). Conceptual problem-solving in highly verbal, nonretarded autistic men. *Journal of Autism and Developmental Disorders, 15,* 23–36.

Rutter, M. (1978). Diagnosis and definition of childhood autism. *Journal of Autism and Childhood Schizophrenia, 8,* 139–161.

Rutter, M. (1983). Cognitive deficits in the pathogenesis of autism. *Journal of Child Psychology and Psychiatry, 24,* 513–531.

Schopler, E. (1983). New developments in the definition and diagnosis of autism. In B. B. Lahey & A. E. Kazdin (Eds.), *Advances in clinical child psychology* (Vol. 6, pp. 93–127). New York: Plenum.

Schopler, E. (1988). Concerns about misinterpretation and uncritical acceptance of exaggerated claims. *American Psychologist, 43,* 658.

Schopler, E., & Mesibov, G. B. (Eds.). (1983). *Autism in adolescents and adults.* New York: Plenum.

Schopler, E., Reichler, R. J., & Renner, B. R. (1988). *The Childhood Autism Rating Scale (CARS).* Los Angeles: Western Psychological Services.

Schreibman, L., O'Neill, R. E., & Koegel, R. L. (1983). Behavioral training for siblings of autistic children. *Journal of Applied Behavior Analysis, 16,* 129–138.

Silliman, E. R., Campbell, M., & Mitchell, R. S. (1989). Genetic influences in autism and assessment of metalinguistic performance in siblings of autistic children. In G. Dawson (Ed.), *Autism: Nature, diagnosis, and treatment* (pp. 225–259). New York: Guilford.

Simeonsson, R. J., Olley, J. G., & Rosenthal, S. L. (1987). Early intervention for children with autism. In M. J. Guralnick & F. C. Bennett (Eds.), *The effectiveness of early intervention for at-risk and handicapped children* (pp. 275–296). New York: Academic Press.

Smith, M. D. (1989). *Autism and life in the community: Successful interventions for behavioral challenges.* Baltimore: Paul H. Brookes.

Strain, P. S., Jamieson, B. J., & Hoyson M. H. (1986). Learning Experiences . . . An Alternative Program for Preschoolers and Parents: A comprehensive service system for mainstreaming of autistic-like preschoolers. In C. J. Meisel (Ed.), *Mainstreaming handicapped children: Outcomes, controversies, and new directions* (pp. 251–269). Hillsdale, NJ: Lawrence Erlbaum Associates.

Surratt, J. E. (1984). Advocacy: Effectively changing the system. In E. Schopler & G. B. Mesibov (Eds.), *The effects of autism on the family* (pp. 129–141). New York: Plenum.

Tommasone, L., & Tommasone, J. (1989). Adjusting to your child's diagnosis. In M. D. Powers (Ed.), *Children with autism: A parents' guide* (pp. 31–50). Rockville, MD: Woodbine.

Ungerer, J. A. (1989). The early development of autistic children: Implications for defining primary deficits. In G. Dawson (Ed.), *Autism: Nature, diagnosis, and treatment* (pp. 75–91). New York: Guilford.

Volkmar, F. R., & Anderson, G. M. (1989). Neurochemical perspectives on infantile autism. In G. Dawson (Ed.), *Autism: Nature, diagnosis, and treatment* (pp. 208–224). New York: Guilford.

Walters, A. S., Barrett, R. P., & Feinstein, C. (1990). Social relatedness and autism: Current research, issues, and directions. *Research in Developmental Disabilities, 11,* 303–326.

Watson, L. R., Lord, C., Schaffer, B., & Schopler, E. (1989). *Teaching spontaneous communication to autistic and developmentally handicapped children.* New York: Irvington.

Wing, L. (1981). Language, social, and cognitive impairments in autism and severe mental retardation. *Journal of Autism and Developmental Disorders, 11,* 31–44.

Wing, L., & Gould, J. (1979). Severe impairments of social interaction and associated abnormalities in children: Epidemiology and classification. *Journal of Autism and Developmental Disorders, 9,* 11–29.

2 Perspectives on Research in Autism: Current Trends and Future Directions

Raymond G. Romanczyk
Mary Ekdahl
Stephanie B. Lockshin
State University of New York at Binghamton

Research is a sophisticated and complex endeavor, quite independent of the subject matter. It is not always performed well and all too often biased, ill conceived observations are improperly portrayed as research. The complexity and difficulty increases even further when the focus is human behavior and disorders. Autism, therefore, represents perhaps an extreme case, in that clearly it is not a unitary disorder caused by a single factor, but rather most likely it is the result of the confluence of events that serve to impair the individual to greater and lesser degrees. Also, autism may coexist with other disorders. Therefore, it is not surprising that whereas over the last four decades there has been a great deal of research conducted on autism, indeed our knowledge base is actually quite small.

Research in this area can be roughly clustered into (a) basic research into the causes and expression of autism, and (b) applied research that seeks to identify and evaluate treatment approaches. Because progress on the first area has been slow and erratic, this clearly influences the second area of research. Treatment research thus becomes all the more complex. Because causal factors are still elusive, it is problematic both to compare subject populations across various research studies (Kistner & Robbins, 1986) and to attempt to integrate the large body of research into a coherent whole.

This has resulted in some interesting problems and dilemmas, such that previous research is often forgotten or dismissed. Some researchers, service providers, and legislators as a result tend to forget the past and continue to make errors as well as proceed in a very inefficient manner. This is perhaps most clearly the case in evaluating treatment research where often extensive basic research is ignored or discarded as not being relevant or not being an appropriate philosophical match for certain broad service delivery philosophies. The difficulty here is one of context and time. That is, when initial research is begun in a difficult problem area, the most common strategy is to employ relatively nonsubtle variables in an attempt to see if in fact any effects can be obtained. It is not a wise use of resources to begin with the subtle, prior to knowing if a particular approach or variable has any merit. Thus, in retrospect, when evaluating research of previous decades, one should not be tempted to say that it was archaic or misguided or irrelevant, but rather one should place it in its proper historical perspective, noting not only the specific procedures utilized but also the conceptualization of the problem at that time. Also, historical perspective is critical in evaluating current procedures and expectations. For instance, at present there is strong emphasis on integration into appropriate social and work environments. This is often seen as the antithesis of the molecular analysis of learning and generalization in more laboratory and tightly controlled learning situations. However, these differences should not be seen as antagonistic, but as complementary. Clearly, information gained from previous research, both basic and applied, can help point to the difficulties that will accrue in various efforts to continue to expand the range of treatment services and the environments in which they are conducted. Thus the full constellation of research provides balance to what otherwise would be a non-self-correcting system.

Because of the various controversies concerning the false dichotomy between research and applied practice, there arises at times almost an antagonism from those involved in day-to-day service delivery concerning the "ivory tower" research conceptualizations, or the feeling that the research information is simply too abstract and too limited to be of practical value. On the other side of the coin, it is also unfortunate that many researchers choose strategies to address important questions without enough regard to the needs of service providers. It is therefore important for service providers to become well-educated in the process of scientific research and also for researchers to be well-versed in the type of pragmatic and contextual problems that face service providers.

It is not easy for either group to acquire these skills and knowledge, but for both the quality of service provision as well as the quality of research concerning basic understandings of the mechanisms that serve to produce the phenomena with which we are all concerned, such mutual understanding and interaction is absolutely critical.

It is often because of this lack of research and interaction that the service provision field moves with erratic progress. Because outcome information is often not provided that is subject to critical evaluation, weeding out false hopes and approaches from those that are truly beneficial is not the norm. This same process and problem can be seen in other fields. For instance, currently in the area of learning disabilities, there is great debate about the use of special lenses (Irlen colored lenses) to assist individuals with learning disabilities. The effects reported in the media are nothing short of phenomenal and anecdotal reports often appear miraculous. However, when one reviews the existing research, (e.g., Parker, 1990) the data are much more mixed. Further, when one takes a critical eye to not only the conclusions of the research, but also its actual structure and methodology, then even more grave concern is registered. Just as one needs to learn specific skills and acquire specific knowledge to be a good consumer when shopping for groceries or a new television set, in like manner one needs to learn specific skills and acquire specific knowledge to be an adequate consumer of research information. All too often when statements are made such as "research has shown that . . . ," what is being cited are simply the selective conclusions that have been drawn from the research without careful regard to the methodological and design integrity. This can be extremely dangerous. That is, the conclusions are only as strong as the methodology that produced the research, and if the methodology is flawed, no matter how desirable the conclusions or no matter how much one would "wish" the conclusions to be true, they are in fact flawed and cannot be trusted. For the reader who wishes to pursue questions of becoming a good consumer of research, there are numerous excellent books and articles on the topic. A relatively short but comprehensive article that addresses such issues recently appeared in the *Journal of Learning Disabilities* (Parker, 1990).

Thus, service providers should guard against being misled by popularization or misrepresentation of research by acquiring those skills to allow themselves to make independent judgments. As has been clear in the history of autism, the field is often jostled and propelled by various philosophies, movements, and agenda that are not in the best interests of individuals with autism or their families, and have little or nothing to do with research concerning treatment efficacy and causal processes. The need for intensive services and the need to provide meaningful and accurate answers to questions from families about this disorder is so great that every effort must be made to present them with accurate factual information. This will allow them to make important decisions and to insure that service providers and researchers can continue in their mutually dependent and critical work.

This approach is sometimes abandoned by individuals who choose to utilize a more narrow evaluation of research in autism. This is unfortunate but is not unlike issues and controversies that have arisen historically in other disciplines, including physics, chemistry, and biology. To the degree that the basic scientific approach is utilized and accepted however, such issues eventually do become clarified and progress is, in fact, made. Thus, our intent in this chapter is to provide a small sampling and broad overview of a few current research areas in autism (excluding current research in diagnosis and etiology) that we feel are important, and to attempt to provide a perspective on those areas where we feel the greatest progress will come and that will serve to provide improved perspective on the research that has been accumulated to date.

COGNITIVE DEVELOPMENT

Considerable heterogeneity exists within the population of individuals with autism in regard to range and severity of cognitive deficits. Whereas levels of intellectual functioning range from profound mental retardation to above average, the majority, 70%–90%, fall within the range of mental retardation (Romanczyk, Lockshin, & Harrison, 1991). However, the pattern of cognitive deficits is not identical for individuals with mental retardation and individuals with autism, as those with autism are most commonly characterized by cognitive inconsistencies and language deficits (Rutter, 1978). Both parents and professionals have rated these difficulties as the most severe and as causing greater stress than other difficulties exhibited by children with autism (Bebko, Konstantareas, & Springer, 1987). Recently, there has been an effort to pinpoint specific areas in which difficulties are most prevalent.

Cognitive Functioning

Ohta (1987) compared 16 autistic children, aged 6 to 14, to a performance IQ and age-matched control group, and to 189 preschool children on measures of intelligence, size comparisons, and spatial relationships, and gestural imitation skills. Autistic subjects received performance IQ scores that were significantly higher than their verbal IQ scores. The age-matched controls showed no such discrepancy. The pattern of responses of the autistic subjects suggested relatively good rote memory skills. The autistic subjects displayed difficulty in abstracting, conceptualizing, and sequencing visual and auditory information.

On the measure of size comparisons and spatial relationships, the responses of the autistic children were comparable to those of typical children less than 3 years of age. However, mean verbal mental age of the autistic group was higher than for the 3-year-old control group, suggesting that delays in size comparisons and spatial relationships were not simply a function of overall delays in language development.

Finally, autistic subjects in this study performed more poorly than either of the control groups on a gestural imitation task. In addition, 3 of the 16 autistic subjects engaged in partial imitation (i.e., the child imitated only part of the gesture) whereas none of the control subjects engaged in partial imitation. Autistic subjects who engaged in partial imitation did not differ from subjects who did not engage in partial imitation in terms of mental age or in their ability to make size comparisons and spatial relationships.

Jones and Prior (1985) compared the motor imitation abilities of 10 autistic children with 10 children matched on chronological age and 10 children matched on mental age. Results showed the autistic children to be impaired in ability to imitate gestures and dynamic body movements when compared to both control groups, although considerable heterogeneity was present in the autistic group.

Maltz (1981) analyzed performance on subscales of a general IQ test for 7 autistic, 7 mentally retarded, and 11 typical children matched for overall scores on the same IQ test. Autistic subjects performed better than the other two groups on concrete discrimination tasks, which involved the ability to discriminate on the basis of concrete information alone (size, color, form). Autistic subjects performed more poorly than the other groups on formal discrimination tasks that involved the ability to discriminate relationships underlying concrete information (e.g., car and plane are both means of transportation).

Ungerer and Sigman (1987) assessed categorization and receptive language skills for autistic children, aged 39 to 74 months, to mental age-matched mentally retarded children, aged 32 to 80 months, and mental age-matched typical children, aged 16 to 25 months. The autistic children's knowledge of function, form, and color categories was comparable to that of both control groups. Significant correlations were found between category knowledge and receptive language for the mentally retarded and typical children, but not for the autistic children. All of the autistic children but one demonstrated category knowledge, but only seven of these children demonstrated clear receptive language skills.

Whereas it appears that some autistic individuals display a relative strength in tasks requiring concrete discriminations (Maltz, 1981; Ungerer & Sigman, 1987), other autistic individuals may have difficulties in this area that are independent of delays in language development. A relative weakness displayed by autistic individuals occurs in the area of abstract reasoning and in the ability to imitate. This latter deficit may result in severe delays in other areas, as imitation is a prerequisite for learning a wide range of skills.

Rumsey (1985) compared the intellectual and social functioning of nine autistic men of average intelligence to that of nine control subjects matched on the basis of highest level of education completed. The autistic subjects and controls did not differ significantly in age, education, or performance IQ. The autistic group had a lower mean verbal IQ. The autistic group showed greater numbers of perseverative responses, perseverative errors, and total errors on a measure of conceptual problem solving. Scores on a measure of social functioning were below average for the autistic group and were not correlated with conceptual problem-solving scores.

Hobson and Lee (1989) compared the specific responses on a picture vocabulary test of nonautistic retarded adolescents with those of adolescents matched for age and overall performance on the same picture vocabulary test. The autistic group performed more poorly than the nonautistic group on the emotion-related items and on items with human content. Interestingly, no difference existed for nonhuman content items and emotion-unrelated items. Further, no difference existed between groups in a comparison of social versus nonsocial items nor abstract versus concrete items.

Beisler, Tsai, and Vonk (1987) found no differences between autistic and nonautistic subjects matched for chronological age, mental age, and sex on a measure of receptive language skills. This apparent inconsistency with the findings of Ungerer and Sigman (1987) and Hobson and Lee (1989) may reflect heterogeneity within the autistic population. An alternate explanation may be that autistic children display inconsistent abilities within a given area (e.g., receptive language skills), and it is therefore necessary to examine component skills.

Remediational Strategies

The learning patterns of autistic individuals are characterized by difficulties responding to complex stimuli and in generalization to novel stimuli (cf. Gilburg, 1989). It is therefore crucial to provide educational programs that specifically address these deficits. Burke and Cerniglia (1990) assessed the responses of four autistic children, aged 8 to 15 years, to one-, two-, three-, and four-component stimuli. For all children, correct responding decreased as the number of stimulus components increased from one to four. Teaching the children to respond to the one-component instructions had minimal effect on responses to the multicomponent instructions. A treatment program designed to increase the children's responses to single and multicomponent stimuli increased responding to multicomponent stimuli, which generalized to responses to complex cross-modal multicomponent stimuli in the natural environment and in two structured settings.

Hedbring and Newsom (1985) compared three approaches to remediate visual overselectivity in 21 students with autism. Prior to participation in the study all subjects met specified criteria for performance on a match to sample task. In addition, subjects all demonstrated visual overselectivity on a task requiring matching of a one component stimulus (e.g., a bowl *or* a spoon) to a two component stimulus (e.g., a bowl *and* a spoon). Visual overselectivity was defined by a discrepancy between performance with one of the component stimuli (e.g., matching the spoon to the bowl and the spoon) to performance with the other component stimulus (e.g., matching the bowl to the bowl and the spoon).

Subjects were randomly assigned to one of three discrimination training procedures: (a) equivalence training, which utilized a four-step sequence of easy stimuli (i.e., actual objects) to difficult stimuli (i.e., colored drawings of objects); (b) functional object-use, which emphasized hands-on use of objects to highlight their relevant features; and (c) repeated practice with test materials alone. Results indicated that equivalence training was more effective in reducing visual overselectivity than repeated practice training, which was in turn more effective than functional object-use training. Neither mental nor chronological age was related to changes in overselectivity.

Berkowitz (1990) compared the effectiveness of a delayed prompting technique to that of a fading-of-prompt technique in training discrimination of communication book pictures. Four autistic students ranging in age from 12 to 20 years served as subjects. The delayed prompting procedure utilized 1-second increments, with delay to prompt increasing after three correct responses to each of three items. The delay to prompt decreased following one incorrect response. The systematic fading-of-prompts procedure consisted of manual guidance faded to a light physical prompt faded to a gestural prompt faded to no prompt. The same criterion for the delayed-prompting procedure was used for the fading of prompts procedure. Results showed the delayed-prompting technique to be more efficient and more effective than the fading-of-prompts procedure. In addition, for the two children requiring the most trials and making the most errors, aggression during training sessions occurred only when errors occurred and only in the fading-of-prompts condition.

LANGUAGE DEVELOPMENT

Individuals with autism typically present with profound difficulties in language development. Several studies have been published in the last decade that specifically address the remediation of language deficits in autistic children. Smith, McConnell, Walter, and Miller (1985) observed the incidence of appropriate verbalization, signing, and social behavior of 14 autistic children ranging in age from 4.5 to 16.5 years. Each child wore an auditory trainer for an average of 24 minutes per day over two 5-week periods, interspersed with five-week control periods in a time series design. After two treatment periods, time spent in a withdrawn state decreased from a baseline of 26.3% to 12.7%, appropriate behaviors increased from 67.4% to 82.1%, and rate of signing increased from 10.2% to 21%. No change was observed in verbalizations.

Koegel, O'Dell, and Koegel (1987) compared the effects of a natural language-teaching paradigm and an analog-teaching condition for two nonverbal, autistic children, ages 4 years, 5 months and 5 years, 8 months. In the analog teaching condition the experimenter-selected items were presented serially until the child reached criterion performance. Instructions and prompts to name the item were utilized. Correct responses were rewarded with food and praise. In the natural teaching condition, child-selected items were presented, resulting in the stimulus items being varied from trial to trial. Instead of presenting specific instructions or prompts, the experimenter played with the toy and modeled the target response. All attempts to vocalize were rewarded with opportunities to play with the instructional stimulus. Results showed higher rates of imitative utterances and spontaneous speech in both clinic and nonclinic settings following implementation of the natural language teaching paradigm.

Koegel, O'Dell, and Dunlap (1988) assessed the specific effects of the reinforcement of attempts. Four autistic children, aged 3 years, 5 months, 8 years, 4 months, 11 years, 9 months, and 9 years, were instructed in each of two conditions. In the reinforcement of motor speech condition, only a child's motor speech production that met or exceeded a phonetic criterion was reinforced. In the verbal attempts condition, any vocal–verbal response that included an observable attempt to speak that was nonself-stimulatory was reinforced. Results showed consistently more positive child affect in the attempts versus motor speech condition. In addition, all four children showed greater phonemic improvements in the verbal attempts condition, while two of the four children showed deterioration in the motor speech condition.

Curcio and Paccia (1987) found a significant relationship between the type of adult verbal input and the quality of autistic children's responses. Dyadic conversations between four autistic boys, aged 7 years, 4 months, 7 years, 7 months, 11 years, and 12 years, 8 months, and their mothers and a female primary school teacher were observed. Adult verbal input that included yes/no questions, low conceptual complexity and/or topical contingency (statement made in reference to the child's previous utterances), resulted in more adequate child responses than did adult verbal input that included "Wh" questions, high conceptual complexity, and no topical contingency. Mothers and teachers did not differ in the quality of their verbal input. Following inadequate child responses, adults were more likely *not* to modify their subsequent question. When adults did modify the subsequent question they also were most likely to increase quality. When the child gave an adequate response to an initial adult question, adults were more likely to decrease the quality of their verbal input as defined by the three dimensions just listed.

Harris, Handleman, Kristoff, Bass, and Gordon (1990) compared rate of progress of young children with autism in two language training settings. The research indicated no difference for the two groups, which differed in the participation of typical peers. However, what was of most interest was that the typical peers showed accelerated language gain as a function of participating in the language emphasis classroom of their peers with autism. Such benefit to the "hosts" has important implications for design and promulgation of least-restrictive classroom models.

SOCIAL DEVELOPMENT

Sigman and Ungerer (1984) compared the social interactions between autistic and normal children and their adult caregivers. Fourteen autistic children with a mean age of 4 years, 4 months and a mean mental age of 2 years, and 14 typical children served as subjects. Social interactions were observed during a free-play situation with caregiver and experimenter present, during caregiver separation, during separation from a stranger (the experimenter), during reunion with the caregiver, and during reunion with the stranger. Functional and symbolic play behaviors were also observed and receptive language was assessed. The typical children showed a strong preference for interacting with the caregiver, whereas the autistic children showed no such preference. Autistic children did show increased proximity-seeking behavior to the caregiver during both reunion periods. Autistic children who interacted more with their mothers demonstrated more symbolic play with greater diversity of such play. Typical children who showed more diverse play demonstrated fewer attachment behaviors. No correlation was found between social behavior and receptive language, chronological age or mental age.

Dawson, Hill, Spencer, Galpert, and Watson (1990) compared social interactions between autistic and nonautistic children and their mothers. Sixteen autistic children, aged 30 to 70 months, were compared with 16 normal children matched for sex, race, receptive language, and mother's SES and educational level. Interactions were assessed in a free-play setting (low communicative demand), a put-toys-away setting (high communicative demand), and a snack time setting (face-to-face interaction). Child behavior was coded as social and interactive/noninteractive, or nonsocial and toy-directed, or other directed. Frequency and duration of gazes at mother's face, and affective behavior of both mother and child were also coded.

During free play, autistic and typical children did not differ in the amount of time spent interacting with toys or mother, or in the frequency or duration of gaze at their mother's face. Autistic children spent more time engaging in nonsocial activities that did not involve toys. During the put-toys-away condition, typical children spent more time watching their mother's activities. Again, frequency and duration of gaze at mother's face did not differ. During the face-to-face interaction, frequency and duration of smiling or gaze at mother's face did not differ. Autistic children, however, were significantly less likely to *combine* smiles and gaze. Autistic and typical children did not differ in the percentages of smiles elicited by nonsocial versus social events. However, autistic children showed significantly fewer smiles in response to mother smiles. Mothers of autistic children displayed significantly fewer smiles and were less likely to smile in response to children's smiles than mothers of typical children.

Dawson and McKissick (1984) assessed visual self-recognition, object permanence, and motor imitation skills of 15 autistic children aged 4 to 6 years. Eleven out of 15 subjects exhibited self-recognition (i.e., when in front of a mirror, they touched their own rouge-covered nose, which is a typical self-recognition test). Two of the subjects displayed imitative behavior in response to their reflection and two of the subjects showed little or no response to their reflection. When compared to the responses of typical children aged 21 and 24 months, the autistic children engaged in fewer vocalizations and less self versus mirror directed behavior. Thirteen of the 15 autistic children demonstrated object permanence, whereas only 8 of 15 demonstrated good imitation skills. The two children who demonstrated no object permanence also demonstrated no self-recognition. There was no relationship between imitation ability and self-recognition.

Dawson and Fernald (1987) administered a perspective-taking task, a measure of receptive language, two measures of social behavior, a measure of intelligence and a measure assessing specific symptoms of autism to 16 autistic children ranging in age from 6 to 14 years. Perspective-taking ability was negatively correlated with measures of social behavior and the severity of autistic symptoms. Social behavior was not correlated with receptive language, intelligence, or chronological age.

Mesibov (1984) reported positive results in the attempt to improve social skills in verbal autistic adolescents. Fifteen adolescents with autism, aged 14 to 25, participated in an individual 30-minute practice session and in a 60-minute group session consisting of group discussion, listening and talking, role playing, and appreciation of humor. Assessment of skills was conducted through role play of social situations, self-report, and skill measures. Parents of participants reported improved social skills (e.g., listening in groups, maintaining eye contact, responding appropriately to strangers). Role plays showed an improvement in initiating and maintaining a one-to-one conversation. Self-concept changes were suggested by improved scores on two self-report measures.

McGee, Krantz, and McClannahan (1984) assessed positive and negative assertions made by three autistic males, aged 4.2, 4.10, and 6.3, in a card game and in a ball game. All children participated in a teaching session prior to each game designed to increase assertive responding. The teaching sessions consisted of modeling, behavioral rehearsal, and praise. All three children demonstrated an increase in both positive and negative assertions in both settings. These effects were present at a $4\frac{1}{2}$ month followup. The responses did not generalize across response types or settings. However, trained assertions did generalize to spontaneous assertions. This generalization was evident at the follow-up.

Coe, Matson, Fee, Manikam, and Linarello (1990) taught two autistic 6-year-old males to initiate and play a ball game with an adult. Target behaviors selected for treatment included ball contact, play initiation, cooperative play, and compliment delivery. Instruction included physical and verbal prompts. Correct responses were rewarded with praise and an edible. Aggression and noncompliance were punished with time out. Both subjects showed an increase in all target behaviors. Introduction of compliment delivery training occurred following training of the other components. For one subject, introduction of this skill appeared to enhance performance on the other three target behaviors, whereas for the other subject, performance on these behaviors appeared to be impeded by the introduction of compliment delivery.

PARENTS

Wolf, Noh, Fisman, and Speechley (1989) assessed the stress levels of the parents of 31 autistic, 31 Down syndrome, 31 chronological age and gender-matched developmentally average and 31 mental age and gender-matched developmentally average children. Mothers of autistic children were significantly more depressed than mothers of normal children. Mothers of children with Down syndrome did not differ significantly in degree of depression from the mothers of either autistic or normal children. Fathers of autistic children showed slightly higher levels of depression compared to other fathers, but the difference was not statistically significant.

Mothers and fathers of autistic children scored significantly higher on a measure of stress than did parents of any of the controls. No differences existed between the control groups. For fathers only, the level of stress seemed to be related to dysphoria more often than in the control groups. For all groups dysphoria and level of stress were related whereas socio demographic variables were not related to stress levels. The impact of stress on depression was suppressed by social support among mothers of handicapped children. For fathers, social support was related to lower levels of depression.

Milgram and Atzil (1988) assessed overall parenting task difficulty, number of parenting tasks performed by each parent, fairness of and satisfaction with the division of parenting tasks, and personal life satisfaction, of 46 parents of 23 autistic children via a self-report measure. Both mothers and fathers perceived as least difficult tasks of daily living and self-care (bathing, bedtime, eating) and as most difficult tasks associated with social behavior (public behavior, anger, protection against injury) and educability. Both mothers and fathers agreed that the mother does more than the father in terms of child care. Mothers reported wanting to do less child care and fathers reported wanting to do more. The less the mothers' share of overall burden, the more fair they believed it to be and the more satisfied they were with the arrangement. No such relationship existed for the fathers.

Fathers reported more life satisfaction than mothers although the satisfaction of one parent was related to that of the other. Mothers' life satisfaction was most highly correlated with their share of the parenting burden and the difference between one's current share and fair share. For fathers, correlations of life satisfaction with parenting, fairness, and parenting satisfaction were lower; the highest correlation was a negative correlation with the number of parenting tasks on which fathers claimed they did more than their wives. Life satisfaction for both mothers and fathers was *not* correlated with teacher ratings of the child's adaptive behavior or symptomatic behavior.

Harris, Handleman, and Palmer (1985) compared the perceptions of family members that were held by the parents (19 mothers, 14 fathers) and grandparents (26 maternal, 17 paternal) of autistic children. There were neither significant differences nor significant correlations between the responses given by mothers and fathers, nor was there any relationship between the responses made by grandmothers and grandfathers. However, when mothers were compared with maternal grandmothers, grandmothers gave a significantly more positive response than mothers to items concerning the child. Mothers were more likely to view the child as more demanding, as having a negative impact on the family, as causing her embarrassment, and as not being a full member of the family. Grandmothers' and mothers' ratings of the mothers' self-description correlated significantly. Both women agreed on the degree of helpfulness of the child's father and on the degree to which the mother had had to make important sacrifices in her life.

When mothers were compared to maternal grandfathers, no significant differences were found. There was a significant correlation between the mothers' and grandfathers' description of the child. They agreed on whether the child had a pleasing personality, whether the child was a full member of the family, and whether achievement of the child gave them pleasure.

Fathers and paternal grandmothers differed in their response to items concerning the child, with grandmothers giving significantly more positive responses than fathers. Grandmothers also described their relationship with their son (the father) as more positive than did the fathers. Fathers' and paternal grandfathers' responses did not differ significantly nor were they significantly correlated.

Stone and Rosenbaum (1988) compared the responses of 47 teachers of autistic students and the responses of 47 parents of autistic children to the responses of 22 specialists in the field of autism on a questionnaire assessing beliefs about etiology, diagnosis, and specific features of autism. Results indicated that the specialists' responses were consistent with empirically based conceptualizations of autism. Parents and teachers were less likely than specialists to believe that autistic children are mentally retarded, were more likely to agree that autistic children possess special talents or abilities, and are more intelligent than tests indicate. Parents were significantly less likely than teachers to agree that most autistic children are mentally retarded.

Parents and teachers were more likely than specialists to view autism as an emotional disorder, to believe that emotional factors play a major role in etiology, and to regard autism and schizophrenia as difficult to differentiate. Teachers and parents were less likely than specialists to view autism as a developmental disorder. Parents were more likely than teachers and specialists to believe that autism exists only in childhood and that children eventually outgrow autism.

Bebko, Konstantareas, and Springer (1987) had parents of autistic children rate their children on severity of various symptoms of autism as well as the degree of parental stress associated with each symptom. Professionals in the field of autism who were familiar with these children also completed the same rating scale. This scale did not include ratings of aggression and self-injury.

The symptoms rated as most severe by parents were cognitive and communication impairments—specifically, inconsistency in child abilities and deficits in verbal expressive language. Relating to people was also rated as severe whereas reaction to environmental change was rated as the least abnormal. Professionals also saw as most severe cognitive and communicative deficits, with nonverbal communication skills being most deviant. Agreement between mother and father symptom ratings was high, as was agreement between parents and professionals.

Verbal expressive difficulties and cognitive inconsistencies were rated as most stressful by both parents. Fathers also rated the child's social impairment as quite stressful. The child's difficulty with change was rated as least stressful. Mothers of older children reported significantly less stress than fathers of older children; however, overall correlations between mothers and fathers was high. Symptom severity was related to the level of stress associated with that symptom and overall severity was associated to overall levels of stress. Professionals' ordering of stressors was identical to that of parents. However, professionals estimated family stress to be higher than the stress levels reported by the families.

Pickering and Morgan (1985) analyzed the responses of 119 parents (73 with nonhandicapped children, 13 with autistic children, and 33 with other handicapped children) to questionnaires evaluating four treatment descriptions all accompanied by the same case description. All three groups rated differential reinforcement and time-out as more effective and more likely to lead to permanent improvement than overcorrection, which in turn was rated as more effective and more likely to lead to permanent improvement than use of contingent electric shock (CES). All groups rated CES as significantly more potent and active than the other three treatments, but all groups also viewed shock as likely to result in negative side effects, and viewed the other three treatments as unlikely to result in negative side effects.

Parents of autistic children rated differential reinforcement more positively than parents of children with other handicaps, who in turn rated differential reinforcement more positively than parents of nonhandicapped children. Parents of autistic and other handicapped children rated shock more negatively than parents of nonhandicapped children.

CHALLENGING BEHAVIORS

Challenging or maladaptive behaviors are often associated with autism. The range and diversity of topography of such behaviors is extremely broad and this presents very significant challenges to not only service providers but also those involved with research into the mechanisms that serve to elicit and maintain such behavior patterns. Because this area represents such a challenge, there are exhaustive reviews of the literature concerning various treatment approaches and hypotheses about causal mechanisms. We do not review vast literature in the present chapter, but rather offer some examples of issues that are often neglected.

One of the recent dominant themes in research in maladaptive behavior has been the recognition that such behavior can stem from a multitude of causes and that even the most severe and seemingly bizarre behavior patterns, such as self-injurious behavior, can be the result of its functional value in the individual's environment (Romanczyk, 1989, 1990a). In particular, in recent years research from individuals such as Edward Carr and Mark Durand have pointed out the functional value of such behavior, particularly in the context of escape paradigms. That is, such maladaptive behavior can serve to remove demands from the environment and thus allow the person to "escape" from these perceived aversive stimuli. This type of model has been extended recently to include both escape and avoidance parameters and to also integrate the important, but until recently neglected, issues of anxiety and arousal (Romanczyk, 1986, 1989).

Durand and Crimmins (1987) assessed the psychotic speech of a 9-year-old boy diagnosed with autism. A functional analysis suggested that this behavior might be motivated by escape from demands. Specifically, time-out from demands reinforced psychotic speech and increased demands resulted in increased levels of psychotic speech. Psychotic speech was reduced by teaching an appropriate escape response "help me" and providing assistance. A condition in which the "help me" response was accompanied by praise without assistance did not decrease psychotic speech. Generalization of the "help me" response occurred in appropriate classroom situations. At a 6-month follow-up, psychotic speech remained at below baseline levels and the classroom teacher reported that psychotic speech no longer interfered with classroom tasks.

Often, the possible useful role of "maladaptive" behavior in the treatment process is overlooked. As an example of utilizing a "maladaptive" behavior, Wolery, Kirk, and Gast (1985) reinforced the correct responding of two autistic children, ages 8 years 10 months and 5 years 10 months, with the opportunity to engage in stereotypic behavior combined with praise. Correct responding increased in this condition relative to a praise-only condition. Use of the stereotypic behavior as a reinforcer did not affect stereotypic behavior in other settings, which is often expressed as a concern.

Often, intervention effects are very precise and specific, as illustrated by Maag, Wolchik, Rutherford, and Parks (1986), who assessed the effects of sensory extinction on the nontargeted self-stimulatory behaviors of two autistic boys ages 7 and 12. Sensory extinction significantly reduced targeted behaviors (i.e., gazing and string waving) and reduced topographically similar, nontargeted behaviors. Suppression did not occur for topographically dissimilar, nontargeted self-stimulatory behaviors. Suppression effects were not maintained following the removal of the sensory extinction procedure.

The Bio-Behavioral Interface

Physical insult, dysfunction, and ailments can result in irritation, discomfort, and pain. Dermatitis and skin lacerations are often found to cause "vicious circle" behavior that most of us experience at one time or another. For example, scratching an itch feels good for a few moments, but scratching produces more irritation, which in turn will prompt further itching, which leads to further scratching. Carr and McDowell (1980) describe the treatment of self-injurious behavior initially elicited by dermatitis, which evolved to be maintained by social reinforcement.

Otitis media is a type of ear infection that can be extremely painful, sometimes resulting in permanent damage and hearing loss. Unlike common earaches (otitis externa) otitis media is a very painful form of earache and appears related in some instances to the elicitation of self-injurious behavior. Self-injurious behavior may reduce the pain produced by otitis media by producing stimulation (pain) in one part of the body that serves to reduce pain from a second site. This "gate" model of pain is familiar to most people and can be seen when confronted by intense, localized pain such as, when in the dentist chair, one squeezes the handles or presses fingernails into the palm. This is probably not a frequent cause of self-injurious behavior, but may be significant and has support in research with humans (DeLissovoy, 1963), and infrahumans (Harkness & Wagner, 1975).

Biological and physiological models of self-injurious behavior have stimulated exploration of pharmacological treatment. However, based on excellent reviews (Farber, 1987; Lapierre & Reesal, 1986; Singh & Millichamp, 1984) at present the efficacy of pharmacological treatment of self-injurious behavior has not been demonstrated. There are many reported instances of positive effects, but such effects are not consistently replicated. The result is that pharmacology is used much more frequently than the results of controlled research would support.

However, current lack of efficacy indicates that more emphasis must be placed upon understanding the biological basic mechanisms of self-injurious behavior. It is likely that the motivation of self-injurious behavior and the varied topography and intensity observed are a function of interaction between biological and environmental learning factors (Romanczyk, in press). Thus, we digress somewhat from this brief overview to examine a few important subtopics in more detail to provide a further degree of appreciation for the potential subtle process that may play a contributing role, although not a role at present easily amenable to clinical measurement or intervention.

Endorphins

Endogenous opioid peptides represent a potentially very important mechanism for understanding certain maladaptive behavior patterns. Among the endogenous opioid peptides, endorphins are hypothesized to maintain addictive-like behavior because of their analgesic effects. For example, the "runner's high" that some athletes who engage in intense and prolonged physical exercise (and thus a particular form of stress) experience, is most likely the result of the endogenous opioid peptides. As stress and pain serve to release endorphins enabling an individual to tolerate higher and higher intensities of pain, it has been hypothesized that self-injurious behavior may thus be influenced by the endorphin mechanism.

Stress-Induced Analgesia

According to Selye (1952), "emergency" situations are met by a number of autonomic adjustments including changes in heart rate, muscle vasodilation, pupillary dilation, glucose and fat mobilization, constriction of capillary beds in the skin, and altered respiration. In addition, these situations activate a complex neuroendocrine response involving the pituitary–adrenal–cortical and sympatho-medullary activity. There is now sufficient experimental evidence to suggest that endogenous pain inhibitory systems are activated during stressful situations. Three families of endogenous opioid peptides have been identified (i.e., the enkephalins, dynorphin, and beta-endorphin), each having a distinct anatomical distribution within the nervous system (Bausbaum & Fields, 1984). Endogenous endorphins have been found to interact with the opiate receptors in the brain and produce an analgesic effect similar to morphine (Hughes, Smith, Kosterlitz, Fothergill, Morgan, & Morris, 1975). Lewis, Cannon, and Liebeskind (1980) have indicated that certain forms of stress may act as natural inputs into the endogenous opiate system. The term *stress-induced analgesia* refers to the phenomenon of increased pain thresholds in response to stressful events.

A variety of experimental manipulations, considered to be stressors, have been employed in investigations of stress-induced analgesia with animals. These include footshock (Mayer & Watkins, 1981), restraint (Amir & Amit, 1979), elevation of blood pressure (Dworkin, Filewich, Miller, Craigmyle, & Pickering, 1979), and food deprivation (Bodnar, Kelly, Spiaggia, & Glusman, 1978). Analysis of the analgesic response has been measured via pre/post response latencies to noxious stimulation following exposure to the putative stressor, measurement of response latencies following interventions expected to block the analgesic effect (i.e., removal or lesion of anatomical substrates thought to be involved in the response and administration of opiate antagonists such as naloxone), as well as via brain assays to assess peptide binding by opiate receptors.

With respect to footshock, the mechanism of this effect is complex and varies with the location of the stimulus on the animal's body, the duration of the stimulus, and the degree of control the animal has over the stimulus. The efficacy of naloxone in blocking analgesia appears to be related to these variables.

An investigation conducted by Lewis, Cannon, and Liebeskind (1980) demonstrates the differential results obtained when the temporal characteristics of footshock are manipulated. The findings indicated that inescapable footshock in rats caused profound analgesia that was reversed by naloxone or dexamthosone under conditions of intermittent footshock applied for a duration of 30 minutes. However, naloxone-reversible analgesia was not found when the stimulus was presented continuously for 3 minutes. The authors concluded that depending on the temporal characteristics, footshock appears to activate opiod or non-opiod analgesia.

Maier, Drugan, and Grau (1982) demonstrated that in a yoked control paradigm, identically shocked rats responded differentially to naloxone treatment following shock. More specifically, rats, unable to escape from tail shock, developed potent, naloxone-reversible analgesia. Another interesting finding was that the effect was reinstated 24 hours later by brief shocks that would otherwise not cause analgesia. This finding underscores the importance of the history of stimulus contact.

Recent evidence also suggests that naloxone-sensitive analgesia can be produced by previously innocuous stimuli following classical conditioning. Chance, White, Krynock, and Rosecrans (1978) found that rats repeatedly exposed to aversive shock became hypoalgesic (i.e., they exhibited significantly longer tail-flick latencies than did control subjects) when placed in the same experimental situation without additional shock. In addition, the binding of exogenous enkephalin was significantly reduced in the fear-conditioned rats, suggesting competition with endogenous peptides.

Thus both painful and nonpainful environmental events have been demonstrated to activate endorphin-mediated networks in the central nervous system that result in analgesia. Furthermore, these networks may be activated directly via ascending nociceptive pathways, or indirectly as a function of stress, conditioning, or hypertension (Bausbaum & Fields, 1984). This clearly relates to the research previously described on escape and avoidance behavior.

Research examining the effects of psychological stimuli on the pituitary–adrenal–cortical system are also relevant. Specifically, Mason (1968) reported that there is evidence to suggest that specific conditions tend to elicit responses of unusual intensity. These include elements of novelty, uncertainty, and unpredictability, anticipation of an event previously experienced as unpleasant, and expenditure of effort to master a difficult task to delay aversive stimulation. In addition, situations in which familiar strategies are no longer functional in achieving mastery may result in disorganized behavior patterns associated with increased ACTH (adrenocorticotropic hormone) release. Further evidence that stressful events may produce analgesia is the finding that beta-endorphin and ACTH are released concomitantly from some cells in the pituitary (Amir & Amit, 1979), a structure whose role in adaptive behavior has been well-documented (Mason, 1968).

Stress-Induced Stereotypies

In light of the discussion of stress-induced analgesia, it is interesting to note that direct injection of beta-endorphin and ACTH into the brain produces excessive grooming in rats (Jolles, Rompa-Barendregt, & Gispen, 1979). The stereotyped response to ACTH was found to be a particularly strong one and was only affected by strong motivational states such as severe hunger, thirst, or anxiety. The authors concluded that the excessive grooming observed is a secondary response that serves to dearouse the organism after activation by ACTH. It has also been demonstrated that the pituitary–adrenal response may persist until the previously arousing stimulus is attenuated (Hennessey & Levine, 1979).

The dopaminergic system of the brain has been implicated in ACTH-induced grooming (Cools, Weigant, & Gispen, 1978) and it has been demonstrated that substances that cause an increase in dopaminergic activity in the striatum (e.g., morphine, ACTH, and beta-endorphin) will result in increased stereotypies (Ahtee, 1974; Valenstein, 1976).

Implications for Self-Injury

Given the interrelationship between stress, pain responsivity, and the release of endogenous opioid peptides and the propensity of the endogenous opiates to elicit stereotyped behavior, Lewis and Baumeister (1982) have speculated that the endogenous opiates may be implicated in the self-injurious and self-stimulatory behavior observed in individuals with severe developmental disabilities. Similarly, Sandman, Datta, Barron, Hoehler, Williams, and Swanson (1983) have speculated that self-injury may be related to aberrations in the endogenous opiate system that result in pain insensitivity. Support for this notion is found in the investigation of the role of the endogenous opiates in individuals with congenital insensitivity to pain. Dehen, Willer, Boureau, and Cambier (1977) found that administration of naloxone dramatically reduced the pain threshold as measured by the nociceptive flexion reflex. In a more recent investigation, Manfredi et al. (1981) failed to find increased pain sensitivity in response to naloxone administration. However, the abnormally high opioid activity found in the cerebral spinal fluid suggests a possible role of endogenous opiates in cases of congenital indifference to pain.

Additional evidence providing support for the role of the endogenous opiates in the genesis of self-injury is provided by the finding that excessive levels of beta-endorphin have been reported in human fetuses experiencing hypoxia, acidosis, and bradycardia (Gautray, Jolivet, Vielh, & Guillemin, 1977). In addition, there is evidence in the animal literature that neonatal exposure to beta-endorphin irreversibly alters pain thresholds (Sandman et al., 1979).

An alternative hypothesis for the role of endogenous opiates in the maintenance of self-injury (Sandman et al, 1983) suggests that self-injury may function as a catalyst for increasing endorphin levels in the central nervous system. Within this context, various pharmacological properties of the endorphins, for example analgesia, tolerance with repeated exposure, physical dependence, and euphoric effects (Belluzi & Stein, 1977; Hosobuchi, Adams, & Linchitz, 1977; Madden, Akil, Patrick, & Barchas, 1977; Wei & Loh, 1976) have been hypothesized to contribute to the durability of the response and its resistance to treatment (Lewis & Baumeister, 1982).

Based upon the preceding basic research, it would seem reasonable to employ naloxone in the treatment of self-injurious behavior. However, extrapolation from basic research can be a complex endeavor, and a multitude of maintaining factors must be considered in the complex world of clinical applications (Romanczyk, Lockshin, & O'Connor, 1991).

Naloxone in the Treatment of Self-Injurious Behavior

Sandman et al. (1983) studied the effects of naloxone on the self-injury of two individuals with an extensive history of self-abuse. Three dosages, .1, .2, and .4 mg, were compared with the vehicle solution in a double-blind crossover design. Naloxone greatly attenuated the self-abusive episodes for one subject and eliminated self-injurious behavior entirely for the other. For one subject the .1 mg dosage appeared to be the most effective. However, the other subject was reported to be equally responsive at all three dosage levels. Although the study demonstrated reduced rates of self-injury, several methodological problems can be identified. These results must be interpreted cautiously as the authors did not include baseline rates of self-injurious behavior. Additionally, no description of the typographies of self-injurious behavior observed in the clients was reported. It is particularly important in the treatment of self-injury to monitor behavior change with specific attention to its various typographies. As discussed earlier, Carr (1977) and others have reported that different typographies of a particular behavior may be influenced by different controlling stimuli and, as such, may be differentially responsive to treatment.

Davidson, Kleene, Carroll, and Rockowitz (1983) reported the effect of naloxone on self-injurious behavior (in the form of head banging) of one subject using a double-blind crossover design that compared two dosages of naloxone (.75 and 1.5 mg) with saline solution placebo. No quantitatively measurable change was observed with naloxone treatment when compared to either baseline or placebo. However, a reduction of intensity was reported clinically.

Szymanski, Kedesdy, Sulkes, Cutler, and Stevens-Our (1987) have discussed limitations of naloxone, and suggest use of naltrexone, a different opiate receptor antagonist, because of its greater half-life and absence of significant side effects. Two subjects participated in their double-blind research design, which was conducted over a period much longer than previous research. The results indicated no effect of naltrexone on self-injurious behavior.

COMPUTER TECHNOLOGY

For several decades there has been interesting speculation about the potential positive use of computer technology for individuals with autism. Almost since computers became reasonably affordable and small, there have been innumerable anecdotal reports of positive responses by individuals with autism to instruction via computer. Perhaps the basis for this long-standing fascination with the possibilities of computer instruction has been the characteristic fascination of individuals with autism for mechanical and repetitive activities.

At present the use of computers in treatment and educational programs for autism is ubiquitous. However, the question arises as to whether in fact the use is justified based on positive outcome. A number of years ago, Panyon (1984) reviewed the appropriate literature at that time and was able to express significant optimism for this technology. However, as with any form of research, it is the long term that produces the best perspective and at this time it would appear that much more caution needs to be expressed (Romanczyk, 1990b). One of the reasons for this caution is that often success of computer instruction is measured by general child reaction and interest rather than actual performance compared to a precise baseline. In our own laboratory over the last 10 years, one of the most consistent findings has been that children reliably express the preference to work with a computer for instructional purposes versus a teacher. This finding appears quite independent of the type of task and independent of the manner in which the question is asked, such as which is nicer, which is more fun, which is easier, and so forth. However, just as consistently, we tend to find that actual performance is better with the teacher than the computer on the specific activities. As a brief overview of the importance of not overgeneralizing the positive effects of the computer utilization, a few studies are reviewed.

First, Plienis and Romanczyk (1985) compared, under highly controlled and well-matched conditions, performance of children with a computer that had full voice synthesis versus a teacher. Interestingly, the performance by the children was equivalent for the two types of training conditions. The children were presented with a simple visual discrimination task of geometric shapes, and the finding of equivalence was important in that often the provision of instruction for simple repetitive tasks is one not enjoyed by human instructors. However, upon closer analysis of the results of this study, it was found that children as a group tended to be more disruptive with the teacher than with the computer. In some instances, this difference was extremely striking. At a more formal level, the relationship between self-stimulation and performance, which is typically negative for children with autism (i.e., as self-stimulation increases, performance decreases, cf. Runco, Charlop, & Schreibman, 1986), was in fact found to be the case but *only* for teacher instruction. That is, with the computer, this relationship with self-stimulation did not hold. Also, observations of classroom behavior for general compliance to instructions by the children was positively related to performance in the human instructor condition and, not surprisingly, was not so related to the computer condition. Thus, the study was important in that it pointed to the possibility that some long-held assumptions about child reaction to task demands may in fact be associated *not* with the task demands themselves, but rather with the instructor and the social learning history associated with human instructors.

A follow-up study was conducted (Plienis, 1987) that attempted to further delineate their findings. In this study, a human and computer instructor were utilized as well as two different types of teaching methodologies, that of positive practice and stimulus fading. The positive practice was a typical instructional procedure whereby when the child made an error, the correct response was indicated to the child and then the task continued in a trial and error fashion. For the stimulus fading method, the task (sight vocabulary instruction) was presented through the mechanism of exaggerating and highlighting the salient characteristics of the correct sight vocabulary words and then gradually fading the emphasis of the salient portion of the word until it was presented in a normal fashion. Interestingly, once again there were no differences between the teacher and computer instructional modality, but there was superiority of the stimulus fading procedure over the positive practice procedure. Also, once again, more disruptive behavior occurred with the teacher than the computer, but this occurred only under the positive practice instructional condition, indicating that this finding of increased disruptive behavior with the human instructor is potentially an interaction with a type of instructional methodology, rather than a simple finding of difference between human and computer instructors. Also, the inverse relationship between maladaptive behavior and performance was again found for teacher instruction but not for computer instruction. However, this was only the case for the positive practice procedure and not for stimulus fading. Thus, the relative superiority of the computer is specific to the type of instructional method and not a function solely of the instructional modality.

In a further extension of this work, Lockshin and Romanczyk (1991) conducted a large-scale study with 22 children, comparing adult versus computer presentation and also varied task difficulty. Given these sets of parameters, interestingly the results indicated that in general the teacher was more effective than the computer, although not to a high degree. Consistent with previous research however, interesting differences were found in that subjects tended to engage in more nonresponding with the computer and particularly in the high demand task. Thus, some of the differences can be accounted for by the teacher's ability to elicit responding attempts under instances of high difficulty where the computer condition appeared unable to as effectively elicit such attempts. Also of interest was that various measures of development, particularly social development, did not serve to predict child performance. This was actually quite surprising, as it would appear to be a reasonable hypothesis to assume that children who have better social functioning might be more responsive to the teacher than to the computer, but this was not in fact the case. Significant correlations did exist, however, between the degree to which an individual child had a strong preference for type of reinforcer used in the tasks, but this correlation held only for the computer and did not exist with the teacher. Thus, once again it appears that some of the very interesting relationships between child behavior and performance are very specific and interact with the modality and method of instruction, and cannot be seen as general child traits.

Another recent study by Ekdahl and Romanczyk (in preparation) attempted to construct an analog computer simulation of the variables that might influence child escape and avoidance behavior. As mentioned such responding appears to have very significant etiological and maintaining effects with respect to maladaptive behavior. Precisely studying such maladaptive behavior in the natural environment is extremely difficult as one cannot provide precise control over the potential variables at work and thus an analog situation was created. A computer was programmed to present an instructional task that consisted of identification of letters or numbers in their proper sequence. The study focused upon manipulation of delay associated with escape and avoidance (which were operationally defined as the child pressing a key on the computer to terminate the particular task presentation and proceed to the next one, either while the task was being displayed on the screen [escape] or just prior to [avoidance] the task being presented on the screen) and whether neutral or negative feedback was utilized. Interestingly, given the common observation that children with severe behavioral problems have difficulty in making temporal discriminations, that is, delaying gratification and inhibiting impulsive responding, and that they also appear to be relatively insensitive to social feedback, the results of the present study were striking. That is, delay did not appear to be a significant variable, but the presence or absence of negative feedback strongly influenced escape behavior. This then may serve also as the basis for interpretation of the mixed results on computer instruction. It would appear that the type of feedback presented to the child would be important especially as it relates to escape from the task, which could also be observed as nonresponding.

At a clinical level, we have also observed very striking examples of this specificity of reaction, such as the instance of a young girl who had a previous history of severe sexual and physical abuse who performed extremely well with the computer but did not generalize the skills she learned to the classroom environment. After rather elaborate task analysis of the failure to generalize, it became clear that in fact the lack of generalization had nothing to do with the task parameters, but rather was simply associated with the absolutely neutral tone of voice of the computer when feedback was given for incorrect responding, versus the child's reaction to extremely subtle connotations of negative feedback in the voice of the human instructor. When this sensitivity was dealt with directly in a desensitization process, generalization from the computer skill level to the classroom was virtually immediate.

Computer technology also can have profound effects upon individuals involved in service delivery by freeing them from many of the repetitive and mundane administrative tasks associated with appropriate record keeping and compliance with regulation. These effects can occur at extremely high levels of magnitude, such that one can observe doubling of staff efficiency and extreme reduction in citations by external review bodies (Romanczyk, 1991). However, there are also numerous anecdotal reports of great failures when it comes to the utilization of such technology, and there is great potential for the abuse of this technology, ranging from its use as "electronic babysitters" to the inappropriate generating of habilitative goals and impressive looking, but content irrelevant, progress reports and documentation of educational and treatment programs.

TREATMENT OUTCOME

Without question, the most significant research study conducted in the last decade was the long-term treatment outcome research by Lovaas (1987). This was a remarkable research project at many levels, and it is the type of research project that is so important that the reader is urged to read the original report in its entirety. Often referred to as the "young autism project," Lovaas conducted a multi-year treatment outcome study that focused upon young children (less than 4 years of age) in an intensive behavioral treatment program. Of great interest was the fact that the children were independently diagnosed as having autism prior to entering the study and that the control group, that is the group to which comparisons were made, actually received up to 10 hours of intensive one-to-one treatment per week. In contrast, however, the experimental group received more than 40 hours of intensive treatment per week and the parents of the children were trained as therapists to provide a consistent and intensive treatment and habilitation package.

The striking result of this study, that 47% of the treatment group achieved normal intellectual and educational functioning as compared to 2% of the control group, is remarkable. Further, of the 10 children in the experimental group who did not recover, 8 were classified as aphasic by their respective school systems. Thus, the overall success of the experimental group is extraordinary.

There have been some criticisms of this research project with respect to its design and conclusions, but such criticisms have been clearly answered very directly and comprehensively by Lovaas (Lovaas, Calouri, & Jada, 1989). Further, subsequent follow-up of these children (McEachin, 1987) has indicated the permanence and comprehensiveness of their recovery and the degree to which these children are indistinguishable from their now-teenage peers. What this research has done therefore is to set a new standard and a new marker by which to evaluate treatment outcome. Certainly in the past decade there has been great progress made in creating new educational and habilitative programs for individuals with autism. Clear progress has been made in enhancing the ability of such individuals to participate in more and more normalized settings. However, even given these very positive changes, one must always be cautious in evaluating outcome research in that it must produce measurable change in the individual's skills and abilities, and not simply be indexed by the degree to which the individual now participates in settings that have been altered and enhanced to support the ability of the individual to meaningfully participate. This is not to say that these are not important goals and important programs, but rather it is research such as that by Lovaas and his colleagues that set the absolute markers that indicate that in fact individuals with autism can recover to the point where they are indistinguishable from their typical peers, and that they can function fully in typical environments without support services and can achieve the same broad spectrum of typical functioning associated with their peers.

The next decade must focus research on establishing the critical components of such treatment strategies as they relate to outcome. The process of establishing programs utilizing the principle of least-restrictive placement must continue in parallel with the imperative to provide the type of intensive, specialized treatment services that will allow more and more individuals with autism to fully recover. Certainly at present such recovery is not a realistic goal for the vast majority of individuals with autism. Much of the service delivery system is ill-prepared to utilize such treatment information and does not have the appropriate resources to implement such comprehensive programs. Nevertheless, the setting of such markers to use as comparison for established and too often entrenched procedures and systems is critical, as it serves to provide impetus to move the norm of service delivery to higher and higher levels.

SUMMARY

This very brief, selective overview of the current status of research in autism has covered a broad array of topics and serves to indicate both the progress being made and our current limitations. Most importantly perhaps, it illustrates that answers will not come from any one narrow field of endeavor and that service providers must undertake the difficult task of keeping abreast of developments in this broad array of fields. Certainly over the next decade we should expect substantial progress to be made in the biological and neurosciences with respect to autism, particularly with respect to etiology and diagnosis. Similarly, well-controlled and well-designed treatment outcome research must increase in number so that we can begin to make rational choices as to the types of treatment strategies that have the best long-term gain for the individual, as opposed to those strategies that are simply easy, comfortable, or cosmetically acceptable to service providers.

Without question, the area of information management and computer science will provide great assistance to service providers not only in their day-to-day habilitative activities, but also to make accessible in a more efficient and rapid manner the wealth of research information being published. It is thus a time of great optimism, if the lessons and information learned in the past can be kept in proper perspective and integrated with our current research findings such that they serve to compliment and enhance one another, rather than being seen as antagonistic or irrelevant. Clearly this large body of research, when seen in proper perspective, indicates that the previous pessimism concerning positive outcome for autism must be radically changed. We are on the brink of being able to provide a broad array of services that significantly and substantially impact upon the life course of individuals with autism, such that we can now speak meaningfully of recovery. However, intensive efforts to find answers to the questions concerning why some individuals are unresponsive to our treatment efforts must continue. Although this is a time of optimism, perspective must be maintained that there remains a very significant number of individuals who currently are not receiving appropriate services, and also that we have not fully identified types of intervention strategies that will allow us to be effective with all individuals with autism. Further, it is clear that autism is not a simple unitary disorder, but rather it is a complex construct that has yet to be fully explicated. The joint partnership between research and service provision must continue and be further enhanced if we are to be successful in answering the myriad of questions remaining.

REFERENCES

Ahtee, L. (1974). Catelepsy and stereotypies in rats treated with methadone, relation to striatal dopamine. *European Journal of Pharmacology, 27,* 221–230.

Amir, S., & Amit, Z. (1979). The pituitary gland mediates acute and chronic pain responsiveness in stressed and non-stressed rats. *Life Sciences, 24,* 439–448.

Bausbaum, A. I., & Fields, H. L. (1984). Endogenous pain control systems: Brainstem pathways and endorphin circuitry. *Annual Review of Neuroscience, 7,* 309–338.

Bebko, J. M., Konstantareas, M. M., & Springer, J. (1987). Parent and professional evaluations of family stress associated with characteristics of autism. *Journal of Autism and Developmental Disorders, 17*(4), 565–576.

Beisler, J. M., Tsai, L., & Vonk, D. (1987). Comparisons between autistic and nonautistic children on the test for auditory comprehension of language. *Journal of Autism and Developmental Disorders, 17*(1), 95–102.

Belluzzi, J. D., & Stein, L. (1977). Enkephalin may mediate euphoria and drive-reduction reward. *Nature, 266,* 556–558.

Berkowitz, S. (1990). A comparison of two methods of prompting in training discrimination of communication book pictures by autistic students. *Journal of Autism and Developmental Disorders, 20*(2), 255–262.

Bodnar, R. J., Kelly, D. D., Spiaggia, A., & Glusman, M. (1978). Biphasic alterations of nociceptive thresholds induced by food deprivation. *Physiological Psychology, 6,* 391–395.

Burke, J. C., & Cerniglia, L. (1990). Stimulus complexity and autistic children's responsivity: Assessing and training a pivotal behavior. *Journal of Autism and Developmental Disorders, 20*(2), 233–253.

Carr, E. G. (1977). The motivation of self-injurious behavior: A review of some hypotheses. *Psychological Bulletin, 84,* 800–816.

Carr, E. G., & McDowell, J. J. (1980). Social control of self-injurious behavior of organic etiology. *Behavior Therapy, 11,* 402–409.

Chance, W. T., White, A. C., Krynock, G. M., & Rosecrans, J. A. (1978). Conditional fear-induced decreases in the binding of (3H)-N-leu-enkephalin to the rat brain. *Brain Research, 141,* 371–374.

Coe, D., Matson, J., Fee, V., Manikam, R., & Linarello, C. (1990). Training nonverbal and verbal play skills to mentally retarded and autistic children. *Journal of Autism and Developmental Disorders, 20*(2), 177–187.

Cools, A. R., Wiegant, V. M., & Gispen, W. H. (1978). Distinct dopaminegic systems in ACTA-induced grooming. *European Journal of Pharmacology, 50,* 265–268.

Curcio, F., & Paccia, J. (1987). Conversations with autistic children: Contingent relationships between features of adult input and children's response adequacy. *Journal of Autism and Developmental Disorders, 17,* 81–93.

Davidson, P. W., Kleene, B. M., Carroll, M., & Rockowitz, R. J. (1983). Effects of naloxone

on self-injurious behavior: A case study. *Applied Research in Mental Retardation, 4,* 1-4.
Dawson, G., & Fernald, M. (1987). Perspective-taking ability and its relationship to the social behavior of autistic children. *Journal of Autism and Developmental Disorders, 17*(4), 487-498.
Dawson, G., Hill, D., Spencer, A., Galpert, L., & Watson, L. (1990). Affective exchanges between young autistic children and their mothers. *Journal of Abnormal Child Psychology, 18*(3), 335-345.
Dawson, G., & McKissick, F. C. (1984). Self-recognition in autistic children. *Journal of Autism and Developmental Disorders, 14*(4), 383-394.
Dehen, H., Willer, J. C., Boureau, F., & Cambier, J. (1977). Congenital insensitivity to pain, and endogenous morphine-like substances. *The Lancet, 2,* 293-294.
DeLissovoy, V. (1963). Head banging in early childhood: A suggested cause. *Journal of Genetic Psychology, 102,* 109-114.
Durand, V. M., & Crimmins, D. B. (1987). Assessment and treatment of psychotic speech in an autistic child. *Journal of Autism and Developmental Disorders, 17*(1), 17-28.
Dworkin, B. R., Filewich, R. J., Miller, N. E., Craigmyle, N., Pickering, T. G. (1979). Baroreceptor activation reduces reactivity to noxious stimulation: Implications for hypertension. *Science, 205,* 1299-1301.
Ekdahl, M., & Romanczyk, R. G. (in preparation). *A computer simulation of escape and avoidance behavior.*
Farber, J. (1987). Psychopharmacology of self-injurious behavior in the mentally retarded. *Journal of American Academy of Child and Adolescent Psychiatry, 16*(3), 296-302.
Gautray, J. P., Jolivet, A., Vielh, J. P., & Guillemin, R. (1977). Presence of immunoassayable beta-endorphin in human amniotic fluid: Elevation in case of fetal distress. *American Journal of Obstetrics and Gynecology, 129,* 211-212.
Gilburg C. (1989). *Diagnosis and treatment of autism.* New York: Plenum Press.
Harkness, J. E., & Wagner, J. E. (1975). Self-mutilation in mice associated with otitis media. *Laboratory Animal Science, 25,* 315-318.
Harris, S. L., Handleman, J. S., Kristoff, B., Bass, L., & Gordon, R. (1990). Changes in language development among autistic and peer children in segregated and integrated preschool settings. *Journal of Autism and Developmental Disorders, 10*(1), 23-32.
Harris, S. L., Handleman, J. S., & Palmer, C. (1985). Parents and grandparents view the autistic child. *Journal of Autism and Developmental Disorders, 15*(2), 127-137.
Hedbring, C., & Newsom, C. (1985). Visual overselectivity: A comparison of two instructional remediation procedures with autistic children. *Journal of Autism and Developmental Disorders, 15*(1), 9-22.
Hennessey, J. W., & Levine, S. (1979). Stress, arousal, and the pituitary-adrenal system. A psychoendocrine hypothesis. In J. M. Sprague & A. N. Epstein (Eds.), *Progress in psychobiology and physiological psychology* (Vol. 8, pp. 133-178). New York: Academic Press.
Hobson, R. P., & Lee, A. (1989). Emotion-related and abstract concepts in autistic people: Evidence from the British Picture Vocabulary Scale. *Journal of Autism and Developmental Disorders, 19*(4), 601-623.
Hosobuchi, Y., Adams, J. E., & Linchitz, R. (1977). Pain relief by electrical stimulation of the central grey matter in humans and its reversal by naloxone. *Science, 197,* 183-186.
Hughes, J., Smith, T. W., Kosterlitz, H. J. W., Fothergill, L. A., Morgan, B. A., & Morris, H. R. (1975). Identification of two related pentapeptides from the brain with potent opiate agonist activity. *Nature, 258,* 577-579.
Jolles, J., Rompa-Barendregt, J., & Gispen, W. H. (1979). ACTH-induced excessive grooming in the rat: The influence of environmental and motivational factors. *Hormones and Behavior, 12,* 60-72.

Jones, V., & Prior, M. (1985). Motor imitation abilities and neurological signs in autistic children. *Journal of Autism and Developmental Disorders, 15*(1), 37–46.

Kistner, J., & Robbins, F. (1986). Brief report: Characteristics of methods of subject selection and description in research on autism. *Journal of Autism and Developmental Disorders, 16*(1), 77–82.

Koegel, R. L., O'Dell, M., & Dunlap. G. (1988). Producing speech use in nonverbal autistic children by reinforcing attempts. *Journal of Autism and Developmental Disorders, 18*(4), 525–538.

Koegel, R. L., O'Dell, M. C., & Koegel, L. K. (1987). A natural language teaching paradigm for nonverbal autistic children. *Journal of Autism and Developmental Disorders, 17*(2), 187–200.

Lapierre, Y. D., & Reesal, R. (1986). Pharmacologic management of aggressivity and self-mutilation in the mentally retarded. *Psychiatric Clinics in North America, 9*(4), 745–754.

Lewis, J. W., Cannon, J. T., & Liebeskind, J. C. (1980). Opioid and non-opioid mechanisms of stress analgesia. *Science, 208,* 623–625.

Lewis, M. H., & Baumeister, A. A. (1982). Stereotyped mannerisms in mentally retarded persons: Animal models and theoretical analyses. *International Review of Research in Mental Retardation, 11*(1), 20–161.

Lockshin, S., & Romanczyk, R. G. (1991). *The interaction of computer versus teacher presentation and task difficulty level on child performance.* Unpublished manuscript.

Lovaas, O. I. (1987). Behavioral treatment and normal educational and intellectual functioning in young autistic children. *Journal of Consulting and Clinical Psychology, 55,* 3–9.

Lovaas, O. I., Calouri, K., & Jada, J. (1989). The nature of behavioral treatment and research with young autistic persons. In C. Gillberg (Ed.), *Diagnosis and treatment of autism* (pp. 285–306). New York: Plenum Press.

Maag, J. W., Wolchik, S. A., Rutherford, R. B. Jr., & Parks, B. T. (1986). Response covariation on self-stimulatory behaviors during sensory extinction procedures. *Journal of Autism and Developmental Disorders, 16,*(2), 119–132.

Madden, J., IV., Akil, H., Patrick, R. L., & Barchas, J. D. (1977). Stress-induced parallel changes in central opioid levels and pain responsiveness in the rat. *Nature, 265,* 358–360.

Maier, S. F., Drugan, R. C. & Grau, J. W. (1982). Controllability, coping behavior, and stress-induced analgesia in the rat. *Pain, 12,* 47–56.

Maltz, A. (1981). Comparison of cognitive deficits among autistic and retarded children on the Arthur Adaptation of the Leiter International Performance Scales. *Journal of Autism and Developmental Disorders, 11*(4), 413–426.

Manfredi, M., Bini, G., Cruccu, G., Accornero, N., Bernardelli, A., & Medolago, L. (1981). Congenital absence of pain. *Archives of Neurology, 38,* 507–512.

Mason, J. W. (1968). A review of psychoendocrine research on the pituitary-adrenal cortical system. *Psychosomatic Medicine, 30,* 576–607.

Mayer, D. J., & Watkins, L. R. (1981). Role of endorphins in endogenous pain control systems. *Modern Problems in Pharmopsychiatry, 17,* 689–696.

McEachin, J. J. (1987). *Outcome of autistic children receiving intensive behavioral treatment: Residual deficits.* Unpublished doctoral dissertation, University of California, Los Angeles.

McGee, G. G., Krantz, P. J., & McClannahan, L. E. (1984). Conversational skills for autistic adolescents: Teaching assertiveness in naturalistic settings. *Journal of Autism and Developmental Disorders, 14*(3), 319–330.

Mesibov, G. B. (1984). Social skills training with verbal autistic adolescents and adults: A program model. *Journal of Autism and Developmental Disorders, 14*(4), 395–404.

Milgram, N. A., & Atzil, M. (1988). Parenting stress in raising autistic children. *Journal of Autism and Developmental Disorders, 18*(3), 415–424.

Ohta, M. (1987). Cognitive disorders of infantile autism: A study employing the WISC, spatial relationship conceptualization, and gesture imitations. *Journal of Autism and Developmental Disorders, 17*(1), 45–62.

Panyon, M. V. (1984). Computer technology for autistic students. *Journal of Autism and Developmental Disorders, 14*(4), 375–382.

Parker, R. M. (1990). Power, control, and validity in research. *Journal of Learning Disabilities, 23,* 613–620.

Pickering, D., & Morgan, S. B. (1985). Parental ratings of treatments of self-injurious behavior. *Journal of Autism and Developmental Disorders, 15*(3), 303–314.

Plienis, A. (1987). *Sources and methods of instruction with atypical children: An investigation of stimulus fading and computer-delivered instruction.* Unpublished doctoral dissertation, S.U.N.Y. at Binghamtom.

Plienis, A., & Romanczyk, R. G. (1985). Analysis of performance, behavior, and predictors for severely disturbed children: A comparison of adult versus computer instruction. *Analysis and Intervention in Developmental Disabilities, 5,* 345–356.

Romanczyk, R. G. (1986). Self-injurious behavior: Conceptualization, assessment and treatment. In K. D. Gadow (Ed.), *Advances in learning and behavioral disabilities* (Vol. 5, pp. 29–56). Greenwich, JAI Press.

Romanczyk, R. G. (1989). *A review of the literature on self-injurious behavior: Factors that should influence clinical decision making.* Paper presented to the National Institute of Health Consensus Development Conference on Treatment of Destructive Behaviors in Persons with Developmental Disabilities, Rockville, MD.

Romanczyk, R. G. (1990a). Aversive conditioning as a component of comprehensive treatment: The impact of etiological factors on clinical decision making. In S. L. Harris & J. Handelman (Eds.), *Aversive and non-aversive intervention: Controlling life-threatening behavior of the developmentally disabled* (pp. 11–35). New York: Springer.

Romanczyk, R. G. (1990b). *Computer technology for providers and recipients of services for developmental disabilities.* Paper presented at the 98th Annual Convention of the American Psychological Association, Boston, MA.

Romanczyk, R. G. (1991). Monitoring and evaluating clinical service delivery: Issues of effectiveness and computer database management. In Alastair Ager (Ed.), *Microcomputers in clinical psychology* (pp. 155–173). Sussex, England: Wiley.

Romanczyk, R. G. (in press). *Self-injurious behavior: Etiology and treatment.* New York: Plenum Press.

Romanczyk, R. G., Lockshin, S. B., & Harrison, K. (1991). Schizophrenia and autism. In J. L. Matson & R. P. Barrett (Eds.), *Psychopathology in the mentally retarded* (2nd ed.). San Antonio, TX: The Psychological Corporation.

Romanczyk, R. G., Lockshin, S., & O'Connor, J. (1991). Psychophysiology and issues of anxiety and arousal. In J. K. Luiselli, J. L. Matson, & N. N. Singh (Eds.), *Assessment, analysis, and treatment of self-injury.* New York: Springer-Verlag.

Rumsey, J. M. (1985). Conceptual problem solving in highly verbal, nonretarded autistic men. *Journal of Autism and Developmental Disorders, 15*(1), 23–36.

Runco, M. A., Charlop, M. H., & Schreibman, L. (1986). The occurrence of autistic children's self-stimulation as a function of familiar versus unfamiliar. *Journal of Autism and Developmental Disabilities, 16*(1), 31–44.

Rutter, M. (1978). Language disorder and infantile autism. In M. Rutter & E. Schopler (Eds.), *Autism: A reappraisal of concepts and treatment.* New York: Plenum Press.

Sandman, C. A., Datta, P. C., Barron, J., Hoehler, F. K., Williams, C., & Swanson, J. M. (1983). Naloxone attenuates self-abusive behavior in developmentally disabled clients. *Applied Research in Mental Retardation, 4,* 5–11.

Sandman, C. A., McGivern, R. F., Berka, C., Walker, J. M., Coy, D. H. & Kastin, A. J.

(1979). Neonatal administration of B-endorphin procedures "chronic" insensitivity to thermal stimuli. *Life Sciences, 25,* 1755–1760.

Selye, H. (1952). *The story of the adaptation syndrom.* Montreal Acta Inc.

Sigman, M., & Ungerer, J. A. (1984). Attachment behaviors in autistic children. *Journal of Autism and Developmental Disorders, 14*(3), 231–244.

Singh, N. N., & Millichamp, C. J. (1984). Effects of medication on the self-injurious behavior of mentally retarded persons. *Psychiatric Aspects of Mental Retardation Reviews, 3*(4), 13–16.

Smith, D. E. P., McConnell, J. V., Walter, T. L., & Miller, S. D. (1985). Effect of using an auditory trainer on the attentional, language, and social behaviors of autistic children. *Journal of Autism and Developmental Disorders, 15*(3), 285–302.

Stone, W. L., & Rosenbaum, J. L. (1988). A comparison of teacher and parent views of autism. *Journal of Autism and Developmental Disorders, 18*(3), 403–414.

Szymanski, L., Kedesdy, J., Sulkes, S., Cutler, A., & Stevens-Our, P. (1987). Naltrexone in treatment of self-injurious behavior: A clinical study. *Research in Developmental Disabilities, 8,* 179–190.

Ungerer, J. A., & Sigman, M. (1987). Categorization skills and receptive language development in autistic children. *Journal of Autism and Developmental Disorders, 17*(1), 3–16.

Valenstein, E. S. (1976). Stereotyped behavior and stress. In G. Serban & J. W. Mason (Eds.), *Psychopathology of human adaptation* (pp. 113–124). New York: Plenum.

Wei, E., & Loh, H. (1976). Chronic intracerebral infusion of morphine and peptides with osmotic minipumps, and the development of physical dependence. In H. W. Kosterlitz (Ed.), *Opiates and endogenous opioid peptides* (pp. 303–318). Amsterdam: Elsevier.

Wolery, M., Kirk, K., & Gast, D. L. (1985). Stereotypic behavior as a reinforcer: Effects and side effects. *Journal of Autism and Developmental Disorders, 15*(2), 149–161.

Wolf, L. C., Noh, S., Fisman, S. N., & Speechley, M. (1989). Brief report: Psychological effects of parenting stress on parents of autistic children. *Journal of Autism and Developmental Disorders, 19*(1), 157–166.

3 Biomedical Research in Autism

Luke Y. Tsai
Mohammad Ghaziuddin
University of Michigan Medical Center

Following Leo Kanner's incisive description of "Infantile Autism" in 1943, it was widely believed that autism was caused by poor parenting and emotional conflicts between mother and child. Some authorities, including Kanner himself, believed that anxiety suffered by the child as a result of bad rearing practices and psychological problems was the underlying cause of the disorder. However, research done over the past four decades has consistently shown that this is simply not true. There is no evidence to suggest that the parents of children with autism are unkind or uncaring, or that poor parenting results in autism. If this were so, all children who suffer from poor parenting would develop autism. Although some people may still believe in the psychogenic hypothesis of autism, most authorities now agree that biological and not psychodynamic factors are of crucial importance.

An important piece of evidence that supports the biomedical hypothesis is the association of mental retardation with autism. Kanner believed that most children with autism were of normal intelligence. However, research has repeatedly shown that out of every four persons, with autism three have coexisting mental retardation.

In addition to the presence of global mental retardation, certain specific *neurological disorders* are also commonly seen in autistic persons, which further provides evidence to the biomedical model of autism. Some of these conditions include: epilepsy, tuberous sclerosis, cytomegalovirus infections, encephalitis and meningitis.

Moreover, certain *neurological abnormalities* have also been reported in 30% to 75% of several series of autistic persons. These include hypotonia or hypertonia, clumsiness, abnormal posture and gait, tremors, drooling, and so on (Tsai, 1987). Autistic children also show a high incidence of congenital physical anomalies (Campbell Geller, Small, Petti, & Fernes, 1978).

Despite the strong evidence pointing to an organic etiology of autism, the nature of the basic defect remains unclear. To attempt to clarify this, a number of studies using a variety of techniques have been undertaken over the last few decades. These are summarized in this chapter.

GENETIC STUDIES

Genetic factors seem to play a major role in the etiology of autism. Several studies have shown that siblings of autistic persons have increased rates of the disorder (Minton Campbell, Green, Jennings, & Samit, 1982; Rutter, 1967; Tsai, Stewart, & August, 1981). It has been estimated that the pooled frequency of autism in the siblings is about 3% (Rutter, in press; Smalley, Asornow, & Spence, 1988), which is about 50 times higher than that of the general population (based on 4–5 per 10,000 rate of autism).

Studies of twins also provide support to the etiological role of genetic factors in autism. However, in view of the fact that twin-births are rather uncommon in the general population, few major studies have been done. An important, carefully designed study was undertaken by Folstein and Rutter in 1977. They studied 21 same-sex autistic twin pairs and found that 4 of the 11 (36%) monozygotic (MZ) twin pairs were concordant for autism, as compared with none of the dizygotic (DZ) pairs. In addition, they found an 82% concordance for serious cognitive abnormalities in MZ pairs and 10% in DZ pairs. On the basis of this finding, they suggested that what was inherited in autism was a pattern of cognitive deficits that included, but was not restricted to, autism. Autism was hypothesized as lying on an extreme pole of a spectrum of cognitive-language disorders, with some learning and/or language disorders being milder variants of the same continuum (Folstein, 1985). A follow-up of Folstein and Rutter's sample has revealed that the nonautistic MZ co-twins in discordant pairs tend to show marked social deficits in adult life, suggesting that the inherited deficit is social as well as cognitive (Le Couteur, Bailey, Rutter, & Gottesman, 1989).

Ritvo, Freeman, Mason-Brothers, Mo, and Ritvo (1985) studied 23 pairs of MZ and 17 pairs of DZ twins drawn from the UCLA Registry for Genetic Studies in Autism. Of the 23 MZ pairs, 22 were found to be concordant for autism compared to 4 of the 17 DZ pairs. This yields a 96% concordance rate for MZ pairs and 24% for DZ pairs. The higher concordance for DZ pairs (24%) probably reflects the fact that the sample studied was not representative of twinships in the population of autistic patients. Also, only 12 pairs of MZ twins and 5 pairs of the 12 pairs of same-sex DZ twins had blood grouping done (Folstein & Rutter, 1987; Smalley et al., 1988). Other twin studies have also found higher concordance rates for MZ pairs and no concordance for DZ pairs, supporting the role of genetic factors in autism (Steffenburg et al., 1989).

Apart from the increased prevalence of autism in siblings and the MZ–DZ differences in concordance, additional support for the importance of genetic factors comes from the finding of increased rate of cognitive disabilities in siblings of autistic persons. August, Stewart, and Tsai (1981) found a 15% rate of cognitive abnormalities in the siblings of autistic probands as against 3% among the siblings of Down's syndrome controls. Of the 11 siblings of autistic probands, 4 showed problems in the comprehension or production of language, 9 had IQs below 80, and 2 had reading disabilities. Similar observations have been made by other investigators (Ritvo, Spence et al., 1985). In another study, Minton, Campbell, Green, Jennings, and Samit (1982) found that nonautistic siblings of autistic children had significantly lower verbal scores than performance scores on Wechsler Intelligence Scales, and 10% were mentally retarded. It has been suggested that the familial loading for cognitive disabilities is most evident in the families of mentally retarded autistic children (Baird & August, 1985). However, other studies have shown that most of the familial loading for cognitive disabilities is not accounted for by mental retardation (Piven, Gayle et al., 1990) and that a family history of reading or language disabilities is present in a quarter of families with an autistic child whose IQ is 70 or more (Bartak, Rutter, & Cox, 1975). A recent study has confirmed that most of the cognitive disabilities in siblings consist of specific disorders of speech and language, rather than global mental retardation (Macdonald, Rutter, Rios, & Boltor, 1989).

Association of autism with certain genetic syndromes also provides support to the importance of genetic factors in this disorder. Thus, a proportion of autistic individuals have been found to exhibit a fragile site on the X chromosome (Brown et al., 1986; Levitas, McBogg, & Hagerman, 1983). Some investigators have suggested that the rate of chromosomal anomalies in autistic individuals is at least 47% with about 20–25% showing the fragile X chromosome (Gillberg & Wahlström, 1985). Although the issue is not yet decided, most recent studies have produced figures of below 5% (Payton, Steele, Wenger, & Minshaw, 1989). In addition to fragile X syndrome, occasional reports have described the association of autism with single gene disorders, both autosomal recessive (such as phenylketonuria) and autosomal dominant (such as tuberous sclerosis). These reports, though not based on systematic series of cases of these single gene disorders, do provide further support to the importance of genetic factors in autism.

Based on these studies, possible modes of inheritance have been proposed. Ritvo, Spence et al. (1985), on the basis of a segregation analysis of

46 families with multiple cases of autism, produced results that were consistent with autosomal recessive inheritance. However, this is inconsistent with the observed marked excess of autistic males. Tsai and his colleagues (August et al., 1981; Tsai & Beisler, 1983; Tsai, Stewart, & August, 1981) proposed a multifactorial model with different thresholds for males and females. Vertical transmission has been implied by some authors (Ritvo, Mason-Brothers, & Freeman, 1988); however, most studies have found no evidence of personality abnormalities in parents (Cantwell, Baker, & Rutter, 1978).

Thus, whereas familial aggregation is noted in case series, and the data from the twin studies indicate that genetic factors are likely to be important in autism, these studies tell us little about the nature of the genetic defect, or whether one or more genetic mechanisms are operating, or whether the genetic mechanism(s) operate(s) in the whole group of autism or just in some subgroups. A delineation of just what is inherited will provide a better understanding of genetic implications in autism. Now that "gene maps" are being made of the positions of genes on human chromosomes, new possibilities are arising for studies called *linkage studies,* which can determine whether genes for a given disorder lie on a chromosome in close proximity to known genetic markers, such as the gene for color blindness or certain blood types. If two genes lie close together, the two traits they cause are likely to be inherited together. Finding clear evidence of linkage between a given psychiatric disorder and a trait caused by a known genetic marker would provide hard evidence that the psychiatric disorder is genetically caused and would lay to rest any doubts left by loopholes in twin and adoption studies. Furthermore, through the identification of genetic markers, a clearer pattern of genetic transmission may be elucidated, etiologic subgroups may be identified, and the pathophysiology of a disorder may be determined (Smalley et al., 1988). For example, in utilizing this approach in medical genetics, different enzymatic defects have been identified to elucidate the existence of many subtypes of mucopolysaccharidoses.

To date, there is one linkage study of autism using blood polymorphisms in a subset of multiple-incidence families (Spence et al., 1985). Spence and colleagues (1985) found no evidence for linkage for autism with 30 blood polymorphisms and could rule out linkage with 19 of these markers. They also found no evidence for an association of HLA and autism. They, however, suggested that potential markers may be found in chromosome 9 in the region of the ABO blood group.

The finding of fragile X chromosome among autistic patients led Tsai and colleagues (Tsai, Crowe, Patil, Murray, & Quinn, 1988) to use six DNA probes in the Xq26-q28 region to search for DNA markers for autism. Although clinically useful markers have not been found, such a research approach may provide a potentially fruitful means of increasing our understanding of the relationship between genetic factors and autism.

In summary, the last decade of genetic research in autism has found strong evidence suggesting that there may be different genetic mechanisms that result in the syndrome of autism, hence suggesting genetic heterogeneity in autism. Several different kinds of studies are needed in order to sort out the various mechanisms. A study should begin with a detailed family analysis based on a systematically ascertained sample. Each autistic proband and all first-degree relatives should have a detailed clinical examination and laboratory tests including social, cognitive, and language assessment. The goal is to identify genetic markers so that the autism phenotype can be redefined using such markers. Then comparative studies of autistic and nonautistic individuals who have the same subclinical marker (e.g., unaffected relatives) should be conducted. In this way, genotype–genotype interaction or genotype–environment interactions may be elucidated in the etiology of autism (Smalley et al., 1988). The ultimate goal is to be able to apply gene therapy to those who are affected with autism, as well as to be able to practice prevention of autism.

OBSTETRIC AND POSTNATAL FACTORS

There is strong evidence that complications of pregnancy and delivery are associated with autism. Twin pairs discordant for autism provide convincing evidence for an association between obstetric/postnatal factors and autism. For example, in the Folstein and Rutter study previously quoted (1977), the authors found that the nonautistic but cognitively disabled MZ co-twins had normal or near-normal birth histories compared with their autistic co-twins, several of whom had a history of significant perinatal problems. Steffenburg et al. (1989) confirmed this finding in a more recent study. They described 11 twin pairs in which only one twin was autistic. In eight of these discordant pairs, the autistic twin had suffered more perinatal and neonatal complications than the nonautistic co-twin.

In addition to twin studies, other data also suggest that autistic singleton experience significantly more obstetric and neonatal complications than matched controls, with complications of pregnancy being more common than complications of delivery (Deykin & MacMahon, 1980; Gillberg & Gillberg, 1983). A number of pre-, peri-, and neonatal factors appear to be more frequent in autistic subjects than in their siblings or matched controls (see review by Tsai, 1987). These include increased maternal age, birth order (first and fourth or later born), bleeding after the first trimester, use of medication, and meconium in amniotic fluid. It has been suggested that pre-

or perinatal insults to the brain are the biological causation of autism in persons whose autistic symptoms are present from birth, and that postnatal cerebral infections or injuries cause the disorder when symptoms appear after a period of apparent normal development. Despite this suggestion, research done so far does not indicate a causal relationship between obstetric and neonatal factors and autism. Nor does it suggest that the association is specific, in the sense that a number of factors of a variable severity have been implicated. This implies that either obstetric and neonatal factors can sometimes convert an entirely normal fetus into an autistic person (Steffenburg et al., 1989), or they can sometimes unmask or potentiate a preexisting genetic liability (Folstein & Rutter, 1977). Clearly, more research is needed before a causal link can be proposed between autism and obstetric/postnatal complications.

NEUROPATHOLOGICAL STUDIES

In view of the high prevalence of neurological signs in persons with autism, attempts have been made to relate these signs to underlying brain pathology. However, due to various ethical and practical reasons, very few neuropathological studies in autism have been done. Initial postmortem brain studies of seven cases were largely negative (Darby, 1976; Williams, Hauser, Purpura, DeLong, & Swischer, 1980). Bauman and Kemper (1985) reported the autopsy findings of a 29-year-old man with clear autism who had died by drowning. The findings included major cellular and structural changes in hippocampus, amygdala, and cerebellum (including Purkinje cell loss). In the following year, Ritvo and colleagues (Ritvo et al., 1986) reported autopsy findings in four autistic patients. They too found Purkinje cell loss in the cerebellum of all the patients. Recently, Kemper (1990) reported further autopsy results of six autistic individuals. The forebrain in all six showed a reduction in neuronal size and increased cell-packing density in the hippocampal formation, entorhinal cortex, amygdala, and medial septal nuclei. In the hindbrain, there was a decreased number of Purkinje and granule cells in the cerebellum. However, in view of the small numbers involved, it is not clear what weight should be attached to the findings of these studies.

NEURORADIOLOGICAL STUDIES

Computerized Tomographic (CT) Scan Studies

Computerized tomography is a radiological technique that uses computerized processing of X-ray transmission data and allows for a greatly enhanced visualization of the brain in living persons. Because of its noninvasive nature, it has been used in a broad range of psychiatric research. Several CT studies have been done on autistic individuals. In a minority of patients, gross abnormalities (e.g., porencephalic cyst) have been identified (Damasio, Maurer Damasio, & Chui, 1980; Gillberg & Svendsen, 1983). Apart from gross abnormalities, smaller focal defects have also been found. For example, an early study (Hier, LeMay, & Rosenberger, 1979) reported a high incidence of abnormal anterior or posterior cerebral asymmetry in autistic children; however, four additional studies have since failed to confirm this finding (Damasio et al., 1980; Gillberg & Svendsen, 1983; Rumsey et al., 1988; Tsai, Jacoby, Stewart, & Beisler, 1982). Damasio et al. (1980) reported ventricular asymmetries in autistic patients with neurological disease, but the finding could not be replicated in idiopathic cases of autism (Rosenbloom et al., 1984). Enlargement of the lateral and third ventricles in physically healthy autistic patients has been reported by some studies (Campbell, 1982; Caparulo, Cohen, Rothman, Shaywitz, & Shaywitz, 1981; Rosenbloom, 1984), but others have failed to confirm this finding (Creasey 1986; Prior, Tress, Hoffman, & Boldt, 1984). No significant group differences have been found in the volumes of cerebrospinal fluid, white matter, gray matter, the caudate and lenticular nuclei or the thalamus (Creasey, 1986). Increased fourth ventricular width and cerebellar atrophy have also been reported in autistic children (Bauman, LeMay, Bauman, & Rosenberger, 1985), though a recent study could not replicate this finding (Rumsey et al., 1988). Enlargement of the third ventricle with significantly lower mean density of the caudate nucleus has also been reported (Jacobson, LeCouteur, Howlin, & Rutter, 1988).

Magnetic Resonance Imaging (MRI) Studies

Magnetic resonance imaging is a new technique that has many strengths compared to CT scanning. It requires no ionizing radiation and whereas CT scanning is limited to one plane, the magnetic resonance technique can provide images in three planes: sagittal, coronal, and transverse. It is free of bony artifact and can permit better visualization of relatively tiny structures and also allows better delineation of the posterior fossa, a region that is observed by bony artifacts on CT scan. Also, fine shades of tissue abnormality (e.g., plaques in multiple sclerosis) can be better identified with this technique. Because of these advantages, it is rapidly displacing CT scanning for clinical and research purposes.

As the patient is required to remain still during scanning, sometimes necessitating the use of sedation, only a few head MRI studies have been done in autism. Minshaw and associates (1986) found that the cerebellum and fourth ventricle were normal in all 10 autistic subjects with IQs of 71 or above. However, three of the six subjects with IQs of 70 to 85 had abnormalities: enlarged lateral ventricles in two and decreased cortical volume with increased subarachnoid space and normal ventricles in one. In a series of 14 autistic patients with IQs of 60 or greater, Gaffney and colleagues (Gaffney, Kuperman, Tsai & Minchin, 1988; Gaffney, Kuperman, Tsai, Minchin, & Hassanein, 1987; Gaffney & Tsai, 1987; Gaffney, Tsai, Kuperman, & Minchin, 1987), found that 6 of the 14 patients had brain lesions including heterotopic gray matter and basal ganglia abnormalities. No single, circumscribed lesion was common to all patients. The fourth ventricle was found to be significantly larger and the entire brainstem significantly smaller than the control group in midsagittal scans. In the coronal scans, the cerebellum of the autistic patients was found to be proportionally smaller and the fourth ventricles proportionally larger. Courchesne, Yeung-Courchesne, Press Hesselink, and Termgon (1988) reported that the cerebellar lobules VI and VII were significantly smaller in a group of 18 autistic patients; however, Garber et al. (1989) did not find any difference in the measurements of these lobules in a group of 15 autistic patients and 15 normal controls. And in a recent study, Piven, Berthier et al. (1990) reported the presence of cerebral cortical malformations in 7 out of 13 high-functioning autistic males. Thus, although the link between structural pathology of the brain and autism is yet to be determined, it is clear that MRI scanning has opened up a new era of research in autism.

Positron Emission Tomography (PET) Studies

This is a new investigative technique that provides a three-dimensional view of a variety of biochemical processes such as brain energy, metabolism, regional blood volume, blood flow, tissue drug levels, and receptor binding. Only a few PET studies have been done in autism because of the risk of radiation exposure in children. In one study, Rumsey and others found elevated utilization of glucose throughout many parts of the brains of 10 autistic men, as compared with controls (Rumsey et al., 1985). Similar findings were reported in a group of 18 autistic children by DeVolder, Bol, Michel, Cogneau, and Goffinet (1988), although the mean brain glucose metabolism did not differ significantly between autistic cases and controls. More recently, Heh (1989) used PET to examine the cerebellum in a group of seven adult autistic patients and eight age-matched controls. The results observed no significant differences in mean cerebellar glucose metabolism between the two groups, though all mean glucose rates of autistic patients were either equal to or greater than those of the controls. Although the significance of these findings is unclear, it is likely that PET will become an important tool of research in autism.

NEUROPHYSIOLOGIC FACTORS

Neurophysiologic studies in autism have focused on the measurement of electrical and other impulses in the brain. It has been hypothesized that two main types of dysfunction occur in autism—a primary cortical dysfunction and a primary brainstem dysfunction. According to the first type of dysfunction, autism results from a disorder of hemispheric lateralization in which parts of the left hemisphere required for information processing fail to develop (Blackstock, 1978; Prior, 1979; Tanguay, 1977). The second type of dysfunction posits that pathophysiologic influences originate in the brainstem and diencephalic structure in autism (Ornitz, 1985). Support for cortical dysfunction in autism comes from studies of event-related potentials (ERPs), in which a reduced P3b wave has been found (Courchesne, Kilman, Galambos, & Lincoln 1984; Courchesne, Lincoln, Kilmon, & Galambos, 1985). This component represents purely cognitive functions and occurs at 300 to 900 milliseconds after stimulus. In addition, another long-latency evoked potential component, Nc, also appears to be smaller in Autism (Courchesne, 1987).

Further support for the cortical dysfunction hypothesis comes from electroencephalographic (EEG) studies in autism. In general, these studies have found bilateral hemispheric abnormalities (Tsai & Tsai, 1984), and are characterized by focal or diffuse, spike, slow wave, or slow dysrhythmic patterns. However, no abnormalities have been found to be specific. Unusually low voltage patterns suggesting a state of chronic hyperarousal have also been found in some studies (Hutt, Hutt, Lee, & Ounstead, 1965; Kolvin, 1971), a finding not confirmed by others (Hermelin & O'Connor, 1988; Creak & Pampiglione, 1969). Sleep EEG studies in autistic children have found that the eye movements of these children more resemble those of normal infants than those of age-matched controls, suggesting immaturity (Ornitz, 1965; Tanguay, Ornitz, Forsythe, & Ritvo, 1976). Computerized EEG studies in autism also indicate abnormal patterns of cerebral lateralization (Cantor, Thatcher, Hrybyk, & Kaye, 1986; Ogawa, Sugiyama, & Ishiwa, 1982; Small, 1975; Tanguay, Edwards, Buchwald, Schwafel, & Allen, 1982). Studies on measurement of ongoing EEG activity during the administration of various cognitive tasks, such as those involving language or other left hemisphere-mediated functions, also suggest abnormal patterns of functional brain lateralization (Dawson, Warrenburg, & Fuller, 1982, 1983).

Auditory evoked-response (AER) studies have also been done in autism. By and large, these studies have shown maturational deviation in a subgroup of autistic children (Fein, Skoff, & Musky, 1981; Gillberg, Rosenthall, & Johansson, 1983; Skoff, Musky, & Tunes, 1980; Student & Sohmer, 1978; Tanguay, Edwards, Buchwald, Schwafel, & Allen, 1982).

Studies have also suggested that AERs are irregular and variable in autistic subjects with smaller amplitudes (Lelord, Laffont, Jusseaurne, & Stephant, 1973). These findings suggest defective integration between visual and auditory pathways in autism.

Studies exploring the role of brainstem dysfunction in autism have focused on autonomic response studies. A variety of disturbances in autonomic function have been found to occur in autistic children. These include cardiac arrhythmias (Hutt, Forrest, & Richer, 1975), inadequate galvanic skin responses to auditory and visual stimuli (Bernal & Miller, 1970), and so on. Dysfunction of the vestibular system, which is said to be involved with self-monitoring, have also been reported. For example, Ritvo et al. (1969) found a decrease in duration of nystagmus after vesticular stimulation by rotation or by caloric irrigation in a group of autistic children. Prolongation of brainstem transmission time has also been reported in autism (Rosenblum et al., 1980; Taylor, Rosenblatt, & Linschoten, 1982), although some investigators have failed to replicate this finding (e.g., Rumsey, Grimes, Pikus, Duara, & Ismond, 1984).

NEUROCHEMICAL FACTORS

Studies focusing on the neurochemical and neurotransmitter substances secreted in the brains of autistic persons have also been done. Three main reasons are responsible for the recent increase in interest in this area of autism research; (a) lack of gross brain pathology, suggesting that microscopic or functional factors may be responsible; (b) relative success in the pharmacological treatments for certain limited aspects of autism; and (c) recent advances in basic neurosciences as applied to psychiatric disorders. Accordingly, all the major neurotransmitters have been studied in autism. Although the studies are usually preliminary, often compounded by problems inherent in neurochemical research (such as assay methods, measurements of body fluids, confounding variables of age and sex), overall evidence strongly suggests that neurochemical factors play a major role in the presentation of autism. The following section focuses on each of the major neurotransmitters separately, although there is a considerable overlap between their functions.

Serotonin

Serotonin (5-hydroxytryptamine of 5 H-T) is an important neurotransmitter whose activity has been implicated in a variety of important processes such as temperature regulation, pain, sensory perception, sleep, sexual behavior, appetite, learning, and memory (Young, Kavanagh, Anderson, Shaywitz, & Cohen, 1982). It is synthesized from the amino acid tryptophan and metabolized to 5-hydroxyindoleacetic acid. The cell bodies of the neurons are located in the hindbrain from where they project widely. Apart from the brain, serotonin also occurs in the intestine and blood platelets.

Several studies have reported that about 30% to 50% of patients with autism have increased levels of serotonin in their blood (Anderson & Hoshino, 1987; Anderson et al., 1987). In fact, of all the biochemical findings in autism, this has been the most replicated. Attempts have been made to clarify the mechanisms involved, as increased serotonin in the blood could result from (a) increased synthesis by the intestine, (b) increased degradation, and/or (c) enhanced uptake and storage of 5-HT by platelets.

Studies of intestinal synthesis of 5-HT have focused on the measurement of the urinary excretion rates of the endpoint metabolite, 5-hydroxyindoleacetic acid (5-HIAA), with or without tryptophan loading. In the latter method, large amounts of oral tryptophan are given to test the metabolic pathway. The results have been conflicting. Most studies have not found any difference between autistic and normal subjects (Minderaa et al., 1987; Partington, Tu, & Wong, 1973), although some have found higher (Hanley, Stahl, & Freedman, 1977) and some lower (Sutton, Read, & Arbor, 1958) excretionary rates of 5-HIAA in autistic patients. Thus, it appears that increased intestinal synthesis of 5-HT is not the mechanism underlying the increased levels of serotonin seen in some autistic individuals.

Degradation of 5-HT occurs as a result of the activity of the enzyme monoamine oxidase (MAO). Several studies have reported that the functioning of this enzyme is normal in autism, as reflected by the lack of differences in the urinary excretion rates between autistic and normal subjects (Boullin et al., 1982; Cohen, Young, & Roth, 1977; Minderaa et al., 1987). Thus, the occurrence of increased serotonin blood levels in autistic persons does not appear to be the result of decreased catabolism of serotonin.

Previous studies found that the handling of 5-HT by platelets is normal in autism (Anderson, Schlicht, & Cohen, 1985; Boullin et al., 1982). However, recent work has suggested that this may not be so (Katsui, Okuda, Usuda, & Koizumi, 1986; Rotman, Caplan, & Szekely, 1980).

Correlations between serotonin levels and specific symptoms of autism have not yet been fully established. Some associations with level of intelligence and level of activity (Campbell, Friedman, De Vito, Greenspan, & Collins, 1974; Partington, Tu, & Wong, 1973) has been reported. Interest in the role of serotonin in autism has increased following the recent reports of improvement in autistic symptoms after administration of fenfluramine, which is a potent 5-HT depleting agent (Geller, Ritvo, Freeman, & Yuwiler, 1982). However, the basic mechanisms underlying the raised serotonin levels in autism still remain unclear.

Dopamine

Dopamine is synthesized from the amino acids phenylolamine and tyrosine, and is metabolized to homovanillic acid (HVA) and dihydroxyphenylacetic acid. The dopaminergic system has most of its cell bodies in the midbrain and is particularly important in the regulation of motor function, eating and drinking behaviors, sexual behavior, selective attention, and so on (Young et al., 1982). Dysfunction in this system has been implicated in such diseases as schizophrenia and Parkinson's disease. The fact that agents that block the dopamine receptors (e.g., neuroleptics such as haloperidol) reduce stereotypies and other motor symptoms in autism, whereas agents that stimulate the receptors (e.g., stimulants) make the symptoms worse, strongly suggests a role of this neurotransmitter in autism (Young et al., 1982).

Most studies of dopamine metabolism in autism have focused on the measurement of HVA. Some studies have found that autistic children do not differ significantly from other diagnostic groups so far as the HVA levels in the cerebrospinal fluid is concerned, although the levels show some correlation with the degree of locomotor activity and stereotypes (Cohen, Caparulo, Shaywitz, & Bowers, 1977; Cohen, Shaywitz, Johnson, & Bowers, 1974). However, others have reported elevated CSF HVA levels in some autistic children (Gillberg, Svennerholm, & Hamilton-Heilberg, 1983).

Peripheral measurement of HVA, either in the plasma or in the urine, is of course a more convenient way of assessing dopaminergic activity. However, most of the peripheral dopamine is not derived from the brain stores and, therefore, does not truly reflect the activity of the central dopaminergic system. Nevertheless, studies have looked at peripheral dopamine levels in autism and the results have been conflicting. Some have found no significant differences between autistic subjects and controls (Minderaa et al., 1987), whereas others have reported increased levels of HVA in autism, especially in those who are more severely impaired (Garreau et al., 1980). It has been suggested that drugs that block the peripheral production of dopamine metabolites such as debrisoquin may make the measurement of central dopaminergic activity more feasible (Riddle et al., 1986).

Epinephrine and Norepinephrine

These two neurotransmitters are often discussed together because of their overlapping actions. Norepinephrine acts as a central and peripheral neurotransmitter and is synthesized from dopamine by the action of the enzyme dopamine beta (β) hydroxylase (DBH). Most of the neurons are located in the hindbrain. Central norepinephrine is metabolized to 3-methoxy-4-hydroxy-phenylglycol (MHPG), whereas peripheral norepinephrine gets converted to both MHPG and vanillylmandelic acid (VMA). The adrenal medulla is the site of synthesis of most of the peripheral epinephrine. Both these neurotransmitters are associated with the regulation of cardiovascular function, attention, memory, anxiety, sleep, and learning (Young et al., 1982). Norepinephrine has been implicated in the causation of various psychiatric disorders such as depression.

Some studies have reported increased plasma norepinephrine levels in autistic patients (Lake, Ziegler, & Murphy, 1977), whereas others have found lower levels (Launay et al., 1987).

MHPG levels in the urine have been found to be decreased in autistic subjects (Young et al., 1982), which is not consistent with the hypothesis that levels of norepinephrine might be increased in autism. So far as CSF MHPG is concerned, three recent studies have found no difference between autistic subjects and controls (e.g., Gillberg, Svennerholm, & Hamilton-Heilberg, 1983).

Levels of the enzyme DBH, which controls the conversion of dopamine to norepinephrine, have also been studied, but the results have been, again, conflicting. Thus, Goldstein, Mahanand, Lee, and Coleman (1976) and Lake et al. (1977) found decreased DBH levels in autistic subjects, whereas Young, Kyprie, Koss, and Cohen (1980) found no difference between autistic and control groups.

Because the level of norepinephrine activity is also affected by two metabolic enzymes, catechol-o-methyl transferase (COMT) and MAO, Giller et al. (1980) studied COMT activity in cultured fibroblasts and in red blood cells of autistic children, and found no difference compared to controls. MAO activity also appears normal in autism (Lake et al., 1977; Young et al., 1982).

Peptides

Certain peptides have been shown to act as neurotransmitters and affect pain perception, emotion, appetite, and sexual behavior. Certain peptides such as enkephalins and endorphins appear to act as endogenous opioids. It has been observed that some opiate-induced behaviors in animals resemble autistic behaviors, which has led to the clinical use of opiate antagonists such as naltrexone, for the control of severe self-injurious behaviors (Deutsch, 1986). Weizman et al. (1984) reported low H-endorphin levels in the blood of a group of autistic children as compared to schizophrenic children or normal controls. However, Gillberg, Terenius, and Lönnerholm

(1985) reported that the mean CSF endorphine fraction II levels were higher in autistic children compared to normal children. Thus, the limited evidence for the role of peptides in autism is again conflicting. Nevertheless, there is a need for further research in this field because of the clinical efficacy of opioid antagonists in the control of some autistic symptoms.

Other Neurochemical Factors

A number of other neurochemical abnormalities have also been reported in autism, although their significance remains unclear. These include elevated CSF creatinine phosphokinase levels (Katz & Liebman, 1970), lower blood adenosine triphosphatase activity in assays of red blood cells (Sankar, 1971), and so on.

In summary, a variety of neurochemical abnormalities have been reported in autism. Of all, perhaps the most widely replicated has been the finding of raised levels of serum serotonin in a sizeable proportion of autistic persons. A direct application of the study of neurochemical factors has been the successful use of certain types of drugs, such as opioid antagonists, in the treatment of some of the symptoms of autism. Clearly, more research is needed to explore further the role of underlying neurochemical factors in autism.

IMMUNOLOGICAL FACTORS

Immune system dysfunction has also been implicated in autism. Earlier studies sought to explore the role of various infectious agents in the etiology of autism. Chess (1977) reported increased frequency of autism in individuals with congenital rubella. Deykin and MacMahon (1979) evaluated a number of infectious agents as possible etiological agents in autism and found that the disorder was associated with prenatal rubella or influenza virus infection in only about 5% of cases. Other studies have also confirmed this low rate of maternal infections during pregnancy in autistic individuals (Finegan & Quarrington, 1979; Gillberg & Gillberg, 1983; Mason-Brothers et al., 1987).

Later studies have focused on the immunoglobulin levels in autism. For example, Young, Caparulo, Shaywitz, Johnson, and Cohen (1977) studied CSF immunoglobulin levels in 15 autistic children and did not find any abnormalities of glucose, protein cells, or folate. The authors concluded that slow virus infection probably does not play a role in autism. Stubbs (1976) gave rubella vaccine challenge to 15 autistic children and 8 age-matched controls in order to retrospectively diagnose prenatal rubella, and found that the challenge did not differentiate autistic children from controls. However, 5 of the 13 autistic children had undetectable hemagglutination-inhibition antibody titers despite previous vaccination. The author speculated that these autistic children might have an altered immune response. Warren, Margaratten, Pace, and Foster (1986) and Warren again in 1990 with Yonk, Burger, Cole, Odell, Warren, White, and Singh, found several immune-system abnormalities including decreased number of T lymphocytes, altered ratio of helper to suppressant T cells, and the like. They further reported (Warren, Foster, & Margaratten, 1987) impaired activity of natural killer (NK) cells, which are large granular lymphocytes active against virus-infected cells and malignancy. Weizman, Weizman, Szekely, Wijsenbeck, and Livni (1982) suggested that a cell-mediated immune response to brain antigen occurred in some autistic individuals. However, Todd, Hickok, Anderson, and Cohen (1988), in an attempt to test for the presence of a generalized antibrain antibody response in autistic patients, failed to find such a response, and others (Todd & Ciaranello, 1985; Westall & Root-Bernstein, 1983) emphasized the role increased serotonin levels might play in the immune response of some autistic individuals.

Thus, a variety of immune system abnormalities occur in autism. More studies are needed to link these abnormalities to the etiology and presentation of the syndrome.

SUMMARY

Since the description of autism by Kanner (1943) about half a century ago, research has convincingly shown that neurobiological factors are of critical importance in its causation. Support for this view comes from a number of painstaking studies originating from a variety of disciplines ranging from genetics and immunology to neuropathology and radioimaging. Despite several important discoveries, it must be admitted that no abnormalities have been found to be specific for the disorder. Besides, the etiological implications of quite a few of the findings are not clear, nor is it clear if some of the abnormalities reflect chance associations without any significance. Although some of the inconsistencies are due to methodological shortcomings, they also reflect that autism is a heterogenous behavioral disorder with several different but distinct subtypes. Future research in autism should continue to emphasize its further subclassification. Such an approach will enable investigators to select more homogeneous group of subjects for future neurobiological research. From this approach, more consistent results could be derived from various independent research groups to further clarify the role of the various factors that contribute to autism.

REFERENCES

Anderson, G. M., Freedman, D. X., Cohen, D. J., Volkmar, E., Hoder, L., McPhedran, P., Minderaa, R. B., Hansen, C. R., & Young, J. G. (1987). Whole blood serotonin in autistic and normal subjects. *Journal of Child Psychology and Psychiatry, 28,* 85-900.

Anderson, G. M., & Hoshino, Y. (1987). Neurochemical studies of autism. In D. J. Cohen & A. Donnellan (Eds.), *Handbook of autism and pervasive developmental disorders* (pp. 166-191) New York: Wiley.

Anderson, G. M., Schlicht, K. R., & Cohen, D. J. (1985). Two dimensional high-performance liquid chromatographic determination of 5-hydroxyindoleacetic acid and homovanillic acid in urine. *Analyst Biochemistry, 144,* 27-31.

August, G. J., Stewart, M. A., & Tsai, L. (1981). The incidence of cognitive disabilities in the siblings of autistic children. *British Journal of Psychiatry, 138,* 416-422.

Baird, T. D., & August, G. J. (1985). Familial heterogeneity in infantile autism. *Journal of Autism and Developmental Disorders, 15,* 315-321.

Bartak, L., Rutter, M., & Cox, A. (1975). A comparative study of infantile autism and specific developmental receptive language disorder. I. The children. *British Journal of Psychiatry, 126,* 127-145.

Bauman, M., & Kemper, T. L. (1985). Histoanatomic observations of the brain in early infantile autism. *Neurology, 35,* 866-874.

Bauman, M., LeMay, M., Bauman, R. A., & Rosenberger, P. B. (1985). Computerized tomographic (CT) observations of the posterior fossa in early infantile autism. *Neurology, 35* (Suppl. 1), 247.

Bernal, M. E., & Miller, W. H. (1970). Electrodermal and cardiac responses of schizophrenic children in sensory stimuli. *Psychophysiology, 7,* 155-168.

Blackstock, E. G. (1978). Cerebral asymmetry and development of early infantile autism. *Journal of Autism and Developmental Disorders, 8,* 339-353.

Boullin, D. J., Freeman, B. J., Geller, E., Ritvo, E., Rutter, M., & Yuwiler, A. (1982). Toward the resolution of conflicting findings. *Journal of Autism and Developmental Disorders, 12,* 97-98.

Brown, W. T., Jenkins, E. C., Cohen, I. L., Fisch, G. S., Wolf-Schein, E. G., Gross, A. Waterhouse, L., Fein, D., Mason-Brothers, A., Ritvo, E., Ruttenberg, B. A., Bentley, W., & Castells, S. (1986). Fragile-X and autism: A multicenter survey. *American Journal of Medical Genetics, 23,* 341-352.

Campbell, M., Friedman, E., DeVito, E., Greenspan, L., & Collins, P. J. (1974). Blood serotonin in psychiatric and brain-damaged children. *Journal of Autism and Developmental Disorders, 4,* 33-41.

Campbell, M., Geller, B., Small, A. M., Petti, T. A., & Ferries, S. H. (1978). Minor physical anomalies in young psychotic children. *American Journal of Psychiatry, 135,* 573-575.

Campbell, M., Rosenbloom, S., Perry, R., George, A., Kricheff, I., Andersson, L., Small, A., & Jennings, S. (1982). Computerized axial tomography in young autistic children. *American Journal of Psychiatry, 139,* 510-512.

Cantor, D. S., Thatcher, R. W., Hrybyk, M., & Kaye, H. (1986). Computerized EEG analyses of autistic children. *Journal of Autism and Developmental Disorders, 16,* 169-187.

Cantwell, D., Baker, L., & Rutter, M. (1978). Family factors. In M. Rutter & E. Shopler (Eds.), *Autism: A reappraisal of concepts and treatment* (pp. 269-296). New York: Plenum Press.

Caparulo, B. R., Cohen, D. J., Rothman, S. L., Shaywitz, S., & Shaywitz, B. (1981). Computed tomographic brain scanning in children with developmental neuropsychiatric disorders. *Journal of the American Academy of Child Psychiatry, 20,* 338-357.

Chess, S. (1977). Follow-up report on autism in congenital rubella. *Journal of Autism and Developmental Disorders, 7,* 69-81.

Cohen, D. J., Caparulo, B. K., Shaywitz, B. A., & Bowers, M. (1977). Dopamine and serotonin metabolism in neuropsychiatrically disturbed children: CSF homovanillic acid and 5-hydroxyindoleacetic acid. *Archives of General Psychiatry, 34,* 545–550.

Cohen, D. J., Shaywitz, R. A., Johnson, W. K., & Bowers, M. (1974). Biogenic amines in autistic and atypical children: Cerebrospinal fluid measure of homovanillic acid and 5-hydroxyindole acetic acid. *Archives of General Psychiatry, 31,* 845–853.

Cohen, D. J., Young, J. G., & Roth, J. A. (1977). Platelet monoamine oxidase in early childhood autism. *Archives of General Psychiatry, 34,* 534–537.

Courchesne, E. (1987). A neurophysiological view of autism. In E. Schopler & G. B. Mesibov (Eds.), *Neurobiological issues in autism* (pp. 285–324). New York/London: Plenum Press.

Courchesne, E., Kilman, B. A., Galambos, R., & Lincoln, A. J. (1984). Autism: Processing of novel auditory information assessed by event-related brain potentials. *Electroencephalography and Clinical Neurophysiology, 59,* 238–248.

Courchesne, E., Lincoln, A. J., Kilman, B. A., & Galambos, R. (1985). Event-related brain potential correlates of the processing of novel visual and auditory information in autism. *Journal of Autism and Developmental Disorders, 15,* 55–75.

Courchesne, E., Yeung-Courchesne, B. A., Press, G. A., Hesselink, J. R., & Jernigan, T. L. (1988). Hypoplasia of cerebellar vermal lobules VI and VII in autism. *New England Journal of Medicine, 318,* 1349–1354.

Creak, M., & Pampiglione, G. (1969). Clinical and EEG studies in a group of 35 psychotic children. *Developmental Medicine and Child Neurology, 11,* 218–227.

Creasy, H., Rumsey, J., Schwartz, M., Duara, R., Rapoport, J. L., & Rapoport, S. I. (1986). Brain morphometry in autistic men as measured by volumetric computed tomography. *Archives of Neurology, 43,* 669–672.

Damasio, H., Maurer, R. G., Damasio, A. R., & Chui, H. C. (1980). Computerized tomographic scan findings in patients with autistic behavior. *Archives of Neurology, 37,* 504–510.

Darby, J. C. (1976). Neuropathologic aspects of psychosis in children. *Journal of Autism and Child Schizophrenia, 6,* 339–352.

Dawson, G., Warrenburg, S., & Fuller, P. (1982). Cerebral lateralization in individuals diagnosed as autistic in early childhood. *Brain Language, 15,* 353–368.

Dawson, G., Warrenburg, S., & Fuller, P. (1983). Hemisphere functioning and motor imitation in autistic persons. *Brain and Cognition, 2,* 346–354.

Deutsch, S. I. (1986). Rationale for the administration of opioid antagonists in treating infantile autism. *American Journal of Mental Deficiency, 90,* 631–635.

DeVolder, A. G., Bol, A., Michel, C., Cogneau, M., & Goffinet, A. M. (1988). Cerebral glucose metabolism in autistic children. *Acta Neurologica Belgica, 88,* 75–90.

Deykin, E. Y., & MacMahon, B. (1979). The incidence of seizures among children with autistic symptoms. *American Journal of Psychiatry, 126,* 1310–1312.

Deykin, E. Y., & MacMahon, B. (1980). Pregnancy, delivery, and neonatal complications among autistic children. *American Journal of Diseases of Children, 134,* 860–864.

Fein, D., Skoff, B., & Mirsky, A. F. (1981). Clinical correlates of brainstem dysfunction in autistic children. *Journal of Autism and Developmental Disorders, 11,* 303–315.

Finegan, J. A., & Quarrington, B. (1979). Pre-, peri-, and neonatal factors and infantile autism. *Journal of Child Psychology and Psychiatry, 20,* 119–128.

Folstein, S. E. (1985). Genetic aspects of infantile autism. *Annual Review of Medicine, 36,* 415–419.

Folstein, S. E., & Rutter, M. (1977). Infantile autism: A genetic study of 21 twin pairs. *Journal of Child Psychology and Psychiatry, 18,* 297–321.

Folstein, S. E., & Rutter, M. (1987). Autism: Familial aggregation and genetic implications. *Journal of Autism and Developmental Disorders, 18,* 3–30.

Gaffney, G., Kuperman, S., Tsai, L., & Minchin, S. (1988). Morphological evidence for

brainstem involvement in infantile autism. *Biological Psychiatry, 24,* 578–586.
Gaffney, G., Kuperman, S., Tsai, L., Minchin, S., & Hassanein, K. M. (1987). Midsagittal magnetic resonance imaging of autism. *British Journal of Psychiatry, 151,* 831–833.
Gaffney, G., & Tsai, L. (1987). Magnetic resonance imaging of high level autism. *Journal of Autism and Developmental Disorders, 17,* 433–438.
Gaffney, G., Tsai, L., Kuperman, S., & Minchin, S. (1987). Cerebellar structure in autism. *American Journal of Diseases of Children, 141,* 1330–1332.
Garber, H. J., Ritvo, E. R., Chiu, L. C., Griswold, V. J., Lashanian, A., Freeman, B. J., & Oldendorf, W. H. (1989). A magnetic resonance imaging study of autism: Normal fourth ventricle size and absence of pathology. *American Journal of Psychiatry, 146,* 532–534.
Garreau, B., Barthelemy, C., Domanech, J., Sauvage, D., Num, J. P., Lelord, G., & Callaway, E. (1980). Disturbances in dopamine metabolism in autistic children: Results of clinical tests and urinary dosages of homovanillic acid (HVA). *Acta Psychiatrica Belgica, 80,* 249–265.
Geller, E., Ritvo, E. R., Freeman, B. J., & Yuwiler, A. (1982). Preliminary observations on the effect of fenfluramine on blood serotonin and symptoms in three autistic boys. *New England Journal of Medicine, 307,* 165–169.
Gillberg, C., & Gillberg, I. C. (1983). Infantile autism: A total population study of reduced optimality in the pre-, peri- and neonatal periods. *Journal of Autism and Developmental Disorders, 13,* 153–166.
Gillberg, C., Rosenthall, U., & Johansson, E. (1983). Auditory brainstem responses in childhood psychosis. *Journal of Autism and Developmental Disorders, 13,* 181–195.
Gillberg, C., & Svendsen, P. (1983). Childhood psychosis and computed tomographic brain scan findings. *Journal of Autism and Developmental Disorders, 13,* 19–32.
Gillberg, C., Svennerholm, L., & Hamilton-Hellberg, C. (1983). Childhood psychosis and monoamine metabolite in spinal fluid. *Journal of Autism and Developmental Disorders, 13,* 383–396.
Gillberg, C., Terenius, L., & Lonnerholm, G. (1985). Endorphin activity in childhood psychosis. *Archives of General Psychiatry, 42,* 780–783.
Gillberg, C. & Wahlstrom, J. (1985). Chromosome abnormalities in infantile autism and other childhood psychoses: A population study of 66 cases. *Developmental Medicine & Child Neurology, 27,* 293–304.
Giller, E. L., Jr., Young, G., Breakefield, X. O., Carbonari, C., Braverman, M., & Cohen, T. J. (1980). Monoamine oxidase and catechol-O-methyltransferase activities in cultured fibroblasts and blood cells from children with autism and Gilles de la Tourette Syndrome. *Psychiatric Research, 2,* 187–197.
Goldstein, M., Mahanand, P., Lee, J., & Coleman, M. (1976). Dopamine-beta-hydronylase and endogenous total 5-hydroxyindate levels in autistics and controls. In M. Coleman (Ed.), *The autistic syndrome* (pp. 56–63). Amsterdam: North-Holland.
Hanley, H. G., Stahl, S. M., & Freedman, D. X. (1977). Hyperserotonemia and amine metabolites in autistic and retarded children. *Archives of General Psychiatry, 34,* 521–531.
Heh, C. W. C., Smith, R., Wu, J., Hazlerr, E., Rusel, A., Asarnow, R., Tanguay, P., & Buchsbaum, M. S. (1989). Positron emission tomography of the cerebellum in autism. *American Journal of Psychiatry, 146,* 242–245.
Hermelin, B., & O'Connor, N. (1968). Measures of the occipital alpha rhythm in normal, subnormal, and autistic children. *British Journal of Psychiatry, 114,* 603–610.
Hier, D. E., LeMay, M., & Rosenberger, P. B. (1979). Autism and unfavorable left-right asymmetries of the brain. *Journal of Autism and Developmental Disorders, 9,* 153–159.
Hutt, C., Forrest, S. J., & Richer, J. (1975). Cardiac arrhythmia and behavior in autistic children. *Acta Psychiatrica Scandinavica, 51,* 361–372.
Hutt, S., Hutt, C., Lee, D., & Ounsted, C. (1965). A behavioral and electroencephalographic study of autistic children. *Journal of Psychiatric Research, 3,* 181–197.

Jacobson, R., LeCouteur, A., Howlin, P., & Rutter, M. (1988). Selective subcortical abnormalities in autism. *Psychological Medicine, 18,* 39–48.

Kanner, L. (1943). Autistic disturbances of affective content. *Nervous Child, 2,* 217–230.

Katsui, T., Okuda, M., Usuda, S., & Koizumi, T. (1986). Kinetics of H-serotonin uptake by platelets in infantile autism and developmental language disorder (including five pairs of twins). *Journal of Autism and Developmental Disorders, 16,* 69–76.

Katz, R. M., & Liebman, W. (1970). Creatinine phosphokinase activity in central nervous system disorders and infections. *American Journal of Diseases of Children, 120,* 543–546.

Kemper, T. L. (1990, November). Neuropathology of infantile autism. *Program and Abstract of Conference on Neurobiology of Infantile Autism,* a satellite meeting of the 5th International Child Neurology Congress, Tokyo.

Kolvin, I. (1971). Psychoses in childhood – A comparative study. In M. Rutter (Ed.), *Infantile autism: Concepts, characteristics, and treatment* (pp. 7–25). London: Churchill Livingston.

Lake, R., Ziegler, M. G., & Murphy, D. L. (1977). Increased norepinephrine levels and decreased DBH activity in primary autism. *Archives of General Psychiatry, 35,* 553–556.

Launay, J. M., Bursztejn, C., Ferrari, P., Dreux, C., Braconnier, A., Zarifian, E., Lancrenon, S., & Fermanian, J. (1987). Catecholamine metabolism in infantile autism: A controlled study of 22 autistic children. *Journal of Autism and Developmental Disorders, 17,* 333–347.

Le Couteur, A., Bailey, A. J., Rutter, M., & Gottesman, I. (1989, August). *An epidemiologically based twin study of autism.* Paper presented at the *First World Congress on Psychiatric Genetics,* Cambridge, England.

Lelord, G., Laffont, F., Jusseaume, P., & Stephant, J. L. (1973). Comparative study of conditioning of averaged evoked responses by coupling sound and light in normal and autistic children. *Psychophysiology, 10,* 415–425.

Levitas, A., McBogg, P., & Hagerman, R. (1983). Behavioral dysfunctions in the fragile X syndrome. In R. Hagerman & P. McBogg (Eds.), *The fragile X syndrome: Diagnosis, biochemistry, and intervention* (pp. 153–173). Dillon, CO: Spectra Publications.

Macdonald, H., Rutter, M., Rios, P., & Bolton, P. (1989, August). *Cognitive and social abnormalities in the siblings of autistic and Down's syndrome probands.* Paper presented at the First World Congress on Psychiatric Genetics, Cambridge, England.

Mason-Brothers, A., Ritvo, E., Guze, B., Mo, A., Freeman, B. J., Funderburk, S. J., & Schroth, P. C. (1987). Pre-, peri-, and postnatal factors in 1981 autistic patients from single and multiple incidence families. *Journal of the American Academy of Child and Adolescent Psychiatry, 26,* 39–42.

Minderaa, R. B., Anderson, G. M., Volkmar, F. R., Harcherk, D., Akkerhuis, G. W., & Cohen, D. J. (1987). Urine 5-hydroxyindoleacetic acid, whole blood serotonin, and tryptophan in autistic and normal subjects. *Biological Psychiatry, 22,* 933–940.

Minshaw, N. J., Payton, J. B., Wolf, G. L., & Latchaw, R. E. (1986). H NMR imaging of autistics: Implications for neurology. *Annals of Neurology, 20,* 417.

Minton, J., Campbell, M., Green, W. H., Jennings, S., & Samit, C. (1982). Cognitive assessment of siblings of autistic children. *Journal of the American Academy of Child and Adolescent Psychiatry, 21,* 256–261.

Ogawa, T., Sugiyama, A., Ishiwa, S., Suzuki, M., Ishihara, T., & Sato, K. (1982). Ontogenic development of EEG-asymmetry in early infantile autism. *Brain Development, 4,* 439–449.

Ornitz, E. M. (1965). Dreaming sleep in autistic twins. *Archives of General Psychiatry, 12,* 77–79.

Ornitz, E. M. (1985). Neurophysiology of infantile autism. *Journal of the American Academy of Child Psychiatry, 24,* 251–262.

Partington, M. W., Tu, J. B., & Wong, C. Y. (1973). Blood serotonin levels in severe mental retardation. *Developmental Medicine and Child Neurology, 15,* 616–627.

Payton, J. B., Steele, M. W., Wenger, S. L., & Minshaw, N. J. (1989). The fragile X marker in perspective. *Journal of the American Academy of Child and Adolescent Psychiatry, 28,* 417-421.

Piven, J., Berthier, M. L., Starkstein, S. E., Nehme, E., Pearlson, G., & Folstein, S. (1990). Magnetic resonance imaging evidence for a defect of cerebral cortical development in autism. *American Journal of Psychiatry, 147,* 734-739.

Piven, J., Gayle, J., Chase, G., Fink, B., Landa, R., Wzorek, M. M., & Folstein, S. (1990). A family history of neuropsychiatric disorders in adult siblings of autistic individuals. *Journal of the American Academy of Child and Adolescent Psychiatry, 29,* 177-183.

Prior, M. R. (1979). Cognitive abilities and disabilities in infantile autism: A review. *Journal of Abnormal Child Psychology, 7,* 357-380.

Prior, M. R., Tress, B., Hoffman, W. L., & Boldt, D. (1984). Computer tomographic study of children with classic autism. *Archives of Neurology, 41,* 482-484.

Riddle, M. A., Shaywitz, B. A., Lechman, J. F., Anderson, G. M., Hardin, M. T., Ort, S., & Cohen, D. J. (1986). Brief debrisoquin loading to assess central dopaminergic function in children. *Life Sciences, 38,* 1041-1048.

Ritvo, E. R., Freeman, B. J., Mason-Brothers, A., Mo, A., & Ritvo, A. M. (1985). Concordance for the syndrome of autism in 40 pairs of afflicted twins. *American Journal of Psychiatry, 142,* 74-77.

Ritvo, E. R., Freeman, B. J., Scheibel, A. B., Duong, T., Robinson, H., Guthrie, D., & Ritvo, A. (1986). Lower Purkinje cell counts in the cerebella of four autistic subjects: Initial findings of the UCLA-NSAC autopsy research report. *American Journal of Psychiatry, 143,* 862-866.

Ritvo, E. R., & Mason-Brothers, A. (1982). Genetic and immunohematologic factors in autism. *Journal of Autism and Developmental Disorders, 12,* 109-114.

Ritvo, E. R., Mason-Brothers, A., & Freeman, B. J. (1988). Eleven possibly autistic parents. *Journal of Autism and Developmental Disorders, 18,* 139-143. (letter)

Ritvo, E. R., Ornitz, E. M., Evitar, A., Markham, C. H., Brown, M. B., & Mason, A. (1969). Decreased postrotatory nystagmus in early infantile autism. *Neurology, 19,* 653-658.

Ritvo, E. R., Spence, A., Freeman, B. J., Mason-Brothers, A., Mo, A., & Marazita, M. L. (1985). Evidence of autosomal recessive inheritance in 46 families with multiple incidences of autism. *American Journal of Psychiatry, 142,* 187-192.

Rosenbloom, S., Campbell, M., George, A. E., Kricheff, I., Taleporos, E., Anderson, L., Reuben, R., & Korein, J. (1984). High resolution CT scanning in infantile autism: A quantitative approach. *Journal of the American Academy of Child Psychiatry, 1,* 72-77.

Rosenblum, S. M., Arick, J. R., Krug, D. A., Stubbs, E. G., Young, N. B., & Pelson, R. O. (1980). Auditory brainstem evoked responses in autistic children. *Journal of Autism and Developmental Disorders, 10,* 215-225.

Rotman, A., Caplan, R., & Szekely, G. A. (1980). Platelet uptake of serotonin in psychotic children. *Psychopharmacology, 67,* 245-248.

Rumsey, J. M., Creasy, H., Stepanek, J. S., Dorwart, R., Patronas, N., Hamburger, S. D., & Duara, R. (1988). Hemispheric asymmetries, fourth ventricular size, and cerebellar morphology in autism. *Journal of Autism and Developmental Disorders, 18,* 127-137.

Rumsey, J. M., Duara, R., Grady, C., Rapoport, J. L., Margolin, R. A., Rapoport, S. I., & Cutler, N. (1985). Brain metabolism in autism: Resting cerebral glucose utilization rates measured with positron emission tomography. *Archives of General Psychiatry, 42,* 448-455.

Rumsey, T. M., Grimes, A. M., Pikus, A. M., Duara, R., & Ismond, D. R. (1984). Auditory brainstem responses in pervasive developmental disorders. *Biological Psychiatry, 19,* 1403-1418.

Rutter, M. (1967). Psychotic disorders in early childhood. Special publication in press, *British Journal of Psychiatry,* 133-158.

Rutter, M. (1990). Autism as a genetic disorder. In P. McGuffin (Ed.), *The new genetics of mental illness.* London: Heinemann Medical.

Sankar, D. V. (1971). Studies in blood platelets, blood enzymes, and leukocyte chromosome breakage in childhood schizophrenia. *Behavioral Neuropsychiatry, 2,* 2–10.

Skoff, B. F., Mirsky, A., & Turner, D. (1980). Prolonged brainstem transmission time in autism. *Psychiatry Research, 2,* 157–166.

Small, J. G. (1975). EEG and neurophysiological studies of early infantile autism. *Biological Psychiatry, 10,* 385–397.

Smalley, S. L., Asarnow, R. F., & Spence, M. A. (1988). Autism and genetics: A decade of research. *Archives of General Psychiatry, 45,* 953–961.

Spence, M. A., Ritvo, E. R., Marazita, M. L., Funderburk, S. J., Sparkes, R. S., & Freeman, B. J. (1985). Gene mapping studies with the syndrome of autism. *Behavior Genetics, 15,* 1–13.

Steffenburg, S., Gillberg, C., Hellgren, L., Andersson, L., Gillberg, I. C., Jakobsson, G., & Bohman, M. (1989). A twin study of autism in Denmark, Finland, Iceland, Norway, and Sweden. *Journal of Child Psychology and Psychiatry, 30,* 405–416.

Stubbs, E. G. (1976). Autistic children exhibit understandable hemagglutination-inhibition titers despite previous rubella vaccination. *Journal of Autism and Childhood Schizophrenia, 6,* 269–274.

Student, M., & Sohmer, H. (1978). Evidence from auditory nerve and brainstem evoked responses for an organic brain lesion in children with autistic traits. *Journal of Autism and Developmental Disorders, 8,* 13–20.

Sutton, H. E., Read, J. H., & Arbor, A. (1958). Abnormal amino acid metabolism in a case suggesting autism. *American Journal of Diseases of Children, 96,* 23–28.

Tanguay, P. E. (1976). Clinical and electrophysiological research. In E. Ritvo (Ed.), *Autism, diagnosis, current research, and management* (pp. 75–84). New York: Spectrum Publications.

Tanguay, P. E., Edwards, R. M., Buchwald, J., Schwafel, J., & Allen, W. (1982). Auditory brainstem evoked responses in autistic children. *Archives of General Psychiatry, 39,* 174–180.

Tanguay, P. E., Ornitz, E. M., Forsythe, A. B., & Ritvo, E. (1976). Rapid eye movement (REM) activity in normal and autistic children during REM sleep. *Journal of Autism and Childhood Schizophrenia, 6,* 275–288.

Taylor, M. J., Rosenblatt, B., & Linschoten, L. (1982, November). Auditory brainstem response abnormalities in autistic children. *Canadian Journal of Neurological Sciences,* 429–433.

Todd, R. C., & Ciaranello, R. D. (1985). Demonstration of inter- and intraspecies differences in serotonin binding sites by antibodies from an autistic child. *Proceedings of the National Academy of Sciences of USA, 82,* 612–616.

Todd, R. D., Hickok, J. M., Anderson, G. M., & Cohen, D. J. (1988). Antibrain antibodies in infantile autism. *Biological Psychiatry, 23,* 644–647.

Tsai, L. Y. (1987). Pre-, peri-, and neonatal factors in autism. In E. Schopler & G. B. Mesibov (Eds.), *Neurobiological issues in autism* (pp. 179–189). New York/London: Plenum Press.

Tsai, L. Y., & Beisler, J. M. (1983). The development of sex differences in infantile autism. *British Journal of Psychiatry, 142,* 273–378.

Tsai, L. Y., Crowe, R. R., Patil, S. R., Murray, J., & Quinn, J. (1988). Search for DNA markers in two autistic males with the fragile X syndrome. *Journal of Autism and Developmental Disorders, 18,* 681–685.

Tsai, L. Y., Jacoby, C. G., Stewart, M. A., & Beisler, J. M. (1982). Unfavorable left-right asymmetries of the brain and autism: A question of methodology. *British Journal of Psychiatry, 140,* 312–319.

Tsai, L. Y., Stewart, M. A., & August, G. (1981). Implications of sex differences in the familial transmission of infantile autism. *Journal of Autism and Developmental Disorders, 11,* 165–173.

Tsai, L. Y., & Tsai, M. C. (1984, July). *Using EEG diagnosis to subtype autistic syndrome. Proceedings of the International Conference of the National Society for Children and Adults with Autism,* San Antonio, TX.

Warren, R. P., Foster, A., & Margaratten, N. C. (1987). Reduced national killer cell activity in autism. *Journal of the American Academy of Child and Adolescent Psychiatry, 26,* 333–335.

Warren, R. P., Margaratten, N. C., Pace, N. C., & Foster, A. (1986). Immune abnormalities in patients with autism. *Journal of Autism and Developmental Disorders, 16,* 189–197.

Warren, R. P., Yonk, L. J., Burger, R. A., Cole, P., Odell, J. D., Warren, W. L., White, E., & Singh, V. K. (1990). Deficiency of suppressor-inducer (CD4+CD45RA+) T cells in autism. *Immunological Investigations, 19,* 245–251.

Weizman, A., Weizman, R., Szekely, G. A., Wijsenbeek, H., & Livni, E. (1982). Abnormal immune response to brain tissue antigen in the syndrome of autism. *American Journal of Psychiatry, 139,* 1462–1465.

Weizman, R., Weizman, A., Tyano, S., Szekely, B., Weissman, B. A., & Sarne, Y. (1984). Humoral endorphine blood levels in autistic, schizophrenic, and healthy subjects. *Psychopharmacology, 82,* 368–370.

Westall, F. C., & Root-Bernstein, R. S. (1983). Suggested connection between serotonin and myelin basic protein. *American Journal of Psychiatry, 140,* 1260–1261.

Williams, R. S., Hauser, S. L., Purpura, D. P., DeLong, G. R., & Swischer, C. N. (1980). Autism and mental retardation. *Archives of Neurology, 37,* 749–753.

Young, J. G., Caparulo, B. K., Shaywitz, B. A., Johnson, W. T., & Cohen, D. J. (1977). Childhood autism: Cerebrospinal fluid examination and immunoglobulin levels. *Journal of the American Academy of Child and Adolescent Psychiatry, 16,* 174–179.

Young, J. G., Kavanagh, M. E., Anderson, G. M., Shaywitz, B. A., & Cohen, D. J. (1982). Clinical neurochemistry of autism and associated disorders. *Journal of Autism and Developmental Disorders, 12,* 147–165.

Young, J. G., Kyprie, R. M., Ross, N. T., & Cohen, D. J. (1980). Serum dopamine-beta-hydroxylase activity: Clinical applications in child psychiatry. *Journal of Autism and Developmental Disorders, 10,* 1–14.

II EDUCATION AND TREATMENT FOR PERSONS WITH AUTISM

4 Assessment for Curriculum Planning

Jan S. Handleman
Douglass College

The complex characteristics of students with autism pose a challenge to educational planning. Diverse school, home, and community needs dictate an individualized and comprehensive assessment, planning, and monitoring process. Successful execution of the educational plan requires input and participation by both professionals and family members.

Recent years have witnessed increased interest in interdisciplinary service delivery, and as a result, input from various professionals is now viewed as a necessary component of educational planning and programming. Medicine, psychology, social work, and speech are a few of the many professions currently contributing to educational decision making. The particular contribution of psychology to testing and evaluation has resulted in a united effort that is referred to as *psychoeducational assessment*.

Discussions of psychoeducational assessment practices with students with autism typically include a focus on both traditional testing practices and behavioral assessment. Whereas the merits and weaknesses of each approach have been argued, current strategies tend to reflect a blending of these two components. This combined approach produces information about a student's relative standing and individual performance. The ultimate focus of assessment on planning and programming makes this process more compatible with the specialized needs of these students.

This chapter focuses on these and other issues pertaining to the comprehensive educational assessment of students with autism. Various components of systematic assessment are presented, along with a discussion of the complementary roles of traditional and behavioral assessment. Emphasis is placed on the direct link between curriculum planning and evaluation. In addition, descriptions are included of the many challenges that these students place on the educational system.

THE ASSESSMENT CHALLENGE: IDIOSYNCRATIC PERFORMANCE BY STUDENTS WITH AUTISM

Educators and clinicians practicing in today's agencies are faced with the complex task of assessing students with autism (Fein, Waterhouse, Lucci, & Snyder, 1985; Handleman & Harris, 1986). The intricacy of diagnosis, the diversity of needs, and the often idiosyncratic performance styles of these students require careful consideration by professionals. The efficacy and value of the assessment process is often dependent on the most accurate match of response style and evaluative strategy.

Learning and performance characteristics of students with autism are generally described in four areas: (a) communication, (b) interpersonal responsiveness, (c) information processing, and (d) developmental and associated cognitive abilities (Powers & Handleman, 1984). The pattern of these characteristics typically results in highly individual student profiles, each requiring very specialized considerations for assessment.

Communication

Difficulties that students with autism demonstrate with the acquisition and refinement of communication skills are widely discussed (Harris, 1975; Lovaas, 1981; Ungerer & Sigman, 1987). Descriptions of problems with the structural aspects of communication, such as disorders of articulation and voice, are provided in the literature, as well as accounts of difficulties with the interpersonal nature of the process (Carrow-Woolfolk & Lynch, 1982; Kirk & Gallagher, 1983; Mundy, Sigman, Ungerer, & Sherman, 1987). Common language deficits of this student population include the complete absence of speech, echolalic responding, sing-song speech patterns, and reversals of word order and pronouns (Hinerman, Jenson, Walker, & Petersen, 1982). Each of these elements related to the development of communication increases the complexity of the assessment process.

Interpersonal Responsiveness

Deficits in interpersonal and social development are endemic to students with autism and often compound those difficulties with communication (Handleman & Harris, 1986; Ollendick & Oswald, 1989). Issues involving motivation, compliance, impulse control, and attending all have a direct impact on the assessment process.

Difficulties with interpersonal responding can be manifested in many different ways. For example, it is not uncommon for students with autism to exhibit a variety of maladaptive behaviors. They may insist on environmental sameness (Baumeister, 1978; Birnbrauer, 1977), avoid eye contact (Howlin, 1978), prefer objects to people (O'Gorman, 1967), engage in perseverative activities (Devany & Rincover, 1982), or display self-injurious behavior (Edelson, 1984). Combined with little curiosity (Koegel & Schreibman, 1976), the person with autism is often very difficult to engage.

Information Processing

Central processing disorders of students with autism have been considered widely and viewed by many to be a major characteristic of the syndrome (Handleman & Harris, 1986). Specific difficulties with interpretation of auditory or visual information and translation of that sensory input into motor responses have been linked to many developmental problems (Kirk & Gallagher, 1983; Nakamura, Toshima, & Takemura, 1986). The information-processing difficulties by these students can interfere with the comprehension of both simple and complex environmental stimuli and need to be considered when planning assessment strategies.

There are a number of manifestations of inconsistent responding to sensory information by students with autism. For example, some students may respond in an overselective fashion by perseverating on a single stimulus to the exclusion of others (Boucher, 1977; Hermelin, 1971) or to a narrow range of sensory input (Lovaas, Koegel, & Schreibman, 1979). The pervasive difficulties that many demonstrate with the generalization of information also exemplify these deficits in responding (Handleman, 1979, 1981; Handleman & Harris, 1986; Westling & Floyd, 1990). In addition, self-stimulation and self-injury have been related to processing difficulties of students with autism and reported to further interfere with educational planning and intervention (Favell, McGimsey, & Schell, 1982; Johnson & Koegel, 1982).

Developmental and Associated Cognitive Abilities

Most students with autism demonstrate developmental delays or discontinuity, and often, as they grow older, the discrepancy between chronological age and developmental level tends to increase (Brown et al., 1979; Donnellan, Gossage, LaVigna, Schuler, & Traphagan, 1977; Ohta, 1987). Many of these students lack self-help skills, are not toilet trained, and often fail to engage in appropriate play. The uneven developmental profiles that result, which typically include various splinter skills, contribute to the intricacies of assessment.

PERSPECTIVE ON THE ROLES OF TRADITIONAL AND BEHAVIORAL ASSESSMENT

Recent years have witnessed growing support for the concept of interdisciplinary service delivery. Input from various professionals is viewed as a critical element of educational planning and programming (Kirk & Gallagher, 1983; Powers & Handleman, 1984). For example, the specific contribution of the field of psychology to testing and evaluation practices has facilitated the unified effort mentioned earlier, psychoeducational assessment (Powers & Handleman, 1984).

Psychoeducational assessment of students with autism typically emphasizes both traditional testing and behavioral assessment (Powers & Handleman, 1984). The merits and weaknesses of each of these components have been argued, and current practice tends to blend both approaches. This comprehensive effort produces a student profile that includes relative standing and individual performance (Harris, Handleman, & Burton, in press).

The reported decline in the utility of traditional testing and the devaluing of its role for students with various developmental disabilities (Scott, 1980; Smith & Knoff, 1981) have prompted the expansion of assessment practices to include behavioral strategies. This redirection has promoted a greater emphasis on the functional as opposed to the descriptive nature of assessment (Tucker, 1985). Focusing assessment in this way on the educational goals of planning and programming has become much more consistent with the needs of students with autism.

Discussions of traditional psychological and educational assessment practices with students with developmental disabilities typically focus on three major goals: (a) observation and evaluation of behavioral repertoires during standardized testing; (b) analysis of test data to provide a profile of strengths and weaknesses; and (c) synthesis of findings to assist diagnosis and guide educational interventions (Handleman & Harris, 1986; Powers & Handleman, 1984). By emphasizing these goals, educators, clinicians, and examiners are encouraged to integrate both performance and behavioral measures.

Although there is agreement that the sanctity of the test protocol should be highly regarded (Alpern, 1967), maintenance of standardized procedures is being considered by many to be secondary in assessment of students with autism (Powers & Handleman, 1984). In an attempt to focus on individual strengths and weaknesses, the comparative nature of testing may be deemphasized. In addition, it may also be necessary to control interfering behaviors and employ strategies that promote optimal test-taking behaviors. All of these modifications can produce important information about students who were traditionally described as "untestable."

Repeated confirmation of the efficacy of the behavioral assessment of students with developmental disabilities has resulted in an increased respect for behavioral practices (Powers & Handleman, 1984). Behavioral assessment strategies serve to objectify observations of student behavior and facilitate a more comprehensive learning profile. By emphasizing present functioning, the specificity of these techniques can greatly facilitate educational planning and programming.

There are several widely accepted components in behavioral assessment of students with autism (Powers & Handleman, 1984). An initial screening of the student can serve to identify global behavioral excesses and deficits and target priority areas. Rank ordering of these concerns can then lead to the development of operational descriptions to guide the assessment of important antecedents and consequences of behavior and learning. Analysis of the results of this systematic gathering of information can ultimately prompt the design of educational interventions. Further implementation of behavioral assessment strategies can then facilitate the monitoring of educational effectiveness, generalization of learning, maintenance of performance, and fine tuning of programming (Powers & Handleman, 1984).

THE PROCESS OF COMPREHENSIVE PSYCHOEDUCATIONAL ASSESSMENT

The combination of traditional psychometric testing, educational evaluation, and behavioral assessment has resulted in a comprehensive psychoeducational assessment process that is highly consistent with the needs of students with autism. The strategies of behavioral assessment can complement more traditional evaluative techniques and minimize some of their limitations (Powers & Handleman, 1984). In addition, comprehensive psychoeducational assessment can result in a testing–teaching cycle that will guide the complex developmental and behavioral programming required by the student with autism.

Comprehensive psychoeducational assessment practices can assist in the initial identification of specific areas of learning difficulty. Confirmation of a discrepancy between current functioning and expected performance can then guide further diagnostic assessment to uncover particular deficits. Standardized tests, combined with clinical observation and informal measures, can facilitate the evaluation of various areas of performance and can result in an index of general ability and achievement. The process emphasizes traditional variables of learning, as well as consideration for issues such as instructional control, generalization, and maintenance.

The ability to focus on the environment, to respond to the multitude of stimuli, and to not engage in competing behaviors are fundamental to skill acquisition by students with autism (Cook, Anderson, & Rincover, 1982; Lovaas, 1981). Compiling information on a student's ability with these critical instructional control behaviors is an important part of the comprehensive assessment process. Interpersonal and environmental attending are basic to all areas of learning, as well as to a student's ability to sit and respond to instructional demands.

Regardless of the nature of the disability, there exists concern about generalizing responses by students with autism (Handleman, 1981; Westling & Floyd, 1990). Assessment of the components of generalization, such as setting, teacher, and material, is important in order to complete a student's learning profile. Information about a student's reliance on prompts or the situationally specific nature of responding can be useful in planning assessment strategies and in guiding current and future educational interventions.

The comprehensive psychoeducational assessment process is also sensitive to individual information-processing styles and to the many possible correlates of learning. After a global screening of the reception and expression of information, a more systematic analysis of learning modalities and motor functioning can be conducted. In addition, the influence of motivational, environmental, and physiological factors can be identified and considered in educational planning.

A systematic functional analysis of performance and behavior is considered a critical component of comprehensive educational assessment (Durand & Crimmins, 1987). The identification of variables that contribute to effective communication by students with autism can facilitate clinical decision making in areas of skill acquisition and behavior reduction. Appreciation for those environmental and physiological factors that impact on learning and an understanding of variables that effect student motivation can help to promote thorough educational evaluation and planning.

Careful analysis and interpretation of results are hallmarks of comprehensive psychoeducational assessment. The consideration of test validity and reliability will either heighten or minimize the findings, and variables such as motivation or consistency of responding will affect the ultimate utility of these results.

The relationship between assessment and educational programming is strengthened when the results of evaluation and observation direct planning and programming (Powers & Handleman, 1984). A curriculum that emphasizes behavioral excesses, skill deficiencies, and contributing factors will effectively promote individualization. In addition, a teaching methodology that includes sensitivity to individual differences and the importance of variables such as functionality and community application will further facilitate optimal performance and progress. This assessment-teaching cycle is further enhanced by ongoing evaluation and performance monitoring.

These additional practices will help to keep the assessment of student needs current and ensure effective goal setting and educational programming.

Ongoing monitoring of performance is one of the most valuable components of the assessment process for students with autism. Criterion-referenced nature of behavioral assessment techniques can typically reflect changing and immediate student needs and promote thorough educational planning. For example, probes can evaluate learning in all curriculum areas and can help determine if a skill or behavior has been generalized or maintained. Probes can also be repeated to assess the durability or consistency of responding. In addition, charts and graphs can visually present information and provide a permanent record of progress. Each of these techniques provides a valuable tool for ensuring teaching effectiveness and accountability.

ISSUES AND CONSIDERATIONS REGARDING THE ASSESSMENT OF STUDENTS WITH AUTISM

The ability to transfer and apply information outside the teaching setting underscores most areas of learning (Handleman, 1979, 1981). Without the ability to generalize, performance becomes situationally specific and of limited use for the student. Not only do difficulties with generalization affect basic skill acquisition by students with autism, a number of related issues are involved. For example, the effect of unfamiliar examiners on the assessment process needs to be considered, as well as the impact that generalization difficulties have on mainstreaming efforts. In addition, current discussion on the importance of extended-year programming for these students is founded on the need to facilitate this important skill.

Successful assessment of students with autism is typically accomplished by familiar professionals in comfortable surroundings (Handleman & Harris, 1986). When more traditional or formal evaluation is attempted, there are numerous issues to consider. For example, it is usual to expect some reluctance or hesitancy by the student with novel examiners or with professionals who have ongoing, yet infrequent contact. It is also useful to consider the student's comfort with unfamiliar settings such as hospitals and unusual assessment procedures or equipment.

The teacher or primary clinician can be a very influential person in the assessment process (Swanson & Watson, 1982). This individual can provide the examiner with valuable information concerning a number of variables, such as a student's communication ability, general level of compliance, or idiosyncratic response patterns. Behavioral records and videotapes may be made available to the examiner before the evaluation and preassessment visits to the setting, and may provide reassurance for the more fearful student. Other helpful preparations might include teaching a new response or increasing tolerance to novel equipment. Often just having the child's teacher present during the session to help motivate, manage, or simply interpret responses can make the difference between a successful and unsuccessful effort.

Initial preparation time will vary from student to student; however, it is important for examiners to consider a number of other factors. A detailed intake or referral record can provide a useful structure for the assessment process. Questions can be answered during preassessment conferences with parents and other professionals, and additional information can be obtained by visits to the student's home or class. These preassessment experiences will better equip examiners to conduct successful assessments.

Rapport building is a critical first step in the assessment process. The amount of time needed to build a relationship with a student with autism will depend on variables such as age and ability, thus student comfort is an important prerequisite to a productive session. Initial participation by parents, for example, can help to make students more comfortable and can help to identify preferred rewards or interpret responses. This involvement can also serve to reduce the anxiety that many parents bring to the assessment session (Powers & Handleman, 1984).

Examiners also need to consider many variables when selecting instruments and planning assessment experiences (Powers & Handleman, 1984). Formal and informal activities should be planned with regard to student interests, age, and initial sense of ability; however, developmental level is often a more valuable index for individuals with autism. Multiskill testing can provide a comprehensive view of strengths and weaknesses, and administering a variety of tests that assess similar areas helps to confirm performance levels.

Administration of standardized tests may have to be modified to accommodate the complex needs of students with autism and their idiosyncratic response patterns (Powers & Handleman, 1984). For example, it is important for the examiner to assess the style of stimulus presentation and response format and make adjustments if necessary. Whereas these modifications must be noted, using alternative forms of presentation or accepting different responses, such as signs or gestures, can often provide important information and maximize the utility of results.

Examiner sensitivity to individual learning styles can greatly contribute to the success of assessment sessions. Sitting quietly, maintaining eye contact, and attending to test materials are important test-taking behaviors, and it may be necessary to provide occasional encouragement or initial training in these instructional control areas. In addition, using identified rewards also serves to heighten student performance and motivation.

It is important for examiners to determine whether benefits will be derived from the testing process (Handleman & Harris, 1986). Ability to understand directions, difficulty with generalization, and the ability to be taught a specific response mode are all important variables to consider. Despite commitment and preparation by examiners, some students will not be amenable to formal evaluation, and a reliance on behavioral observations and on the reports of third-party assessments will be necessary. Careful planning and sensitivity to the structure and tempo of assessment sessions will provide optimal results and individualization of testing practices (Powers & Handleman, 1984). All deviations from standardized procedures must be reported to avoid misunderstanding and to increase usefulness to other professionals.

In addition to the various issues involved in the actual assessment process, there are a number of broader concerns to consider. For example, the initial response to the complex needs of students with autism resulted in the development of highly specialized facilities, often with limited opportunities for mainstreaming (Handleman, 1981). Creating strategies for the eventual re-entry of these students into the mainstream of the general and educational community has, therefore, become a priority for service providers (Handleman, 1979; Hanrahan, Goodman & Ropagna, 1990; Russo & Koegel, 1977).

Planning for these important transitional experiences requires systematic assessment and conscientious programming (Handleman, 1979; McEvoy, Twardosz, & Bishop, 1990). The identification of variables such as staff/student ratio, contingencies, school or community life activities, classroom organization, and physical plant can guide approximating the new environment in order to facilitate generalization and optimal adjustment. Follow-up services that are based on ongoing assessment of student progress and performance can then promote continued success of future transitional experiences.

Recent legal, parental, and professional attention has been focused on extended year programming for students with autism (Handleman & Harris, 1986). Assessing a student's need for a 12-month program has, therefore, become an important, yet difficult task. Because particular students may regress during vacation periods, skill recovery time is an important variable to consider. Another issue refers to the degree to which different skills are vulnerable in the absence of instruction. Disability severity, specific type of learning difficulty, extent of regression, and availability of support to prevent regression are additional considerations for this important educational decision. Decision making that results from extended school year and transitional planning ultimately facilitates the provision of the comprehensive educational services required by students with autism.

SUMMARY

In recent years, assessment practices have assumed a major role in the diagnosis and education of students with autism. Current efforts are providing a stronger foundation for educational planning and programming. The strategies of comprehensive psychoeducational assessment can facilitate an accurate student profile and lead to planning in areas such as community integration and extended-year programming. The assessment process has also created a more functional relationship between evaluation and remediation, and this link continues to strengthen through the evolution of an assessment-teaching cycle.

Assessment of students with autism is an intricate process and requires consideration of many factors. Examiners must bring to the process personal training and a willingness to individualize experiences. The resulting process becomes one that goes beyond traditional practices to include a greater reliance on observation, analysis of behavior, and most importantly, input from other professionals and parents. It is this partnership between teacher, parent, and examiner that will promote appropriate assessment, careful planning, and effective programming for this special group of students.

REFERENCES

Alpern, G. D. (1967). Measurement of "unstable" autistic children. *Journal of Abnormal Psychology, 72,* 478–496.

Baumeister, A. A. (1978). Origins and control of stereotyped movements. In C. E. Meyers (Ed.), *Monographs of the American Association on Mental Deficiency,* 18–23.

Birnbrauer, J. S. (1977). Applied behavior analysis, service, and the acquisition of knowledge. *The Behavior Analyst, 2,* 15–21.

Boucher, J. (1977). Alternation and sequencing behavior, and response to novelty in autistic children. *Journal of Child Psychology and Psychiatry, 18,* 67–72.

Brown, L., Branston, M. B., Hamre-Nietupski, S., Pumpian, I., Certo, N., & Gruenewald, L. (1979). A strategy for developing chronological age appropriate and functional curricular content for severely handicapped adolescents and young adults. *Journal of Special Education, 13,* 81–90.

Carrow-Woolfolk, E., & Lynch, J. (1982). *An integrative approach to language disorders in children.* New York: Grune & Stratton.

Cook, A. R., Anderson, N., & Rincover, A. (1982). Stimulus overselectivity and stimulus control: Problems and strategies. In R. L. Koegel, A. Rincover, & A. L. Egel (Eds.), *Educating and understanding autistic children* (pp. 90–105). San Diego: College Hill Press.

Devany, J., & Rincover, A. (1982). Self-stimulatory behavior and sensory reinforcement. In R. L. Koegel, A. Rincover, & A. L. Egel (Eds.), *Educating and understanding autistic children* (pp. 127–141). San Diego: College Hill Press.

Donnellan, A., Gossage, L. D., LaVigna, G. W., Schuler, A., & Traphagan, J. (1977). *Teaching makes a difference.* Sacramento, CA: California State Department of Education.

Durand, V. M., & Crimmins, D. B. (1987). Assessment and treatment of psychotic speech in an autistic child. *Journal of Autism and Developmental Disabilities, 17*(1), 17-28.

Edelson, S. M. (1984). Implications of sensory stimulation in self-destructive behavior. *American Journal of Mental Deficiency, 89,* 140–145.

Fein, D., Waterhouse, L., Lucci, D., & Snyder, D. (1985). Cognitive subtypes in developmentally disabled children: A pilot study. *Journal of Autism and Developmental Disorders, 15*(1), 77-95.

Favell, J. E., McGimsey, J. F., & Schell, R. M. (1982). Treatment of self-injury by providing alternate sensory activities. *Analysis and Intervention in Developmental Disabilities, 2,* 83-104.

Hanrahan, J., Goodman, W., & Ropagna, S. (1990). Preparing mentally retarded students for mainstreaming: Priorities of regular class and special school teachers. *American Journal on Mental Retardation, 94*(5), 470–474.

Handleman, J. S. (1979). Transition of autistic-type children from highly specialized programs to more "normal" educational environments. *Journal for Special Educators, 15,* 273–279.

Handleman, J. S. (1981). Transfer of verbal responses across instructional settings by autistic-type children. *Journal of Speech and Hearing Disorder, 46,* 69–76.

Handleman, J. S., & Harris, S. L. (1986). *Educating the developmentally disabled: Meeting the needs of children and families.* San Diego, CA: College Hill Press.

Harris, S. L. (1975). Teaching language to nonverbal children – With emphasis on problems of generalization. *Psychological Bulletin, 82,* 565–580.

Harris, S. L., Handleman, J. S., & Burton, J. L. (1990). The Stanford-Binet profiles of young children with autism. *Special Services in the Schools, 6,* 135–143.

Hermelin, B. (1971). Rules of language. In M. Rutter (Ed.), *Infantile autism: Concepts, characteristics and treatment* (pp. 98-111). London: Churchill Livingstone.

Hinerman, P. S., Jenson, W. R., Walker, G. R., & Petersen, P. B. (1982). Positive practice overcorrection combined with additional procedures to teach signed words to an autistic child. *Journal of Autism and Developmental Disorders, 12,* 253-263.

Howlin, P. (1978). The assessment of social behavior. In M. Rutter & E. Schopler (Eds.), *Autism: A reappraisal of concepts and treatment* (pp. 63–70). New York: Plenum Press.

Johnson, J., & Koegel, R. L. (1982). Behavioral assessment and curriculum development. In R. L. Koegel, A. Rincover, & A. L. Egel (Eds.), *Educating and understanding autistic children* (pp. 1-33). San Diego: College Hill Press.

Kirk, S., & Gallagher, J. (1983). *Educating exceptional children* (4th ed.). Hopewell, NJ: Houghton Mifflin.

Koegel, R. L., & Schreibman, L. (1976). Identification of consistent responding to auditory stimuli by a functionally "deaf" autistic child. *Journal of Autism and Childhood Schizophrenia, 6,* 147–156.

Lovaas, O. I. (1981). *Teaching developmentally disabled children: The me book.* Baltimore: University Park Press.

Lovaas, O. I., Koegel, R. L., & Schreibman, L. (1979). Stimulus overselectivity in autism: A review of research. *Psychological Bulletin, 86,* 1236–1254.

McEvoy, M. A., Twardosz, S., & Bishop, N. (1990). Affection activities: Procedures for encouraging young children with handicaps to interact with their peers. *Education and Treatment of Children, 13*(2), 159–167.

Mundy, P., Sigman, M., Ungerer, J., & Sherman, T. (1987). Nonverbal communication and play correlates of language development in autistic children. *Journal of Autism and Developmental Disorders, 17*(3), 349-364.

Nakamura, K., Toshima, T., & Takemura, I. (1986). The comparative and developmental study of auditory information processing in autistic adults. *Journal of Autism and Developmental Disorders, 16*(2), 105–118.

O'Gorman, G. (1967). *The nature of childhood autism.* New York: Appleton-Century-Crofts.

Ohta, M. (1987). Cognitive disorders in infantile autism: A study employing the WISC spatial relationship conceptualization and gesture imitations. *Journal of Autism and Developmental Disorders, 17*(1), 45–62.

Ollendick, T. H., & Oswald, D. P. (1989). Role taking and social competence in autism and mental retardation. *Journal of Autism and Developmental Disorders, 19,* 119–127.

Powers, M. D., & Handleman, J. S. (1984). *Behavioral assessment of severe developmental disabilities.* Rockville, MD: Aspen.

Russo, D. C., & Koegel, R. L. (1977). A method for integrating an autistic child into a normal public school classroom. *Journal of Applied Behavior Analysis, 10,* 579–590.

Scott, M. (1980). Ecological theory and methods for research in special education. *Journal of Special Education, 14,* 279–294.

Smith, C., & Knoff, H. (1981). School psychology and special education students' placement decisions: IQ still tips the scale. *Journal of Special Education, 15,* 55–64.

Swanson, H. L., & Watson, B. L. (1982). *Educational and psychological assessment of exceptional children.* St. Louis: C. V. Mosby.

Tucker, J. A. (1985). Curriculum-based assessment: An introduction. *Exceptional Children, 52,* 199–204.

Ungerer, J. A., & Sigman, M. (1987). Categorization skills and receptive language development in autistic children. *Journal of Autism and Developmental Disorders, 17*(1), 3–16.

Westling, I. L., & Floyd, J. (1990). Generalization of community skills: How much training is necessary? *Journal of Special Education, 23*(4), 386–406.

5 Instructional Planning: Goals and Practice

Dianne E. Berkell
C. W. Post Campus, Long Island University

8:30 a.m. Steven disembarks from the school bus, a tall, lanky, 14-year-old youth with a fixed silly smile. His disheveled appearance, awkward gait, and the faraway look in his eyes make him appear oblivious to the school surroundings. The teacher is waiting. She accompanies him and his classmates to their room.

An assistant teacher helps the youngsters find their seats at the table in the center of the room. Large communication cards filled with pictures are taped onto the table directly in front of several students' seats. Steven looks at his communication card, points to the picture of a sandwich, and makes several loud noises to draw his teacher's attention. Around the table are four boys and two girls, each of whom has autism and moderate mental retardation. They sit, three engaging in stereotypic behaviors (arm flapping, nose flicking, and rocking), two staring into space, and Steven still pointing to the sandwich, as the teacher begins the day's first lesson.

Imagine you are Steven's teacher. What are your plans for your class today? How do these plans relate to the annual goals and short-term objectives in each youngster's Individualized Education Plan (IEP)? Most importantly, how do the objectives and goals included in the students' IEP's contribute to the development of skills required for successful community living in the mainstream of society?

Children and youth with autism exhibit complex and intense learning problems that often require specialized instructional programming. These children may exhibit severe language deficits, uneven skill development, ment, extreme behavior problems, and other disabilities in learning and relating to people (Norsworthy & Sievers, 1981). During the past two decades, researchers have gathered much new information pertaining to the characteristics and needs of students with autism as they progress through the educational process. This body of knowledge can provide guidance and structure for designing instructional programs that are directed toward meeting the unique learning needs associated with autism.

Improved educational programming is needed in order to increase the likelihood that persons with severe disabilities will be able to lead productive lives. Change is especially necessary if people with autism are to live full, meaningful lives with dignity in the mainstream of their communities. The ultimate goal of education is to prepare individuals to be contributing members of society. Toward this most crucial outcome, educators must redirect their efforts and utilize strategies and techniques that research has demonstrated to be effective in teaching children with autism.

The present chapter discusses best practices for instructional planning for students with autism. Recommendations are provided to assist teachers, administrators, and support personnel in developing basic curriculum and methodology strategies. The chapter is intended to offer systematic instructional guidelines for the design and implementation of educational programming.

In order to achieve maximum benefit from the presented information, teachers will need an appreciation of the philosophies in which the described training procedures are grounded. Specifically, there are two basic tenets upon which this chapter is based: (a) the majority of instruction received by students with autism must be provided in the context of natural settings in which students will ultimately have to function, and (b) persons with autism need frequent opportunities for interaction with nondisabled individuals in the mainstream of school and society.

A word of caution pertaining to the adoption of any instructional strategy is in order here. Curriculum should be based on realistic goals and must be functional and chronologically age-appropriate. It is imperative that when choosing educational activities and environments, teachers consider the student's age, ability level, and learning style. Also, when determining which skills to teach, educators must consider the types of demands being placed upon the learner in relation to any behavior/communication deficits that may interfere with the student's acquisition and performance of those skills. In other words, teachers must select educational goals and objectives that are attainable and usable.

INTEGRATED SCHOOLS

Preparation for integrated community living begins with integrated schools. There is widespread recognition that educational integration is overdue. All students with disabilities—without exception—have the right to receive an education in their neighborhood public school, in proximity to nondisabled peers. This perspective has been widely supported in the literature (see, e.g., Brown et al., 1979; Sontag, Certo, & Button, 1979). In addition, empirical evidence has shown that such integration has a positive impact on both the quality of services provided to these students (Gaylord-Ross & Holvoet, 1985) and their acceptance by nondisabled children (Voeltz, 1984).

In spite of research findings and the existence of many successful integrated programs, resistance to integration still remains (Janney & Meyer, 1990; Meyer & Kishi, 1985). Many school districts throughout the country continue to insist on serving students with autism in segregated, handicapped-only schools. A continuum of placements based on student characteristics, in which students with the most severe learning and behavior problems remain grouped together in specialized segregated public schools, is still often advocated by administrators (e.g., Colella & Pucciarelli, 1990).

Proponents of segregated schools claim that they are justified based on the number of skills learned and behaviors managed in specialized centers. However, data are available to show greater skill development and generalization in integrated public school settings (e.g., Gaylord-Ross, Haring, Breen, & Pitts-Conway, 1984). In fact, it has been shown that isolation from nonhandicapped peers is detrimental to the growth and development of students with autism (Donnellan, 1984). Clearly, the question is no longer whether these students should be educated alongside their nondisabled peers, but rather how to best accommodate their unique needs in integrated public school settings.

CURRICULUM DEVELOPMENT FOR STUDENTS WITH AUTISM

Curriculum planning for students with autism and other severe developmental disabilities has undergone a metamorphosis since the passage of Public Law 94-142 (Education for All Handicapped Law) in 1975. This law, sometimes referred to as the *Magna Carta of Special Education,* mandates that all children, regardless of their disability, be provided with a free and appropriate education in the least restrictive environment. Upon passage of P.L. 94–142, efforts were made to comply with its directives to provide effective public school education for all children; however, in 1975 relatively little technical information pertaining to instruction for students with severe developmental disabilities was available.

Children were placed in segregated classrooms, often in separate buildings that had been relegated to special education students, or in isolated locations, such as basements or back halls of public schools, with little or no opportunity for interaction with nondisabled peers. Instruction typically focused on developing process-type abilities (e.g., visual discrimination, fine motor coordination, auditory sequencing) through the use of materials specific to the classroom, neglecting direct instruction of practical skills necessary for community living. Thus, persons with autism were prepared for dependent lives, and continued to exist in isolation from society.

Recent research has yielded more information about how to teach individuals with autism, and federal initiatives have helped to motivate teachers and parents to begin planning for lifelong educational outcomes. Today, the need to provide direct skill instruction in natural environments (i.e., real-life settings in which learned skills will later have to be performed) is recognized. In view of voluminous research findings in the area of generalization (e.g., Baer, 1981; Coon, Vogelsberg, & Williams, 1981; Hill, Wehman, & Horst, 1980; Horner, Bellamy, & Colvin, 1984; Stokes & Baer, 1977; Storey, Bates, & Hansen, 1984), special educators have been encouraged to extend their teaching efforts beyond the limitations of classroom walls and school buildings, to incorporate community-based instruction into their programming. As a result of recent research and federally supported model programs, much information has become available to educators to help prepare students with autism for meaningful and satisfying lives within their communities.

CURRICULAR DOMAINS

In keeping with the philosophy that instructional programming should be focused on building a repertoire of skills needed to function productively in society's mainstream, three major curricular areas are discussed in this chapter: (a) life skills for integrated community living, (b) vocational preparation, and (c) functional academics. Based on the work of Brown et al. (1979), these three areas provide a framework through which curriculum theory may be studied. The initial work of Brown and his colleagues dissected curriculum for persons with severe disabilities into life space domains, and contributed significantly toward improving instructional effectiveness.

In many ways similar to the domains delineated by Brown and his colleagues, the broad curriculum areas presented here are not situation specific; skills from each category may be employed in a variety of settings and domains, and for a variety of purposes, thereby transcending particular situations. In other words, the skills included in any one category may be applied across school, home, neighborhood, employment, and community domains.

Life Skills for Integrated Community Living

The Life Skills Domain encompasses three subdomains. In order to enjoy the benefits of community integration, individuals need to have some degree of competence in each of these three subdomains:

1. social interaction,
2. self-preservation, and
3. activities of daily living skills.

Proficiency in these skill areas can enhance the quality of life for individuals with autism by enabling them to participate in neighborhood residential programs (Smith & Belcher, 1985), as well as in other integrated activities in their communities.

Social Interaction Skills

Difficulty in forming relationships with other people constitutes a central feature of autism, and considerable effort has been devoted to designing strategies for improving social functioning (Rutter, 1978; Williams, 1989). Whereas most people acquire social interaction ability through various daily living experiences, individuals with autism are not able to absorb this kind of knowledge without the benefit of direct skill instruction (Berkell, 1986). In fact, in order to develop skill in this area, instruction must be extremely structured and highly systematic.

Curriculum content for building interpersonal social interaction skills should be based on a combination of developmental (Dyer & Peck, 1987) and behavioral (Dunlap, Koegel, & Egel, 1979; Smith & Coleman, 1986) theory. In addition, recent advances in the study of autism indicate the importance of analysis and identification of the communicative intent of interactive behaviors (Christof & Kane, 1991; Donnellan, Miranda, Mesaros, & Fassbender, 1984; Durand, 1990), in recognition of the fact that every interpersonal behavior, regardless of its outward form, is inherently meaningful.

When teaching social interaction skills to students with autism it is necessary to be familiar with and to understand the manner and sequence in which nondisabled individuals acquire social skills. In order to prepare persons with autism to engage in interpersonal activities, a series of developmental steps based on normal developmental theory should be loosely followed. As is often the case with individuals with autism, less sophisticated or lower level skills may remain unmastered although skills ascribed to more advanced stages already exist in the student's repertoire. Decisions as to whether the more basic skills will have to be taught in such cases depend on their relationship to higher level skills, as well as on the necessity of specific lower level skills for continued social growth.

Seven stages through which students progress as they develop socially are listed and explained in this section. These stages constitute a large portion of early childhood education and continue throughout the school years for students with severe developmental disabilities.

Stage 1: Social Interaction Readiness. In order to benefit from instruction in specific social interaction skill training, certain prerequisite behaviors are helpful. Specifically, students should demonstrate the ability to sustain some form of eye contact, or visual interpersonal attention, with the instructor. Sitting behavior should be present, and the student should comply with simple commands and be able to imitate one-step actions (e.g., touch nose).

Stage 2: Exploratory Play. As students begin to follow basic commands and to demonstrate an awareness of other people, as well as of objects, it becomes the teacher's role to increase exploratory interaction with objects. Students should be encouraged to notice objects and to reach for, grasp, and study them. Nondisabled children at this stage typically reach for and shake items, seemingly attempting to learn more about what is inside of them.

Stage 3: Solitary Play. When youngsters with autism begin to "check out" objects in their immediate environment through inquisitive behaviors, they need to be directed to use materials appropriately. For example, rather than sitting and spinning the wheels of toy trucks without purpose, students should be encouraged to push or pull trucks. The role of the teacher is now to model appropriate play behavior (actually play with the truck while the child observes) and to prompt the child to imitate the teacher's actions. If the student has mastered the abilities listed in the first two stages, appropriate object interaction is more likely to occur.

Stage 4: Parallel Play. Students entering Stage 4 are able to play independently and to interact appropriately with several designated objects, but may have difficulty sustaining this interaction when other children are introduced into play settings. Often youngsters with autism are so easily distracted and disruptive that they are unable to continue their play activities when in the presence of other children. Further, they are unable to allow other children to play without disturbing their activity. Practice in playing in close proximity to peers is useful in increasing tolerance to other children, as well as for increasing time on task and reducing distractability.

As soon as children are able to play in parallel dyad situations, teachers should arrange play settings so that two children are playing with the same materials in an associative parallel fashion. In other words, they are not playing cooperatively but are sharing a common pool of materials and are sitting in close proximity to each other.

Stage 5: Directed Cooperative Play. During this stage students learn to play with the teacher or with another adult or peer tutor when prompted to do so. They progress to a level at which they can actually initiate play activities and engage themselves cooperatively with other individuals.

Cooperative play activities should include children from varied functioning levels. One of the least sound educational expectations regarding children with autism is based on the belief that they will learn how to play cooperatively by playing with other children who are also autistic. By definition, the syndrome of autism precludes the occurrence of such positive interaction between autistic individuals, unless they have already received training with nondisabled persons.

Stage 6: Peer Play. Following acquisition of some basic cooperative social interaction skills in Stage 5, it becomes easier to teach students how to interact with other individuals in social situations. They must learn to attend to other people visually and aurally and to perform such actions as turn taking, item passing, and rule compliance.

Peer play experiences are best provided in integrated environments with opportunities to interact with nondisabled children. Such experiences lead to increased understanding and acceptance on the part of nondisabled learners, as well as more appropriate interaction skills by students with autism.

Stage 7: Utilization of Community Facilities/Resources. People who live, work, and play in the community need to be able to navigate the neighborhood and to utilize local facilities. Although all persons with autism may not be capable of the same degree of independence, each person should be helped to develop to his or her fullest potential. In so doing, teachers will need to train students in such skills as the use of money, telephone competence, and appropriate behaviors for public places, including restaurants, supermarkets, and other community settings.

All too often parents of children with severe behavior problems find it too difficult to take their children to restaurants or even to supermarkets because of the child's unacceptable behaviors. By prioritizing targeted skills and providing instruction in necessary community living skill areas, teachers can help youngsters to more often accompany their parents, siblings, or other caregivers (some could even go alone), and school training would be more likely to be reinforced after school hours.

Self-Preservation Skills

Self-preservation, or safety skill, training is designed to improve students' ability to recognize and appropriately respond to dangerous, and possibly life-threatening situations. Additionally, this subdomain includes certain abilities associated with one's lifelong maintenance in society.

Self-preservation skills should be assessed for each student prior to beginning instruction. Based on an ecological inventory of the environments in which individuals spend significant portions of their daily life, these skills should be prioritized and taught with long-term planning in mind. Ecological inventory strategies require that teachers visit and secure relevant information about the environments in which students are or may be expected to function. Some examples of frequently needed self-preservation skills are listed below:

1. Student keeps foreign objects out of eyes, ears, nose, and mouth.
2. Student maintains safe distance from stove.
3. Student refrains from touching electrical outlets or wires.
4. Student dials police emergency number.
5. Student follows rules during fire drill without assistance.
6. Student handles sharp objects carefully.
7. Student recognizes and follows safety signs and signals (e.g., red light).
8. Student looks both ways before leaving sidewalk to cross street.
9. Student remains seated in car or bus.
10. Student keeps seat belt fastened while in car or bus.

Daily Living Skills

Preparing students with autism to become contributing members of their home environment requires that families and educators work together to develop appropriate programming in daily living skills that are suited to each student's particular situation (Harris & Handleman, 1980). Daily living skills include basic living activities and domestic care. Eating, toileting, dressing, and grooming constitute basic living activities. Domestic care involves responsibilities related to maintaining a clean and pleasant home environment. Proficiency in these activities will enable individuals to function as independently as possible. Instruction in daily living skills should start early in life and be developed systematically with the changing needs of the student (Eshilian, Haney, & Falvey, 1989) and the home environment.

Critical to successful instruction in activities of daily living is the utilization of the student's own home, to ensure that the student will be able to perform these activities when and where necessary. In order to select and prioritize instructional objectives, information from the student and the family must be obtained regarding preferences, current living arrangements and future plans, and present level of functioning. Assessment of the student's daily living skill repertoire is required prior to the onset of training, and throughout the training process.

Vocational Preparation

Preparation for the transition from school to work is crucial to community integration. A person's status in our society is often determined by the type of job held and the salary earned (Budnick, 1985). Work is especially important for persons with disabilities. It generates the respect of others (Terkel, 1974) and can be a source of pride, self-satisfaction, personal fulfillment, and, of course, income. Yet, for persons with autism, the gap between traditional special education programming and effective vocational preparation presents a major obstacle to successful community integration.

Nearly two decades have passed since the passage of Public Law 94–142, and growing numbers of students, who as a result of this legislation had gained access to public school programs, have been exiting the schools as they reach 21. Unfortunately, graduates with autism are often placed in day activity centers, and remain isolated from nondisabled community members. The vast majority remain unemployed and nonproductive in their adult years, although it has been clearly demonstrated that many of these individuals can learn and acquire skills when appropriate instructional methods and procedures are utilized (Boles, Bellamy, Horner, & Mank, 1984; Gold, 1972; Karan, 1978; Koegel, Rincover, & Egel, 1982; Sailor & Guess, 1983).

Transition from school to working life is a process encompassing years of learning experiences and often requiring ongoing follow-up and support services for persons with disabilities (Will, 1984). Typically, it includes secondary school years, the point of graduation, additional post-secondary education or adult services, and the initial years of employment. For persons with autism, however, vocational preparation must begin earlier and may include lifelong ongoing support services. Whenever feasible, training should be provided at community-based worksites with attention directed toward reinforcing appropriate work behaviors and improving job-related skills.

Instructional techniques that are helpful in facilitating the development of work proficiency and appropriate work behaviors include task analysis and behavioral instructional procedures. An essential component of the instructional process is an assessment inventory of both the work training site and the required job tasks. This inventory should include an analysis of the physical layout of the site, including lavatories, potential dangers, exits, and entrances (Berkell, 1987). The inventory also should delineate skills needed to perform designated jobs within particular environments, and any necessary adaptations of the work sites should be specified.

Elementary School Programming for Vocational Preparation. Students with disabilities should begin receiving career/vocational training at the elementary school level (Anderson & Strathe, 1987; Moore, Agran, & McSweyn, 1990). Classroom responsibilities such as collating papers, cleaning tables, caring for plants, serving snacks, and delivering messages are useful in developing career awareness and feelings of job satisfaction. These behaviors should be continually reinforced throughout the school years (Kochany & Keller, 1981). Promotion of these behaviors and attitudes during the school years greatly enhance the likelihood of successful employment in adulthood.

Cook (1983) concurred that career development should begin in early childhood and extend into the adult years for all exceptional children. She maintained that although vocational education should be required in all programs for students with disabilities, it need not be provided through separate programming but can, instead, be an integral part of the ongoing curriculum.

In order to determine the content for elementary-level vocational curricula, including procedures for integrating vocational training into the general curriculum, teachers need to visit secondary and adult programs (Wehman, 1981). Observation of older students and clients involved in vocational training programs provides useful information regarding the types of skills that will be most important to the vocational success of students with autism.

Intermediate School Years. Development of general work habits and skills that can eventually lead to various types of employment should be included in Individual Education Plans (IEPs) once youths with autism reach age 11. Work habits, such as attention to task and rule compliance, can be taught through functional and age-appropriate activities concurrently in both classrooms and community-based settings.

In addition to the development of proper work habits, during the middle school years teachers should provide exposure to a variety of jobs, available in the local job market. The purpose of this instructional stage is to provide an array of experiences representing a wide range of jobs and to develop a broad skill base upon which secondary and post-secondary teachers may build.

Secondary School Programming for Transition to Work. If students have received adequate vocational training in the elementary and middle school years, by age 15 they will have been exposed to several types of jobs and work settings. Students will have acquired positive work habits and will also be able to demonstrate appropriate interpersonal skills for use on job sites.

Secondary school vocational special education teachers must first determine which vocational tasks are best suited to each student's learning and behavior characteristics, and next identify community work training sites at which these skills may be taught. During the secondary school years students should receive a combination of classroom instruction and training at varied worksites. Data pertaining to the quality of production, interpersonal relationships, and student satisfaction and behaviors at each job training site can be maintained and analyzed. Consideration of this information will be helpful later when deciding upon a particular placement in the competitive job market.

The secondary school student, the teacher, and the parent require the guidance of a vocational rehabilitation counselor. The role of the counselor is one of assistance and support in case management to the special education teacher (Reubens, 1981). Counselors serve as a resource for placement opportunities in the community. They can also contribute to vocational preparation through participation in the planning stages of the vocational component of IEPs.

Teaching Functional Academics to Students with Autism

Although a small percentage of persons with autism demonstrate intellectual ability at average or higher levels, the majority of these individuals function within the moderate-to-severe mental retardation range. Therefore, material presented in this chapter is directed primarily toward persons who have autism with moderate-to-severe mental retardation. Accordingly, the functional academics addressed in this section are presented for students with limited intellectual functioning.

Curricula for students with severe disabilities has traditionally been organized into categories such as fine and gross motor coordination; self-help skills; language development; recreation, leisure, and social skills;

and functional academics (Barudin & Hourcade, 1990). Basic reading and math skills needed for everyday living usually constitute the core of functional academic programs. Academics are functional when they involve such skills as knowing coin values, using a calculator to add up purchases, telling time, or reading words like "in," "out," "exit," and "walk" when they are encountered outside of school (Ferguson, 1987).

Many functional academic skills are useful in several life space domains. For example, making change might be useful in a restaurant, supermarket, clothing store, on a vending machine, at a pay telephone, or on a bus. Because generalization is often a problem for individuals with autism, functional academics should be taught in particular environments in which they will later need to be performed.

Also, using naturally occurring cues and reinforcers can lead to increased transfer of skills. When instruction is provided in environments where the targeted skills naturally occur, difficulties in generalizing skills from simulated to natural environments are minimized (Falvey, 1989). By employing direct instruction in a variety of community-based sites, educators make no inferences regarding skill generalization from the training site to real-life situations. Students taught to perform skills in artificial settings, such as simulated supermarkets, have really not been taught to perform functional skills because they may not be able to transfer the skills to nonschool environments.

Educators hold the keys to instructional effectiveness. It is time to put this knowledge to use in teaching the functional academics needed for everyday living. Most current texts that deal with education for students with severe disabilities tend to omit the area of academics. Perhaps viewing academic content as a part of the various life space domains, these texts focus on the more basic adaptive living skills. Functional academics, however, are a crucial aspect of curriculum and, although they may be taught as part of other curriculum domains, these academic skills often apply across domains.

STRATEGIES FOR FACILITATING LEARNING

Persons with severe disabilities, such as autism, often exhibit slow learning, poor retention, and generalization problems (Bull, Cochran, & Snell, 1988). These characteristics have real implications for teaching. Teacher effectiveness can be enhanced through the utilization of methods that take into account the need for direct instruction designed to match the unique learning styles of students with autism. Specifically, generalization strategies, including teaching skills across settings, materials, and people, are crucial to successful instruction (Evans, Evans, Gable, & Schmid, 1991). In addition, ecological inventories, ongoing assessment, and task analysis procedures enhance learning by providing a systematic approach to education.

Selection of Instructional Settings

In order for students to gain competence in skills required for community integration, the amount of instructional time spent within the confines of the classroom must decrease. Training should take place, as often as possible, in the specific locations in which students will be expected to function following their exit from the educational system at age 21 (Bates & Cuvo, 1984; Brown, Nieutupski, & Hamre-Nieutupski, 1976; Brown et al., 1983). Students need to learn to interact not just with teachers and family members, peers, and school personnel, but also with strangers, such as waiters, store clerks, bus drivers, physicians, and numerous other persons within the community. Community environments offer a rich variety of situations to which students must learn to respond (Ford & Mirenda, 1984). Teaching procedures that draw the student's attention to relevant cues as they naturally occur in the community can facilitate learning, as well as skill maintenance and retention. Only through the provision of on-site community-based training will educators attain success in teaching community living skills.

When selecting community environments for instruction several factors should be considered (Falvey, 1989). Specifically, the following questions should be addressed:

1. Is the type of environment being considered frequented by students with family members/caretakers during nonschool hours?
2. Is the environment frequented by nondisabled peers?
3. What type of environments are preferred by particular students?
4. Does the environment involve skills that would be required in other community environments?

Input from other teachers, administrators, and, especially parents is beneficial in determining community-based training environments. Parental input is tremendously valuable for insights into the student's lifestyle, preferences, interfering and/or dangerous behaviors, and financial resources available for visiting particular places. School administrators may lend support to community-based training through budget allocation, as well as through personal interest and activity in the program. In order for administrators to understand and appreciate the benefits of such training, on-site observation is helpful.

Task Analysis

The second step in the instructional process, following curriculum development, is the design of instructional procedures. Curriculum deals with the question of "what to teach," and task analysis answers questions regarding "how to teach." Task analysis is the breaking up of a task into its component parts, or subskills, and placing these subskills in sequential order. The task analysis organizes the activity, or task, into teachable steps and strategies for instruction.

Task analyses enhance instruction through (a) insuring that essential subskills are taught, (b) tailoring instruction to individual functioning, and (c) keeping the teacher and student on track by reducing the likelihood of teaching unnecessary skills. When properly utilized, task analysis can thus lead to more efficient programming.

Behaviors in a task analysis must be stated operationally (i.e., in terms of observable movement that is measurable). All behaviors should be stated in terms of learner action so that what is to be learned rather than how it is to be taught is the focus. In addition, each step of the task analysis should be stated discretely so that it can be lifted from the other steps and can stand alone for instructional purposes.

A complete task analysis includes the following types of information:

1. Statement of the performance object, or task to be learned.
2. Antecedent cue to let the student know what is expected.
3. List of subskills necessary to master the performance objective.
4. List of necessary resources and materials.

SUMMARY

The ultimate aim of education is to prepare individuals to lead productive and satisfying lives. Toward this end, educators need to take advantage of new information and advances in the field of special education. A redirection of educational efforts can lead to increased integration for students with the most severe disabilities, including those with autism.

Curriculum content should include life skills for integrated community living, vocational preparation, and functional academics. When planning IEPs, teachers must consider lifelong goals for their students. And finally, learner styles should be accommodated as teachers systematically prepare students, through instruction in natural environments, to function in the real world.

REFERENCES

Anderson, R. J., & Strathe, M. I. (1987). Transitional programming: Suggesting an adaptability model. In S. E. Breuning & R. A. Gable (Eds.), *Advances in mental retardation and developmental disabilities* (Vol. 3, pp. 179–208). Greenwich, CT: JAI Press.

Baer, D. M. (1981). *How to plan for generalization.* Lawrence, KS: H & H Enterprises.

Barudin, S. I., & Hourcade, J. J. (1990). Relative effectiveness of three methods of reading instruction in developing specific recall and transfer skills in learners with moderate and severe mental retardation. *Educating and Training in Mental Retardation, 25,* 287–291.

Bates, P. E., & Cuvo, A. J. (1984). Simulated and naturalistic instruction of community functioning skills with mentally retarded learners. *Direct Instruction News, 4* (2).

Berkell, D. E. (1986). A new look at the scope and sequence of social interaction training for autistic students. In J. Levy, P. Levy, & B. Niven (Eds.), *Model programs and new technologies for people with disabilities.* New York: Young Adult Institute.

Berkell, D. E. (1987). Issues in vocational preparation for severely handicapped adolescents and young adults. In J. Gottlieb & B. W. Gottlieb (Eds.), *Advances in special education* (Vol. 6, pp. 151–170). Greenwich, CT: JAI Press.

Boles, S. M., Bellamy, G. T., Horner, R. H., & Mank, D. (1984). Specialized training programs: The structured employment model. In S. C. Paine, G. T. Bellamy, & B. Wilcox (Eds.), *Human services that work: From innovation to standard practice* (pp. 181–208). Baltimore: Paul H. Brookes.

Brown, L., Branston, M. B., Hamre-Nietupski, S., Johnson, F., Wilcox, B., & Gruenewald, L. (1979). A rationale for comprehensive longitudinal interactions between severely handicapped students and nonhandicapped students and other citizens. *AAESPH Review, 4,* 3–14.

Brown, L., Nieutupski, J., & Hamre-Nieutupski, S. (1976). The criterion of ultimate functioning. In M. A. Thomas (Ed.), *Hey, don't forget about me!* (pp. 2–15). Reston, VA: CEC Information Center.

Brown, L., Nisbet, J., Ford, A., Sweet, M., Shiraga, B., York, J., & Loomis, R. (1983). The critical need for nonschool instruction in educational programs for severely handicapped students. *Journal of the Association for the Severely Handicapped, 8,* 71–77.

Budnick, A. (1985). *Autism. The state of the art.* Albany, NY: New York State Education Department.

Bull, G. L., Cochran, P. S., & Snell, M. E. (1988). Beyond CAI: Computers, language, and persons with mental retardation. *Topics in Language Disorders, 8*(4), 55–76.

Christof, K. J., & Kane, S. R. (1991). Relationship-building for students with autism. *Teaching Exceptional Children, 23*(2), 49–51.

Colella, H., & Pucciarelli, C. (1990). *Least restrictive environment and the center-based school.* Paper presented at the meeting of the New York State Federation of Chapters of the Council for Exceptional Children, Uniondale, NY.

Cook, I. D. (1983). Career development for exceptional children. *Teaching Exceptional Children, 15,* 220–225.

Coon, M. E., Vogelsberg, R. T., & Williams, W. (1981). Effects of classroom public transportation instruction on generalization to the natural environment. *Journal of the Association for the Severely Handicapped, 6,* 46–53.

Donnellan, A. (1984). The criterion of the least dangerous assumption. *Behavioral Disorders, 9,* 141–150.

Donnellan, A. M., Mirenda, P. L., Mesaros, R. A., & Fassbender, L. L. (1984). Analyzing the communicative functions of aberrant behavior. *Journal of the Association for Persons with Severe Handicaps, 9,* 201–212.

Dunlap, G., Koegel, R. L., & Egel, A. L. (1979). Autistic children in school. *Exceptional Children, 45,* 552–558.
Durand, V. M. (1990). *Severe behavior problems: A functional communication training approach.* New York: Guilford Press.
Dyer, K., & Peck, C. A. (1987). Current perspectives on social/communication curricula for students with autism and severe handicaps. *Education and Treatment of Children, 10,* 338–351.
Eshilian, L., Haney, M., Falvey, M. A. (1989). Domestic skills. In M. A. Falvey (Ed.), *Community-based curriculum: Instructional strategies for students with severe handicaps* (2nd ed., pp. 115–140). Baltimore: Paul H. Brookes.
Evans, W. E., Evans, S. S., Gable, R. A., & Schmid, R. E. (1991). *Instructional management.* Boston: Allyn & Bacon.
Falvey, M. A. (1989). *Community-based curriculum: Instructional strategies for students with severe handicaps* (2nd ed.). Baltimore: Paul H. Brookes.
Ferguson, D. L. (1987). *Curriculum decision making for students with severe handicaps: Policy and practice.* New York: Teachers College Press.
Ford, A., & Mirenda, P. (1984). Community instruction: A natural cues and corrections decision model. *Journal of the Association of Persons with Severe Handicaps, 9,* 79–88.
Gaylord-Ross, R. J., Haring, N. G., Breen, C., & Pitts-Conway, V. (1984). The training and generalization of social interaction skills with autistic youth. *Journal of Applied Behavior Analysis, 17,* 229–248.
Gaylord-Ross, R. J., & Holvoet, J. F. (1985). *Strategies for educating students with severe handicaps.* Boston: Little, Brown.
Gold, M. (1972). Stimulus factors in skill training of the retarded on a complex assembly task: Acquisition, retention, and transfer. *American Journal of Mental Deficiency, 76,* 517–526.
Harris, S. L., & Handleman, J. S. (1980). Programming for generalization: Educating autistic children and their parents. *Education and Training of Children, 3,* 51–63.
Hill, J. W., Wehman, P., & Horst, G. (1980). Acquisition and generalization of leisure skills in severely and profoundly handicapped youth: Use of an electronic pinball machine. In P. Wehman & J. W. Hill (Eds.), *Instructional programming for severely handicapped youth: A community integration approach* (pp. 43–62). Richmond, VA: Virginia Commonwealth University.
Horner, R. H., Bellamy, G. T., & Colvin, G. T. (1984). Responding in the presence of nontrained stimuli: Implications of generalization error patterns. *Journal of the Association for Persons with Severe Handicaps, 9,* 287–295.
Janney, R. E., & Meyer, L. H. (1990). A consultation model to support integrated educational services for students with severe disabilities and challenging behaviors. *Journal of the Association for Persons with Severe Handicaps, 15,* 186–199.
Karan, O. C. (1978). *Habilitation practices with the severely disabled* (Vol. 2). Madison, WI: University of Wisconsin Research and Training Center in Mental Retardation.
Kochany, L., & Keller, J. (1981). An analysis and evaluation of the failures of severely disabled individuals in competitive employment. In P. Wehman (Ed.), *Competitive employment: New horizons for the severely disabled* (pp. 181–198). Baltimore: Paul H. Brookes.
Koegel, R. L., Rincover, A., & Egel, A. L. (1982). *Educating and understanding autistic children.* San Diego, CA: College-Hill Press.
Meyer, L. H., & Kishi, G. S. (1985). School integration strategies. In K. C. Lakin & R. H. Bruininks (Eds.). *Strategies for achieving community integration of developmentally disabled citizens* (pp. 231–252). Baltimore: Paul H. Brookes.
Moore, S. C., Agran, M., & McSweyn, C. A. (1990). Career education: Are we starting early enough? *Career Development for Exceptional Individuals, 2,* 129–134.
Norsworthy, K., & Sievers, P. (1981). The teacher's perspective: The struggle to provide quality education to autistic children. In B. Wilcox & A. Thompson (Eds.), *Educating*

autistic children and youth (pp. 207–219). Washington, DC: National Society for Children and Adults with Autism.

Reubens, B. G. (1981). *From school to work: A European perspective* (National Institute of Health Contract No. C. 400760122). Columbus, OH: National Center for Research in Vocational Education.

Rutter, M. (1978). Diagnosis and definition of childhood autism. *Journal of Autism and Childhood Schizophrenia, 5,* 57–70.

Sailor, W., & Guess, D. (1983). *Severely handicapped students: An instructional design.* Boston: Houghton Mifflin Company.

Sontag, E., Certo, N., & Button, J. E. (1979). On a distinction between the education of the severely and profoundly handicapped and a doctrine of limitations. *Exceptional Children, 45,* 604–616.

Smith, M. D., & Belcher, R. (1985). Teaching life skills to adults disabled by autism. *Journal of Autism and Developmental Disorders, 15,* 163–175.

Smith, M. D., & Coleman, D. (1986). Managing the behavior of adults in the job setting. *Journal of Autism and Developmental Disorders, 16,* 145–154.

Stokes, T. F., & Baer, D. M. (1977). An implicit technology of generalization. *Journal of Applied Behavior Analysis, 10,* 349–367.

Storey, K., Bates, P., & Hansen, H. B. (1984). Acquisition and generalization of coffee purchase skills by adults with severe disabilities. *Journal of the Association for Persons with Severe Handicaps, 9,* 178–185.

Terkel, S. (1974). *People talk about what they do all day and how they feel about what they do.* New York: Pantheon.

Voeltz, L. M. (1984). Program and curricular adaptations to prepare children for integration. In N. Certo, N. Haring, & R. York (Eds.), *Public school integration of severely handicapped students: Rational issues and progressive alternatives* (pp. 155–183). Baltimore: Paul H. Brookes.

Wehman, P. (1981). *Competitive employment: New horizons for severely disabled individuals.* Baltimore: Paul H. Brookes.

Will, M. (1984). *OSERS programming for the transition of youth with disabilities: Bridges from school to working life.* Washington, DC: Department of Education.

Williams, T. I. (1989). A social skills group for autistic children. *Journal of Autism and Developmental Disorders, 19,* 143–155.

6 Facilitating Language and Communication Development in Autism: Assessment and Intervention Guidelines

Amy M. Wetherby
Florida State University

Barry M. Prizant
Emerson College

The acquisition of language and communicative abilities is a major challenge faced by persons with autism. The significance of this challenge is reflected in current conceptualizations of the autism syndrome, which include language and communicative impairments as primary diagnostic features (American Psychiatric Association, 1987). Communicative impairment of autistic children is one of the greatest sources of stress for the family (Bristol, 1988), and level of communicative competence has been found to be an important predictor of more positive outcomes. Therefore, the development of language and communication abilities needs to be a major focus in the provision of education and treatment for individuals with autism and their families. This chapter provides an overview of the nature of communication and language impairments in autism. Guidelines for assessing communication and related symbolic abilities using ecologically-based strategies are presented, and best practices for facilitating language and communication for individuals with autism are suggested.

NATURE OF THE COMMUNICATION AND LANGUAGE IMPAIRMENT IN AUTISM

The communication and language disturbances of persons with autism range from failure to develop any functional speech, with approximately 50% of these individuals remaining mute or nonverbal, to the development of functional but idiosyncratic use of spontaneous speech and language

(Rutter, 1978). Individuals with autism show impairments in verbal and nonverbal communication, not just in speech and language (Ricks & Wing, 1975). Impairments in language and communication have been found to be related to deficits in social and cognitive development. Numerous studies of children have demonstrated that impairments in symbolic play and imitation are related to language level (see Prizant & Wetherby, 1989), indicating that speech and language problems are secondary to underlying impairments in reciprocal social interaction and social cognition.

Anecdotal reports of these children's limited abilities to use speech' and gestures for communicative purposes pervade the literature (e.g., Baltaxe & Simmons, 1975; Kanner, 1943; Ricks & Wing, 1975; Rutter, 1978). However, research has demonstrated that most children do not lack communicative intent, but rather show limitations in the ability to use communicative signals for a full range of purposes, including social purposes; for example, to direct another's attention to an object or event for the purpose of sharing the experience (Mundy, Sigman, Ungerer, & Sherman, 1986; Wetherby & Prutting, 1984). Persons with autism have particular difficulty following and using indicating strategies to establish a joint focus of attention (e.g., showing, pointing). The emerging intentional communication of these children appears to express primarily or exclusively relatively nonsocial intentions, such as to request an object or assistance (Curcio, 1978; Wetherby & Prutting, 1984). Idiosyncratic and unconventional means to communicate (e.g., self-injurious behavior, echolalia) may also be developed, which indicates that the children may be motivated to communicate but are limited in their use of conventional signals and in their ability to consider what the listener needs to know to understand their message. Even in older, cognitively higher functioning individuals with advanced grammatical skills, problems in following social rules of conversation persist (Baltaxe, 1977). Thus, rather than viewing persons as noncommunicative or noninteractive, current understandings suggest that social–cognitive limitations result in particular difficulties acquiring social communicative intentions and conventional communicative means (Mundy & Sigman, 1989; Prizant & Wetherby, 1987; Wetherby, 1986).

Certain common characteristics have been identified among autistic individuals who develop language. Kanner (1943, 1946) identified characteristics of language associated with autism including immediate and delayed echolalia and resultant pronominal reversals, extreme literalness, private and original frame of reference, and affirmation by repetition. The vast majority of autistic children who do speak go through a period of using echolalia, the imitation of the speech of others, either immediately after it was said or at some later time (Prizant, 1983; Schuler & Prizant, 1985). Echolalic utterances appear to be used as a label for a situation or event, apparently because of difficulties in decoding and segmenting utterances into meaningful units (Baltaxe & Simmons, 1975; Prizant, 1983). Prizant and associates (Prizant & Duchan, 1981; Prizant & Rydell, 1984) have demonstrated that immediate and delayed echolalia may be used to express many different communicative functions (e.g., request, protest, affirmation, declarative, calling, rehearsal, and self-regulation). Thus, echolalic utterances should not simply be dismissed as deviant or nonfunctional, but rather should be viewed as efforts to communicate.

MAJOR CONSIDERATIONS IN COMMUNICATION PROGRAMMING

Several major factors need to be taken into consideration in developing an individualized communication program for persons with autism. The issue of chronological age and impending transitions that the individual and the family are facing is one major consideration that will influence most decisions made in developing a communication program. Decisions about goals to target and strategies to use for developing communication will differ for infants and toddlers, preschool children, school-age children, adolescents, and adults.

Communication programming must also be driven by functional considerations. Donnellan and Neel (1986) emphasized the importance of a functional curriculum for students with autism. Factors to consider in establishing functional curricular priorities include teaching skills that: (a) are required regularly in the student's everyday environments (i.e., home, school, and community); (b) are appropriate for the individual's chronological age; and (c) need to be performed by someone else if the student cannot perform the task (Falvey, Grenot-Scheyer, & Luddy, 1987). Decision-making based on functional considerations does not need to be mutually exclusive from that based on developmental considerations. At younger ages, developmental appropriateness does not usually conflict with chronological-age appropriateness, and therefore, developmental issues become paramount. For older children, adolescents, and adults, functional considerations may need to take priority. However, the individual's developmental level in communication and language can be used as a frame of reference for targeting functional skills.

Another factor influencing communication programming is the social supports available to the family. Caregivers' ability to enhance communication will be influenced by formal and informal supports available to them (Bristol & Schopler, 1983; Dunst, Lowe, & Bartholomew, 1990). Stresses on the family change with the child's age, thus issues regarding family support are related to the child's chronological age. For younger children, families may just be beginning to experience a grieving process, and may be undergoing dramatic shifts in emotional well-being (Moses, 1981; Prizant & Tiegerman, 1984). Development of communication is critical for younger children, as it relates to day-to-day stresses of the family and to long-term prognosis. For older children and adolescents, stresses on the family have been found to be even greater, due to the family's acceptance of their child's disability and their pessimism regarding outcome, and the great demands on family involved in caring for an autistic youth (Bristol & Schopler, 1983). Because of the severity of the handicapping condition associated with autism, it is critical that communication programming addresses skills that will enhance the individual's ability to be a more effective communicator.

Another important factor is the setting or context in which communication programming will occur. For younger children, communication programming is usually either center-based or home-based, therefore, decisions pertain to how to best address the communication needs of the family (see Prizant & Wetherby, 1988). For school-age children, considerations depend on whether the child is educated in an integrated versus segregated setting. With the trend toward mainstreaming and education within integrated settings, issues relating to the chronological age of the child and peers become more critical for school-age children. In adolescence and adulthood, programming issues relate to whether educational, vocational, and living environments are segregated or located within community settings. Communication development should be facilitated in all natural settings, the issues pertaining to the setting will affect communication goals and strategies.

ASSESSMENT GUIDELINES

Traditional formal language assessment instruments focus primarily on the structure of language and rely on elicited responses. Because language impairments associated with autism are most apparent in the area of pragmatics (i.e., the social conventions governing language and communication), formal assessment instruments have limited utility (Prizant & Schuler, 1987; Wetherby & Prizant, 1992). Therefore, professionals must rely on the systematic use of informal procedures to assess language and communication. In designing an assessment plan, the key content areas to be addressed need to be determined first, and then strategies to explore these areas can be selected. Communicative abilities of persons with autism need to be examined in natural communicative exchanges, with his/her symbolic abilities serving as a developmental frame of reference (Prizant & Wetherby, 1988). This section provides a framework for an individualized assessment of communication and symbolic abilities for persons with autism.

Assessment of Communicative Abilities

Communicative Profile of the Individual with Autism. Assessment of communication should determine the communicative functions expressed by the individual as well as the repertoire of behaviors used for communicating. If an individual is at a preintentional level (i.e., does not demonstrate any deliberate, goal-directed communication), assessment should identify any behaviors that serve a communicative function based on others' interpretation of these behaviors. For individuals demonstrating intentional communication, assessment should identify the range of communicative functions expressed. A framework that is useful in assessment is based on Bruner's (1981) categories of communicative functions that emerge in development prior to the onset of speech:

1. Behavior regulation, which includes signals used to regulate another's behavior for purposes of obtaining or restricting environmental goals (e.g., request or protest object/action);
2. social interaction, which includes signals used to attract and maintain another's attention to oneself for affiliative purposes (e.g., request social game, greet, call, show off); and
3. joint attention, which includes acts used to direct another's attention for purposes of sharing the focus on an entity or event (e.g., comment on object/action, request information).

Children with autism in the early stages of communication and language development have been found to show limitations in the range of communicative functions expressed (Wetherby & Prutting, 1984). Wetherby (1986) suggested that the easiest and first emerging category of functions for these children is regulating others' behavior, whereas the most difficult is referencing joint attention, presumably because of the differing social underpinnings of these abilities.

The communicative means or behaviors used to express intentions should be identified. Research has demonstrated that children may use unconventional, idiosyncratic, or aberrant behavior to communicate for a variety of functions (Carr & Durand, 1986; Donnellan, Mirenda, Mesaros, & Fassbender, 1984; Wetherby & Prutting, 1984). Therefore, a lack of conventionality or social acceptability should not preclude the possibility that a behavior is used purposefully to communicate. The degree of conventionality and social acceptability should be considered in the communicative behavior.

Additionally, the sophistication of gestural and vocal communication should be considered. Gestures may range from primitive contact gestures, in which a person physically manipulates another person's hand, to pointing, or depictive (i.e., pantomime) gestures. Vocalizations may range from vowels that are differentiated based on the affective state expressed (e.g., pleasure versus distress) to articulated speech. Gestures and vocalizations may range from presymbolic behaviors to symbolic, referential communication. For individuals who are verbal, the communicative functions of echolalia should be identified and compared to creative word combinations. Autistic persons may show discrepancies in the sophistication of communicative means for different functions (Wetherby, 1986). For example, a child with autism may use creative speech to regulate others' behavior, echolalic speech, or primitive gestures to engage in social interaction, and show no intentional communication to reference joint attention. In assessment it is critical to compare the quality and complexity of communicative means for each communicative function.

In addition to assessing communicative functions and means, it is important to assess the individual's ability to repair communication breakdowns. That is, when an individual's attempt to communicate is unsuccessful, what strategies are used to repair? Does the individual at least repeat the communicative signal (nonverbal or verbal) to persist in communicating, or is the individual able to modify the signal to clarify the communicative intention? Because individuals with autism may be faced frequently with communication breakdowns, repair strategies are critical for successful communicative interactions.

Persons with autism also evidence difficulty with the reciprocity of communication, ranging from impairments in synchronizing and regulating turn-taking interactions (Dawson & Galpert, 1986) to difficulty with conversational contingency (Baltaxe, 1977; Prizant & Wetherby, 1988). They may initiate topics without identifying the referent and have difficulty clarifying what the listener needs to know. Maintaining a topic of joint focus typically is problematic when conversing with autistic individuals and should be evaluated in assessment.

Assessment of Social Relatedness. Language and communicative abilities are acquired and used in the context of social interactions and social relationships. Although persons with autism have traditionally been thought of as noninteractive and unrelated, current views recognize the great variability of social competence and social relatedness (Wing & Attwood, 1987). Thus, assessment of social relatedness is an important component of a thorough communication assessment because communicative competence will depend, to a great extent, upon an individual's social knowledge and social relationships. Social relatedness may be defined as an individual's motivation to be with, to be like, to share feelings with, and to learn from others (Prizant, 1986). Social relatedness also entails knowledge of social conventions of behavior, and an understanding of others' motivations and intentions.

Dimensions of social relatedness that may be assessed vary according to chronological age and developmental level. Dimensions to be assessed may include social orientation (i.e., interest in being with or observing others), attachment (i.e., selective orientation towards an individual who may serve as a base of security), joint reference (i.e., the ability to establish and maintain shared attention with others), imitation (i.e., the ability to repeat actions or speech of others for social ends, or to learn from others), emotional expression (i.e., the ability to express emotional states in a readable manner), empathy (i.e., the ability to understand the emotional perspective of others), and knowledge of social rules and conventions (i.e., understanding rules of social behavior in different contexts and modifying behavior accordingly: Prizant, 1986). Appropriateness of nonverbal behavior in communicative interactions may also be assessed as to its role in supporting or inhibiting social exchange and communicative interactions (Lapidus, 1985; Wetherby & Prizant, 1990).

Interaction Style of Significant Others. Successful communication involves reciprocity and mutual negotiation between at least two individuals. The quality of a child's social environment influences the child's socioemotional, communication, and language development. Joint action routines between the child and caregiver form the social context in which children learn to use more sophisticated and conventional means to communicate (Bruner, 1978). The successful acquisition of communication and language are influenced by the developmental interaction of the readability of a child's communicative signals and the caregiver's contingent social responsiveness to the child (Dunst et al., 1990). However, compared to mothers of normally developing children, mothers of communicatively impaired children, including children with autism, have been found to use a lower proportion of utterances that are semantically related to the child's previous verbal or nonverbal behavior, and a higher proportion of topic initiations and directives (see Cross, 1984, and Tiegerman & Siperstein, 1984, for review of this literature). Thus, mothers of children with communication impairments typically provide a more controlling and less responsive language learning environment than mothers of normally developing children. Although a directive interactional style may be the result of communicative limitations, it may also contribute to the difficulties that a child is having in developing communication and language (Newhoff & Browning, 1983).

In considering the role of the social context on language development, it is critical to examine the effect each communicative partner has on the other in language and communication assessment (MacDonald, 1985; Prizant & Wetherby, 1988). The interaction style used by significant others (i.e., persons who interact with the individual with autism on a regular basis, such as parents, siblings, teachers, peers) when interacting with the individual with autism should be identified. Mirenda and Donnellan (1986) found that, compared to a "directive" style, the use of a "facilitative" style resulted in higher rates of student-initiated interactions, question asking, and initiation of conversational topics. The operational definitions proposed by Mirenda and Donnellan (1986) can be used to evaluate interaction style with verbal individuals, and are presented in Table 6.1. Facilitative strategies have also been found to increase the initiation of communication and appropriate nonverbal behavior of autistic persons with limited or no language abilities (Dawson & Adams, 1984; Peck, 1985; Tiegerman & Primavera, 1984). For preverbal autistic persons, a facilitative interaction style entails waiting to allow the person to initiate a behavior, interpreting the person's behavior as communicative and meaningful, and then responding in a manner that will encourage continued communicative interactions (Fey, 1986; MacDonald, 1985; Prizant & Wetherby, 1988).

In addition to identifying facilitative versus directive styles of interaction, it is critical to assess the ability of significant others to adjust their language to the developmental level of an individual with autism during natural interactions. When interacting with developmentally younger children, adults match the complexity of their language to the level of the child. However, significant others may have great difficulty adjusting their language to that of the person with autism because development typically is characterized by an uneven profile. Adjusting language to persons who are echolalic is particularly difficult because they may produce sentences containing many words, yet be functioning at a one- or two-word expressive language stage. Using language that is beyond an individual's comprehension is likely to be confusing and frustrating for that individual, and may lead to withdrawal or behavioral outburst.

TABLE 6.1
Operational Definitions of Directive and Facilitative Interaction Styles

Directive Style	*Facilitative Style*
Does not allow sufficient time for initiation or language processing	Allows lags of up to 30 seconds to occur
Initiates more than half of all topics	Initiates less than one third of all topics
Uses direct questions to initiate majority of all topics	Uses no direct questions to initiate topics
Uses direct questions for topic continuation majority of time	Uses direct questions for no more than one fourth of topic continuations
Does not ask for clarification	Requests clarification when needed

Note: Adapted from Mirenda and Donnellan (1986)

Assessment of Symbolic Abilities

Numerous studies of autistic children have found impairments in cognitive–social correlates of language, indicating a limited capacity to use symbols (e.g., Dawson & Adams, 1984; Sigman & Ungerer, 1984; Wetherby & Prutting, 1984). Therefore, a communication assessment should compare the individual's ability to use symbols across verbal and nonverbal domains. It is important to consider the symbolic capacity of an autistic individual because many skills that need to be taught deal with symbolic systems. The individual's expressive language and communication should be compared with their symbolic level in language comprehension as well as nonverbal symbolic domains to obtain an accurate picture of symbolic functioning.

Verbal Symbolic Level. A developmental framework summarizing major milestones in language production and comprehension is presented in Table 6.2 and can be used to identify an individual's language level and to prioritize intervention goals. However, determining the level of language production for individuals with autism may be difficult, particularly when rote memory capacity for learning language forms exceeds comprehension of these forms as is observed in echolalia. It is not simply a matter of determining whether an individual is preverbal or verbal, but rather, examining how he or she uses gestures, sounds, words (spoken or signed), and word combinations.

Professionals and caregivers need to be knowledgeable about the language level of a person with autism in order to form reasonable expectations about the individual's language capabilities. Four major questions should be asked in considering level of language production. First, what communicative means (i.e., gestures, sounds, and/or words) does a person use that serve communicative purposes, and are these used intentionally? Second, are words used, and if so, do the words have referential meaning? That is, are words used to refer to specific objects or events, and only those objects or events? Individuals who use words or word combinations communicatively but not referentially will typically cycle through their repertoire of utterances in an attempt to request an object until they happen upon the name and get the object.

A third question to be explored in considering an individual's language level is how many different words and word combinations are used referentially. For an individual with autism who is producing spontaneous or echolalic utterances, the inventory of utterances used referentially may be a better measure of language level than utterance length or complexity. If an individual spontaneously produces less than 20 different utterances, it is likely that his or her overall language level is within *first words,* rather than *first word combinations.* A fourth question for persons who use word

TABLE 6.2
Major Developmental Stages in Language Acquisition

Intentional Communication: 9–13 Months

- Uses gestures and/or sounds to communicate, with evidence of intentionality, to regulate other's behaviors, to engage in social interaction, and to reference joint attention
- Demonstrates prelinguistic comprehension response strategies, that is, comprehension of nonverbal (gestures, facial expression, and directed eye gaze), situational (immediate environment and knowledge of what to do with objects), and paralinguistic (intonation) cues

First Words: 13–18 Months

- Repairs unsuccessful communicative interactions by repeating, modifying the form, or using an alternative strategy
- Uses a small number of conventional signals referentially, that is, to refer to objects or classes of objects, but shows slow vocabulary growth (uses about 10 to 20 single words at one time)
- Develops comprehension of single words to direct attention to relevant objects or to suggest actions appropriate to the immediate environment

First Word Combinations: 18–30 Months

- Begins to engage in conversation by providing new information about the previous speaker's topic, requesting information, and providing information about things in the past
- Uses word combinations based on semantic relations, shows a sudden surge in vocabulary growth (from about 20 to more than 200), and shows an expansion of semantic relations for predication, that is, to describe a state or quality of an object or event (e.g., action, attribute, denial, location, possession)
- Comprehends word meanings but depends on immediate environment, knowledge of prior similar experience, and knowledge of semantic reltions to know how these elements go together

Sentence Grammer: 30 Months–5 Years

- Uses language to regulate own and other's actions, plan and anticipate outcomes, report on present and past experiences, comment on imagined context, project own and other's feelings, and regulate interactions, expresses more than one function in a single utterance
- Develops semantic relational terms to encode spatial, dimensional, temporal, causal, quantity, color, age, and other relations
- Uses a grammar to construct sentences, that is, produces grammatical morphemes (e.g., prepositions, tense markers, plural endings, pronouns, articles), and uses syntax (i.e., rules of word order) to construct declarative, negative, imperative, interrogative, passive, and complex sentences
- Comprehends sentences based on morphological and syntactic rules (e.g., uses word-order strategy for agent-action-recipient relations)

Discourse Grammer: 5–8 Years

- Abides by conversational rules to be clear, informative, and polite
- Produces connected discourse by setting up transitions between sentences and clarifying shifts in reference form one clause or sentence to another to convey personal experiences and tell stories
- Comprehends connected discourse by using knowledge of scripts and story grammars to comprehend narratives

Note: Adapted from Lord (1985) and Prizant and Wetherby (in press)

combinations is, do they use the individual words alone and in other word combinations, or is an utterance equivalent to a single word for that person? It is likely that persons who do not combine words creatively are functioning within first words, rather than first word combinations. Although this seems paradoxical, it is important to determine an individual's generative language capabilities and not be misled by the surface form of utterances.

It is also important to assess level of language comprehension so that professionals and significant others can use this information to adjust their language level to promote successful interactions. As outlined in Table 6.2, it should be determined whether the child's language comprehension is at a prelinguistic or linguistic level (see Lord, 1985). At prelinguistic levels, an individual may comprehend and respond to a message based on nonverbal, situational, and/or paralinguistic cues. It is important for professionals and significant others to be aware of whether these nonlinguistic cues are necessary to understand the message. For individuals who comprehend linguistic aspects of the message, it is important to determine whether the individual is able to comprehend single words within the message, multiwords guided by semantic relations (i.e., understanding based on knowledge about word classes and relations), grammatical constructions (i.e., syntactic and morphological rules), or connected discourse.

Nonverbal Symbolic Level. In development, cognitive and social skills contribute to the foundation for the emergence of symbols, which is seen in children's use of language and play (Bates, 1979). Early childhood development literature has described growth in play skills along cognitive and social dimensions (e.g., Fewell & Kaminski, 1988; Rubin, Watson, & Jambor, 1978), which underscores the interdependence of language and play. Level of play reflects advances in cognition that may also enhance language acquisition, and participation in play activities provides a learning context for social, cognitive, and language development.

The developmental literature distinguishes between symbolic and constructive play (Piaget, 1962). Symbolic play is make-believe play in which the child uses one object to stand for or represent an absent object. Cognitive advances in symbolic play progress from exploratory actions on objects to pretending with objects that are not realistic, using others as agents and recipients of actions, and organizing action schemes in planned sequence (Fewell & Kaminski, 1988; Westby, 1988). Constructive play is the systematic manipulation of materials to create a product, and includes playing with drawing materials, clay, blocks, and puzzles. Cognitive advances in constructive play progress from manipulating the physical properties of the materials to creating a product with detailed features.

Play development has also been characterized by the degree of social participation among children. Parten (1932) described sequential stages of social participation from individual play (i.e., unoccupied behavior, onlooker behavior, solitary) to group play (parallel, associative, and cooperative), which are used widely as a measure of social maturity of play. Use of a nested play scale that rates cognitive level of symbolic or constructive play as well as degree of social participation has been found to be useful to distinguish between the quality of individual and group play in preschoolers and kindergarteners (Rubin et al., 1978).

Several research studies have demonstrated that children with autism show significant deficits in symbolic play (Dawson & Adams, 1984; Sigman & Ungerer, 1984; Wetherby & Prutting, 1984). Compared to normally developing children at the same language level, children with autism have been found to perform at lower levels on symbolic play but at higher levels on aspects of constructive play (i.e., combining objects in ordinal relations) (Wetherby & Prutting, 1984). This is presumably because of the greater social demands of symbolic play compared to constructive play. In autistic children at preschool and early school age, it is important to assess play skills, and to compare their cognitive level of symbolic and constructive play, as well as degree of social participation in play.

Because children's participation in symbolic play diminishes during late childhood, it is not appropriate to evaluate symbolic play in autistic adolescents and adults, even if they are cognitively impaired. Many constructive play activities become recreation and leisure activities for the older individual and can be evaluated using age-appropriate materials. It is also possible to assess level of sequential organization in daily living skills, such as setting the table and doing laundry, to provide information about nonverbal mental representation.

Assessment Strategies

Due to the difficulty in assessing communicative, social, and related symbolic behavior of autistic individuals, a combination of assessment strategies are recommended (Wetherby & Prizant, 1992). Ecologically based theories of child development address the relationship between the child and his/her natural environment and, therefore, have important implications for communication and language assessment strategies. Ecologically sound assessment strategies involve assessing an individual's language in dyads or groups involving people with whom he or she has meaningful relationships (MacDonald, 1985). Therefore, the assessment of language, communication, and related abilities should occur in the home, the classroom, and the community involving significant others because these are the natural environments in which an individual will need to use these abilities.

A useful initial method for gathering information about an individual's communicative and symbolic behaviors is to interview significant others. The interview should include questions about and solicit examples of behaviors as outlined. Peck and Schuler (1987) and Lapidus (1985) have developed interviews addressing communicative means and functions that may be referred to for this purpose. The use of significant others as informants ensures that the assessment will address the communicative needs of the individual with autism and of people interacting with that individual in everyday situations. Ecological inventory strategies can be used to determine communication, language, and related symbolic skills needed for domestic, vocational, recreation/leisure, and community domains (see Falvey et al., 1987).

Based on the information obtained from the interview, a checklist or inventory of possible communicative and symbolic behaviors and the functions they serve can be developed to measure behaviors that an individual uses spontaneously in natural contexts. Observations during regularly scheduled activities provide information about that individual's communicative, social, and symbolic behavior, as well as the adequacy of the natural environment to provide opportunities that foster spontaneous communication. Checklists, such as those developed by Donnellan et al. (1984) and Lapidus (1985), are particularly useful to establish which communicative means are used to express different communicative functions across settings with various partners. It is important to compare the communicative behavior of an autistic child or adolescent while interacting with a familiar adult to that with a familiar peer. Usually a peer will be a less competent interactant than an adult, and therefore the communication skills of the individual with autism may appear more limited with a peer.

Although observational checklists provide critical information about an individual's spontaneous communicative behavior, it may be rather time consuming to wait for behaviors to occur naturally, and some of an individual's abilities or potential may not be demonstrated even during an extended observation period. A third method to supplement the observational checklist is behavior sampling. The purpose is to collect a representative sample of behavior typical of an individual's range of functioning in a relatively short period of time, preferably on videotape for later analysis. Structured communicative situations may be staged to entice an individual to interact and use a variety of communicative functions (see Schuler & Prizant, 1987; Wetherby & Prizant, 1989). Opportunities can also be set up for the use of toys or objects instrumentally and symbolically to evaluate an individual's level of symbolic representation. In sampling spontaneous behavior, we have found that it is critical not only to provide the opportunity to initiate behavior but also to wait and look expectantly at the individual.

Assessment should be done on an ongoing basis over an extended period of time, not solely at one point in time. This is especially pertinent when assessing unconventional and primitive communicative acts. Furthermore, to assure representativeness, the behaviors of concern should be examined in different environments with a variety of interactants. Thus, assessment should be considered an exploratory process that is ongoing rather than episodic.

Assessment of communication and related symbolic abilities, as outlined provides a profile of an individual's strengths and needs in communication, social relatedness, and symbolic capacity, as well as information about the interaction style of significant others and adequacy of natural environments to provide opportunities for communicating. These assessment findings provide the basis from which to derive intervention goals.

CONSIDERATIONS FOR SELECTING A COMMUNICATION/ LANGUAGE SYSTEM

Decision making for selection of a communication and/or language system should be based on an individual's social, communicative, cognitive, and motoric abilities. Table 6.3 lists specific questions that should be considered about an individual's abilities and limitations in order to develop the most optimal system or systems for communicating. First consideration needs to be given to whether an individual has the communicative abilities to support a language system, as identified under requirements for communication in Table 6.3. For individuals who do not yet have the potential for language or speech, as identified in Table 6.3, emphasis should be placed on developing a nonlanguage (i.e., nonsymbolic) communication system (see Mirenda & Schuler, 1988, for further discussion). Options include using natural gestures (e.g., giving, pushing away, manipulating others' hands) or real objects to communicate. Both of these systems can be graded in sophistication. Natural gestures can progress to indicative (e.g., pointing) and depictive (i.e., pantomimes) gestures, which are foundations for the development of language, spoken or signed. Using real objects can progress to using more sophisticated systems to refer to objects, including parts of objects (e.g., key to a wind-up toy), labels from objects or containers of objects (e.g., label from box of raisins), or pictures of objects. These systems can lead to the development of a picture or tangible symbol system laying the foundation for written or other language systems.

For individuals who communicate spontaneously and have the symbolic capacity for a language system, as identified in Table 6.3, consideration needs to be given to whether speech is a viable immediate goal. For individuals who demonstrate most or all of the abilities listed in Table 6.3

TABLE 6.3
Questions to Consider in the Selection of a Communication and/or Language System

Requirements for Intentional Communication
• Does the social environment provide opportunities for the individual to communicate for a variety of reasons?
• Does the individual use communicative signals (gestural or vocal) intentionally for one or more functions (i.e., behavior regulation, social interaction, joint attention)?
• Does the individual demonstrate repair strategies when communicative intentions are not understood?
• Is the individual's current communication system readable to familiar people (combination of nonverbal and vocal/verbal communication)?
Requirements for Language
• Does the individual demonstrate the nonverbal and/or verbal (e.g., spoken, written, signed) symbolic capacity for a language system?
Requirements for Speech
• Does the individual use differentiated vocalizations intentionally to communicate?
• Does the individual demonstrate the ability to imitate speech?
• Does the individual demonstrate the sensory abilities to comprehend speech?
• Does the individual demonstrate the motor abilities to produce speech (consider oral reflexes, breath support, control of phonation, differentiation and independent muscular control of jaw, lips, and tongue)?
• Does the individual demonstrate motivation and interest in speech?
• Does the individual's age and educational history indicate a good prognosis for speech?

Note: Adapted from Mirenda and Schuler (1988) and Wetherby and Hayden (1990)

under requirements for speech, spoken language would be the system of choice because it is completely portable and universal. However, for individuals who do not demonstrate the abilities required for speech but have the symbolic capacity for language, there are many choices of nonspeech language systems varying in complexity. Nonspeech gestural language system options include sign language. Iconic signs (i.e., signs that resemble the objects/actions that they represent, such as the sign for *eat* or *tree*) may be chosen initially to minimize symbolic demands, but can only represent concrete objects or events. Nonspeech visual language system options include, from simplest to most complex, color photographs, black-and-white photographs, miniature objects, black-and-white line drawings, Bliss symbols, and written words (Mirenda & Schuler, 1988). These symbols can be represented on communication boards, communication books, or electronic communication devices.

In making decisions about communication and/or language systems for individuals with autism, it is critical to keep in mind that any language system is a sophisticated tool for communicating. An individual needs to have the communicative competence and a supportive environment to use a language system. Decisions about the selection of a system should not be viewed as permanent but rather as a developing process. Selection of more than one system is preferable to develop a repertoire of communicative means that an individual can use to initiate communicative interactions and to repair communicative breakdowns. One system may be developed as a primary means of communicating (e.g., speech or signs) and a different system may be used to repair communicative breakdowns (e.g., natural gestures, picture system). Emphasis should be placed on the flexible and creative use of language or nonlanguage systems for communication.

INTERVENTION GUIDELINES

Advances in our understanding of autism as a developmental disorder involving impairments of social interaction, communication, and symbolic abilities have had a great influence on approaches to language intervention (Prizant & Wetherby, 1988). Contemporary language intervention approaches for autistic individuals differ dramatically from traditional behavioral approaches that dominated in the 1970s and early 1980s. One of the most critical differences is the emphasis on successful communicative interactions, which is indicated in both developmental and behavioral contemporary literature. The priority on successful communicative interactions affects all aspects of programming, from targeting goals to designing the contexts of intervention. Following are some of the major principles that should be considered in communication programming with autistic persons based on "best practices" identified in contemporary developmental and behavioral literature.

Communication Goals Should be Selected on the Basis of *Developmental* and *Functional* Criteria

Because autism is a developmental disorder, information on language and communication development offers an organizational framework for assessment and language and communication enhancement. Too rigid an interpretation of a developmental model has resulted in "readiness models" that indicate that a certain level of cognitive or language ability *must* be reached in order for an individual to learn certain skills or information. A distinction must be made between working within a developmental model, which is the approach advocated here, as opposed to teaching to a developmental checklist. Rather than merely offering a guideline for sequencing communication objectives, developmental information can provide a frame of reference for understanding a child's behavioral competencies and for setting appropriate goals.

In a more detailed discussion of the application of developmental information, we delineated three significant principles that the developmental literature has contributed to understanding and enhancing the communication abilities of persons with autism (Prizant & Wetherby, 1989). First of all, communication development involves continuity from preverbal to verbal communication. That is, the development of preverbal communication is a necessary precursor to the development of the intentional use of language to communicate. Second, being a competent communicator is the outcome of a developmental interaction of cognitive, social-affective, and linguistic capacities. A child's developmental profile across these domains should provide the basis for decision making. Third, in a developmental model, all behavior should be viewed in reference to the child's relative level of functioning across developmental domains. Many of the behavior problems displayed by autistic children can be understood as attempts to communicate if they are interpreted with the child's developmental level in mind.

Intervention goals and contexts for communication enhancement should be selected on the basis of functional as well as developmental criteria. Functional criteria should be based on the assessment information obtained from caregivers' and professionals' knowledge of an individual's communicative needs. For example, an appropriate goal for a preverbal 3-year-old may be acquisition of communicative signals to request specific social games (e.g., chase games, peek-a-boo), which clearly would be an inappropriate goal for a preverbal 12-year-old. On the other hand, developmental considerations will have great bearing on the specific communicative means targeted. In the example just given, use of natural gestures or a picture communication board may be an appropriate goal for the 3-year-old or the 12-year-old who both may be at similar developmental expressive and receptive levels, as long as goals address communicative needs in daily life routines. Without careful attention to developmental issues, communication enhancement efforts can target competencies considerably above or below an individual's capabilities.

Emphasis Should be Placed on the *Functional Use* of Language and Communication, Not Simply on Advancing Language Forms (e.g., Vocabulary, Grammar) in All Natural Settings

A first *priority* in education should be in helping individuals with autism develop communication, with verbal and/or nonverbal means, and not simply learn a set of verbal behaviors. These individuals need to be motivated to communicate, and need to have opportunities to communicate through verbal and nonverbal means. The emphasis in communication programming should be on using language and communication spontaneously for a variety of functions. We recommend beginning with an emphasis on behavior regulation functions because of the minimal social demands. Once an individual is capable of communicating to regulate others' behavior, greater emphasis should be placed on communicating for social interaction and then for joint attention functions. If language forms are addressed, they should be serving an important communicative function to the autistic person.

Enhancing functional communication should be a priority in all settings. Using and developing language and communication should be an *integral* part of an individual's ongoing educational, work, and living experiences to ensure ecological soundness. Communication programming needs to occur in natural environments to enhance generalization. Many opportunities for choice making and initiating communication can be provided throughout the day (see Halle, 1984; Shevin & Klein, 1984). The individual's attempts at communicating with socially acceptable means should be responded to contingently and consistently.

The Natural Environment Should be Designed to Foster Communicative Interactions that are *Balanced and Reciprocal*

Both developmental and behavioral literature have emphasized the importance of teaching strategies that encourage individuals with communicative impairments to initiate communication and language. In the developmental literature, the pragmatics movement in the 1970s has led to strategies that *follow the child's lead* to develop communication and conversational abilities (Fey, 1986; MacDonald, 1985, 1989). The developmental literature emphasizes the importance of using a facilitative style to enhance communication and language and shifting the balance of power or control to the child (see MacDonald, 1989; Prizant & Wetherby, 1988). If there is not a balance of power in interactions with a child, that child may become a passive partner or use aggression to claim power (MacDonald, 1989).

The behavioral literature has described "incidental language teaching" as a method of achieving a more naturalistic approach to language training. In contrast to a discrete trial format in which the trainer controls the interaction, an incidental teaching episode is initiated by the child. The adult waits for a child to initiate a communicative behavior (i.e., gesture, vocalization), focuses attention on the child and the child's topic, asks for a language elaboration or models a verbal response for the child to imitate, and then indicates the correctness of the child's language or gives the child what is asked for. Incidental teaching has been found to enhance generalization in teaching language to children with severe handicaps, including autism (see Hart, 1985, and Warren & Kaiser, 1986, for review).

Numerous strategies are described in the literature to design the environment to encourage the initiation of communication (Prizant & Wetherby, in press). The developmental literature has emphasized the importance of "engineering" the environment to provide opportunities and reasons for the child to initiate communication. The behavioral literature has described specific strategies to occasion language use, such as to delay at critical moments in natural routines and to interrupt chains of behavior by removing an object needed to complete the chain (see Halle, 1984). By making the initiation of communication a priority, natural opportunities for communicating can be capitalized upon in all settings.

The Autistic Individual Should Not be the Sole Focus of Intervention/Education. Goals Should be Targeted to Improve *Facilitative* Interaction Styles of Significant Others

Because communication involves the cooperative interaction of two members of a dyad, communication goals should address changing the behavior of both members of the dyad. In addition to providing opportunities for communicating, goals for significant others need to include learning to wait for the initiation of communication, to read the communicative attempts of the autistic individual, and then to respond in a facilitative manner. Additionally, significant others need to understand an autistic individual's language level in order to adjust their language and to foster language and communication goals that are developmentally appropriate.

Peer relationships can be fostered by teaching peers how to interact more effectively with a person with autism. It is important to be aware that directing communication to other children may place greater social demands on an autistic individual, and therefore, in developing peer-directed communication, other social demands should be minimized. For example, for a young autistic child, communication with peers can be enhanced initially for behavior regulation functions during constructive play activities because of the relatively minimal social demands of these behaviors. Relatively simpler communicative means may be acceptable when directed toward peers.

The Management of *Behavior Problems* Should be Fully Integrated with Communication Programming

Positive/nonaversive approaches to the management of challenging behaviors are becoming widely accepted as best practice for individuals with severe handicaps (see Horner, et al., 1990). The expanded use and improved technology of *functional analysis* of problem behaviors has led to a variety of alternatives to the use of punishment (see Horner et al. 1990; Meyer & Evans, 1986). One of the most effective interventions derived from a functional analysis has been to teach *functional equivalents* of the challenging behaviors (Carr & Durand, 1985; Horner et al., 1990). For example, for behaviors that are determined to serve a *communicative function* (e.g., to request an object, to request assistance, to express frustration or boredom, to seek attention), teaching appropriate communicative means to express the function(s) served by the problem behaviors has been associated with a reduction in the problem behavior. However, Evans and Meyer (1990) warn that "lifestyle enhancement, such as teaching communication within responsive environments, not 'functional communication training' in isolation, is the fundamental intervention" (p. 135). Thus, communication programming should impact on the individual's lifestyle by enhancing meaningful progress in communication abilities that increases access to a variety of people, places, and events.

The Individual's *Level of Emotional Arousal* and its Effect on Communication and Social Interactions Needs to be Considered

An area of increasing interest to educators and clinicians is the relationship between emotional arousal and communicative competence. In reference to normally developing children, Tronick (1989) has emphasized the importance of infants' development of self- and mutual-regulatory capacities to regulate emotional arousal in potentially overstimulating and anxiety-arousing situations. Recently, Dawson and Lewy (1989) proposed that problems in *modulation of arousal* in autism detrimentally influence attentional capacities and may ultimately account for limitations in social interaction and socioemotional development. More specific to communication, a number of researchers have discussed behavioral problems of persons with autism in reference to the use of unconventional communicative means (Carr & Durand, 1985; Prizant & Wetherby, 1987). Socially unacceptable means to communicate may be used to exert social control during states of high negative arousal. Furthermore, inability to apply *self-regulatory strategies* to control arousal may interfere directly with social and nonsocial learning.

In planning intervention approaches, the issue of emotional arousal and its effect on communication and social participation should be addressed. First, individuals should have as a primary intervention goal the acquisition of socially acceptable means to protest or reject (Prizant, 1988; Prizant & Wetherby, 1987). It has been hypothesized that such communicative skills may serve to preclude or mitigate the development of behavior problems (Carr & Durand, 1986; Prizant & Wetherby, in press). Second, for situations known to be stressful or anxiety arousing for an individual, strategies that the individual can ultimately use independently should be developed; for example, the use of picture stimuli or picture schedules to prepare individuals for stressful situations (Prizant & Wetherby, 1989), or relaxation (Cautela & Groden, 1978), or other calming activities may be implemented to help reduce arousal. Finally, educators and clinicians must be prepared to identify situations when communication may not be a successful means to reduce high levels of arousal, and when humane and respectful strategies be applied to assure the safety of the individual and of others in the environment. It is our belief, however, that when language and communicative interactions are adapted to an appropriate level for an individual, when environments and activities are structured in predictable and understandable manner, and when opportunities for decision making and social control are provided, behavioral problems due to negative emotional arousal can be minimized.

CASE EXAMPLES

Three case examples of individuals with autism were selected for presentation to illustrate how information gained from communication assessment can be used for intervention planning. These examples are used to characterize the heterogeneity of communication abilities in the autistic population and to consider needs of individuals at different ages from early childhood to adulthood.

Case Example 1. Jamie is a 4½-year-old boy with autism. He lives at home with both parents and has attended a self-contained preschool class for children with emotional handicaps at a regular elementary school for the past 6 months. He uses echolalia and some single words to request and protest objects and actions. He has recently begun to use echolalia to greet and call, to describe pictures in a book, and to refer to events that he experiences. Jamie is an example of a child who produces sentences but is functioning at a *first words* level. He produces some phrases but they function as single words (e.g., "let me taste your wares," which was from a nursery rhyme and was used to protest; "open the door" was used to request help). He has a repertoire of less than 20 different spontaneous words and phrases used referentially. He has very limited symbolic play abilities but has strengths in constructive play (e.g., block building, puzzles, nesting cups) and gross motor activities. He displays some problem behaviors including aggression, screaming, and mild self-injury when he does not get his own way or when his communicative attempts are not understood. Jamie displays very limited ability to interact with peers and to participate in group activities in the classroom, but he is beginning to observe peers from a distance and play with them on the playground.

An immediate need for Jamie is to identify an integrated school setting to provide models of appropriate language, play, and social behavior, and opportunities for interacting with typical peers. Within an integrated setting, priority goals for language development include expanding range of communicative functions, developing repair strategies, replacing problem behaviors with words and/or gestures to express these functions, and breaking down echolalia and developing more flexible and creative speech. Because of Jamie's capacity to imitate speech, incidental language teaching strategies can be used with appropriate language models provided by adults and peers. Additional priority goals include developing symbolic play and social interaction with peers. A combination of peer modeling of appropriate behaviors, structuring the environment to encourage appropriate behaviors, and adult guidance of interactions will be needed. If Jamie makes progress on these goals in an integrated setting, it is likely that he would enter regular kindergarten next year. In the home setting, Jamie's parents need assistance in learning how to adjust their language to his level, to replace problem behaviors with appropriate communicative means, and to provide appropriate language models to break down his echolalia and develop creative language.

Case Example 2. David is a 10-year-old boy with autism and moderate mental retardation. He is living at home with both parents and has been attending a self-contained class for children with mental handicaps since the age of 5. He communicates only to regulate the behavior of others (i.e., to request and protest actions and objects). His means of communicating include vocalizations, gestures, and on occasion, self-injury and tantrums. His parents reported that he requests objects or assistance by leading them by the hand to the desired source. He also shakes his head or pushes an object away to indicate rejection. Traditional behavioral approaches have been used in his classroom to teach speech, sign language, total communication, and written words, with minimal success using any of these communication systems. He does not produce any spoken words and his repertoire of conventional signs used spontaneously consists of nut, apple, orange, cracker, drink, shoe, car, book, and ball. However, he uses only the signs for book and ball referentially (i.e., to request these and only these specific objects). In requesting other objects, he typically cycles through several of the signs in his repertoire in an apparent effort to guess the name of the desired object. His expressive language level is best characterized as emerging *first words,* rather than true *first words.* If he is not able to use the correct sign to make a choice, he usually is able to repair by manipulating another's hand to indicate what he wants. David is not able to comprehend language without nonverbal cues. David has strengths in nonverbal symbolic abilities as evidenced by his ability to draw pictures and to play video games.

Immediate needs for David include developing the use of a symbolic system for communicating (e.g., picture communication, signs). David has the communicative foundation and nonverbal symbolic capacity to learn a language system. Because he initiates communication with natural gestures, it is recommended that incidental teaching strategies be used to map language onto his preverbal gestures. Additional language and communication needs include expanding the range of communicative functions using natural gestures, increasing opportunities to interact with peers, and expanding education to community-based instruction. His parents are effective at reading his communicative signals and responding contingently, but need assistance in structuring the home environment to provide more opportunities for David to initiate communication and build a language system.

Case Example 3. Nona is a 20-year-old woman with autism. She lives at home with both parents and has been attending a self-contained class in a center school for students with mental handicaps. She uses both echolalia and creative speech to request objects and actions, to protest, greet, comment, and to describe events that she has experienced. Nona uses over 100 different object names referentially, some in the phrase "want some more ______ please," to request these items. These phrases are equivalent to two-word combinations for her. She also uses a number of delayed echolalic utterances, such as "stop doing that" to protest and "time to say goodbye" to greet, which are equivalent to single words. Nona's language level is best characterized as emerging *first word combinations.* On occasion she displays very volatile behavior, including self-injury, aggression, and destructive behavior. These behavioral outbursts occur when she is corrected for an error, her communicative attempts are not understood, or when an expected routine is violated. In her school and home setting, these behavioral outbursts are consequated by sending her to a time out area. Nona has learned to ask for a deck of cards when she is upset to play a game of "Fish" or solitaire; dealing and handling cards has a calming effect on her. She is able to organize multiple steps in sequence for daily living activities (e.g., obtaining and sorting materials to set the table; preparing, stirring, and serving frozen juice drink; dealing cards for game of "Fish"). A relative strength for Nona is apparent in her constructive play, as demonstrated by her ability to put together a 1,000-piece jigsaw puzzle. Her parents' interaction style is characterized by frequent question-asking, particularly ones that they already know the answer to, and using language that is beyond Nona's comprehension level. They are beginning to seek residential placement in a group home setting in preparation for her transition into adulthood.

Immediate needs for Nona include replacing her problem behaviors with simple verbal means to express the function(s) served and developing repair strategies. Additionally, language goals may expand her use of a variety of words to increase the informativeness of her utterances and help break down her echolalia into meaningful units. Because her language level appears much higher on the surface, it may be tempting to increase her utterance length by targeting pronouns and specific grammatical structures. However, she does not have the pragmatic and semantic language base for sentence grammar. It is unlikely that her educational setting will change in the next year. However, her parents need information that will assist them in making decisions about group home and job placements. Her parents also need assistance in adjusting their language to her language level, using a facilitative interaction style, as well as encouraging Nona to provide needed "information" when talking with them.

SUMMARY AND CONCLUSIONS

The communication and language impairments associated with autism have a significant impact on the outcome of individuals with autism and on their family. Current understandings of communication and language development in autism suggest that difficulties acquiring conventional communicative behaviors to express intentions effectively are related to underlying social-cognitive limitations. In this chapter we identified the following factors as important for individualizing a communication program: the individual's chronological age; functional as well as developmental considerations in targeting goals; social supports available to the family; and the setting or context in which communication programming will occur.

Communication and language abilities of a person with autism need to be examined in natural communicative interactions. Assessment of communicative abilities should examine the communicative functions expressed as well as the range of behaviors used for communication, the ability to repair communication breakdowns, aspects of social relatedness, and the interaction style used by significant others. A communication assessment should also compare the individual's ability to use symbols across verbal and nonverbal domains. Because formal assessment tools do not assess these areas, a variety of informal assessment strategies were recommended. Guidelines for decision making for the selection of a communication and/or language system should be based on the individual's communicative and symbolic profile.

Major principles that need to be considered in communication programming with autistic persons should be based on "best practices" identified in the contemporary literature and discussed in this chapter. That is, communication and language intervention programs for individuals with autism should target goals focusing on communicative competence in natural language learning environments with the emphasis on acquisition of functional skills that support successful communicative interactions.

REFERENCES

American Psychiatric Association. (1987). *Diagnostic and statistical manual of mental disorders* (rev. 3rd ed.). Washington, DC: Author.

Baltaxe, C. (1977). Pragmatic deficits in the language of autistic adolescents. *Journal of Pediatric Psychology, 2,* 176–180.

Baltaxe, C., & Simmons, J. (1975). Language in childhood psychosis: A review. *Journal of Speech and Hearing Disorders, 40,* 439–458.

Bates, E. (1979). *The emergence of symbols: Cognition and communication in infancy.* New York: Academic Press.

Bristol, M. M. (1988). Impact of autistic children on families. In B. Prizant & B. Schaechter (Eds.), *Autism: The emotional and social dimensions.* Boston: The Exceptional Parent.

Bristol, M. M., & Schopler, E. (1983). Stress and coping in families of autistic adolescents. In E. Schopler & G. B. Mesibov (Eds.), *Autism in adolescents and adults* (pp. 251–278). New York: Plenum Press.

Bruner, J. (1978). From communication to language: A psychological perspective. In I. Markova (Ed.), *The social context of language.* Chichester: Wiley.

Bruner, J. (1981). The social context of language acquisition. *Language and Communication, 1,* 155–178.

Carr, E. G., & Durand, V. (1985). Reducing behavior problems through functional communication training. *Journal of Applied Behavior Analysis, 18,* 111–126.

Carr, E. G., & Durand, V. (1986). The social-communicative basis of severe behavior problems in children. In S. Reiss & R. Bootzin (Eds.), *Theoretical issues in behavior therapy* (pp. 219–254). New York: Academic Press.

Cautela, J., & Groden, J. (1978). *Relaxation: A comprehensive manual for adults, and children with special needs.* Champaign, IL: Research Press.

Cross, T. (1984). Habilitating the language-impaired child: Ideas from studies of parent-child interaction. *Topics in Language Disorders, 4*(4), 1–14.

Curcio, F. (1978). Sensorimotor functioning and communication in mute autistic children. *Journal of Autism and Childhood Schizophrenia, 8,* 181–189.

Dawson, G., & Adams, A. (1984). Imitation and social responsiveness in autistic children. *Journal of Abnormal Child Psychology, 12,* 209–226.

Dawson, G., & Galpert, L. (1986). A developmental model for facilitating the social behavior of autistic children. In E. Schopler & G. B. Mesibov (Eds.), *Social behavior in autism* (pp. 237–261). New York: Plenum Press.

Dawson, G., & Lewy, A. (1989). Reciprocal subcortical-cortical influences in autism: The role of attentional mechanisms. In G. Dawson (Ed.), *Autism: Nature, diagnosis, and treatment* (pp. 144–173). New York: Guilford Press.

Donnellan, A. M., Mirenda, P., Mesaros, R., & Fassbender, L. (1984). Analyzing the communicative functions of aberrant behavior. *Journal of the Association for Persons with Severe Handicaps, 9,* 201–212.

Donnellan, A. M., & Neel, R. S. (1986). New directions in educating students with autism. In R. Horner & L. Meyer (Eds.), *Education of learners with severe handicaps* (pp. 99–126). Baltimore: Brookes.

Dunst, C., Lowe, L. W., & Bartholomew, P. C. (1990). Contingent social responsiveness, family ecology, and infant communicative competence. *National Student Speech Language Hearing Association Journal, 17,* 39–49.

Evans, I. M., & Meyer, L. H. (1990). Toward a science in support of meaningful outcomes: A response to Horner et al. *Journal of the Association for Persons with Severe Handicaps, 15,* 133–135.

Falvey, M. A., Grenot-Scheyer, M., & Luddy, E. (1987). Developing and implementing integrated community referenced curricula. In D. Cohen & A. Donnellan (Eds.), *Handbook of autism and pervasive developmental disorders* (pp. 238–250). New York: Wiley.

Fewell, R., & Kaminski, R. (1988). Play skills development and instruction for young children with handicaps. In S. Odom & M. Karnes (Eds.), *Early intervention for infants and children with handicaps* (pp. 145–158). Baltimore: Brookes.

Fey, M. E. (1986). *Language intervention with young children.* San Diego: College Hill Press.

Halle, J. W. (1984). Arranging the natural environment to occasion language: Giving severely language-delayed children reasons to communicate. *Seminars in Speech and Language, 5,* 185–197.

Hart, B. (1985). Naturalistic language training techniques. In S. Warren & A. K. Rogers-Warren (Eds.), *Teaching functional language: Generalization and maintenance of language skills* (pp. 63–88). Baltimore: University Park Press.

Horner, R. H., Dunlap, G., Koegel, R. L., Carr, E. G., Sailor, W., Anderson, J., Albin, R. W., & O'Neill, R. E. (1990). Toward a technology of "nonaversive" behavioral support. *Journal of the Association for Persons with Severe Handicaps, 15,* 125–132.

Kanner, L. (1943). Autistic disturbances of affective contact. *Nervous Child, 2,* 217–250.

Kanner, L. (1946). Irrelevant and metaphorical language in early infantile autism. *American Journal of Psychiatry, 103,* 242–245.

Lapidus, D. (1985). *Developing communication and language skills in autism.* Unpublished manuscript.

Lord, C. (1985). Autism and the comprehension of language. In E. Schopler & G. B. Mesibov (Eds.), *Communication problems in autism* (pp. 257–281). New York: Plenum Press.

MacDonald, J. D. (1985). Language through conversation: A model for intervention with language-delayed persons. In S. Warren & A. K. Rogers-Warren (Eds.), *Teaching functional language: Generalization and maintenance of language skills* (pp. 89–122). Baltimore: University Park Press.

MacDonald, J. D. (1989). *Becoming partners with children: From play to conversation.* San Antonio: Special Press.

Meyer, L., & Evans, I. (1986). Modification of excess behavior: An adaptive and functional approach for educational and communicating contexts. In R. Horner, L. Meyer, & H. Fredericks (Eds.), *Education of learners with severe handicaps: Exemplary service strategies* (pp. 315–350). Baltimore: Paul Brookes.

Mirenda, P. L., & Donnellan, A. M. (1986). Effects of adult interaction style on conversational behavior in students with severe communication problems. *Language, Speech, and Hearing Services in the Schools, 17,* 126–141.

Mirenda, P., & Schuler, A. L. (1988). Augmenting communication for persons with autism: Issues and strategies. *Topics in Language Disorders, 9,* 24–43.

Moses, K. (1981). *Mourning theory as related to parents of autistic children.* Paper presented at National Society for Autistic Children Midwest Regional Conference, Chicago, IL.

Mundy, P., & Sigman, M. (1989). Specifying the nature of the social impairment in autism. In G. Dawson (Ed.), *Autism: Nature, diagnosis, and treatment* (pp. 3-21). New York: Guilford Press.

Mundy, P., Sigman, M., Ungerer, J., & Sherman, T. (1986). Defining the social deficits of autism: The contribution of nonverbal communication measures. *Journal of Child Psychology and Psychiatry, 27,* 657–669.

Newhoff, M., & Browning, J. (1983). Interactional variation: A view from the language-disordered child's world. *Topics in Language Disorders, 4*(1), 49–60.

Parten, M. B. (1932). Social participation among preschool children. *Journal of Abnormal and Social Psychology, 27,* 243–269.

Peck, C. (1985). Increasing opportunities for social control by children with autism and severe handicaps: Effects on student behavior and perceived classroom climate. *Journal of the Association for Persons with Severe Handicaps, 4,* 183–193.

Peck, C., & Schuler, A. (1987). Assessment of social/communicative behavior for students with autism and severe handicaps: The importance of asking the right question. In T. Layton (Ed.), *Language and treatment of autistic and developmentally disordered children* (pp. 35–62). Springfield, IL: Charles C. Thomas.

Piaget, J. (1962). *Play, dreams, and imitation in childhood.* New York: W. W. Norton.

Prizant, B. M. (1983). Language acquisition and communicative behavior in autism: Toward an understanding of the "whole" of it. *Journal of Speech and Hearing Disorders, 48,* 296–307.

Prizant, B. M. (1986). *Social relatedness and communicatively impaired children.* Paper presented at the Third Sino-American Symposium on Speech Pathology and Communication Disorders, Taipei, Taiwan.

Prizant, B. M. (1988). Communication problems in the autistic client. In N. Lass, L. McReynolds, J. Northern, & D. Yoder (Eds.), *Handbook of speech, language, and hearing* (pp. 1014–1039). Toronto: B. C. Decker.

Prizant, B. M., & Duchan, J. (1981). The functions of immediate echolalia in autistic children. *Journal of Speech and Hearing Disorders, 46,* 241–249.

Prizant, B. M., & Rydell, P. (1984). Analysis of the functions of delayed echolalia in autistic children. *Journal of Speech and Hearing Research, 27,* 183–192.

Prizant, B. M., & Schuler, A. (1987). Facilitating communication: Language approaches. In D. Cohen & A. Donnellan (Eds.), *Handbook of autism and pervasive developmental disorders* (pp. 316–332). New York: Wiley.

Prizant, B. M., & Tiegerman, E. (1984). Working with language-impaired children: Problems/issues often encountered but (too) rarely discussed. *Journal of the National Student Speech Language Hearing Association, 11,* 18–32.

Prizant, B. M., & Wetherby, A. M. (1987). Communicative intent: A framework for understanding social-communicative behavior in autism. *Journal of the American Academy of Child Psychiatry, 26,* 472–479.

Prizant, B. M., & Wetherby, A. M. (1988). Providing services to children with autism (0 to 2 years) and their families. *Topics in Language Disorders, 9,* 1–23.

Prizant, B. M., & Wetherby, A. M. (1989). Enhancing language and communication in autism: From theory to practice. In G. Dawson (Ed.), *Autism: Nature, diagnosis, and treatment* (pp. 282–309). New York: Guilford Press.

Prizant, B. M., & Wetherby, A. M. (in press). Communication in preschool autistic children. In E. Schopler, G. Mesibov, & M. Van Bourgondien (Eds.), *Preschool issues in autism and related developmental handicaps.* New York: Plenum Press.

Ricks, D., & Wing, L. (1975). Language, communication, and the use of symbols in normal and autistic children. *Journal of Autism and Childhood Schizophrenia, 5,* 191–221.

Rubin, K. H., Watson, K. S., & Jambor, T. W. (1978). Free play behaviors in preschool and kindergarten children. *Child Development, 49,* 534–536.

Rutter, M. (1978). Diagnosis and definition of childhood autism. *Journal of Autism and Childhood Schizophrenia, 8,* 139–161.

Schuler, A., & Prizant, B. (1985). Echolalia in autism. In E. Schopler & G. Mesibov (Eds.), *Communication problems in autism* (pp. 163–184). New York: Plenum Press.

Schuler, A., & Prizant, B. (1987). Facilitating communication: Pre-language approaches. In D. Cohen & A. Donnellan (Eds.), *Handbook of autism and pervasive developmental disorders* (pp. 301–315). New York: Wiley.

Shevin, M., & Klein, N. K. (1984). The importance of choice-making skills for students with severe disabilities. *Journal of the Association for Persons with Severe Handicaps, 9,* 159–166.

Sigman, M., & Ungerer, J. (1984). Cognitive and language skills in autistic, mentally retarded, and normal children. *Developmental Psychology, 20,* 293–302.

Tiegerman, E., & Primavera, L. (1984). Imitating the autistic child: Facilitating communicative gaze behavior. *Journal of Autism and Developmental Disorders, 14,* 27–38.

Tiegerman, E., & Siperstein, M. (1984). Individual patterns of interaction in the mother-child dyad: Implications for parent intervention. *Topics in Language Disorders, 4*(4), 50–61.

Tronick, E. (1989). Emotions and emotional communication in infants. *American Psychologist, 44,* 112–119.

Warren, S. F., & Kaiser, A. P. (1986). Incidental language teaching: A critical review. *Journal of Speech and Hearing Disorders, 51,* 291–299.

Westby, C. (1988). Children's play: Reflections of social competence. *Seminars in Speech and Hearing, 9* 1–14.

Wetherby, A. M. (1986). Ontogeny of communicative functions in autism. *Journal of Autism and Developmental Disorders, 16,* 295–316.

Wetherby, A. M., & Hayden, D. (1990). *Profiling social and motor abilities in children with communicative impairments.* Miniseminar presented at the Annual Convention of the American Speech-Language-Hearing Association, Seattle, WA.

Wetherby, A. M., & Prizant, B. (1989). The expression of communicative intent: Assessment issues. *Seminars in Speech and Language, 10,* 77–91.

Wetherby, A. M., & Prizant, B. (1990). *Communication and symbolic behavior scales—research edition.* Chicago: Riverside Publishing.

Wetherby, A. M., & Prizant, B. (1992). Profiling young children's communicative competence. In S. Warren & J. Reichle (Eds.), *Causes and effects in communication and language intervention* (pp. 217–253). Baltimore: Brookes.

Wetherby, A. M., & Prutting, C. (1984). Profiles of communicative and cognitive-social abilities in autistic children. *Journal of Speech and Hearing Research, 27,* 364–377.

Wing, L., & Attwood, A. (1987). Syndromes of autism and atypical development. In D. Cohen & A. Donnellan (Eds.), *Handbook of autism and pervasive developmental disorders* (pp. 3–19). New York: Wiley.

7 A Model for Multielement Treatment Planning and Outcome Measurement

Gary W. LaVigna
Thomas J. Willis
Institute for Applied Behavior Analysis

Despite increased attention to nonaversive procedures in the literature and their apparent effectiveness in dealing with a wide variety of problems for a wide variety of populations (LaVigna & Donnellan, 1986), those opposed to strictly nonaversive approaches challenge their effectiveness. In particular, they question the ability of the nonaversive procedures to deal with the most serious problem behaviors, such as severe aggression and severe self-injury. In fact, if aversive intervention is employed, it is often justified on the basis that less intrusive methods were tried and failed (e.g., Foxx, Bittle, & Bechtel, 1986).

This chapter describes a model for effective behavior management. A case study involving serious self-injury that was successfully treated with nonaversive strategies, after the person was removed from an unsuccessful program employing extreme forms of punishment, is presented. Clinical intervention following a model for multielement treatment planning and outcome measurement resulted in significant behavior improvement.

A CLINICAL MODEL FOR TREATMENT PLANNING AND OUTCOME MEASUREMENT

The multielement treatment plan model includes an expanded view of the outcome criteria for evaluating treatment programs for behavior problems (LaVigna, Willis, & Donnellan, 1989). As illustrated in Fig. 7.1, beyond the traditional criteria of speed and degree of effects, the model requires that intervention be evaluated in terms of the durability and generalization of their effects, the side effects they produce, and their social and clinical validity (AABT, 1982). This complex array of critical outcomes makes it unlikely that any one procedure will be fully effective. Rather, full results are likely to require multielement treatment plans whose various components, in combination, address the full range of outcome requirements. These separate components must be integrated into an organized treatment plan.

The first major distinction within intervention plans is between *proactive strategies* and *reactive strategies* (LaVigna, Willis, & Donnellan, 1989). Proactive strategies are those designed to produce rapid, durable, and generalized suppression of target behaviors with minimal negative side effects and with good social and clinical validity. Included within this category are ecological manipulations (i.e., changes in the person's physical, programmatic, and/or interpersonal environments); positive programming, designed to teach the person more effective and socially acceptable ways of getting their needs met and of coping with and tolerating naturally occurring, everyday frustrations; and direct treatment (i.e., nonaversive behavioral strategies designed to establish rapid control, while the more permanent goals of ecological manipulations and positive programming are pursued).

Reactive strategies to manage individual occurrences of target behavior are provided to minimize staff and client injury or serious property damage. Our model also considers assessment as a major set of independent

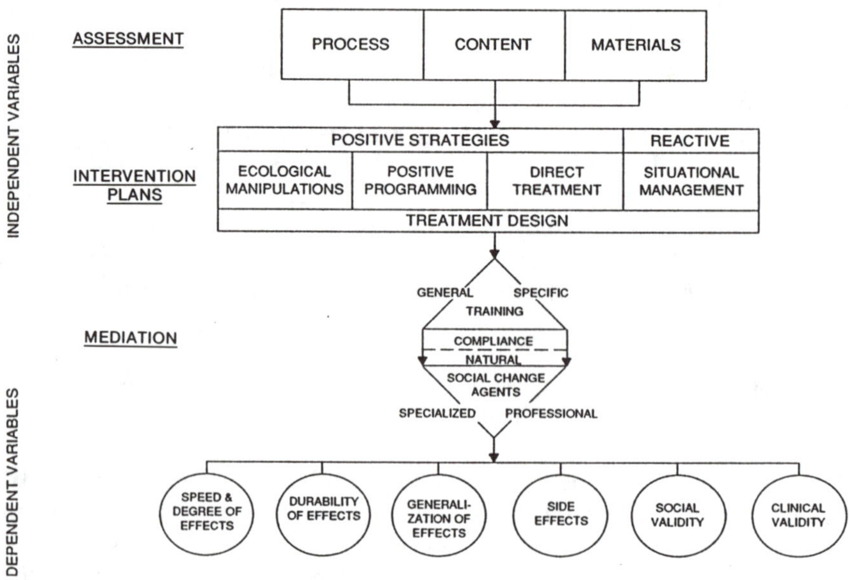

FIG. 7.1 A conceptual framework for research, treatment, and training.

variables. The need for complete information is extended when we consider the possible influence that neurological, medical, or other organic variables may have on behavior. Traditional approaches to behavior modification have tended to minimize or ignore the importance of assessment to effective intervention.

Finally, our model highlights mediation as a separate set of independent variables affecting treatment outcome, and delineates different categories of mediators and different levels of training. This multielement model was applied in the following case study.

METHOD

Client Description

Jeff was a 17-year-old with a profound hearing loss, due to maternal rubella. He also had a diagnosis of autism. Although he had severe deficits in communication in his public school program and with his respite worker at home, Jeff was learning American sign language. His receptive communication included approximately 100 signs, and he had an expressive vocabulary of about four signs. He was able to use signs to label things in his environment and had some symbolic language that was not restricted to an immediate perceptual event. He was also beginning to initiate signs spontaneously. Jeff was only able to follow simple one-part requests, and he had limited self-help skills, requiring physical prompting and supervision for a majority of these activities. He tended to form one strong attachment at a time, usually to a male. He would perform exceedingly well in the presence of that particular person only. At the time of referral, this relationship was with his respite worker.

Jeff resided at home with his parents and three sisters, where he had lived with the exception of a period of 1½ years, when he was approximately 14 years old. During that time, he was in a small group home and attended an associated non-public school program. He was removed from this program by his parents, who felt that the staff were using aversive intervention to an excessive degree and that this treatment was adversely affecting Jeff's behavior.

Jeff's primary problem was his self-injurious behavior. This problem was occurring to such an extent that his parents were unable to meet his needs at home. For this reason, community placement was once again being sought. Jeff was referred for an assessment of his problems and for recommendation of treatment and service strategies to prevent institutional placement pending the availability of an appropriate, community-based residential setting that would be capable of meeting his needs.

Previous Treatment

Jeff's self-injurious behavior (SIB) was of long-standing duration and had occurred sporadically for several years. As described later, the opportunity to be restrained had since become a powerful reinforcer for Jeff. Despite the lack of prior attempts to control these behaviors with sophisticated, consistently implemented nonaversive strategies, punishment was viewed as the last resort in the small group home and private educational program in which he was placed. In that setting, the behaviors were initially controlled by aversive consequences, including bare-bottomed spankings, water squirts, pinches, and the like. Eventually, however, the effectiveness of these procedures diminished, and they acted only to escalate the problem to the point where he was receiving over 100 aversive consequences a day. For example, on one day alone, after more than a year of treatment, he received 177 bare-bottomed spankings.

It was during this period that parental control also deteriorated. Before, family members had good instructional control with Jeff and were able to take him to stores, the beach, the public park, and elsewhere in the community. After Jeff's experience in the punishment program, his parents no longer had this control, and he was virtually 100% noncompliant to any requests that they made. Although his parents reported that it was very rough going when they first removed him from the program, Jeff had established a good relationship with his in-home respite worker, and was reported to be doing well in his public school program.

Assessment and Functional Analysis

Description of Target Behavior

Jeff's SIB was defined as the act of striking his head or nose with his fist or against another object, or the act of abruptly moving his head to the side in order to hit his chin on his shoulder. Despite the fact that he physically restrained himself most of the day and minimal demands were being placed on him, his parents reported that SIB occurred approximately 60 times a day. This rate was confirmed by staff observation.

Antecedents

The primary antecedent to this behavior was Jeff's removal, or threat of removal, from a self-restraining situation. He restrained himself by tangling up with his bed, chair, or other pieces of furniture. Physically, of course, he was able to free himself from these situations anytime he wanted; but, he didn't, and when he was made to, particularly by his mother or father, he was likely to engage in self-injurious behavior. This typically occurred when a demand was being placed on him. Therefore, demands were also observable antecedents to this response.

Self-injurious behavior was less likely to occur at home when his respite worker was present and when he was the one interacting with Jeff. The respite worker reported that when he was alone with Jeff, SIB virtually never occurred. It was also reported not to occur any more at school, although it had occurred when he was first enrolled. These reports were truthful. Observations of Jeff with his respite worker also suggested, however, that he had developed some very subtle and even symbolic forms of self-restraint that were acceptable and that were not immediately viewed as self-restraint by the people involved. For example, Jeff would put a hat on, lay under the coffee table, and even put the person's arm around his neck. Jeff did not spend any significant time without being restrained, at least symbolically.

Consequences

In the past, SIB has been consequated with aversive stimuli and events. Spanks, water squirts, pinches, and a variety of other events had all been applied. In the classroom, he was consequated by being placed in the middle of the room by himself. This, of course, isolated him from the opportunity to self-restrain. This time-out from positive reinforcement procedure appeared to be the operative strategy used by the school program to keep this behavior under control. At home, a variety of consequences were provided for this response. He was told "no" in emphatic sign language, he was physically redirected, the hair on the back of his neck was pulled, and sometimes, because of the press to do other things, he was just left alone to be by himself and to engage in self-restraint.

Initially, Jeff's respite worker had also applied some of these consequences. Now it appeared that he simply had to withdraw his presence to get Jeff to stop. Being with his respite worker was something that Jeff really liked. It is quite conceivable that, in the past, SIB had played a functional role for Jeff in getting out of things he didn't want to do. Task avoidance was almost certainly still part of the picture. The opportunity to be restrained had appeared to become, however, by itself, a powerful reinforcer (Favell, McGimsey, & Stone, 1978). Its intermittent availability was making a significant contribution to the maintenance of this behavior at home.

Mediators

Jeff's family was not able to carry out the intensity of behavioral intervention he required at this time. Ideally, he needed a small group home setting with trained staff in a one-to-one staff–client ratio that would also be able to address his hearing loss and communication needs. Such a program was being developed through a grant obtained by the not-for-profit corporation established by Jeff's parents for this purpose. Pending the development of this program, it was necessary for professional staff to be available in his natural home to carry out intervention. The battles with Jeff at home were getting worse and were becoming more exhausting and frustrating for the family. Help was necessary to avoid the disintegration of the family or to avoid institutional placement.

As an interim arrangement, intensive intervention (Donnellan, LaVigna, Zambito, & Thvedt, 1985) in his parents' home at the level of 30 hours a week was recommended. This represented 26 hours a week of direct intervention and 4 hours a week of parent–consultant discussions. In addition, Jeff's parents carried out the complex treatment procedures when staff were not present. Without their full level of in-home service, placement in a state hospital was likely. Such a placement would have been unnecessarily restrictive for Jeff, given the availability of in-home support and, further, would not have provided him with the behavioral treatment he needed for his problems. A continuation of respite services at the level of 8 hours a week was also recommended.

Procedures

Jeff's treatment program was based on assessment results and was organized around four categories as shown in Table 7.1. The following describes the treatment plan that was implemented by the intensive intervention team.

Ecological Manipulations

There was a general consensus that Jeff's needs could best be met in a community-based group home, providing sophisticated behavior modification services within the context of specialized training in independent living and in community and social integration. Traditionally, pending the availability of such a setting, a person with Jeff's level of SIB would have been placed in a state hospital or a comparable segregated setting. It was felt, however, that congregate living, close proximity with large numbers of individuals also having severe behavior problems, the lack of opportunities to learn and to engage in a rich and wide variety of functional, chronological age-appropriate activities, in natural, socially integrated settings, and the other characteristics of a typical state hospital setting would greatly exacerbate Jeff's problems. Accordingly, a critical ecological decision was made to provide intensive intervention in his home and community settings in the belief that in the interim this would provide the greatest ecological support for the control of SIB.

TABLE 7.1
Jeff's Multielement Treatment Plan

Ecological Manipulations
1. Community-based group home
2. Peer and staff sign language for primary communication
3. Interim intensive intervention: 30 hours/week
4. Token reinforcement program
Positive Programming
1. Chronological age-appropriate and functional skill development
2. Discrete trial, differential reinforcement for compliance
3. General sign communication training
4. Signed request for self-restraint
Direct Treatment Strategies
1. Antecedent control; gradually faded
2. DRO schedules
Reactive Strategies
1. No physical intervention was necessary
2. Signed "no! wrong!"
3. Back-up "self-restraints"

A second major ecological manipulation involved the introduction of a token reinforcement program as a mediating system to motivate Jeff to participate in his various scheduled activities and training sessions. Jeff was taught to operate within the token economy in a number of stages: (a) a simple "star" on a token card was delivered for a select behavior; (b) the "star" was exchanged immediately for a "back-up" reinforcer; (c) a picture menu was developed that depicted a variety of "back-up" events; (d) the number of "stars" required to exchange for increasingly larger "back-up" reinforcers was gradually increased to two, three, and four; and (e) Jeff was gradually taught to delay his selection of "back-up" reinforcers.

Positive Programming

There was also a general consensus that a key to managing Jeff's SIB would be the development of domestic, leisure-time, community, and self-help skills. A major part of the program, therefore, involved training in these areas. Systematic training was conducted to establish skills that were functional and chronologically age-appropriate, such as cooking, loading the dishwasher, making a sandwich, showering, and shopping. Training involved: (a) detailed task analyses of skills to be taught; (b) trial-by-trial progression through each task using a "whole-task" training procedure; (c) prompting of correct responses using a hierarchy of assistance; and (d) positive reinforcement for success.

One of the identified functions of SIB was task avoidance. To address this, a compliance training program was developed. Specifically, Jeff was systematically reinforced with praise, exchangeable tokens, and access to preferred activities (i.e., the opportunity to go to his bedroom to restrain himself, and the opportunity to use the backyard swing) for beginning, maintaining, and completing selected activities. A partial list of these selected activities included getting out of bed, getting into and participating with his bath, going to breakfast, getting on his school bus, getting off his school bus, changing his clothes, taking off and putting on various articles of clothing, going to the bathroom, eating with utensils, clearing and setting the table, washing the table after a meal, washing dishes, and participating in leisure activities.

If Jeff did not respond to a signed report to initiate one of these activities within a period of approximately 10 seconds, the request was repeated. If he didn't respond within 10 seconds of the second request, he was prompted with sufficient physical guidance to ensure that the task was completed. He was positively reinforced with praise, tokens, and access to special privileges for compliance to the first request. Physically prompted compliance was consequated with only praise.

Finally, as a powerful reinforcer for SIB was identified as the opportunity to restrain, a major goal of intervention was to teach Jeff, when he was agitated, to request restraints using sign language. This was an effort to teach a more acceptable way of communicating his request to be restrained and to preclude his need to engage in SIB (Donnellan, Mirenda, Mesaros, & Fassbender, 1984).

Direct Treatment

Direct treatment incorporated a number of strategies, including Antecedent Control. It was obvious that Jeff did not engage in SIB when he was self-restrained. Initial observation in the home clearly indicated that Jeff restrained himself much of the time. He would wrap himself around chairs, around his bed, or wrap himself in his own clothes. This self-restraint frequently resulted in the necessity of taking his bed apart in order to get him out of bed. Certain forms of restraint would result in the cut-off of circulation to parts of his body. For example, when he would wrap himself in straps, he would wrap them so tightly that his arms would turn blue. The self-restraint frequently would prevent his movement from one place to another, would prevent compliance with demands, and would necessitate the use of physical force to move him from one setting to another. Prior to intervention, he would spend most of his day at home self-restraining himself in his bed. The purpose of this self-restraint was unclear, but it may have been the way that he learned to manage his own SIB.

To increase Jeff's participation in his home environment without resulting in a severe increase in SIB, he was taught to use a portable, self-restraining device. Initially, he was given a large plastic truck in which he restrained himself by placing his fingers and arms through various openings. However, this device was abandoned because it caused swelling of his fingers and frequent lacerations. Eventually, several self-restraining devices were used, including plastic rings that Jeff could insert over his fingers, a neck brace, a pair of glasses, and removable casts. These portable restraints were gradually faded (Foxx & Dufrense, 1984) along a variety of dimensions, depending on the nature of the particular device. The speed of fading depended on the level of Jeff's SIB and on the ultimate need to insure his safety. (Total fading was not accomplished until after he was placed in his group home.)

A second direct treatment strategy involved a schedule for the *Differential Reinforcement of Other Behavior (DRO).* Initially, Jeff was reinforced for gradually increased periods during which he was free of SIB. During training sessions, his portable restraints were removed and he was positively reinforced for the absence of SIB. Eventually, however, the initiation of these training sessions was associated with the occurrence of major tantrums. Although Jeff had shown significant progress with this DRO procedure, it was terminated in favor of specified periods of time during which SIB was absent. He was not required to remove his restraints. Throughout the programming day, if SIB had been absent for the specified time interval, he received reinforcement. When SIB occurred, the interval timer was reset.

Reactive Strategies

Initially, all SIB was passively ignored by Jeff's parents and staff. Ignoring was selected because past records and direct observation indicated that contingently signing "no" increased the likelihood of SIB. However, there was one exception. When Jeff hit his head against hard objects, he was signed "No! Wrong!" emphatically. This appeared to stop continued attempts at hitting. Additionally, with this behavior, a shadowing method was used in which Jeff was prevented from contacting an object with his head by placing oneself between him and the object.

During treatment, a series of events occurred that led to an overriding need to protect Jeff's physical well-being. In the first place, Jeff's "neck snapping" resulted in a small laceration. This laceration was subsequently invaded by staphylococcus bacteria, a quite serious problem. As a result, in order to protect Jeff, a "neck brace" was placed on him to prevent additional damage and to allow his chin to heal. Second, approximately 2 weeks later, Jeff caused serious damage to his head while he was at school.

As a result of repeated head hittings, he lacerated his scalp. Therefore, to protect his head, Jeff was given a "helmet" to wear. Third, soon after its introduction, Jeff lacerated his fingers on the helmet. Those lacerations were also invaded by staphylococcus, which subsequently necessitated his hospitalization for a period of 10 days.

Based on these incidents in which Jeff injured himself through intense, high-rate SIB, it was agreed that his need for physical protection should override behavioral programming when necessary. Thus, a variety of methods was explored that could be used to prevent damage, but with the ultimate goal of fading those devices as soon as possible. Therefore, neck braces to prevent neck snapping and removeable casts to prevent head hitting were used. Such protective devices could not be construed as treatment. They were merely a temporary means of protecting Jeff from physical damage while treatment was applied. For example, one of Jeff's neck braces was faded along the dimensions of height and thickness. The intention was to gradually fade any protective device that was used.

Approximately 1 year after initial assessment and the beginning of intensive intervention, Jeff was admitted to a university hospital in order to have corrective foot surgery. He was out of school for a 3½-week period, and when he returned, he was still in his wheelchair. After surgery, several medical complications developed that resulted in considerable physical discomfort and emotional upheaval. The many medical changes Jeff experienced during this period clearly influenced the rate of SIB. As a result, it became necessary to implement another reactive strategy to reduce instances of actual hand-to-head contact. This procedure involved two components: (a) if Jeff began to initiate a hit, an attempt was made to prevent him from making actual contact, especially during tantrums which typically included multiple blows, and (b) when he attempted to hit, staff used a brushing action of the hands in which their lower arm and wrist were placed between Jeff's elbow and wrist, and with a sweeping motion, the hand was brushed down smoothly. Eventually, as Jeff's health improved, SIB was once again ignored, unless he made contact repeatedly for three times and appeared to be escalating.

Group Home Placement

Intensive intervention was provided for Jeff over a period of 61 weeks. At that time, it was possible for him to move into the small group home that had been developed for that purpose by his parents. Whereas the initial treatment plan in the group home setting incorporated the procedures applied by the intensive intervention team, these procedures were progressively revised by the group home staff to reflect their skills, particularly their ability to communicate fluently using sign language, Jeff's continued improvement, and the opportunity to provide treatment for a full program day. The following describes the group home program.

Ecological Manipulations. The major ecological manipulation during this phase was placement in a small group home. Jeff shares this residence with five other young adult men, all of whom also rely on sign language for communication. Further, staff were hired for their ability to sign or willingness to learn this method of communication and, in fact, a number of staff are deaf. For these individuals, signed communication is in fact their first language. The staff–client ratio in the group home is 1:2 during programming hours (14 hours a day, 7 days a week), except for that time Jeff spends in his day program. This level of staffing has allowed for more community integration and more comprehensive programming.

Positive Programming. At 7:30 a.m. Jeff gets up and begins his daily self-care routine comprised of showering, shaving, toothbrushing, hair combing, and dressing. He then assists in bed making and straightening his bedroom. Afterward, he participates in meal preparation by selecting foods (usually a preferred item, such as a burrito), then cooks the food in the microwave. Upon completion of the meal, he cleans his place setting. While waiting for the bus to his day program, Jeff engages in preferred and previously mastered leisure skills. Arriving home at 4 p.m. Jeff prepares a snack and beverage for himself. Programming begins with structured communication sessions and throughout the remainder of the day he receives training on purchasing/money management, preparing a sack lunch, table manners, and a variety of recreational and leisure skills. Community activities on some evenings and during weekends include shopping, swimming, amusement parks, water parks, museums, walks/hikes, bowling, miniature golf, puzzles, restaurants, the beach, car rides, and so on. The day concludes at approximately 10 p.m. with Jeff's preparation for bed.

Jeff has received training on such skills as toileting, toothbrushing, showering, preparing food items (Rice-a-Roni, juice, and sandwich), table manners, and community walks. In his most recent IPP, skill programs focused on: (a) table manners: serving himself, cutting foods, and not eating with fingers; (b) preparing a simple sack lunch consisting of a sandwich, fruit, vegetable, chips, drink, and dessert; (c) participating in a variety of sports and leisure activities such as ball games, skating and bowling, aerobic isometric and body toning exercise routines, and independent skills such as puzzles, computer games, and photo albums; and (d) money management and purchasing skills.

Perhaps most important has been the emphasis on communication-training in his group home environment. Jeff's structured communication program includes vocabulary building, learning the names of important people in his environment, and using language effectively to express his personal needs. He is progressing in all of these areas. Although it is difficult to quantify the number of words Jeff can use independently both expressively and receptively, it is evident that he does demonstrate basic language skills. His receptive understanding of language is greater than his ability to express himself using language (like most people). Additionally, the vocabulary words that Jeff has mastered, he uses independently. He seems to have a ready aptitude to learn vocabulary for items that interest him (he learned the sign for 'Cadillac' with minimal coaching—he has a lifelong fascination for these cars), but he does not apply the same zeal to learning the more mundane objects in life, and his success has been uneven. These preferences extend to learning the name signs for the staff and the other residents in the home. He has mastered the names of a few staff members, his mother, and even his own name, but has not yet learned the names of the residents.

Direct Treatment. Initially, *Antecedent Control* was also used in the group home. Portable restraints were continued and eventually faded out. The only restraint presently used is symbolic and consists of eye glasses, which Jeff wears propped on the top of his head. Similarly, the schedules of reinforcement have been revised to reflect his dramatic improvement. Two separate *DRO schedules* are currently employed. The first involves hourly intervals, at the end of which he receives an exchangeable token if he has not engaged in SIB *and* if he has not been noncompliant. The second DRO schedule provides additional tokens at the end of each day during which he did not ask for restraints or engage in tantrum behavior.

Reactive Strategies. Physical intervention is no longer necessary to protect Jeff from self-injury. If he engages in SIB, he is emphatically told (signed) "Wrong! Hurt! No!" This is now sufficient to prevent further escalation.

Observation and Recording Procedures

The intervention specialists acted as primary observers throughout the course of treatment. On a prepared form, they recorded the discrete frequency of each topography of self-injury. The total frequency of self-injury was summed at the end of each day. Reliability checks were conducted throughout the course of intervention yielding indices in excess of 85%.

RESULTS

Intensive Intervention

Figure 7.2 shows that Jeff engaged in SIB 50 times per hour during the first week of intensive intervention. This was a rate of almost one incident of

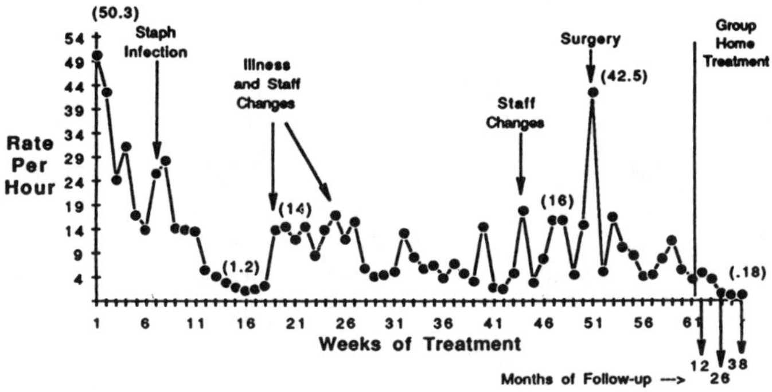

FIG. 7.2 Jeff's self-injurious behavior.

self-injury every minute. Progress was steady but marked by considerable variability in the target response during the course of treatment. Illnesses and staff changes help explain some of this variability. Relatively steady progress was made in the first 18 weeks. However, the spikes in his behavior shown for Weeks 7 and 8 were associated with his staph infection and subsequent 2-week hospitalization. In Week 19, he became ill and this was followed by a period of several weeks during which there were a number of personnel changes on the intervention team. Changes surrounding Week 43 are harder to explain but were also thought possibly to be associated with changes in personnel. The last major spike in Jeff's behavior in Week 51 was associated with the period of time following his surgery. From that point on, his SIB continued to improve and by the end of the intensive intervention was occurring only about five times an hour. This represents a 90% reduction when compared to rates exhibited when intervention began.

Group Home Placement

Figure 7.2 also shows the rates of Jeff's behavior in his group home setting after intensive intervention was terminated. Figure 7.2 shows representative rates during sample weeks approximately 1 year after placement and then approximately every 6 months for the following 2½ years. Jeff's SIB has essentially been eliminated in the group home program. Further, in contrast to what was accomplished in intensive intervention, he no longer requires portable restraints and is content with simply being allowed to wear his glasses propped on top of his head, giving him a rather jaunty look. Group home staff report that SIB and self-restraint were always strongly intertwined behaviors, and it seems clear that the home's success in fading out restraints played a major role in finally controlling SIB. Jeff is also under good instructional control, responding to the first request over 95% of the time. This is considered to be within normal limits and is acceptable to Jeff's parents and the staff who work with him.

SUMMARY

The results show that Jeff's severe self-injurious behavior was successfully treated using strictly nonaversive procedures. These results are particularly significant given Jeff's previous placement in a program that considered punishment to be the last resort and, therefore, justified. In fact, punishment not only failed to solve the problem but also led to its exacerbation.

One challenge to nonaversive approaches is that it requires very specialized knowledge that would not be accessible to most settings. In Jeff's case, outside consultation and intensive staff were only available and provided during the first phase of intensive intervention. During this phase, only a 90% reduction in the problem behavior was achieved. In contrast, Jeff's most significant progress occurred in his group home setting, where the staff were able to communicate with Jeff using sign language, where they related to him as a competent and self-actualizing individual, and where they were able to revise and modify the procedures developed by the intensive intervention team based on their on-going assessment, and based on Jeff's continued progress.

In fact, staff and Jeff's parents are not willing to rest on their laurels yet. They believe that Jeff has only begun to realize his potential. For example, after graduation from school, Jeff was placed in a day activity program that specializes in dealing with severe behavior problems. The general consensus is that in contrast, Jeff could do well in a supported work program. For example, he could wash and do detailing for Cadillac limousines for a local rental agency.

The major implication of this case study is that aversive procedures may not be necessary, even for the most challenging and severe behaviors. Those who would propose punishment for individual cases have a major responsibility to document that previous attempts to solve problems nonaversively were comprehensive, well-designed, and consistently implemented. This level of accountability is missing from today's literature. Rather than relying on the unsubstantiated claims that previous attempts failed, the specifics of those previous attempts should be described in sufficient detail to allow for their independent evaluation. Our model suggests that to accomplish enduring and important clinical outcomes, comprehensive assessment and complex multielement treatment plans may be needed. Jeff represents only one example of this possibility.

ACKNOWLEDGMENT

The authors wish to thank Jean Rothfelder for her assistance and support.

REFERENCES

AABT Task Force Report. (1982). The treatment of self-injurious behavior. *Behavior Therapy, 13,* 529–554.

Donnellan, A. M., LaVigna, G. W., Zambito, J., & Thvedt, J. (1985). A time-limited intensive intervention program model to support community placement for persons with severe behavior problems. *Journal of the Association for Person with Severe Handicaps, 10*(3), 123–131.

Donnellan, A. M., Mirenda, P. L., Mesaros, R. A., & Fassbender, L. L. (1984). Analyzing the communicative functions of aberrant behavior. *Journal of the Association for Persons with Severe Handicaps, 9*(3), 201–212.

Favell, J. E., McGimsey, J. F., & Jones, M. L. (1978). The use of physical restraint in the treatment of self-injury and as a positive reinforcement. *Journal of Applied Behavior Analysis, 11,* 225–241.

Foxx, R. M., & Dufrense, D. (1984). "Harry": The use of physical restraint as a reinforcer, time-out from restraint, and fading restraint in treating a self-injurious man. *Analysis and Intervention in Developmental Disabilities, 4,* 1–13.

Foxx, R. M., Bittle, R. G., & Bechtel, D. R. (1986). The successful treatment of a dually-diagnosed deaf man's aggression with a program that included electric shock. *Behavior Therapy, 17,* 170–186.

LaVigna, G. W., & Donnellan, A. M., (1986). *Alternatives to punishment: Solving behavior problems with nonaversive strategies.* New York: Irvington.

LaVigna, G. W., Willis, T. J., & Donnellan, A. M. (1989). The role of positive programming in behavioral treatment. In E. Cipani (Ed.), *Behavioral approaches to the treatment of aberrant behavior* (pp. 59–82). AAMD Monograph Series, American Association on Mental Deficiency.

8 Medical Treatment in Autism

Luke Y. Tsai
University of Michigan Medical Center

The primary aim of medical care of autistic persons is to ensure physical and psychological health. To accomplish this goal, preventive medical care is crucial. Generally speaking, a good preventive health care system should include regular physical checkups to monitor somatic growth, vision, hearing, and blood pressure; administering immunization according to schedule; arranging regular visits to the dentist, and paying attention to diet and hygiene.

The secondary aim is early detection and treatment of the unappealing and irritating behaviors, disturbing sleep and eating problems, and discomfortable medical/dental conditions associated with autism hence to improve the quality of life of individuals with autism.

From previous chapters we have learned that Infantile Autism is a behaviorally defined syndrome that may have a variety of etiologies. Both behavioral and biological studies have generated sufficient evidence suggesting neurobiologic etiologies of autism. At present, however, no specific biological markers have been identified. In the absence of an understanding of the causes of autism, it is not surprising that attempts at treatment have inevitably been haphazard and poorly organized. Nowadays, no single treatment modality has been shown to be effective in *curing* autism. However, the comprehensive treatment program (comprising parental counseling, behavior modification, and special education in a highly structured environment) has demonstrated significant treatment effect in target symptoms of many individuals with autism. Parents of autistic children and other caregivers who work with autistic people rarely have any grave concern in terms of accepting this kind of comprehensive treatment approach. Often, however, they feel uneasy about medical treatment, particularly drug treatment (pharmacotherapy) for their autistic children/clients. Such feeling, no doubt, comes from past abuses of psychotropic drugs in persons with developmental disabilities. Unfortunately, the current severe shortage of child psychiatrists who specialize in developmental disorders further impedes the availability of experienced and sensitive physicians. As a result, advances in pharmacotherapy in autism have been limited.

Today, in the eyes of many parents and other caregivers, drug therapy is often viewed as a treatment of last resort to be used only when other types of treatment have been unsuccessful. However, there is now enough evidence to suggest that certain drugs may be effective as a first-line treatment of other mental disorders as well as some of the maladaptive behaviors caused by organic brain disease in autistic people. In addition, an effective drug will increase the response of these patients to other forms of treatment.

MEDICAL ASSESSMENT

The effective medical and pharmacological treatments begin with a thorough medical assessment including a comprehensive physical and neurological examination. Information should be collected using behavior rating scales, direct observation, and various tests such as electroencephalogram (EEG), electrocardiogram (EKG), and neuroradiological imaging; other laboratory tests, when appropriate, include chromosome studies, amino acid screening on blood and urine, thyroid function tests, liver function tests, viral antibodies, blood lead levels, complete blood count (CBC), and differential blood count; simple measures such as recording of blood pressure, pulse, height, and weight should not be ignored. The pretreatment assessment is essential for detecting many medical conditions such as seizure disorder, meningitis, lead poisoning, brain tumors, endocrinological disorders, and chromosomal abnormalities that can cause or exacerbate an autistic individual's behavioral, emotional, or cognitive problems. Furthermore, it should be emphasized that assessment procedures are continuous throughout the course of the treatment.

It should be pointed out that administering the physical and neurodevelopmental assessment in some individuals with autism can be a real challenge. Because of their rather low cognitive and communicative functioning, it may be impossible even to explain the examination procedure. The assistance of a parent or therapist who is familiar with the individual's behavior patterns and means of communication can be most helpful. Some autistic people may resist any physical contact and may even react violently to the usual examination procedure. The physician sometimes will have to determine how many physical and neurological procedures are actually essential rather than doggedly follow the standard examination procedure (Dalldorf, 1983).

GENERAL APPROACHES TO PHARMACOTHERAPY

Pharmacotherapy begins with an establishment of relationship between behavioral abnormalities (i.e., symptoms) and underlying biochemical abnormalities. The goal of pharmacotherapy is to correct both with an effective chemical agent (i.e., drug). However, based on the contemporary definition and classification systems, autism is viewed as a heterogeneous syndrome (Tsai & Ghaziuddin, 1991). Hence it is heterogeneous both behaviorally and biochemically. Until the cause–effect relationship in autism becomes clear, the aim of pharmacotherapy of autism will be for a rational treatment. To achieve such a goal, it is essential to learn about the basic principles of pharmacotherapy, the workup for use of various drugs, the basic categories of drugs, their indications, contraindications, and side effect profiles, and the measuring of drug effects.

Basic Principles of Pharmacotherapy

1. Drug treatment must be based on a sound diagnosis. Choosing a specific drug must base on the patient's diagnosis. It should be kept in mind that autistic persons may develop the full range of psychiatric disorders. When the symptom/behavior reflects an underlying organic brain syndrome/neurological disorder (e.g., Tourette disorder), drug selection must be based on the presence of specific types of psychopathology (e.g., vocal tics).

2. Drug treatment should be reserved for individuals with severe behavioral problems or emotional disturbances who do not respond to other forms of treatment.

3. The individual should be involved in the treatment process as much as possible, despite his or her age and level of functioning. Every effort should be made to help the individual to understand the reason and purpose of taking the medication(s). This approach will prevent the development of negative attitude or misperception toward the use of the drug(s) in these individuals. When this is done, the individual becomes a useful and helpful ally in the treatment.

4. The family or responsible care provider (e.g., school or residential group home) should always be included in the process. The parent and other direct caretaker's attitude toward the use of medication and ability to work with the physician and autistic person is extremely important. A parent or

caretaker is a necessary source of information about the individual's functioning and response to medication. They need to be informed about the reasons for drug therapy, the likely therapeutic effects, side effects, etc.

5. Placebo effect often exists and should be weighed carefully to determine the continuation of the medication. The placebo effect can be produced by the individual taking the drug, the family members, or the caretakers, including the prescribing physician.

6. Medication should never be used as the sole intervention. Drug use should be a part of a comprehensive program of treatment that includes psychosocial, behavioral, and special education interventions. Without additional therapy, the improvement associated with the medication usually disappears after the drug is discontinued.

7. Therapeutic gains need to be weighed carefully against side effects, and all efforts must be made to minimize risks to the individual.

8. Children differ significantly from adults in their pharmacokinetic capacities due to relatively large liver size in proportion to body weight. Hence, children tend to need higher doses relative to body weight when compared to adults. On the other hand, children tend to have less adipose tissue and less protein binding, when compared to adults, and may have more drug available for bioactivity and, potentially, more side effects (Rapoport & Mikkelsen, 1978).

9. Appropriate drug selection requires comprehensive information about the individual, including current functioning, family history, and medical history. It is crucial that the autistic individual's family maintains an up-to-date medical record because the prescribing physician needs to know whether the individual has seizure, previous use of and response to any drug, and current medications. Many drugs may lower the threshold for seizure, or can interact either to potentiate or to diminish their individual effectiveness.

10. In general, if an individual has not responded to a drug within 4 weeks while in the therapeutic range, it is unlikely he or she will respond at a later date. In the cases with therapeutic response, drug treatment should proceed at optimal dosage for periods of 2 and up to 6 months. The drug should then be discontinued for at least a 1- to 2-month drug holiday to permit evaluation of the need for continued treatment as well as assessment of the development of side effects such as growth changes or dyskinesias.

11. During the initial phases of drug therapy, the individual should be seen at least once a week. Once the individual has been stabilized, usually after several weeks, a drug maintenance program can begin. Individuals can be seen less frequently, such as monthly, to review therapeutic response and development of side effects.

12. Medication should be aimed at altering specific symptoms and should be carefully evaluated for these effects using reliable measures described in the following section.

Measures of Drug Effects

To determine the optimal dosage, many researchers and clinicians prefer to titrate dosage for each individual patient. Usually, this entails starting with a low dosage and raising by standardized increments every 2 or three days until the "optimal" clinical effect is seen or therapeutic range is reached, or until the side effects begin to interfere with desired changes. Others prefer to employ standardized doses based on the subject's body weight. Still, certain drugs can be measured in the blood to guide their clinical use. However, it should be pointed out that there is some disagreement in the research literature as to whether there is a clear relationship between drug concentration in the blood and clinical response to that drug (Curry, 1978). Another concern in the use of blood level is the lack of agreement on the clinically useful range of blood concentration indicative of therapeutic change. Nonetheless, measurement of blood levels may provide a drug index that can be related to changes in specific behaviors, to prevent serious side effects, and to identify nonresponders.

It is clear that dosage regulation of any drug depends on reliable measurement of changes or improvements of targeted behaviors. However, in most cases of autism, patients are unable to report their symptoms or their response to treatment accurately. Furthermore, a positive treatment effect may be a decrease in the frequency or severity of long-standing maladaptive behavior, and this change may not be readily apparent in the clinician's office. Therefore, the measuring of treatment response must rely on objective techniques that are reliable (i.e., repeatable over time or across observers) and valid (i.e., reflect what is actually being measured) for data collection from caregivers. There are various measurement techniques that can be employed. These techniques include global impression, direct behavioral observations, behavioral rating scales, self-reports, standardized tests, learning and performance measures, and mechanical movement monitors. On the other hand, it is also crucial that the assessment strategies are sensitive to changes produced by the drug and are practical, economic, safe, and ethical.

Global Impression. An individual's overall behavior is judged by global impression. This is the most frequently used and least reliable method of evaluating the drug efficacy. It fails to capture day to day variability, and it can not be replicated across time or clinicians. Clinical Global Impressions (Campbell & Palij, 1985) and Nurse's Global Impression (Campbell, Anderson, Meier, Cohen, Small, Samit, & Sachar, 1978) are examples of the scales that have been used in previous studies.

Direct Behavioral Observations. Behavior is recorded as it happens with frequent reliability checks, and assessment results are often graphed to aid interpretation. This type of assessment can be carried out either in an artificial situation (e.g. a child taking an intelligence test) or in a natural situation (e.g., a child's home or classroom). The major limitation with this procedure is that it is expensive in terms of staff time.

Behavioral Rating Scales. These are generally problem-oriented checklists that are completed by parents or caretakers familiar with the autistic individual. This is a quick, efficient, inexpensive, and practical procedure that is used frequently in almost all clinical settings. There are many rating scales with established reliability, validity, and sensitivity to medication changes, for example, the Conners checklist (Conners, 1973) and the Ritvo-Freeman Real Life Rating Scale for Autism (Freeman, Ritvo, Yokota, & Ritvo, 1986).

Self-Reports. This procedure has a limited application in the autistic population due to general difficulties in cognitive and communicative functionings of autistic people. In addition, the self-report tends to have low agreement with other's evaluation of the behavior.

Standardized Tests. All the standardized clinical tests such as intelligence tests, school-attainment tests, language and speech tests, and specific psychological tests (e.g., visual–motor integration test) have been used to assess drug efficacy. However, these tests are generally insensitive to behavioral changes produced by medications.

Learning and Performance Measures. These include assessments of short-term memory, task completion, and rate of performance before and after administration of certain drug. These measurements are appropriate for short-term drug trials. For long-term studies, standardized intelligence tests may be utilized.

Mechanic Monitors. These are devices (e.g., computerized activity monitor and videotapes) used primarily to measure the changes of functions and activities of autonomic nervous system caused by certain drug. However, most devices are presently too cumbersome and expensive for routine clinical use. (Bio-Feed back)

Monitoring of Other Drug Effects. Periodic laboratory screening should be done on a regular basis during the entire duration of drug therapy. It is judicious practice to repeat CBC and differential, urinalysis, and basic chemistry screening at 3 months and every 6 months for each of the medications. Blood pressure and pulse rate should be checked weekly. Serial EKG should take place whenever drug with significant cardiovascular effects is prescribed. Weight and height should be recorded on a monthly or quarterly basis.

Classes of Drugs

anti-psycotatics

Neuroleptics. Neuroleptics or major tranquilizers include six major classes: (a) phenothiazines, (b) thioxanthenes, (c) butyrophenones, (d) dihydro-indolones, (e) dibenzoxazepines, and (f) diphenylbutylpiperidines. In adults, neuroleptics are prescribed almost exclusively for the treatment of schizophrenia and other psychoses. In children, neuroleptics are used less specifically, that is, they have been used in reducing hyperactivity, stereotypies, tics, and aggressiveness. However, agreement over indications for the use of neuroleptics in children is not uniform (Rutter, 1985).

Among the neuroleptics, butyrophenone (Haloperidol or Haldol), aliphatic phenothiazines (Chlorpromazine or Thorazine), and piperidine phenothiazines (Thioridazine or Mellaril) are the most frequently used drugs. The bulk of the studies, however, have been with haloperidol (Campbell, 1982). Low-potency neuroleptics, such as chlorpromazine, have little, if any, therapeutic effect because they yield excessive sedation, even at low doses. On the other hand, haloperidol, a high-potency neuroleptic, has demonstrated both short-term and long-term efficacy.

Haloperidol is a dopaminergic blocking agent. Despite the extensive use of the drug in children with developmental disorders, pharmacokinetic data are available only in adults. Absorption is rapid following both oral and intramuscular injection. Plasma half-life of elimination phase varies from 12–36 hours. Both high (0.05 mg/kg/day) and low (0.025 mg/kg/day) doses are effective in reducing behavioral symptoms in hyperactive and aggressive outpatients of normal intelligence (Werry & Aman, 1975; Werry, Aman, & Lampen, 1976). In another study of children with conduct disorder, haloperidol in doses ranging from 1.0 to 6.0 mg/day or 0.04–0.21 mg/kg/day was highly effective in reducing aggressiveness, negativism, explosiveness, and hyperactivity (Campbell et al., 1984).

Haloperidol, in doses ranging from 2 to 16 mg/day, was shown to be effective in reducing symptoms of acute schizophrenia in adolescents (Pool, Bloom, Mielke, Roniger, & Gallant 1976).

Haloperidol has been systematically studied in autistic children. It has been reported that haloperidol, at doses ranging from 0.25 to 4.0 mg/day, is helpful in improving coordination, self-care, affect, and exploratory behavior (Engelhardt, Polizos, Waizer, & Hoffman, 1973), in reducing stereotypies, withdrawal hyperactivity, and fidgetiness (Anderson et al., 1984; Campbell et al., 1978). Perry (1989) reported that haloperidol remained effective when given over a period of 6 months to 60 autistic children.

At optimal doses, no untoward effects of haloperidol are noted. Above optimal doses or during dose regulation, excessive sedation is most common, followed by acute dystonic reactions (i.e., abrupt, frightening muscular contractions usually involving the head and neck and causing oculogyric crises, facial grimacing, torticollis, opisthotonos, and speech and swallowing difficulties), Parkinson-like movements (i.e., tremor, cogwheel rigidity, excessive salivation, masklike face, and stiffness of voluntary movement), and akathisia (i.e., motor restlessness). Acute dystonic reactions usually occur within 72 hours of the first dose of haloperidol; Parkinsonian movements and akathisia usually occur during the first 3 months of treatment. Acute dystonic reactions can be treated with Benadryl orally or intramuscularly. Parkinsonian movements and akathisia can be ameliorated by the administration of antiparkinsonian agents.

Long-term side effects of haloperidol include weight gain, withdrawal dyskinesia, and tardive dyskinesia. Symptoms of dyskinesia include slow involuntary movements of facial, buccal, and lingual muscles, and choreoathetoid movements of the trunk, limbs, or facial muscles. Withdrawal dyskinesia usually occurs within 2 weeks of haloperidol or other neuroleptics withdrawal and lasts for 4 months or less (Polizos & Engelhardt, 1978). Tardive dyskinesia may be permanent; currently no satisfactory treatment is available. Perry et al. (1985) noted that a minimum of 3 months' total cumulative exposure to drug is necessary for the development of dyskinesia. Hence, it is recommended that the dosage increments be gradual and made on a regular basis. Furthermore, about every 4–6 months the drug should be discontinued in order to determine whether the child needs further drug treatment (Campbell, Adams, Perry, Spencer, & Oveall 1988).

In summary, haloperidol is effective in the treatment of agitation, hyperactivity, aggression, stereotypic behaviors, and affective lability. It is less effective in the treatment of withdrawal behavior and in correcting impairment of cognition, communication, and social interaction.

Diphenylbutylpiperidine (Pimozide or Orap) is a potent dopamine antagonist. It is effective in reducing motor and vocal tics in Tourette disorder (Shapiro & Shapiro, 1984). After an oral dose of Pimozide, peak serum levels occur 6 to 8 hours. The mean serum elimination half-life in schizophrenic patients is approximately 55 hours. However, the correlation between plasma levels and clinical findings is not clear. In the treatment of Tourette disorder, the mean daily dose is about 7 mg and the maximum daily dose was 10 mg. Side effects include sedation, parkinsonian symptoms, and T-wave change of ECGs (Shapiro & Shapiro, 1984). It is recommended that pretreatment laboratory studies should include ECGs, vital signs, blood count, and liver profile. These measures should be monitored periodically (Campbell, Cohen, Perry, & Small, 1989).

In a study that compared haloperidol (0.75–6.75 mg/day) and Pimozide (1–4 mg/day) in 87 autistic children and adolescents, Pimozide was found to be superior to both haloperidol and placebo on behavioral ratings, and on global ratings the two drugs were equally superior to placebo (Naruse et al., 1982).

Stimulants

Since Bradley (1937) discovered in the late 1930s that amphetamines "subdued" behaviorally disordered children, stimulants including dextroamphetamine (Dexedrine), methylphenidate (Ritalin), and magnesium pemoline (Cylert) have gained wide usage in treating children with behavior disturbances.

The amphetamines and methylphenidate may enhance CNS catecholamine (norepinephrine and dopamine) release from sympathetic nerve terminals and inhibition of reuptake in the caudate nucleus. Absorption is fairly rapid following oral administration of both amphetamines and methylphenidate. Peak plasma concentrations are usually observed in 1–3 hours after an oral dose (Ebert, Vankammen, & Murphy, 1976). The mean half-life of amphetamine is about 6 hours. There is some correlation of peak concentration of dextroamphetamine with improvement in behavior variable in children. The half-life of methylphenidate is 2–7 hours. A dose of 0.3 mg/kg/day appears to be effective for short-term learning and testing; however, 0.7–1 mg/kg/day are required for long-term behavioral changes (Werry & Sprague, 1974). A sizeable number of studies of the stimulants in hyperactive/behavior-disordered children have been published from many medical centers. It is now generally accepted that stimulants are efficacious in decreasing restless, impulsive behaviors and improving attention span in these children. However, there is a relative lack of effect of stimulants on academic achievement and on interpersonal functioning.

The effects of stimulants have not been extensively studied in individuals with autism. Campbell et al. (1976) found that stimulants had only a mildly positive effect by improving attention, but showed clinically and statistically significant increases in stereotypic behavior in autistic children. Aman (1982) reviewed stimulants' effect in developmental disorders and concluded that there is no role for the use of stimulants in autistic population. These studies, however, included mostly lower-functioning autistic children. There are now many anecdotal reports of positive effects of stimulants in certain autistic children, particularly those with higher-functioning autism. The present author has prescribed methylphenidate to several higher-functioning autistic children. They all respond positively to the medication. In summary, stimulants may be considered in a higher-functioning autistic child without seizure or other neurological disorders, but for those in whom short attention span, distractibility, impulsivity, and excitability are significant symptoms.

Sedatives

The sedative–hypnotic group of medications such as benzodiazepines (diazepam or Valium) and diphenhydramine (Benadryl) have been studied for their effectiveness in a variety of conditions in childhood, including aggressiveness, hyperactivity, behavior disturbances, and anxiety disorder. In general, these drugs have been found to be no better than placebo or psychotherapy without medication. These drugs, however, seem to have a role in the treatment of sleep disorders in children. An initial dose of 5 mg per night of Valium is recommended in the treatment of sleep disorders including pavor nocturnis, somnambulism, and somniloqui. It can be increased by 5 mg until therapeutic effect is achieved. For other sleep disturbances such as increased sleep latency, excessive wakefulness, and excessive restlessness, Benadryl 1 mg/kg given 30 minutes before bedtime for 2–3 nights may alleviate or correct the disorder. However, in daily practice, it is not unusual that parents of autistic children report paradoxical excitatory responses with these sedatives. In these cases, Imipramine may be considered.

Side effects of the sedatives include CNS depression, drowsiness, and dizziness. There also have been reports of "paradoxical" aggressive reaction in some children (Kraft, Ardali, Duffy, Hart, & Pearce, 1965).

Beta Blockers

Propranolol (Inderal) has been reported as being effective in reducing severe and treatment-resistant aggressiveness directed against others or oneself. These reports, however, are based on uncontrolled trials or case reports involving nonautistic subjects. Furthermore, the patients were heterogeneous diagnostically (Campbell et al., 1989). Further studies are needed to determine the effects of beta blockers in autistic population. It would be very helpful to identify as many effective drugs as possible when dealing with severe aggressive behavior and/or self-injurious behavior in individuals with autism. Without effective treatments, these individuals most likely would be placed in mental institutions for long-term restricted treatment.

Antidepressants

There are two major classes of antidepressants: the *monoamine oxidase inhibitors* (MAOIs) and the *tricyclics*. There is no solid evidence of MAOIs therapeutic efficacy or of their safety in children (for a review, see Annell, 1972).

The tricyclic antidepressants presumably act on the CNS by inhibiting the uptake of neurotransmitters at adrenergic nerve terminals, resulting in an increase of monoamine neurotransmission. Imipramine (Tofranil) is the tricyclic most frequently used in children. After a single oral dose of 50 mg, relatively rapid absorption at steady-state conditions with peak level was seen in 1.5–3 hours. Half-lives for the terminal phase of elimination of imipramine range from 25 to 60 hours in children (Winsberg, Perel, Hurwic, & Klutch, 1974). A relationship between dose and plasma level cannot be clearly defined due to possible genetic differences in metabolism. However, a correlation between response and plasma concentration has been demonstrated in certain psychiatric disorders. Studies in children with behavior disorders show that clinical response roughly parallels the plasma level (Winsberg, Yepes, & Bialer, 1976).

In daily practice, many children who suffer from depression seem to respond to tricyclics. However, the superiority of these drugs over placebo has not been established in children (Campbell et al., 1989).

Tricyclics, specifically of imipramine, has been shown to be effective in enuresis (Rapoport et al., 1980), in attention deficit disorder with hyperactivity (Werry, Aman, & Diamond, 1980), and in school phobia (Gittleman-Klein & Klein, 1971). Onset of clinical response varies with the condition treated. In the treatment of enuresis, an effect can be seen in hours to a few days whereas a response in school phobia may not be apparent until 3–6 weeks.

In the treatment of enuresis in children over 7 years who fail to respond to nonmedical means, the usual starting dose of imipramine is 25 mg given at bedtime. This can be increased every other night until there is a clinical effect or to a total of 75 mg.

When imipramine is used in hyperactive children who cannot tolerate or do not respond to stimulants, the starting dose is 25 mg/day with increase at a rate of 25 mg every other day until there is clinical improvement or the maximum dose of 5 mg/kg/day has been reached.

There has been no controlled study of tricyclic use in the autistic population. However, in daily practice, tricyclic should be considered when there is clear evidence of depression in certain individuals with autism, or in autistic persons with severe hyperactivity and impulsivity who fail to respond to other means.

Side effects of tricyclics include dry mouth, nausea, anorexia, constipation, lethargy, tremors, sweating, insomnia, irritability, tachycardia, t-wave abnormalities, prolongation of P-R interval, widening of QRS, ventricular extrasystoles, bundle branch block, and hypotension. When tricyclics are used with amphetamines, hypertensive crises may develop (Kupfer & Detre, 1978). When tricyclics are used with Ritalin, serum level of the tricyclic may increase (Rapoport & Mikkelsen, 1978).

In recent years, several nontricyclic antidepressants had been introduced in the United States. Fluoxetine (Prozac) has been promoted as causing fewer adverse effects than other antidepressants. Fluoxetine is a selective inhibitor of serotonin reuptake in the CNS. Following a single oral 40 mg dose, peak plasma concentration of fluoxetine is observed after 6 to 8 hours. The elimination half-life is 1 to 3 days. The drug usually begins to act about 1 to 3 weeks after beginning treatment. It appears to be as effective as tricyclic antidepressants for treatment of depression in adults. There were also reports suggesting that fluoxetine might be effective in decreasing symptoms of Obsessive–Compulsive Disorder (OCD) (Fontaine & Chouinard, 1986). However, the effectiveness of fluoxetine in children has not been established. Recently, Riddle, Hardin, King, Seahill, & Woolson, (1990) reported significant decrease of obsessive–compulsive symptoms in 10 children and adolescents with OCD and/or Tourette disorder. Mehlinger, Scheftner, and Poznanski (1990) reported that fluoxetine appeared to improve the mood and ritualistic behavior in a 26-year-old autistic female. The present author and his associates have noted that fluoxetine seems to be most effective when a clear-cut superimposed depression is present in the autistic patients. It is not clear whether fluoxetine is effective in ritualistic or stereotyped behaviors in the four autistic patients (Ghaziuddin, Tsai, & Ghaziuddin, 1990).

Adverse effects of fluoxetine include nausea, nervousness, headache, insomnia, dry mouth, constipation, urinary retention, and urticaria or other skin rash. It may rarely precipitate seizures in patients with convulsive disorders.

Tricyclic Antiobsessional Antidepressants

Clomipramine (CMI or Anafranil) is an antiobsessional drug that belongs to the class of tricyclic antidepressants. It is presumed to influence obsessive and compulsive behaviors through its effects on serotonergic neuronal transmission due to its relatively selective capacity to inhibit the reuptake of serotonin. After a single 50 mg oral dose, maximum plasma concentration of CMI occur within 2–6 hours. After a 150 mg oral dose, the half-lives of CMI range from 19 hours to 37 hours.

The effectiveness of CMI for the treatment of obsessive–compulsive disorder was demonstrated in multicenter, placebo-controlled, parallel-group studies, including 10 weeks studies in adults, as well as children and adolescents 10–17 years of age (DeVeaugh-Geiss, Landau, & Katz, 1989; Leonard et al., 1989). The maximum daily dose is 250 mg for most adults and 3 mg/kg for all children and adolescents.

Recently, Gordon, Rapoport, Hamburger, and Mannheim (1990) completed a 10-week double-blind crossover trial of CMI in five children with autistic disorder. CMI was noted to be superior to baseline and placebo ratings for all measures except the NIMH Global Anxiety Scale. Larger studies are warranted to confirm the positive results.

The most common side effects of CMI are dry mouth, somnolence, tremor, dizziness, constipation, and ejaculatory failure. Lowering the dosage often reduces side effects when they occur, usually without loss of therapeutic benefit. CMI may lower seizure threshold.

Opiate Antagonists

Panksepp and Sahley (1987) suggested that there is a similarity between certain maladaptive behaviors in autistic persons and symptoms seen in adults who are opiate addicts. Recently, naltrexone, an opiate antagonist, has been given to two small groups of autistic children and has shown positive effects on social relatedness and self-injurious behavior (SIB) (Campbell, Adams, Perry et al., 1988; Herman, 1987). The therapeutic changes occurred at doses of 0.5 to 2.0 mg/kg/day. However, when the effect of naltrexone on SIB was tested in a larger sample (i.e., 36 autistic children), the naltrexone- and placebo-treated groups did not differ significantly regarding decline of SIB across (Campbell, Magee, Locascio, Lynch, & Anderson, 1990). Nevertheless, naltrexone merits further study in a larger sample of subjects using a double-blind and placebo-controlled research design.

Other Pharmacological Agents

Fenfluramine. It has been noted that about 30% of autistic persons have elevated serotonin levels as compared to normal controls (Ritvo, 1970). It has been known that fenfluramine has potent antiserotonergic activity in animal brains. Geller, Ritvo, Freeman, and Yuwiler (1982) reported preliminary findings of behavioral improvement associated with increased IQs in three autistic boys. In a larger sample of autistic children (14 outpatients) treated with fenfluramine, Ritvo, Freeman, Geller, and Yuwiler (1983) noted behavioral improvements including decreases of motility disturbance, restlessness, and "sensory symptoms" improvements in sleep pattern, increases in eye contact, socialization, and communicative language. IQ scores also seemed to increase.

However, subsequent data from nine medical centers with 81 patients participating showed less positive effects (Ritvo et al., 1986). One of the nine centers reported somewhat negative results (Leventhal, 1985). More recently, several independent research groups reported no significant improvements with fenfluramine as compared to the placebo effect (Campbell, Adams, Small et al., 1988; Ekman, Miranda-Linnè, Gillberg, Garle, & Wetterberg, 1989; Sherman, Factor, Swinson, & Darjes, 1989). There is considerable doubt on the efficacy of fenfluramine in autistic persons as a group (Campbell, Adams, Small et al., 1988).

Lithium. Lithium is a monovalent cation and the lightest alkali me*t*
In adult literature, lithium has a mood-reducing effect in manic disor*-*

may also reduce aggressiveness and hyperactivity in some individuals. Its exact mechanism of action in manic disorder is not fully known. Pharmacokinetic data of lithium in children are not available. In adults, absorption is rapid from the gastrointestinal tract with peak blood concentration at 2–4 hours after a single oral dose (Rapoport, Mikkelsen, & Werry, 1978). The half-life of lithium elimination is 24 hours and the onset of effect is 6–10 days.

The role of lithium in children is unclear. Only a few controlled studies are available. It appears that lithium is effective in reducing aggressive behavior in children of normal intelligence diagnosed as having conduct disorder. The therapeutic doses ranged from 500 to 2,000 mg per day, with plasma levels ranged from 0.32–1.51 mEq/l (Campbell et al., 1989).

There are uncontrolled studies that suggest lithium may have antiaggressive effect in children with mental retardation. To confirm this suggestion, controlled studies are needed.

Lithium has not been systematically studied in any autistic population diagnosed by contemporary criteria, that is, DSM-III or DSM-III-R classification. However, lithium should be considered in the treatment of autistic individuals who have clear bipolar affective illness, or in autistic persons with severe aggressive and/or self-injurious behavior but fail to respond to other antiaggressive medications.

The most common side effects of lithium include stomachache, anorexia, nausea, vomiting, diarrhea, tremor of hands, headache, and weight gain. Leukocytosis with lymphocytopenia, a decrease in thyroxine iodine, urinary frequency, and polyuria have also been reported. These side effects are usually minimal within the therapeutic range and often disappear after several weeks of use.

Clonidine. Clonidine (Catapres), an alpha-adrenergic agonist, has been reported as having therapeutic value in Tourette disorder (Leckman, 1982). It appears that clonidine stimulates alpha-adrenoreceptors in the brain stem, resulting in reduced sympathetic outflow from the central nervous system. However, the exact mechanism of its effect on Tourette disorder is not clear.

After an oral dose, the plasma level of clonidine peaks in approximately 3 to 5 hours and the plasma half-life ranges from 12 to 16 hours. In doses of 0.6–2.0 mg per day, clonidine seems to be helpful in decreasing compulsive behaviors, as well as aggressiveness, hyperactivity, and attentional difficulties. It is less effective in reducing tics as compared with haloperidol and pimozide. However, it has fewer side effects than haloperidol. Most side effects of clonidine are mild and tend to diminish with continued therapy. The frequent side effects include dry mouth, drowsiness, dizziness, constipation, and sedation.

Controlled studies of clonidine have not been conducted extensively in autistic children. Recently, Jaselskis, Cook, and Leventhal (1990) reported that clonidine seemed to be effective in reducing hyperactivity and irritability in some of the eight male autistic children who had not responded to other psychopharmacological treatments.

Further larger studies are warranted to determine whether clonidine is also effective in compulsive and aggressive behaviors.

Vitamins

"Megavitamin" therapy has become a popular form of treatment for a variety of psychiatric disorders. The proponents of orthomolecular psychiatry claim that "mega" doses of certain vitamins will ameliorate or prevent mental disorders such as schizophrenia, mental retardation, and autism.

There were two studies that had reported that autistic individuals showed significant improvement during vitamin B_6 (pyridoxine) treatment (Gualtieri, van Bourgondien, Hortz, Schopler, & Marcus, 1981; Rimland, Callaway, & Dreyfus, 1978). In these studies, the doses of vitamin B_6 ranged from 2.4 to 94.3 mg/kg or 300 to 900 mg per day. The minimum daily requirement of vitamin B_6 for adequate functioning of the nervous system is only about 2–4 mg. The reports of positive effect, however, were criticized for their flaws in research methodology. Subsequently, there were three double-blind crossover studies of the use of vitamin B_6 in autistic subjects (Ellman, 1981; Jonas, Etienne, Barthelemy, Jouve, & Mariotte, 1984; Martineau, Barthelemy, Garreau, & Lelord, 1985). All of the three studies used a combination of pyridoxine and magnesium. The doses of pyridoxine ranged from 15 to 30 mg/kg/day or 700 to 1,000 mg per day; the dose of magnesium ranged from 10 to 15 mg/kg/day or 380 to 500 mg per day. Significant behavior improvements were noted in some autistic children. However, the treatment periods were rather short (2 weeks to 30 days). The behavior scales used to evaluate the outcomes were not specific to autism.

The use of vitamin B_6 and magnesium may be helpful in some individuals with autism. However, there is no solid evidence supporting such a suggestion. Larger and long-term studies are needed to draw a final conclusion. It is strongly recommended that megavitamin treatment should be undertaken only when it is under the supervision of a knowledgeable and experienced physician because such a treatment is not completely free of toxic side effects.

Lowe, Cohen, Miller, and Young (1981) gave folic acid and B_{12} to an unselected group of children with autism. No significant change of behavior was noted in these children. Nonetheless, Hagerman et al. (1986) reported behavioral improvement in prepubertal boys with the fragile X syndrome treated with folate 10 mg per day. This finding calls for a trial of folate in autistic children since about 7.7% of autistic people also have fragile X syndrome (Brown, 1986). Gillberg, Whalstrom, Johansson, Tornblom, and Albertson-Wikland (1986) gave folate to four autistic boy with the fragile X syndrome but found no significant behavioral change. Nevertheless, this treatment warrants further exploration.

Diet

Feingold (1975) suggested that food additives might cause children's behavioral problems including hyperactivity and learning difficulties. He reported positive results in treating hyperactive children with an elimination diet that excluded artificial flavors and colors, as well as salicylates and other additives. Since then the dietary treatment has become quite popular and many clinicians and researchers have reported rather inconsistent results (for a review, see Kruesi & Rapoport, 1986). To date, the majority of the researchers in this field feel that dietary treatment may be helpful to a very small subgroup of children with hyperactivity.

The effect of "diet" on individuals with autism has not been systematically studied, though some parents and professionals enthusiastically advocate for it. Dietary treatment may be relatively safe. However, it should be undertaken only under the supervision of a knowledgeable dietician or physician to ensure the child's nutritional needs.

Anticonvulsants

The anticonvulsants of particular relevance are Phenobarbital and related barbiturates, Phenytoin (Dilantin), Carbamazepine (Tegretal), Ethosuximide (Zarontin), Valproate (Depakene), and Clonazepam (Clonopin). These anticonvulsants may act through two mechanisms to achieve their effect: direct modification of neuronal membrane function and alteration of neurotransmission (Menkes, 1985).

The objective in the treatment of the seizure disorder is complete control of seizures, or at least a reduction in their frequency to the point where they no longer interfere with physical and social well-being. It is not uncommon that a single anticonvulsant is all that is needed to achieve satisfactory seizure control in individuals with seizure disorder. In some cases, complete seizure control may not be possible. The acceptance of the occurrence of an occasional seizure is more appropriate than using multiple anticonvulsants for prolonged periods, which tends to cause cognitive and behavior side effects in persons with seizure disorder.

The general guidelines to anticonvulsant therapy are: (a) treatment should begin with one drug; if the drug does not control seizures, it is discontinued gradually while a second drug is instituted and its dosage is increased; (b) alterations in drug dosage should be made gradually, usually not more frequently than once every 5 to 7 days; (c) once seizures are controlled, the medication should be continued for a prolonged period of time; (d) determinations of anticonvulsant blood levels are necessary in all cases; and (e) anticonvulsant medication should be withdrawn gradually.

The following anticonvulsants are the most commonly used in controlling various types of seizure disorders:

Phenobarbital is absorbed slowly from the gastrointestinal tract, and at a dose of 4 mg/kg, 95% of the maximum serum level is reached in about 2 to 3 weeks (Buchthal, Svensmark, & Simonsen, 1968). The serum half-life of phenobarbital is about 96 hours. In treating grand mal seizures, the drug is effective at levels of 10 to 30 u/ml. These can be achieved by an oral dosage of about 4 to 5 mg/kg/day, given in two divided doses. Toxic levels of phenobarbital vary from one individual to another. However, no permanent sedation has been seen with levels below 35 ug/ml.

Phenobarbital and other barbiturate anticonvulsants may cause hyperactivity or drowsiness. These anticonvulsants may also cause initial impairment in cognitive functions, which disappears after the first year of therapy (Hellström & Barlach-Christoffersen, 1980).

Phenytoin is also slowly absorbed from the gastrointestinal tract. At a dose of 4 to 6 mg/kg/day, equilibrium levels in the blood are established between 7 and 10 days after initiation of therapy (Buchthal & Svensmark, 1960). The serum half-life of phenytoin is 13–46 hours. The average effective dose of phenytoin in children is 5 to 10 mg/kg/day, given at approximately 8-hour intervals. Clinically, phenytoin is effective in controlling tonic-clonic (grand mal) seizures and the therapeutic levels range from 10 to 20 ug/ml. However, it has lost considerable favor as a long-term anticonvulsant for use in children because of the wide variability in its absorption, the effect of other anticonvulsants, and the relatively high incidence of side effects (Menkes, 1985).

About 2% to 5% of patients receiving phenytoin develop fever, a morbilliform rash, and lymphadenopathy within 2 weeks of the start of therapy and with blood levels in the therapeutic range. After discontinuation of the medication, the symptoms clear (Dawson, 1973). At therapeutic level, prolonged phenytoin therapy causes gum hyperplasia, megaloblastic anemia, lower serum folate concentration, disturbed vitamin D metabolism resulting in hypocalcemic rickets, decreased serum calcium and phosphorus, increased alkaline phosphatase (Crosley, Chee, & Berman, 1975), and peripheral neuropathy. At toxic level, phenytoin may cause sedation, impairment of motor coordination and performance (e.g., ataxia), and negative effects on memory and learning, irreversible degeneration of the cerebellar Purkinje cells (Kokenge, Kutt, & McDowell, 1965), and aggravation of underlying behavior disorder.

Carbamazepine is chemically unrelated to any of the other major anticonvulsants. Individuals with psychomotor and grand mal seizures are most likely to benefit from the drug. Steady state blood level of carbamazepine is established between 5 and 10 days. The serum half-life of carbamazepine is 8–20 hours. The starting dosage in children aged 6 to 12 is 20 to 25 mg/kg/day (200 mg/day), and maximum dosage for effective seizure control in that age range is about 800 mg/day. Optimal therapeutic levels are between 4 and 12 ug/ml.

The most common side effect of carbamazepine is diplopia, which may disappear spontaneously or after reduction of drug dosage (Lesser, Pippenger, Ludus, & Dinner, 1984). Other side effects include rashes, hyponatremia, hepatic dysfunction, and leukopenia. Carbamazepine may also cause hyperactivity, irritability, insomnia (Rivinius, 1982), memory impairment, assaultive behavior, agitation, and motor and phonic tics (Evans & Gualtieri, 1985). Such effects may occur at low doses and at low blood levels of such anticonvulsants.

Ethosuximide is the most effective drug for treatment of absence (petit mal) seizures. Starting doses for children are 250 mg twice daily or 20 mg/kg/day. Steady state blood level is reached between 5 and 8 days. The serum half-life of ethosuximide is about 30 hours. Optimal therapeutic plasma levels are between 40 and 100 ug/ml.

Side effects of ethosuximide are rare. They include gastrointestinal upsets, skin rashes, headaches, and occasional reversible leukopenia (Menkes, 1985)

Valproic Acid (VPA) or Valproate (Depakene) is highly effective in controlling minor motor, grand mal, petit mal, and simple partial seizures. Starting dosages for children are 15 to 20 mg/kg/day given two to three times a day. The dose is increased at weekly intervals to a level that provides seizure control, usually in the range of 20 to 70 mg/kg/day. Steady blood level is reached in about 4 days. The serum half-life of VPA is short, about 6 to 15 hours. However, correlation between blood levels and therapeutic effects or adverse reactions has not been established.

Side effects of VPA include gastrointestinal upsets, increased appetite and weight gain, hepatic dysfunction, sedation, tremor, and asterixis. These side effects tend to develop when the patients are receiving polytherapy.

Clonazepam is an effective anticonvulsant for most types of minor motor seizures, particularly akinetic and atypical petit mal seizures. It appears that clonazepam is most effective when given in conjunction with phenobarbital or other anticonvulsants (Wilensky, Ojemonn, Temkin, Troupin, & Dodrill, 1981). The drug is given in gradually increasing dosages beginning at

0.05 mg/kg/day in 3 or 4 divided doses, and increased by 0.05 mg/kg every fifth to seventh day until seizures are controlled or until a dose of 0.25 mg/kg is reached. Thereafter, the dose is raised more slowly to 0.5 mg/kg if needed, or until side effects are encountered (Menkes, 1985). In general, it may need 14 days to reach the steady state blood level. The serum half-life of clonazepam is 22–33 hours. At present, the relationship of blood levels to therapeutic and toxic effects of clonazepam is uncertain.

Clonazepam may cause sedation, memory impairment, depression, excessive weight gain, ataxia, dysarthria, and paradoxical excitement or disinhibition (Rivinius, 1982).

Clinical Indications for Pharmacotherapy in Autism

The following clinical conditions in autism and associated psychiatric disorders are potentially drug responsive. In some of the conditions, administration of the previously mentioned drugs has been based on well-documented research. However, the efficacy of drug therapy in other conditions requires further research. Here, I make suggestions based on the limited clinical, empirical experience and a few other investigators, as little research has been done in this field.

Unusual Patterns of Behavior

Resistance to Change

Autistic children are disturbed by changes in the familiar environment, and tantrums may follow even a minor change of everyday routine. Many autistic children line up toys or objects and become very distressed if these are disturbed. The behavior is twice as common in retarded autistic children as in those with normal intelligence. Almost all autistic children show a resistance to learning or practicing a new activity.

Ritualistic or Compulsive Behaviors

In childhood, ritualistic or compulsive behaviors usually involve rigid routines (e.g., insistence on eating particular foods) or stereotyped repetitive motor acts, such as hand clapping or finger mannerisms (e.g., twisting, flicking movements carried out near the face). Some children develop preoccupations, such as spending a great deal of time memorizing weather information, state capitals, or birth dates of family members. In adolescence, some of these behaviors may develop into obsessional symptoms (e.g., repeatedly asking the same question that must be answered in a specific manner) and compulsive behaviors (e.g., compulsive touching of certain objects). Ritualistic or compulsive behaviors are more often displayed by autistic children of normal intelligence than by autistic children with mental retardation.

Abnormal Attachments

Many autistic children develop intense attachments to odd objects, such as pipe cleaners, small plastic toys, and the like. The child may carry the object at all times and protest or throw tantrums if it is removed.

Unusual Responses to Sensory Experiences

There may be a fascination with lights, patterns, sounds, spinning objects, and tactile sensations. Objects often are manipulated without regard to their usual functions. Thus young autistic children may perseveratively line up, stack, or twirl objects. The children may repetitively flush toilets or turn on and off light switches. There may be a perseverative preoccupation with certain features of objects, such as their texture, taste, smell, color, or shape. Some autistic children may follow extreme food fads.

Drug of Choice. *Haloperidol* or *clomipramine* should be considered for stereotypies and/or compulsive behaviors.

Disturbance of Motility

Many young autistic children are markedly overactive but tend to become underactive in adolescence. Many autistic persons display tic-like symptoms such as grimacing, hand flapping or twisting, toe walking, lunging, jumping, darting or pacing, body rocking and swaying, and head rolling or banging. In some cases they may appear intermittently, whereas in other cases they are continuously present. They are usually interrupted by episodes of immobility and odd posturing with head bowed and arms flexed at the elbow. Many children exhibit body tensing movements when they are excited about or absorbed in some sensory experience, such as watching a spinning toy.

Drug of Choice. Hyperactivity, attention deficit, and impulsiveness: *Haloperidol* for *low*- or *middle*-functioning individuals with or without other neurological disorders such as seizure disorders, Tourette disorder, and the like is recommended. *Clonidine* or *Tofranil* should be considered in patients who either no longer or do not respond to haloperidol. In *high* functioning individuals without other neurological disorders, *stimulants* such as *Ritalin* should be tried first. *Haloperidol, clonidine,* and *Tofranil* should be considered in patients who do not respond to stimulants or in patients with other neurological disorders. For tic-like symptoms: *Haloperidol* should be tried first. *Clonidine* is the next drug of choice.

Social Withdrawal

Although both low-IQ and high-IQ autistic children are similar in terms of the main symptoms associated with autism, those with a lower IQ show a more severely impaired social development and are more likely to display deviant social responses, such as touching or smelling people.

Drug of Choice. For social withdrawal, *naltrexone* should be considered.

Associated Features of Autism

Affect

The affective expression of autistic persons may be flattened, excessive, or inappropriate to the situation. Their mood often is labile; sobbing, crying, or screaming may be unexplained or inconsolable; hysterical laughing and giggling may occur for no obvious reason. Major depression may occur during adolescence and adult life. The depression may be a reaction to partial realization of handicaps. This is more likely seen in those of higher level of ability. However, depression also can be seen in lower functioning individuals.

Drug of Choice. In individuals with strong family history of unipolar affective illness, tricyclic antidepressant such as desipramine or other antidepressant such as fluoxetine should be considered. Lithium may be the drug of choice in patients with family history of bipolar affective illness.

Seizure

Seizure has been noted in between one quarter and one third of autistic persons. Several reports have suggested that many autistic individuals develop first seizures in adolescence (Deykin & MacMahon, 1979; Rutter, 1984). Recently, Volkmar and Nelson (1990) reported that risk for developing seizures in the autistic subjects is highest during early childhood. The seizure types are varied. However, the most common type is the generalized, major motor (tonic–clonic) seizure.

Autistic people who develop seizures are likely to require long-term anticonvulsant treatment. The selection of the drug for the treatment depends on the type of seizure. Drugs of choice are presented in Table 8.1.

TABLE 8.1
Drugs Used in Autism and Associated Medical/Psychiatric Disorders*

Complication or Disorder	*Generic Name (Trade Name)*	*Start Dose (mg)*	*Daily Dosage*	
			Range (mg)	*(mg/kg)*
Attention Deficit & Hyperactivity	Methylphenidate	0.3/kg		0.3-1.0
	Dextroamphetamine (Dexedrine)	0.15-0.3/kg		0.15-0.5
	Magnesium pemoline (Cylert)	37.5/day	56.25-75	0.5-2.5
	Clonidine (Catapres)	0.05/day	0.2-0.4	0.004-0.005
	Imipramine (Tofranil)	0.5/kg	25-200	0.5-3.5
	Desipramine	10-25/day		5
Aggressiveness	Haloperidol (Haldol)	0.02-0.5/kg	0.5-16	0.1-0.5
	Lithium carbonate (Eskalith or Lithobid)	150/day	300-2400	
	Propranolol (Inderal)	30/day	50-960	up to 20
Self-injury & Withdrawal	Naltrexone	0.5/kg		0.5-2.0
Sterotypies & Obsessive-Compulsive Disorder	Clomipramine (Anagranil)	25/day	maximum 200	maximum 3
	Haloperidol	0.02-0.05/kg	0.5-16	0.1-0.5
Tic Disorders	Haloperidol	0.25/day	0.5-10	
	Pimozide (Orap)	1-2/day	maximum 10	maximum 0.2
	Clonidine	0.001-0.002/kg	0.15-0.6	
Major Depression	Imipramine	0.5	100-300	1.0-5.0
	Fluoxetine (Prozac)	20/day	20-80	
Bipolar Affective Disorder	Lithium carbonate	300/day	300-2400	

Anxiety Disorders	Imipramine	0.5/kg	100-200	1.0-5.0
	Chlordiazepoxide (Librium)	5-10/kg	45-90	
	Clomipramine	25/day	maximum 200	maximum 3
Schizophrenia	Haloperidol	0.02-0.5/kg	0.5-16	0.5
	Thiothixene (Navane)	6-10/day	20-30	
	Thioidazine (Mellaril)	20-30/day		maximum 3
	Chlorpromazine (Thorazine)	1/lb	50-200	
Sleep Disorders				
Insomnia	Diphenhydramine (Benadryl)	25-50/day	25-500	2.0-5.0
	Hydroxyzine (Vistaril or Atarax)	0.6/kg	25-100	5
	Chloral Hydrate (Noctec)	500/day	500-1000	
	Imipramine	10/day	10-50	
Night Terrors	Diazepam (Valium)	1/day	1-20	
Enuresis	Imipramine	0.5/kg	25-125	0.5-2.5
Seizure Disorders				
Tonic-clonic (Grand mal)	Phenobarbitol	4-5/kg		2-6
	Phenytoin (Delantin)	4-8/kg		5-10
	Carbamazepine	20-25/kg	400-800	10-30
	Primidone (Mysoline)	50/day	150-500	10-20
Absence (Petit mal)	Ethosuccimide (Zarontin)	20/kg		20-40
	Valproate (Depakene)	15-20/kg		30-60
	Clonazepam (Clonopin)	0.05/kg		0.01-0.15
Psychomotor & Focal	Carbamazepine	20-25/kg	400-800	10-30
	Primidone	50/day	150-500	10-20
	Phenobarbital	4-5/kg		2-6
	Phenytoin	4-8/kg		5-10
	Valproate	15-20/kg		30-60

Aggression

Some autistic individuals may become aggressive and physically attack other people. Some of the aggressive behaviors may relate to frustrations of these individuals. Much of the aggressive behaviors, however, do not seem to have any clear cause. They are of great concern because of their more devastating effect.

Drug of Choice. In individuals who exhibit frequent aggressive behaviors and who do not respond to behavioral interventions, *haloperidol* may be the drug of choice. *Lithium* and *propranolol* may be considered in patients who fail to respond to *haloperidol* treatment.

Self-Injurious Behavior

Self-injurious behavior, such as head-banging, finger-, hand-, or wrist-biting, or face- or extremities-scratching may occur in lower functioning individuals.

Drug of Choice. *Naltrexone* should be the drug of first choice. *Haloperidol* may be considered in individuals who do not respond to naltrexone treatment.

Unusual Sleep Pattern

Unusual sleeping patterns are common. Many autistic children seem to need much less sleep than most normal children. These children tend to keep the whole family awake every night because of their sleep disturbances. Some children develop complete reversed sleep pattern, that is, they sleep during the day and wake during the night.

Drug of Choice. *Chloral hydrate* may be the drug of first choice. Some autistic children may respond to antihistamines such as *diphenhydramine* and *hydroxyzine*. In other more severe cases, tricyclic antidepressant such as *imipramine* may be considered.

Autistic-like Disorders

Rett Syndrome

Children with Rett syndrome develop "autistic features" during Rapid Developmental Regression stage (Stage II, usually appears at 1–2 years of age). The features include: no sustained interest in persons or objects, stereotypic responses to environmental stimuli, absent or very limited interpersonal contact, manifestation of great anxiety and apparent fear when confronted with an unfamiliar situation, or even without evident stimulation, loss of already acquired elements of language, stereotypic hand movements such as "hand-washing" movements in front of the mouth or chest and rubbing motions of the hands, and repetitive blows on the teeth, grabbing of the tongue, and other movements (Rett, 1966). However, the clinical course is quite different, with Rett syndrome progressing from relatively normal development till about 6 months of age, to various forms of progressive neurological impairment that is not seen in autism. Nonetheless, it is most likely that in the near future Rett syndrome and autism will be considered as subtypes of Pervasive Developmental Disorders (PDDs) by the American Psychiatric Association's Diagnostic and Statistical Manual of Mental Disorders, 4th edition (DSM IV), and by the World Health Organization's International Classification of Diseases, 10th revision (ICD-10).

Medical Treatment. Appropriate anticonvulsants should be given to children who develop epilepsy, which is common during Stagnation stage (Stage III, usually appears at 3–4 years of age). Several investigators have reported that *carbamazepine* seems to be the most effective single anticonvulsant, especially in patients with a predominance of complex partial seizures (Trevathan & Naidu, 1988). The medication should be carefully monitored. Most patients become wheelchair-bound during Late Motor Deterioration stage (Stage IV, usually appears during school age). General treatment should be directed toward correction of malnutrition, anemia, and electrolyte disturbances that may be caused by the patient's immobilized status. Exercises and physical therapy should be given to prevent muscle weakness and wasting. The skin over the coccyx and ischial tuberosities must be inspected daily.

Disintegrative Disorders

Disintegrative disorders are a group of childhood disorders that roughly fit Heller's account of dementia infantilis (Heller, 1954): a progressive intellectual deterioration with, ultimately, the appearance of neurologic signs. In these conditions, development usually appears normal or near-normal up to the age of 3 or 4 years, at which time there is a profound regression and behavioral disintegration. There is a loss of speech and language, social skills, and interest in objects. Interpersonal relationships are impaired. There is development of stereotypies and mannerisms. Sometimes these disorders develop after some clear-cut organic brain disease. More often there are no clinical signs of neurologic damage, but the subsequent course and postmortem studies often reveal some kind of organic cortical degeneration (Rutter, 1977). The patterns of symptomatology differ in crucial aspects from autism. Nevertheless, Disintegrative disorders most likely will also be considered as subtypes of PDDs by both DSM IV and ICD-10.

Medical Treatment. Children with Disintegrative Disorder require more general health care including frequent clinic visits, proper diet and nutrition, prevention of infections, dental care, and physical fitness. Close neurologic monitoring and medical follow-up are essential in epileptic individuals receiving anticonvulsant. Medications such as *haloperidol, benzodiazepines,* and *anticonvulsants* have been used to modify behavior, but generally have not been effective (Evans-Jones & Rosenbloom, 1978). Psychotropic, antidepressant, and psychoactive medications should not be used to control "overactive behavior," "noisiness," "aggression," and "agitation" in persons with Disintegrative Disorder. These medications should be used to treat their concomitant psychiatric disorder.

Other Psychiatric Disorders

Obsessive and Compulsive Disorder

Bartak and Rutter (1976) noted that about 68% of the normally intelligent autistic children had shown rituals. About 80% of these children also had "quasi-obsessive behaviors." Difficult adaptation to new situations was found in about 74% of these children. Unusual play activities such as repeating dialogue from radio and television, continually talking about and playing with a single toy, or repetitively writing or drawing numbers, words, and maps, have been observed in higher functioning autistic children (Shea & Mesibov, 1985).

Some of these obsessive and/or compulsive symptoms have obvious similarities to those seen in Obsessive Compulsive Disorder (OCD). However, in the classic OCD, the developmental history is usually within normal limits. People with an OCD struggle against their compulsions, often develop a dysphoric mood, and become irritable, tense, and depressed. Although their symptoms may interfere with their usual social activities or relationships with others, individuals with an OCD almost always develop and maintain an interest in their environment and do not have deviant social skills in terms of relating with other people.

Due to difficulties in communicating with other people, as well as in showing appropriate affect, autistic individuals do not seem to resist their compulsions, or to complain about the compulsive acts, or to manifest distress. This raises the possibility that clinicians may hesitate to diagnose superimposed OCD in persons with Autism. However, it is conceivable that in some higher functioning autistic people "quasi-obsessive behaviors" reflect true symptoms of a coexisting OCD.

Drug of Choice. Clomipramine should be considered in individuals who exhibit "quasi-obsessive and compulsive behaviors" and who do not have seizure disorders.

Gilles de la Tourette Syndrome

Compulsive and ritualistic behaviors (e.g., keeping objects neatly arranged and routines unchanged, compulsive touching of people and things nearby, compulsive shouting and swearing, echoing of words, sounds, and actions) that can occur in the syndrome of Gilles de la Tourette (or the syndrome of chronic multiple tics) resemble some phenomena occurring in autism. Separating the symptoms of Tourette syndrome from the symptoms of autism can be difficult sometimes. However, the examination of the total behavior pattern and developmental history should make the diagnosis clear. Patients with Tourette Syndrome are often aware of their disorder. They are frightened and are distressed because they do not feel that they can control it. They usually do not have significantly delayed and deviant language and speech development and their tics often have a waxing and waning pattern.

However, some recent studies have described the development of Tourette syndrome in autistic individuals (Barabas & Matthews, 1983; Realmuto & Main, 1982). The present author has also seen a few such cases. It is, however, unclear how frequently the two disorders might occur coincidentally. It is also uncertain how this finding might be linked to the etiology of the two disorders. This remains one of many areas requiring further investigation.

Drug of Choice. In patients with the tic-like symptoms described or with a clear diagnosis of Tourette disorder, *haloperidol* should be tried first. The next drugs of choice are *Pimozide* and *clonidine.*

Schizophrenia in Childhood and Adolescence

Most autistic individuals do manifest prodromal or residual symptoms of schizophrenia such as social isolation, impairment in role functioning or grooming, inappropriate affect, and so on. Many higher functioning autistic people exhibit illogical thinking, incoherence, and poverty in content of speech. Their lack of nonverbal communication may be seen as exhibiting blunt affect. Autistic people's inappropriate laughing or weeping due to inability to comprehend the meaning of events may be interpreted as labile or abnormal affect. Some higher functioning verbal autistic persons have strange beliefs (e.g., some may believe there is no air in other states;), idiosyncratic interests (e.g., spending enormous amount of time studying dinosaurs), or sensory experiences (e.g., seeing other people's faces in the air when alone in the room) bordering on delusions or hallucinations. However, one well-established finding is that autistic children almost never develop a thought disorder with delusions and hallucinations. Only a few well-diagnosed autistic children have been reported to have developed schizophrenia during follow-up periods (Petty, Ornitz, Michelman, & Zimmerman, 1984).

Drug of Choice. In individuals who develop clear delusions, hallucinations, and bizarre behaviors including catatonia, haloperidol would be the drug of first choice. Other antipsychotic medications such as Thiothixene (Navan) and Loxapine (Loxitane) are the second line of drugs of choice.

SIDE EFFECTS OF PHARMACOTHERAPY

Many of the side effects of neuroleptic, antidepressant, lithium, and anticonvulsant seen in adult patients also can be seen in children and adolescents. Of particular concern are the short-term anticholinergic (e.g., constipation, tremors, sweating, insomnia, and irritability) and cardiovascular (e.g., tachycardia, hypotension, and arrhythmias) side effects of the tricyclic antidepressants, and the cognitive (e.g., cognitive blunting) and extrapyramidal side effects (e.g., acute dystonia, dyskinesia, parkinsonian reactions, akathisia, rabbit syndrome) of neuroleptics, and the long-term abnormal involuntary movements (i.e., tardive dyskinesia and withdrawal dyskinesias) of neuroleptics, and effects of many drugs on height, weight, blood counts, and liver function. In addition, due to cognitive and communicative impairments, individuals with autism often become frightened or suspicious if a sudden change or dysfunction occurs following the administration of drug(s). Such feelings may trigger tantrums or interfere with compliance.

It is essential that the clinician is knowledgeable of the full range of side effects of the drug(s) being prescribed and knows how to manage side effects should they arise. Nevertheless, the best approach of managing adverse effects is preventive. The following are general guidelines to avoid possible side effects:

1. Obtain a complete family history including drug treatments and responses and a complete medical history (including responses to previous drug treatment) of the patient.
2. Treatment should begin with one drug.

3. Avoid giving the same drug that had demonstrated previous side effects in the individual.
4. Avoid giving *preventive* anti-side effect medication such as antiparkinsonian agent.
5. If the patient does not respond to the drug of first choice, it is discontinued gradually while a second drug is instituted and its dosage is increased.
6. Use the lowest possible maintenance doses in the therapeutic range once it has been established.
7. Regularly monitor the blood level of the drug, blood counts, blood pressure, pulse rate, EKG, liver function, height, and weight.
8. Give periodic drug holidays, at least once every 6 months.
9. In most cases, drugs should be tapered and withdrawn gradually.

SUMMARY

An overview of medical treatment, particularly pharmacotherapy in individuals with autism and related disorders, was presented. Recent advances in drug treatment in autism and other childhood psychiatry disorders were highlighted. The drug treatment of autism is symptomatic. Autistic people are treated with medications for the maladaptive behaviors that may develop during the course of their lives, as well as that may be caused by underlying organic brain syndromes/neurological disorders. Autistic people may also be treated with drugs for the concomitant psychiatric disorders. However, the target symptoms/maladaptive behaviors in autistic people are viewed as results of these individuals' inability to cope with the environmental demands and physical discomfort, as well as their suffering from disturbed neurochemical and neurophysiological function. Further, the use of drugs in this population was viewed only as one component of a total treatment plan for the individuals. Nevertheless, there are data suggesting that with an appropriate evaluation, predrug work-ups, a specific diagnosis, and multiple measures of outcome, pharmacotherapy is a safe and efficacious treatment for some symptoms in autistic persons. The data presented in this chapter, however, were obtained mainly from autistic children treated with neuroleptics. A great deal of work remains to be done with other drugs as well as with adolescents and adults with autism. Future research should also put more emphasis on studying the efficacy of combined treatments such as pharmacothery with behavioral therapy, or group therapy with drug therapy. It is highly unlikely that certain medication(s) can be developed that would be curative for autism. It is, however, highly possible, with improving knowledge of comprehensive treatment including pharmacotherapy, to promote the autistic person's more normal social and linguistic developments as well as to minimize the autistic individual's maladaptive behaviors (e.g., hyperactivity, stereotypies, self-injury, aggressiveness), which interfere with or are incompatible with the individual's functioning and learning.

REFERENCES

Aman, M. C. (1982). Stimulant drug effects in developmental disorders and hyperactivity: Toward a resolution of disparate findings. *Journal of Autism and Developmental Disorders, 12,* 385–398.

Anderson, L. T., Campbell, M., Grega, D. M., Perry, R., Small, A. M., & Green, W. H. (1984). Haloperidol in the treatment of infantile autism: Effects on learning and behavior symptoms. *American Journal of Psychiatry, 141,* 1195–1202.

Annell, A. L. (1972). *Depressive states in childhood and adolescence.* Stockholm: Almquist & Wiksell.

Barabas, G., & Matthews, W. S. (1983). Coincident infantile autism and Tourette syndrome: A case report. *Journal of Developmental Pediatrics, 4,* 280–281.

Bartak, L., & Rutter, M. (1976). Differences between mentally retarded and normally intelligent autistic children. *Journal of Autism and Childhood Schizophrenia, 6,* 109–120.

Bradley, C. (1937). The behavior of children receiving benzedrine. *American Journal of Psychiatry, 94,* 577–578.

Brown, W. T., Jenkins, E. C., Cohen, I. L., Fish, G. S., Wolf-Schein, E. G., Gross, A., Waterhouse, L., Fein, D., Mason-Brothers, A., Ritvo, E., Ruttenberg, B. A., Bentley, W., & Castells, S. (1986). Fragile X and autism: A multicenter survey. *American Journal of Medical Genetics, 23,* 341–352.

Buchthal, F., & Svensmark, O. (1960). Aspects of the pharmacology of phenytoin (Dilantin) and phenobarbital relevant to their dosage in the treatment of epilepsy. *Epilepsia, 1,* 373–384.

Buchthal, F., Svensmark, O., & Simonsen, H. (1968). Relation of EEG and seizures to phenobarbital in serum. *Archives of Neurology, 19,* 567–572.

Campbell, M., Adams, P., Perry, R., Spencer, E. K., & Overall, J. E. (1988). Tardive and withdrawal dyskinesia in autistic children: A prospective study. *Psychopharmacology Bulletin, 24,* 251–255.

Campbell, M., Adams, P., Perry, R., Tesch, L. McV., & Curren, E. L. (1988). Naltrexone in infantile autism. *Psychopharmacology Bulletin, 24,* 135–139.

Campbell, M., Adams, P., Small, A. M., Curren, E. L., Overall, J. E., Anderson, L. T., Lynch, N., & Perry, R. (1988). Efficacy and safety of fenfluramine in autistic children. *Journal of the American Academy of Child and Adolescent Psychiatry, 27,* (4), 434–439.

Campbell, M., Anderson, L. T., Meier, M., Cohen, I. L., Small, A. M., Samit, C., & Sachar, E. (1978). A comparison of haloperidol and behavior therapy and their interaction in autistic children. *Journal of the American Academy of Child Psychiatry, 17,* 640–655.

Campbell, M., Anderson, L. T., Small, A. M., Perry, R., Green, W. H., & Caplan, R. (1982). The effects of haloperidol on learning and behavior in autistic children. *Journal of Autism and Developmental Disorders, 12,* 167–175.

Campbell, M., Cohen, I. L., Perry, R., & Small, A. M. (1989). Psychopharmacological treatment. In T. H. Ollendick & M. Hersen (Eds.), *Handbook of child psychopathology* (2nd ed., pp. 473–497) New York: Plenum Press.

Campbell, M., Magee, H., Locascio, J. J., Lynch, N., & Anderson, L. T. (1990). The effect of naltrexone on self-injurious behavior in autistic children. *American Academy of Child and Adolescent Psychiatry, Scientific Proceedings of the Annual Meeting,* VI:49.

Campbell, M., & Palij, M. (1985). Behavior and cognitive measures used in psychopharmacological studies of infantile autism. *Psychopharmacology Bulletin, 21,* 1047–1053.

Campbell, M., Small, A. M., Collins, P. J., Friedman, E., David, R., & Genieser, N. (1976). Levodopa and Levoamphetamine: A crossover study of young schizophrenic children. *Current Therapeutic Research, 19,* 70–86.

Campbell, M., Small, A. M., Green, W. H., Jennings, S. J., Perry, R., Bennett, W. G., & Anderson, L. (1984). Behavioral efficacy of haloperidol and lithium carbonate: A comparison in hospitalized aggressive children with conduct disorder. *Archives of General Psychiatry, 41,* 650–656.

Conners, C. K. (1973). Rating scales for use in drug studies with children. *Psychopharmacology Bulletin* (Special Issue—Pharmacotherapy with children), 24–84.

Crosley, C. J., Chee, C., & Berman, P. H. (1975). Rickets associated with long-term anticonvulsant therapy in a pediatric outpatient population. *Pediatrics, 56,* 52–57.

Curry, S. H. (1978). Pharmacokinetics and psychotropic drugs. *Psychological Medicine, 8,* 177–180.

Dalldorf, J. S. (1983). Medical needs of the autistic adolescent. In E. Schopler & G. B. Mesibov (Eds.), *Autism in adolescents and adults* (pp. 149–168). New York: Plenum Press.

Dawson, K. P. (1973). Severe cutaneous reactions to phenytoin. *Archives of Disease in Childhood, 48,* 239.

DeVeaugh-Geiss, J., Landau, P., & Katz, R. (1989). Treatment of obsessive-compulsive disorder with clomipramine. *Psychiatry Annal, 19,* 97–101.

Deykin, E. Y., & MacMahon, B. (1979). The incidence of seizures among children with autistic symptoms. *American Journal of Psychiatry, 126,* 1310–1312.

Ebert, M. H., Vankammen, D. P., & Murphy, D. L. (1976). Plasma levels of amphetamine and behavioral response. In L. A. Gotschalk & S. Merlis (Eds.), *Pharmacokinetics of psychoactive drugs.* New York: Spectrum Publications.

Ekman, G., Miranda-Linnè, F., Gillberg, C., Garle, M., & Wetterberg, L. (1989). Fenfluramine treatment of 20 children with autism. *Journal of Autism and Developmental Disorders, 4,* 511–532.

Ellman, G. (1981). *Pyridoxine effectiveness on autistic patients at Sonoma State Hospital.* Paper presented at the Research Conference on Autism, San Diego.

Engelhardt, D. M., Polizos, P., Waizer, J., & Hoffman, S. P. (1973). A double-blind comparison of fluphenazine and haloperidol. *Journal of Autism and Childhood Schizophrenia, 3,* 128–137.

Evans, R. W., & Gualtieri, C. T. (1985). Carbamazepine: A neuropsychological and psychiatric profile. *Clinical Neuropharmacology, 83,* 221–241.

Evans-Jones, L. G., & Rosenbloom, L. (1978). Disintegrative psychosis in childhood. *Developmental Medicine and Child Neurology, 20,* 462–470.

Feingold, B. F. (1975). *Why your child is hyperactive.* New York: Random House.

Fontaine, R., & Chouinard, G. (1986). An open clinical trial of fluoxetine in the treatment of obsessive-compulsive disorder. *Journal of Clinical Psychopharmacology, 6,* 98–101.

Freeman, B. J., Ritvo, E. R., Yokota, A., & Ritvo, A. (1986). A scale for rating symptoms of patients with the syndrome of autism in real life settings. *Journal of the American Academy of Child Psychiatry, 25,* 130–136.

Geller, E., Ritvo., E. R., Freeman, B. J., & Yuwiler, A. (1982). Preliminary observations on effect of fenfluramine on blood serotonin and symptoms in three autistic boys. *New England Journal of Medicine, 307,* 165–169.

Ghaziuddin, M., Tsai, L. Y., & Ghaziuddin, N. (1990). *Fluoxetine in autism: More useful in the presence of depression.* Manuscript submitted for publication.

Gillberg, C., Whalstrom, L., Johansson, R., Tornblom, M., & Albertson-Wikland, K. (1986).

Folic acid as an adjunct in the treatment of children with the autism fragile X syndrome (AFRAX). *Developmental Medicine and Child Neurology, 28,* 624–627.

Gittleman-Klein, R., & Klein, D. F. (1971). Controlled imipramine treatment of school phobia. *Archives of General Psychiatry, 25,* 204–207.

Gordon, C., Rapoport, J., Hamburger, M. S., & Mannheim, G. (1990). *Differential response of autistic disorder to clomipramine.* Scientific Proceeding of the Annual Meeting of the American Academy of Child and Adolescent Psychiatry, VI, 48.

Gualtieri, C. T., van Bourgondien, M. E., Hartz, C., Schopler, E., & Marcus, L. (1981). *A pilot study of pyridoxine treatment in autistic children.* Paper presented at the American Psychiatric Association meeting, New Orleans.

Hagerman, R. J., Jackson, A. W., Levitas, A., Bracken, M., McBogg, P., Kemper, M., McGravian, L., Berry, R., Matus, I., & Hagerman, P. J. (1986). Oral folic acid versus placebo in the treatment of males with the fragile X syndrome. *American Journal of Medical Genetics, 23,* 241–246.

Heller, T. (1954). Dementia infantilis: trans Hulse WC. *Journal of Nervous and Mental Disorder,* (119), 471–477.

Hellström, B., & Barlach-Christoffersen, M. (1980). Influence of phenobarbital on the psychomotor development and behaviour in preschool children with convulsions. *Neuropädiatrie, 11,* 151.

Herman, B. H., Hammock, M. K., Arthur-Smith, A., Egan, J., Chatoor, I., Werner, A., & Zelnik, N. (1987). Naltrexone decreases self-injurious behavior. *Annals of Neurology, 22,* 550–552.

Jaselskis, C. A., Cook, E. H., & Leventhal, B. L. (1990). *Clonidine treatment of hyperactive and impulsive children with autistic disorder.* Scientific Proceeding of the Annual Meeting of American Academy of Child and Adolescent Psychiatry, VI, 46–47.

Jonas, C., Etienne, T., Barthelemy, C., Jouve, J., & Mariotte, N. (1984). Intérèt clinique et biochimique de i'association vitamine B_6 + magnesium dans le traitement de l'autisme résiduel è l'âge adults. *Therapie, 39,* 661–669.

Kokenge, R., Kutt, H., & McDowell, F. (1965). Neurological sequelae following dilantin overdose in a patient and in experimental animals. *Neurology, 15,* 823.

Kraft, I. A., Ardali, E., Duffy, J. H., Hart, J. T., & Pearce, P. (1965). A clinical study of chlordiazepoxide used in psychiatric disorders of children. *International Journal of Neuropsychiatry, 1,* 433–437.

Kruesi, M. J. P., & Rapoport, J. L. (1986). Diet and human behavior: How much do they affect each other? *Annual Review on Nutrition, 6,* 113–130.

Kupfer, D. J., & Detre, T. P. (1978). Tricyclic and monoamine oxidase inhibitor antidepressants: Clinical use. In L. L. Iverson, S. D. Iverson, & S. H. Snyder (Eds.), *Handbook of psychopharmacology* (Vol. 14, pp. 199–232). New York: Plenum Press.

Leckman, J. F., Cohen, D. J., Detlor, J., Young, J. G., Harcherick, D., & Shaywitz, B. A. (1982). Clonidine in the treatment of Tourette syndrome: A review of data. In A. J. Friedhoff & T. N. Chase (Eds.), *Advances in neurology, Gilles de la Tourette syndrome* (Vol. 35, pp. 391–401). New York: Raven Press.

Leonard, H. L., Swedo, S. E., Rapoport, J. L., Koby, E. V., Lenane, M. C., Cheslow, D. L., & Hamburger, S. D. (1989). Treatment of obsessive–compulsive disorder with clomipramine and desipramine in children and adolescents. *Archives of General Psychiatry, 46,* 1088–1092.

Lesser, R. P., Pippenger, C. E., Luders, H., & Dinner, D. S. (1984). High-dose monotherapy in treatment of intractable seizures. *Neurology, 34,* 707–711.

Leventhal, B. L. (1985). *Fenfluramine administration to autistic children: Effects on behavior and biogenic amines.* Paper presented at the 25th Annual Meeting, Key Biscayne, FL.

Lowe, T. L., Cohen, D. J., Miller, S., & Young, J. G. (1981). Folic acid and B_{12} in autism and neuropsychiatric disturbances of childhood. *Journal of the American Academy of Child Psychiatry, 20,* 104–111.

Martineau, J., Barthelemy, C., Garreau, B., & Lelord, G. (1985). Vitamin B_6, magnesium and combined B_6-Mg: Therapeutic effects in childhood autism. *Biological Psychiatry, 20,* 467–468.

Mehlinger, R., Scheftner, W. A., & Poznanski, E. (1990). Fluoxetine and autism. *Journal of the American Academy of Child and Adolescent Psychiatry, 29,* 985.

Menkes, J. H. (1985). *Textbook of child neurology.* Philadelphia: Lea & Febiger.

Naruse, H., Nagahata, M., Nakane, Y., Shirahashi, K., Takesada, M., & Yamazaki, K. (1982). A multicenter double-blind trial of pimozide (Orap), haloperidol and placebo in children with behavioral disorders, using crossover design. *Acta Paedopsychiatrica, 48,* 173–184.

Panksepp, J., & Sahley, T. L. (1987). Possible brain opioid involvement in disrupted social intent and language development in autism. In E. Schopler & G. B. Mesibov (Eds.), *Neurobiological issues in autism* (pp. 357–372). New York: Plenum Press.

Perry, R., Campbell, M., Adams, P., Lynch, N., Spencer, E. K., Curren, E. L., & Overall, J. E. (1989). Long-term efficacy of haloperidol in autistic children: Continuous versus discontinuous drug administration. *Journal of the American Academy of Child and Adolescent Psychiatry, 28,* 87–92.

Perry, R., Campbell, M., Green, W. H., Small, A. M., Die Trill, M. L., Meiselas, K., Golden, R. R., & Deutsch, S. I. (1985). Neuroleptic-related dyskinesias in autistic children: A prospective study. *Psychopharmacology Bulletin, 21,* 140–143.

Petty, L. K., Ornitz, E. M., Michelman, J. D., & Zimmerman, E. G. (1984). Autistic children who become schizophrenic. *Archives of General Psychiatry, 41,* 129–135.

Polizos, P., & Engelhardt, D. (1978). Dyskinetic phenomena in children treated with psychotropic medications. *Psychopharmacology Bulletin, 14,* 65–68.

Pool, D., Bloom, W., Mielke, D. H., Roniger, J. J., & Gallant, D. M. (1976). A controlled evaluation of loxitane in 75 adolescent schizophrenic patients. *Current Therapeutic Research, 19,* 99–104.

Rapoport, J. L., & Mikkelsen, E. J. (1978). Antidepressants. In J. S. Werry (Ed.), *Pediatric psychopharmacology: The use of behavior modifying drugs in children* (pp. 208–233). New York: Brunner/Mazel.

Rapoport, J. L., Mikkelsen, E. J., & Werry, J. S. (1978). Antimanic, antianxiety, hallucinogenic, and miscellaneous drugs. In J. S. Werry (Ed.), *Pediatric psychopharmacology: The use of behavior modifying drugs in children* (pp. 316–355). New York: Brunner/Mazel.

Rapoport, J. L., Mikkelsen, E. J., Zavadil, A., Nee, L., Gruenau, C., Mendelson, W., & Gillin, J. C. (1980). Childhood enuresis: 2. Psychopathology, tricyclic concentration in plasma and antienuretic effect. *Archives of General Psychiatry, 37,* 1146–1152.

Realmuto, G. M., & Main, B. (1982). Coincidence of Tourette's disorder and infantile autism. *Journal of Autism and Developmental Disorders, 12,* 367–372.

Rett, A. (1966). *Ueber ein cerebral-atrophisches syndrome bei hyperammonamie.* Vienna: Bruder Hollinek.

Riddle, M. A., Hardin, M. T., King, R., Scahill, L., & Woolson, J. L. (1990). Fluoxetine treatment of children and adolescents with Tourette's and obsessive compulsive disorders: Preliminary clinical experience. *Journal of the American Academy of Child and Adolescent Psychiatry, 29,* 45–48.

Rimland, B., Callaway, E., & Dreyfus, P. (1978). The effects of high doses of vitamin B_6 on autistic children: A double-blind crossover study. *American Journal of Psychiatry, 135,* 472–475.

Ritvo, E. R., Freeman, B. J., Geller, E., Yuwiler, A. (1983). Effects of fenfluramine on 14 outpatients with the syndrome of autism. *Journal of the American Academy of Child Psychiatry, 22,* 549–558.

Ritvo, E. R., Freeman, B. J., Yuwiler, A., Geller, E., Schroth, P., Yokota, A., Mason-Brothers, A., August, G. J., Klykylo, W., Leventhal, B., Lewis, K., Piggott, L., Realmuto, G., Stubbs, E. G., & Umansky, R. (1986). Fenfluramine treatment of autism: UCLA collaborative study of 81 patients at nine medical centers. *Psychopharmacology Bulletin, 22,* 133–140.

Ritvo, E. R., Yuwiler, A., Geller, E., Ornitz, E. M., Saeger, K., & Plotkin, S. (1970). Increased blood serotonin and platelets in early infantile autism. *Archives of General Psychiatry, 23,* 566–572.

Rivinius, T. M. (1982). Psychiatric effects of the anticonvulsant regimens. *Journal of Clinical Psychopharmacology, 2,* 165–192.

Rutter, M. (1977). Infantile autism and other child psychoses. In M. Rutter & L. Hersov (Eds.), *Child psychiatry: Modern approach* (pp. 717–747). Oxford: Blackwell.

Rutter, M. (1984). Autistic children growing up. *Developmental Medicine and Child Neurology, 26,* 122–129.

Rutter, M. (1985). The treatment of autistic children. *Journal of Child Psychology and Psychiatry, 26,* 193–214.

Shapiro, A. K., & Shapiro, E. (1984). Controlled study of pimozide versus placebo in Tourette syndrome. *Journal of the American Academy of Child Psychiatry, 23,* 161–173.

Shea, V., & Mesibov, G. B. (1985). The relationship of learning disabilities and higher-level autism. *Journal of Autism and Developmental Disorders, 15,* 425–435.

Sherman, J., Factor, D. C., Swinson, R., & Darjes, R. W. (1989). The effects of fenfluramine (hydrochloride) on the behaviors of 15 autistic children. *Journal of Autism and Developmental Disorders, 4,* 533–543.

Trevathan E., & Naidu, S. (1988). The clinical recognition and differential diagnosis of Rett syndrome. *Journal of Child Neurology, 3*(Suppl.), S6–S16.

Tsai, L. Y., & Ghaziuddin, M. (1991). Autistic disorder. In J. Weiner (Ed.), *The comprehensive textbook of child and adolescent psychiatry* (pp. 169–191). Washington, DC: American Psychiatric Press.

Volkmar, F. R., & Nelson, D. S. (1990). Seizure disorders in autism. *Journal of American Academy of Child and Adolescent Psychiatry, 29*(1), 127–129.

Werry, J. S., & Aman, M. G. (1975). Methylphenidate and haloperidol in children: Effects on attention, memory, and activity. *Archives of General Psychiatry, 32,* 790–795.

Werry, J. S., Aman, M. G., & Diamond, E. (1980). Imipramine and methylphenidate in hyperactive children. *Journal of Child Psychology and Psychiatry, 21,* 27–35.

Werry, J. S., Aman, M. G., & Lampen, E. (1976). Haloperidol and methylphenidate in hyperactive children. *Acta Paedopsychiatrica, 42,* 26–40.

Werry, J. S. & Sprague, R. (1974). Methylphenidate in children-effect in dosage. *Australian and New Zealand Journal of Psychology, 8,* 9–19.

Wilensky, A. J., Ojemann, L. M., Temkin, N. R., Troupin, A. S., & Dodrill, C. B. (1981). Chlorazepate and phenobarbital as antiepileptic drugs: A double-blind study. *Neurology, 31,* 1271–1276.

Winsberg, B. G., Perel, J., Hurwic M., & Klutch, A. (1974). Imipramine protein binding and pharmacokinetics in children. In I. S. Forrest, C. J. Carr, & E. Usdin (Eds.), *The phenothiazines and structurally related drugs* (p. 425). New York: Raven Press.

Winsberg, B. G., Yepes, L., & Bialer, I. (1976). Pharmacological management of children with hyperactive/aggressive/inattentive behavior disorders. *Clinical Pediatrics, 15,* 471–477.

III CURRENT DIRECTIONS AND EMERGING TRENDS

9 Meeting the Unique Needs of Families

Thomas H. Powell
Anton Hecimovic
Linda Christensen
Eastern Montana College

Nick just turned 21. His parents have dreamed that despite his autism and moderate mental retardation he would live a full life in his community. Their dream had specific components including:

- *a home in a local neighborhood*
- *a real job*
- *regular recreational opportunities*
- *continuing education*
- *adequate financial support*

Now they face the challenge of realizing that dream without a state or federal mandate for adult services. Nick is one of 900 people on a state waiting list for services, in a state with a small population. Nick and his family, like others who face the challenge of autism, hope that their dreams do not turn into nightmares.

Timmy has severe autism. In addition to major communication problems, he has difficulty sleeping through the night, gets upset easily, and has not yet mastered many self-help skills. Timmy's parents, wrestling with the challenge of meeting his needs while also meeting their other children's needs, have requested from the school an extended day and extended year program for Timmy. The school superintendent has argued that such a request is beyond the school's responsibility and capability. However, the superintendent has said the school will be willing to send Timmy to a residential school. His parents want him to remain at home in the local community and argue that their request would provide the support needed to allow him to stay home and thus cost less to taxpayers. The superintendent refused to implement the parents' request. So, Timmy's parents hired an attorney and began the long, arduous, and expensive process of fighting to secure appropriate schooling for their son.

Sarah just celebrated her fourth birthday, complete with balloons, cake, ice cream, and six of her preschool friends. A year ago Sarah was diagnosed as having autism. She exhibits a number of typical characteristics including language delay, stereotypic behaviors, unresponsiveness to others, and unusual patterns of play. Uncharacteristically, Sarah attends a local preschool program and she receives swimming lessons at the YWCA. Sarah attends preschool Sunday school with her age peers. Sarah's parents have resisted placing her in the special "autism preschool," stating that their daughter is best served in the programs she would attend if she had no label. They work with a number of professionals committed to full inclusion of children with autism.

Three individuals with autism. All three experience this disability called *autism* in unique ways. Each is a member of a family, a unique and complex system of relationships, experiences, values, and expectations. Nick, Timmy, and Sarah share a common diagnosis, autism. However, their life experiences are as different and as individual as any in society.

Nick, Timmy, and Sarah are the typical focus of special education services, yet it is their families who require unique attention and support services. This chapter covers some of the issues involved for professionals who have chosen to support Nick, Timmy, Sarah, and their families, and thousands of other families like theirs, yet also different. This chapter addresses ways for professionals to become aware of, and sensitive to, the needs of families of individuals with autism, including those members of the family whose needs are often forgotten by professionals.

We address the needs of different family members, and consider the whole family as an interrelated, interdependent system. A critical determinant of the family system's support is the nature of the family–professional relationship. It is this relationship, and the sensitivity, skills, and information with which professionals approach the relationship, that defines how much support families receive from the professionals with whom they will need to interact, simply because they happen to have a family member who experiences autism.

CHALLENGING THE OLD ASSUMPTIONS REGARDING FAMILIES

Attitudes and assumptions of professionals in the field of autism have defined the service delivery and support provided to families. Typically professionals, especially educators, physicians, psychologists, and social workers, have assumed roles of authority in working with families of children with autism (Schopler, 1976). Darling (1983) and Seligman (1979) note that the predominant attitudes about families have led to deficiencies in professional preparation programs, with preservice professionals receiving neither information about families nor specific skills to facilitate parent–professional partnerships. As noted by Donnellan and Mirenda (1984), the "implicit message given is that professionals rarely need to be concerned about working with families, and if they do encounter families in the course of their work with the child, they need no special information in order to be effective with them" (p. 17).

Negative stereotypes about parents have contributed to assumptions underlying family services. Gartner, Lipsky, and Turnbull (1991) assert that parents, like their children, are labeled with the disability. The parents become "the autistic parents" to the professional community, and this, in a shorthand way, communicates the wellspring of negative assumptions and expectations about the parents. The damaging consequences of labeling the child are extended to the parents as well (Ferguson & Asch, 1989).

Some key assumptions and misconceptions that have been pervasive in the delivery of services to families with children with autism include the following:

1. The "doctor knows best." Families are expected to listen to the all-knowing professional, without questioning. Families need to trust the wisdom of the professional (Lyon & Preis, 1983).
2. The family should be grateful. Families need to be thankful that *any* service is provided. The service is viewed as a charity function with lessened need for accountability and thus lowered expectations.
3. Parents should follow directions. Ideal parents are those who rigorously follow professional prescriptions without questioning or modifying the professional's advice.
4. Parents contribute to the child's problem. Autism is one area of disability in which parents have been blamed directly for the cause of the disability. Some professionals vigorously argued that autism was the result of cold, schizophrenic parents (Berlin, 1973; Bettelheim, 1967; Tinbergen & Tinbergen, 1972).
5. Parents are unrealistic. Parents have unrealistic expectations about their child with autism. Some professionals believe that parents are not willing to accept the realities of the disability and therefore have fantasies about the child's abilities and future (Cutler, 1981).
6. Parents need professionals to help them solve problems. A commonly held belief among professionals is that the needs of the

child with autism are so great that parents cannot be expected to manage the child without extensive professional intervention. Along with this assumption is the belief that parents do not know how to parent a child with autism, thus needing professional intervention.

7. All parents need counseling. Some professionals believe that the trauma of having a child with autism necessitates counseling for all parents. The child with autism will create such stress that the only way parents can maintain their mental health is with professional counseling.
8. The family is at fault. If professional interactions with the family are negative or nonproductive, the family is at fault. After all, professionals have the training and couldn't be hindering the development of a positive, productive relationship (Donnellan & Mirenda, 1984).
9. The family is dysfunctional. Having a child with autism is so traumatic that the family will be disabled in all of its functions. Because the presence of the child with autism in the family will naturally cause stress and tax the natural resources of the family, there is a predominate belief that nothing positive can come of the experience.

These negative assumptions have not only hindered productive family–professional partnerships, they have led to an established folklore about families and, in particular, parents. All too often these assumptions have resulted in labels being ascribed to parents such as overprotective, guilt-ridden, unaccepting, uncaring, or noncompliant (Seligman, 1979).

If we are to move beyond these limiting and dangerous assumptions and develop productive family–professional partnerships, we must continue to examine and expose the assumptions that underly family treatment and support services. We engage in such an examination through the remainder of this chapter.

A NEW AND HEALTHIER WAY OF THINKING ABOUT FAMILIES

The old assumptions about families that lead to negative interactions and outcomes for persons with autism and their families have been challenged in a manner that has given rise to a new way of thinking about families. Perhaps the most significant change in the assumptions about families of children with autism is a reexamination and rejection of the notion that parents are the causative agents of the disability (see Cantwell, Baker, &

Rutter, 1979; Plienis, Robbins, & Dunlap, 1988). This conceptual shift has refuted the psychogenic theories (e.g., Bettelheim, 1967; Kanner, 1949) with a growing body of knowledge on the biological and organic etiological factors involved in autism (DeMyer, Hingtgen, & Jackson, 1981; Ornitz, 1978; Ritvo & Freeman, 1984). Not only have recent findings refuted the parental blame for autism, parents and other family members are recognized as essential treatment partners and the primary decision makers for their children. These new assumptions have been the result of a recent knowledge base about families and a greater appreciation of the role of families in nurturing children, including those with autism.

One of the major shifts in viewing families has been the growing recognition of the positive contribution of persons with disabilities to their families. Summers, Behr, and Turnbull (1989) described several empirical and anecdotal studies in which families report evidence of positive contributions, such as:

1. increased happiness,
2. greater love,
3. strengthened family ties,
4. strengthened religious faith,
5. expanded social network,
6. greater pride and accomplishment,
7. greater knowledge about disabilities,
8. learning not to take things for granted,
9. learning tolerance and sensitivity,
10. learning to be patient,
11. expanding career development,
12. increased personal growth,
13. assuming personal control, and
14. living life more slowly. (p. 29)

Summers and her colleagues noted that such studies suggest "that children with disabilities contribute positively to their families and that some families not only survive their experience with disability but also grow stronger" (p. 31).

The new, and we think healthier, way of thinking about families is characterized by the 10 points listed here:

1. **Children "grow best" in families.** Children with autism need to be offered the opportunity to live in a family structure, enjoying a rich array of interaction and activity grounded in the family's culture and beliefs.

2. **Family members are interdependent.** Families are best viewed as a system (Turnbull & Turnbull, 1986). The members of a family interact reciprocally and are mutually dependent. As a result, professionals need to understand, appreciate, and work with the entire family system to provide meaningful support.
3. **Parents are the best judges of their children's needs.** Parents, not professionals, know their children better than anyone else and thus are in the best position to judge what services and supports are needed by the child. Parents need to be supported in their efforts to secure needed services and supports.
4. **The family is the best advocate.** The family is the best long-term advocate for the child with autism (Donnellan & Mirenda, 1984). Not only is the family relationship a long-lasting one, but family members are in the position of putting the individual with autism's needs and well-being before the potentially conflicting priorities of other advocates.
5. **Families want involvement.** Families want and need to be actively involved in all aspects of the child's educational programs (Donnellan & Mirenda, 1984). Professionals must fully include families in the educational process and in all other services.
6. **Professionals need to support families.** Professionals need to be engaged in practices that support the family as a system. No longer can professionals afford the luxury of looking solely at the needs of the child. Professionals need to consider all aspects of families to provide services and resources to strengthen the whole family.
7. **Parents should question professionals.** When parents are given confusing and conflicting information about their children with autism, parents must question the professionals' information and, perhaps, values. Assertive parenting implies a questioning of professionals, rather than meek compliance.
8. **Autism need not be negative.** The child with autism can add to a family system and enhance family functions. There is a growing body of evidence from parents, siblings, and extended family members that the experience of autism can have profound, positive effects on the family as a whole.
9. **Concern is for the long term.** Parents and professionals share the concern for the long-term functioning of the child with autism. Although there are many real day-to-day concerns, the future and longer term are everyone's constant, underlying concern.
10. **There is more than autism.** Other issues, besides autism, may be the focus of a family's needs at a given point in time. Families are confronted by numerous issues in addition to those pertaining to the disability. Professionals need to recognize and affirm that

other issues may need to be given priority by the family, and thus need to also be given priority by professionals.

Acting upon these 10 assumptions will empower and enhance the family. When professionals incorporate these assumptions into their clinical practices, true family–professional partnerships can be developed and strengthened and families of persons with autism can be supported.

UNIQUE CHALLENGES FACED BY FAMILIES

We briefly consider the situation of a young man with autism, whom we know, and his family. Christopher lives with his mom, dad, and younger sister, Cate. Christopher, nearly 10, is like many 10-year-olds except that he presents a number of unique and specific challenges to this family. Consider for a moment several of the challenges Christopher presents to his family:

- Christopher usually sleeps in an erratic pattern. Two hours of sleep, 2 hours up, on and off all night.
- Christopher is easily upset by changing family routines, even changes in the television schedule. He shows his distress by screaming and slapping his hand against his head.
- Christopher has been referred to numerous medical, psychological, and educational clinics, taxing not only the family's financial resources, but their time and energy as well.
- Christopher has unusual dietary habits. He only eats steamed vegetables with a side dish of butterscotch pudding and half a banana for dinner.
- Christopher regularly tears his clothes and does not seem content unless his shirt and pants are torn.
- Christopher is still not toilet trained, necessitating strained family routines and a constant supply of expensive adult-sized diapers.
- Christopher likes to run away when he is out of the house. When he runs he likes to hide, and it usually requires an hour of frantic searching to find his latest hiding place.

Now consider that Christopher's family wants to provide a loving, nurturing home for him. Christopher's family, despite the challenges they face, are adamant in their resolve to provide for him at home, just as they do for his sister. How can Christopher's family do what they know is best for him?

A Lack of Support

The dilemma felt by families like Christopher's who are caring for a child with a severe disability could be lessened with an adequate community support system (Cohen, Agosta, Cohen, & Warren, 1989). Unfortunately, many communities lack necessary support services for families who elect to keep their child with autism at home. These families are given the message that their decision to keep their child at home also becomes a decision to be excluded from necessary local, state, and federal support programs. The full set of family support services does not exist uniformly throughout the nation. Lack of support exacerbates problems faced by all families, especially those who happen to have a family member with autism.

The following sections of this chapter address some issues that have been assumed by professionals in the field to be particular sources of difficulty for families of individuals with autism. We attempt to present a balanced look at some of the assumptions that are commonly held. As a general statement, it is safe to say that a systems approach to viewing and supporting families and an orientation that focuses on maximizing the positive, rather than focusing on the negative or pathology, has brought about a new appreciation for the families of individuals with autism.

Stress

Much has been written and surmised regarding stress and families of individuals with autism. By and large, the literature has focused on a deficit approach to the consideration of families. In this way of thinking, the assumption is made that the inclusion of a member with autism in a family must, in and of itself, introduce an inordinate amount of stress for that family, and that this stress must have a negative effect on the family. We primarily consider this issue in relation to parents here. In another section of this chapter, we consider this and other issues for the siblings and members of extended families of individuals with autism.

Rabkin and Streuning (1976) succinctly stated that, among the potential causes of stress, those situations that are characterized by their unpredictability, intensity, magnitude, and duration, tend to present the most life stress. In this light, it is not an overgeneralization to say that all families, at times, face stress related to parenting, no matter which children are involved. Over the years, however, there have been assumptions made that having a family member with autism somehow inherently not only introduces a great deal more stress into the family, when compared to other families, but that this stress, by definition, has negative effects on the family. Studies have attempted to pinpoint specific child behaviors that are related to family stress (Milgram & Atzil, 1988); show how families with a member with autism compare to families with a member with a different kind of disability in regard to stress and its effects (Noh, Dumas, Wolf, & Fisman, 1989); or show which family characteristics are related to stress or its assumed negative effects (Wolf, Noh, Fisman, & Speechley, 1989).

A recent study by Bebko, Konstantareas, and Springer (1987) raises some very interesting and important issues regarding the causes of stress and families' perceptions of stress. In the study, the mothers and fathers of children with autism were asked to rate how stressful they found certain characteristics associated with autism. In addition, these researchers asked therapists who knew the families to estimate the parents' perceptions of stress. Not surprisingly, the professionals who were involved in the study judged the families as more stressed than the parents themselves reported. This finding is enlightening in regard to our professional emphasis on problems, difficulties, and pathology. Professionals should proceed cautiously in regard to their assumptions of the causes and degrees of stress that *might* be felt by families. Parents know what they feel.

The authors have come in contact with increasing numbers of individuals who report anecdotally that having a family member with a disability, including autism, has had a positive effect on their life. They describe feelings of accomplishment and enrichment because of the opportunities associated with living with a person with autism. These experiences further illustrate the danger professionals can encounter should they make a priori assumptions about another individual's, or another family's, experiences and perceptions.

Financial Issues

The financial difficulties related to childrearing that face many families nowadays are very often more intense and long-lasting for families who have a child with autism. Over the past several years more and more two-parent families face the situation of both of those parents needing to work to make economic ends meet. Families who face this situation also find themselves in the bind of having less nonwork time available, which also means less time to provide care to a family member with autism. Typically the family must pay someone to provide the necessary care. Given our current situation in regard to support for families of individuals with disabilities, especially financial support, there can be no doubt that the presence of a family member with autism has an economic impact on the family. As with other issues, financial problems can be overcome. In considering the families of children with a variety of disabilities, Seligman and Darling (1989) have separated direct and indirect costs to families.

Direct costs to families are those expenses that are incurred for the costs of direct care, training, therapies, and medically related equipment and supplies that are not covered by private insurance or public assistance. Additional expenses come in many forms, including costs for medical and psychological assessments, trips to out-of-town clinics, expenses for special diets, special clothing, and furniture. Some families who have children with autism who are not toilet trained report extraordinary expenses with diapers and clothing as well as laundry expenses. Some families report needs for environmental modifications. Such costs can be easily calculated and can total hundreds of thousands of dollars over an individual's lifetime for some families. For other families, direct costs might actually be minimal. A critical thing to keep in mind is that not only are the costs variable from one family to the next, but even the effects of a given cost on the economic situation of a family vary from one family to another and from one point in time to the next.

An often unconsidered set of costs to families who have a member with autism might be called *indirect costs.* Rather than out-of-pocket expenses, indirect costs are those hidden costs that are difficult to estimate. They may include the costs of moving to a particular community because of the availability of specific programs or services. Indirect costs may also include the costs to the family of opportunities foregone because of the needs of the family member with autism. These might include the economic losses to the family when one parent cannot work outside the home in order to be available to provide care. Such costs are often overlooked by families and professionals when they consider the financial effects of the presence of a family member with autism.

Marital Issues

The research on marital problems in families with a child with disabilities has been equivocal. Some researchers show evidence of higher divorce rates and lower rates of remarriage (Crnic, Friedrich, & Guenberg, 1983; Hobbs, Perrin, & Ireys, 1986), whereas others show no difference in these rates when compared with other families (Bristol, Gallagher, & Schopler, 1988; Waisbren, 1980). Harris (1983) cautioned that a family may focus on the child with a disability as the source of the problem when there may be other factors in the marriage that are causing marital discord. Professionals working with families need to discriminate these causes and not necessarily focus on the child as the problem.

Much research is beginning to focus on the strengthening bonds that caregiving and the challenge of having a child with a disability can create in a family (Ferguson & Asch, 1989; Kazak & Marvin, 1984; Turnbull, Guess, & Turnbull, 1988). Positive spousal support, including the understanding of a partner, help in caregiving, the ability to jointly communicate and problem solve, all contribute to the continuation of the family as a positive, effectively functioning system (Friedrich & Friedrich, 1981; Notarius, Benson, & Sloane, 1989; Pahl & Quine, 1987). Professionals should look at the support factors and family characteristics that help families to cope and how those areas can be strengthened.

Shopping

In the past, "shopping behavior" of parents of children with disabilities has been viewed by professionals as an unhealthy behavior. Professionals felt that it was part of the denial stage of grieving, that parents were "shopping around" for second, third, and fourth opinions from professionals to find a more acceptable diagnosis or even a "cure" for their child (Anderson, 1971; Bicknell, 1983; Davidson & Schrag, 1968; Patton, Payne, & Beirne-Smith, 1986). Sometimes shopping has even been initiated by so-called professionals, or popular literature, where false hopes were raised among families through stories that purported to "cure" autism.

More recent consideration of shopping behavior has revealed that parents are actually responding to having a child with a disability in a positive, coping manner. First, they are seeking second opinions, encouraged to do so by practitioners in the medical community, counselors, and even insurance companies (Ackerman, Lyons, Hammer, & Larsen, 1988). They also may be trying to obtain an initial diagnosis, as many physicians and other professionals are at times hesitant or unwilling to provide one. Second, they are often attempting to *clarify* a diagnosis, seeking additional information about what may be an initially unclear, inaccurate, or inconsistent diagnosis and/or explanation of the disability from the first professional they encounter (Avant, 1988; Sample, 1991). Third, they may be looking for the best label to fit the best services for their child or looking for additional services for their child. All of these activities are often encouraged and recommended by the initial professionals they encounter (Miezo, 1983).

Shopping behavior has been identified as a positive coping strategy of parents (Summers, Turnbull, & Brotherson, 1985). There might be so many different needs identified for the family and the child with a disability, that shopping is necessary to meet these needs. Positive coping strategies that entail an active problem-solving approach and a sense of gaining "control" over an overwhelming situation have been identified as promoting family functioning (Antonovsky, 1987; Darling, 1983; Vitaliano, Maiuro, Russo, & Becker, 1987).

As one parent described it,

> I sometimes feel like I am the teacher of the teacher, the doctor of the doctor, the expert in adapting family life to a disability, the source . . . of everything.

If I didn't "shop," as you call it, my kid wouldn't get diddley. And that's the truth! (Sample, 1991)

Frustration with Professionals

Confusing and conflicting professional advice and suggestions are well-known to parents who have children with autism. It is often difficult to get professionals to confirm a diagnosis. A 1981 publication of the National Society for Children and Adults with Autism (now Autism Society of America) expressed the situation faced by many families.

- The pediatric clinic says that the child is "slow in developing," the parents must wait. Try a mental retardation specialist.
- The mental retardation specialist finds the child is not testable. It must be a brain dysfunction. Try a pediatric neurologist.
- The pediatric neurologist comes up with "funny squiggles" on the EEG. Nothing specific. See a psychiatrist.
- The psychiatrist decided the child is too ill for testing and must be retarded. Try a special educator.
- The special educator refers the child back to the pediatric clinic for diagnosis and treatment. (pp. 18f)

Then, professionals, narrowly considering their interactions with a family, wonder why the family who has been on this merry-go-round is frustrated by their interactions with them.

THE FAMILY AS A SYSTEM

Family systems theory (Minuchin, 1974; Neugarten, 1976; Turnbull, Summers, & Brotherson, 1986; Turnbull & Turnbull, 1986) serves as a good foundation for the understanding and examination of dynamics within the family that has a child with autism. The basic premise of family systems theory is that each family is unique and that within the family constellation each member contributes to the overall composition and thus influences all aspects of the family. Likewise, each family member is influenced by all other members of the family system and by the system as a whole.

Turnbull and Turnbull (1986) use family systems theory to conceptualize families with a member who has a disability. Figure 9.1 depicts this conceptual framework, which consists of four major components: (a) family resources, (b) family interaction, (c) family functions, and (d) family life cycles.

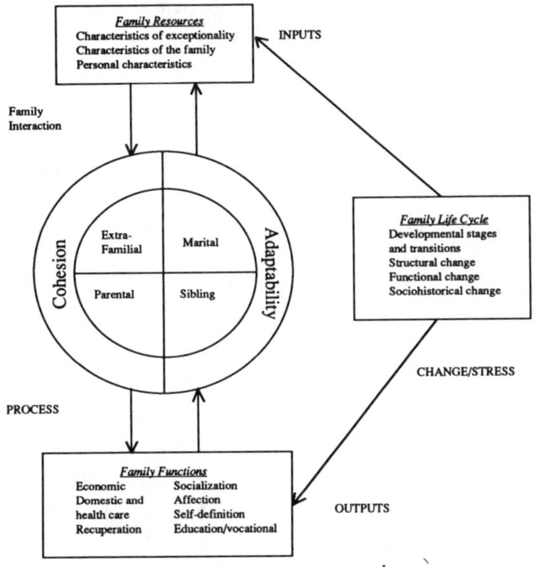

FIG. 9.1. Family systems conceptual framework (from Turnbull & Turnbull, 1986, p. 20).

Family Resources. All individual members have personal characteristics that make them distinct from the others in the family system. These descriptive characteristics, family resources, are the abilities, resources, and capacities of the family to meet the needs of each individual member and the family as a whole (Turnbull & Turnbull, 1986). Characteristics pertaining to the family (e.g., size, socioeconomic status, ethnicity, geographic location), handicapping condition (e.g., type, level of ability), and personal condition (e.g., health, well-being, individual personality characteristics, coping strategies) are considered family resources—those abilities, strengths, and skills the family possesses to meet individual and family needs. Cultural style, ethnicity, and religion, as well as the family members' beliefs and values, contribute to the family system and its resources. Obviously, this constellation of family resources is different from one family to another.

Family Interaction. This is the focal point of the family system and consists of those relationships that are related to the daily activities of the family. Each family is a system with four major *subsystems:* marital, parental, sibling, and extrafamilial (entire family or individual member interactions with family members, friends, professionals, and persons within the community) (Turnbull, Summers, & Brotherson, 1984). As noted by Turnbull et al. (1986), the family systems framework incorporates the premise that all living systems have interdependent components and that the "interaction of these parts creates properties not contained in any separate entities" (p. 46). Therefore, it is difficult, if not impossible, to consider the actions, needs, or desires of one part of the family without first considering the family as an interconnected system. The individual needs of family members can be understood by studying the relationships and interactions among family members. These family subsystems (i.e., parent–child, sibling–sibling) interact according to rules of cohesion, adaptability, and communication. Cohesion describes the degree of closeness or distance among family members. Adaptability is the degree of family stability and reaction to change, and communication is the degree of honesty and frankness among family members.

Family Functions. Family functions are those needs that the family possesses that must be addressed. These functions, tasks, or output may be economic (e.g., generating money), domestic/health care (e.g., locating health care staff), recreation (participating in community sporting events), socialization (developing friendships), self-identity (developing a thorough sense of self), affection (acknowledging others), and educational/vocational (securing a job that a person enjoys).

Family Life Cycle. These needs change across the family life cycle or developmental stages of each family. Turnbull and Turnbull (1986) suggest six stages within the family life cycle: early childhood (birth to age 5), school age (6 to 12 years), adolescence (13 to 21 years), adulthood (21 and older), empty nest, and elderly years. For all families the point at which they find themselves in the family life cycle has great impact on many aspects of their functioning as a system. Professionals need to keep in mind that the family as a whole progresses through these stages and individual families will move along the stages at differing rates. Finally, it is important for professionals to also keep in mind the potential overlapping nature of these described stages.

Conclusion. To meet the needs of family members with compassion and understanding, professionals must consider the dynamics of individual families, their needs, characteristics, strengths, values, resources, and their particular stage within the family life cycle. Families who have a child with autism are like all families because their needs vary. Each family is unique. Within a family, numerous characteristics influence how the family reacts to autism, how family members cope, and how they face the challenge of incorporating the child into the structure and function of the family. It should be remembered that families display both vulnerability and strength. Featherstone (1980) spoke of the solitude, loneliness, and fear of being a parent of a child with a disability. She reminded us, however, that parents and families endure and learn to live with the challenge of the disability, and even flourish because of it.

A Special Part of the Family System: Parents

It generally has been acknowledged that in most families primary child-care responsibilities have been, and often still are, accomplished by mothers (Nye, 1976). Given this situation, in the consideration of parenting of family members with autism, most of the research attention has focused on the activities, needs, and feelings of mothers. Only recently has there been interest in the fathers of children with disabilities, including those children with autism (Lamb, 1983; Meyer, 1986). The nature of this research with fathers has been similar to much of the earlier research conducted with mothers of children with disabilities. It has been focused on differences, such as efforts to determine how fathers differ from mothers in regard to parenting issues (Milgram & Atzil, 1988), or how the fathers of children with a particular disability differ from other fathers (Noh et al., 1989). As an example, among their findings, Milgram and Atzil (1988) stated that the mothers of children with autism expressed that life satisfaction is associated with relative contributions to overall parenting, whereas fathers of children with autism expressed that life satisfaction is associated with their absolute parenting effort. According to Milgram and Atzil, these findings indicated that "mothers' life satisfaction is enhanced by fathers assuming a smaller, but fair, share of child care" (p. 422). One would think that the statement applies to two-parent families in general, rather than being peculiar to families with children with autism or other disabilities.

It is our feeling that research that takes a deficit-oriented approach has limited utility in considerations of how best to support families of individuals with autism. With both mothers and fathers there is a need to refocus attention on strengths and capacities and the contributions of both parents as individuals and as a part of a whole family system. Similarly, much more needs to be known about how best to support single-parent families, regardless of the presence of a family member with a disability.

An important consideration in supporting two-parent families is the change that has been occurring over the recent past in regard to the roles of mothers and fathers in general. Increasing numbers of mothers are working outside of the home. At the same time, there is evidence that fathers are taking increasingly active roles in parenting. There is a less clearly differentiated gender-related role separation in parenting than there has been. These changes are not specific only to families of individuals with autism. They are occurring within all families. At present, because these societal changes in regard to gender-related roles are in flux, it is important for professionals who are attempting to support families to be aware that, not only will there be potentially large differences among families in regard to the involvement of mothers and fathers, but there can also be a great deal of change within a family over time.

Perhaps, as professionals who are interested in supporting families as part of the family system, we should keep in mind a statement made by Ferguson when he was speaking of his son. He said:

> As a father I do not love my son *in spite* of his handicaps as some abstracted, idealized version of reality. The object of my affection is the flesh and blood lad whom I dress every day, put in a wheelchair, and struggle to talk to in words he can understand. (Ferguson & Asch, 1989, p. 114)

Ferguson's statement could have been made by either a mother or a father. It reflects feelings and concern that are very common to parents.

A Special Part of the Family System: Siblings

The family systems framework outlined by Turnbull et al. (1986) stresses the importance of *interactions* among the members of a family group, and the interrelatedness of all family members. Brothers and sisters of persons with disabilities are unique and vital components of such a family system. Sibling relationships, a critical component of a child's overall development, take on special significance when one of the siblings has a disability.

In their analysis of sibling interactions and interdependence, Schvaneveldt and Ihinger (1979) asserted the importance of considering families as systems. They outlined five basic assumptions in regard to sibling relationships:

1. Within most families, there exist three subsystems of interaction. Each of these subsystems (spouse–spouse, parent–child, and sibling–sibling) operates semi-independently of the other two subsystems within the family structure.
2. Siblings both initiate and receive social interactions. Family interaction is dynamic, with husbands and wives affecting each other, parents and children affecting each other, and siblings affecting each other.
3. Sibling interaction is in a continuous process of development that occurs throughout the life span. Thus, the nature and form of the interaction is continually in evolution.

4. The personality development and social behaviors of family members are partially determined by family composition and interaction.
5. Sibling groups have properties similar to other small groups.

As Powell and Ogle (1985) noted, the sibling relationship is perhaps the most long-lasting and most influential relationship of one's life. It begins with the birth of a brother or sister and continues throughout life. The duration of that relationship is certainly substantial. Unlike parental relationships that may last 40 to 60 years, the sibling relationship may last 60 to 80 years. Unlike any other relationship between people, the sibling relationship provides two people with ongoing physical and emotional contact at critical stages throughout their lives. Siblings provide a continuing relationship from which there is no annulment. This permanent relationship allows two people to exert considerable influence over each other through longitudinal interactions (Bank & Kahn, 1982).

Research on sibling relationships provides evidence that there can be both positive and negative effects for the disabled child; that is, living closely and intensely with a sibling with a disability can be rewarding, as well as stressful (Powell & Ogle, 1985). On the positive side, many siblings report satisfaction in learning to live and cope with the demands of a child with a handicap in the family, resulting in feelings of warmth and compassion for all individuals with unique needs (Laureys, 1982; Lettick, 1979; Myers, 1978). Other siblings report negative effects, including feelings of bitterness and resentment because of the extra attention given to the child with the disability, or even guilt over their own good health (Featherstone, 1980; Myers, 1978; Zatlow, 1982).

It is helpful to envision the effects of a child with autism on a sibling as a continuum, with very positive outcomes at one end and some negative outcomes (i.e., psychological disturbance) at the other (Gallagher & Powell, 1989). This continuum of outcomes for siblings is not static. A sibling may have a healthy, positive relationship at one time and yet, at another time, the same sibling may express negative behaviors and feelings toward the child with a disability (Powell & Ogle, 1985). Such adjustment, of course, also affects the overall family system. Several factors contribute to determining where the nondisabled sibling functions on this continuum at various points in time. These factors include family characteristics, characteristics of the nondisabled sibling, and the characteristics of the child with the disability.

Powell and Ogle (1985) described a number of special concerns and unique needs experienced by siblings. Although these concerns and needs are by no means limited to autism, their universal applicability provides a foundation from which to understand and address the needs of this special part of the family system. Siblings of children with disabilities are typically concerned about six broad themes:

1. **The child with the disability,** including the cause of the disability, the child's feelings, needed services, and what the future will hold;
2. **Their parents,** including varying parental expectations, communication, the parents' feelings, and the parents' time;
3. **Themselves,** including their feelings, their health, and their relationship with the siblings;
4. **Their friends,** including informing their friends, handling teasing, their friends' acceptance of the disability, and dating;
5. **The community,** including school services, community acceptance, and community living;
6. **Adulthood,** including guardianship, financial responsibility, continuing their involvement, and genetics.

In addition to these broadly described areas of concern, siblings have expressed a number of unique needs including:

1. The need for information. Often siblings are excluded from the information sources regarding the disability. Consider what Bodenheimer (1979) had to say regarding her brother Chris, who has autism.

> And I remember the turmoil surrounding the pursuit of his elusive diagnosis. The whole family shared in the knowledge that "something" was wrong—he doesn't talk, he doesn't seem to hear, yet he loves music and keeps rhythm, he will only eat bananas, he's fascinated with water, never wants to cuddle, won't sleep through the night . . . Knowing all these things made it even more difficult when those professionals sought out gave confusing and conflicting reports. . . . An especially difficult part of living with an autistic sibling is the ever-present question of etiology. Why??? As a child, it's hard to live with someone who has difficulty learning, gets upset, and acts strangely when no one seems to know why. Children expect adults to have the answers, but so often in the case of the autistic child, the siblings are left on their own to grapple with this question. (pp. 291–292)

2. The need for respect. Like all people, siblings need to be respected as individuals, separate and apart from the disability. They need to be recognized for their own accomplishments.
3. The need for skills. Many siblings report a need to learn specific skills to assist them with their interactions with their brother or

sister with autism. The more severe the autism, the more critical skill training for siblings appears to be.

4. The need to share feelings and experiences. Many brothers and sisters report a need to share their experiences and feelings with others. The national *Sibling Information Network* at the University of Connecticut was created, in part, to provide that exchange of information, feelings, and experiences needed by siblings.

A Special Part of the Family System: Extended Family Members

When professionals consider the family that has a member with autism, we generally concern ourselves with the nuclear family. Consideration is seldom given to the members of the extended family. The research with the concerns and needs of the extended family has been limited to the grandparents who might be involved (Sonnek, 1986). Grandparents are a critical part of the family system, however, there is also the need to consider other members of the extended family, such as aunts, uncles, and cousins. In addition, an appropriately scaled consideration of extended family must go beyond relations by blood or marriage. With the increased mobility of families, the functions that may be served by relatives often are accomplished by friends. Any consideration of extended family must, thus, use the family's definition of members for inclusion.

Extended family members can provide support in a variety of ways. They might provide respite, temporary financial assistance, or an opportunity to listen and reflect family member's feelings. For professionals it is important to recognize the real and potential support that might be available through this extended family network. At times, one of the best types of support a professional can provide to a family is to assist them in activating the support available through an extended family network.

PROVIDING HELP: FAMILY SUPPORT SERVICES

It is clear that families with children with autism need aggressive community support systems. Family supports include both formal and informal networks that can build the family's capacity to successfully meet their various functions (Appoloni & Triest, 1983; Moore, Hamerlynck, Barsh, Spicker, & Jones, 1982). Informal supports, such as friends, extended family members, church, and community service organizations usually offer a form of support that is natural and not burdened with the bureaucracy that is associated with state and federal programs. Such informal, natural supports should be promoted and enhanced (Cohen &

Syme, 1985). However necessary and valuable, these informal family support networks are seldom sufficient in assisting the family. The more severe the autism, or the greater the impact on the family system, the more the family will need more formal supports.

Family support services must be dedicated to strengthening the family's ability to provide care and enhance the individual's opportunity to live in the family without diminishing the family's normal lifestyle (Cohen, Agosta, Cohen, & Warren, 1989). The Center on Human Policy's (Syracuse University) Statement on Support of Families and Their Children (1987) provided the following key principles that should be used to guide the development and delivery of family support services.

- All children, regardless of disability, belong with families and need enduring relationships with adults.
- Families should receive the supports necessary to maintain their children at home. Family support services must be based on the principle of "whatever it takes."
- Family supports should build on existing social networks and natural sources of support.
- Family supports should maximize the family's control over the services and supports they receive.
- Family supports should support the entire family.
- Family support services should encourage the inclusion of all children into the community.
- When children cannot remain with their families for whatever reason, out-of-home placement should be viewed initially as a temporary arrangement and efforts should be directed toward reuniting the family.
- When families cannot be reunited and when active parental involvement is absent, adoption should be aggressively pursued.
- Although it is a preferred alternative to any group setting or out-of-home placement, foster care should only be pursued when children cannot live with their families or with adoptive families.

Key Support Services for Families with Children Who Have Autism

To adequately address the varying needs of families who have children with autism, several key support services are required. These support services must be designed and provided in a manner that facilitates family choices and allows for flexibility. Singer and Irvin (1991) noted that families typically use and appreciate the services that allow them greater choice and that are tailored to their individual circumstances. Family support programs that are rigid and require adherence to inflexible rules or standards may not only fail to provide support, but these services may become yet another source of stress and frustration.

In addition to choice and flexibility, the family support service must allow for full family participation in the design and monitoring of the program. Families bring unique perspectives to the delivery of support services. They help ensure that the support is delivered in respectful and meaningful ways to serve the interest of the family. Giving families the power to monitor the outcomes and quality of the support services empowers them to help make needed changes to ensure that the goals of family support services are realized.

It is impossible in one chapter to provide a complete description of every type of family support service that might be needed by families who have children and adults with autism. However, we emphasize seven specific family support services that can have a beneficial effect in assisting families.

Financial Assistance

There is a clear need for financial assistance for families with a child or adult who has autism, for that family system to maintain life at home. It is not, however, always clear from where these monies should or will come. Many states now offer some form of financial assistance to families who have children with disabilities (Singer & Irvin, 1991). These financial assistance programs are usually in the form of cash assistance to the family, payment for needed support services, or a combination of these services. However, one must note that in reviewing the amount of public resources put into this area, only about 2% of all public funds for persons with developmental disabilities goes to family support services (Braddock, Hemp, Fujiura, Bachelder, & Mitchell, 1989). Approximately 20 states now offer some form of cash assistance to families (Agosta, 1989). For these services to be effective, programs must be family centered, culturally sensitive, community based, and well coordinated (Agosta & Bradley, 1985; Turnbull et al., 1986). Agosta (1989) also pointed out that family-centered approaches to financial assistance need to:

1. enable and empower family members to make their own responsible decisions;
2. be responsive to the needs of the entire family system; and
3. be flexible enough to meet the particular needs of each individual family unit. (pp. 191–192)

Receiving cash assistance in any form enables a family to have control and flexibility over what services they may need to maintain quality of life at home as a family unit.

Parent Education

One of the main supports that has been provided to families is parent education. Parent education programs have been aimed at providing parents with skills and knowledge to help alleviate stress while building the child's skills in the home environment. The importance of these education programs in family support has been described frequently (Baker, 1976; Gordon & Davidson, 1981; O'Dell, 1985; Schopler & Reichler, 1971).

Much of the effort regarding parent education has concentrated on teaching parents skills of applied behavior analysis and is known as *behavioral parent training* (see Kaiser & Fox, 1986; O'Dell, 1985; Schreibman, Koegel, Mills, & Burke, 1984). In this approach, parents are taught learning theory and how to apply its principles and procedures. Typically, parents receive direct guidance in the actual modification of parent–child interactions (Kozloff, 1984; Lilly, 1974).

The use of the behavioral parent training model in family support programs is well supported with research on its efficacy. These procedures have been demonstrated to be both effective and efficient in helping parents learn and use skills to enhance their relationships with their children with autism (Kolko, 1984). It is clear that parents are capable of using behavioral principles and that when applied in home settings, child behavior change can be rapid and dramatic. There is some evidence that parents who use behavioral principles increase their recreational and leisure time and thus may alleviate stress (Koegel, Schreibman, Britten, Burke, & O'Neill, 1982).

The widespread use of behavioral parent training has been seen as a means to extend the educational treatment provided to the child. Whereas most parents teach their children in many informal ways, children with autism seem to benefit from more structured and direct parental instruction. The learning challenges presented by a youngster with autism are formidable and parents usually request assistance learning to improve their instructional efforts. Parents using behavioral teaching tactics have been able to enhance child performance in such diverse areas as communication skills, self-help skills, social skills, and academics, as well as teaching the child acceptable forms of behavior (see Harris, Wolchick, & Weitz, 1981; Snell & Beckman-Brindley, 1984). Behavioral parent training provides a structure to help parents become efficient and effective teachers of their children.

Kaiser and Fox (1986) describe the typical behavioral parent training process. Parents are taught to observe child behaviors and record data on the behaviors that they wish to modify. Parents are then instructed in the principles of applied behavior analysis through readings, videos, role-playing, and lectures. Parents are observed using these tactics and receive feedback from a professional in either home and/or clinical settings. They note, however, that training formats and lengths vary widely. Some programs concentrate on group training and others provide individual instruction. The goals of behavioral parent training are similar, however, the means of instruction vary considerably.

Behavioral parent training is not without its critics. Turnbull and her colleagues (1986) caution that overemphasis of behavioral parent training may relegate the parent to a surrogate teacher position. They warn that these highly structured approaches may distort the parent–child relationship and cause more stress within families. They urge methods that enhance the typical, informal parent–child teaching interactions that include affection, playing, and joking. Because parents have many essential roles to fulfill, behavioral parent training may simply require too much time and energy from the parents. Trying to meet necessary demands as well as those of structured interactions may cause substantial stress.

Singer, Irvine, and Irvin (1989) pointed out a number of additional limitations to behavioral parent training as a sole means of parental support. They raised concerns with the recruitment of parents for these programs, noting that recruitment rates tend to be low and that many parents tend to drop out of the training. They also noted that the research on behavioral parent training does not provide conclusive evidence of parents' ability to generalize learned skills to different behaviors, settings, or over time.

Kaiser and Fox (1986) noted that behavioral parent training approaches must be sensitive to the parents' time, energy, and desires. Behavioral parent training must be provided in the context of the family systems approach discussed earlier in this chapter. The training program must be focused on helping the family meet its needs, as opposed to merely extending the educational treatment provided to the child.

In response to this criticism, some researchers have implemented parent training programs that focus on the use of more natural instruction within the normal family routine. Singer and Irvin (1991) report several successful approaches to help parents improve teaching skills within the natural setting and everyday situations.

The shift from teaching parents highly structured and demanding teaching tactics to more natural and informal teaching interactions will be most helpful in supporting families. Parent training programs must continue to emphasize the primary role of the parent and recognize the many and sometimes competing needs of the family.

A comprehensive parent education program, such as the one advocated by Kozloff (1984), seems to be the most useful for families. In a comprehensive parent education program, behavioral parent training is one of several necessary components. The emphasis is on meeting a number of family needs through education. A comprehensive parent education program will include:

- Information on autism
- Information and community support services available to the family
- Skill development to enhance parent–child, child–child, parent–parent, and parent–professional interaction
- Information on rights, entitlements, and public laws
- Strategies to help parents manage time, resources, and competing needs
- Information on transition and future needs and service options for persons with autism

Naturally, flexibility in delivery, including evening and weekend availability, will facilitate the different needs of families. Access to written and recorded (audio and video cassettes) materials will be useful in allowing parents greater flexibility to gear their learning around their own schedule. Comprehensive parent education programs should provide regular follow-up services to allow parents an opportunity to renew skills, update information, and seek new educational support services. Regular follow-up can also facilitate greater generalization of learned materials.

Parent education must not be conceptualized as one-way delivery with professionals imparting information and skills to parents. Indeed, a comprehensive parent education program allows parents many opportunities to teach professionals and temper professionally accepted approaches with the reality of the family perspective. Parent education programs that make a difference in supporting families reassert that professionals need to learn from parents.

Respite Care

When a child has autism, parents very often have a difficult time finding babysitters to allow them breaks in parenting responsibilities. Most would agree that such breaks are essential for all parents, and even more so when a child has a disabling condition. When natural avenues for relief or respite are not available, a formal respite care program is needed. Respite can be arranged in many ways, from out-of-home services to in-home helpers who assist with the care of the individual with the autism. Unfortunately, many communities lack respite care programs (Salisbury & Intagliata, 1986) despite the persistent need for these services.

Singer et al. (1989) pointed out that although respite care is a necessary support service, in and of itself it may not reduce family stress. Respite care is more likely to be helpful to families if it is delivered as a part of a comprehensive support program. Respite should be designed to allow parents the greatest amount of control over how the respite is provided and flexibility as to when the respite is available and used. Knoll and Bedford (1989) found that parents are most satisfied when they selected the caregiver and the respite was provided on their schedule as opposed to a predetermined time. They also found that parents were least satisfied when the respite service was delivered in inflexible, bureaucratic ways. Again, choice and flexibility seem to be the key for delivery of this needed support service.

Case Management

With a vast array of fragmented and uncoordinated community-based services offered by a number of different private and public agencies, families who have children with autism often, but not always, need a support service to help them receive and coordinate these services. The term most commonly used for this support service is *case management*. Unfortunately, the term itself implies an impersonal approach in helping families select, use, and monitor support services. A father once said to us, "My family is not a case and we don't need to be managed!" He is right. Given the changing attitudes about family support, perhaps this service term will be changed to a more sensitive title, such as "Family Support Coordination."

Case management is typically provided by a human service professional or social worker who works directly with the family to:

1. Develop a support service plan;
2. identify community agencies that will provide the support;
3. assist with enrollment in the service;
4. monitor the quality of the service; and
5. periodically, update the support service plan to reflect changes in the family's needs.

In their analysis of case management services, Dunst and Trivette (1989) called for an enabling model of case management. This model of support service management is designed to strengthen the family via their active involvement in identifying their needs, arranging for resources, and monitoring the quality of services. In this model of case management, the professionals help families mobilize resources in a manner that provides the family with skills and a stronger control over the coordination and delivery of support services. Professionals proactively work with families to anticipate future support needs and promote the competencies that allow families to arrange for these services. Dunst and Trivette (1989) note that an outcome of the case management support should be family empowerment, in which their ability to make effective decisions about support services is strengthened.

Advocacy

Many families of children with autism find that they must fight the system in order to secure services for their children. It is a sad commentary that the system designed to support families often needs to be challenged in order to ensure the provision of appropriate services. Families typically find the proposition of fighting the system a lonely experience, with professionals distancing themselves from the controversy.

Parents are the best long-term advocates for their children (Donnellan & Mirenda, 1984; Vincent, Laten, Salisbury, Brown, & Baumgart, 1981). Hamre-Nietupski, Krajewski, Nietupski, Otercamp, Sensor, and Opheim (1988) note that in the advocacy process parents bring: (a) an intense, energetic commitment to their children and a strong desire for a better life in the community; (b) intimate knowledge of their children's needs and the ability to articulate those needs to the general community; and (c) the ability to network with other parents and influence community leaders through the advocacy process (p. 252).

They continue:

> Parental efforts, however, can be strengthened significantly through sustained assistance from professionals in the community who support integrated services. Professionals can add the following to the partnership: (a) experience with "the system": an understanding of how it works, who to contact, and strategies for overcoming system-imposed obstacles; (b) access to professional literature/research to support family contentions that integration is feasible and in the best interest of all children; and (c) knowledge of strategies to make integration work and resources to implement such strategies. (p. 252)

Mutual Support Networks

Many families report that they find mutual support networks, whether groups or individual supports, to be a critical component in their total support picture. This type of support is common in our society today. Singer and Irvin (1991) estimate that as many as seven million Americans currently belong to mutual assistance groups for a variety of needs. A number of these support networks have arisen among the perceived support needs of families who have a family member with a general or specific disability. There are clear reasons for the development and growth of these groups. Thoits (1986) pointed out that people are most likely to seek support from individuals or groups who have experiences similar to their own. On the other hand, help from those who are seen as different from themselves can be seen as controlling or demanding. A parent of a child with autism can say "I know how you feel" to another parent with a legitimacy that a professional who has not had similar experiences can never achieve. Professionals, however, can support families by being aware of mutual support networks in order to inform families of their existence and availability. Should there not be such a network available in a community, professionals can facilitate the development by putting families in touch with each other or helping bring them together. Professionals can facilitate parent entry into a support network or provide specific information or assistance to the network when it is requested, but such networks function best when they are of the members, by the members, and for the members.

Supports for the Future

Earlier in this chapter reference was made to constant concern in regard to the future of the family member with autism. Professionals can support families in planning and preparation for the future through the activities discussed here:

Transition Planning. As the child with autism matures, the family should be actively involved in planning for the child's transition from one service to another. Ideally, parents and other family members have been oriented to future needs of the child and community service options. A systematic approach to helping families prepare for future has been referred to as *Individualized Transition Planning.*

In this regard the Individuals with Disabilities Education Act, Public Law 101–476, has defined and addressed *transition services* in the following way:

> . . . a coordinated set of activities for a student, designed within an outcome oriented process, which promotes movement from school to post-school activities, including post-secondary education, vocational training, integrated employment (including supported employment), continuing and adult education, adult services, independent living, or community participation. The coordinated set of activities shall be based upon the individual student's needs, taking into account the student's preferences and interests, and shall include instruction, community experiences, the development of employment, and other post school adult living objectives, and when appropriate, acquisition of daily living skills and functional vocational objectives. (Sec 602[a][19])

Estate and Financial Planning. As the child with autism matures, family concerns tend to focus on future arrangements for the individual when parents and other family members are not available. Given the rapid changes in social services policy, benefits, and community services, future estate and financial planning is a strategic step to help ensure this family member's future.

Estate and financial planning are typically done via wills and trusts. However, Fee (1990) noted that simple wills and special needs trusts are typically not sufficient to ensure a secure future for the person with a disability. Fee advocates a life planning approach using a letter of intent (Russell, 1990) that allows the family to specify what they want for the family member in terms of residential, vocational, recreational, religious, medical, and social services. Naturally, the first option is to allow the individual with autism to be actively involved in specification of future life styles and services. However, when the individual has difficulty expressing desires, as is often the case with autism, the family's letter of intent can inform future care providers of their preferences.

Another future planning option for families is the self-sufficiency trust set up in several states to help supplement the individual's government benefits. These trusts are managed in a manner that allows families to set aside resources that do not interfere with the individual's benefits, and are used to provide services and materials to enhance the family member's quality of life.

Apolloni (1989) described a service model called the National Continuity Program, which is aimed at supporting the long term financial, advocacy, and guardianship services for persons with disabilities. This program serves to assist local advocacy programs in ensuring provision of quality services. The National Continuity Program provides seven key services to participants and their families. These include the following:

1. A file is established for each participant and updated to ensure proper services.
2. When a parent dies or becomes permanently disabled, the program monitors the participant's receipt of government benefits.
3. The participant is provided representation at individual habilitation planning sessions with state agencies.
4. The participant is visited twice a month to monitor quality of life standards and advocate on the individual's behalf.
5. The delivery of all services are monitored and an advocate acts to correct problems.
6. A guardian is ensured when a guardian is necessary.
7. Legal, dental, and medical services that supplement government services are made available.

In addition to the obvious long-term support such a program can provide to families, it may offer more immediate support in alleviating some parental stress about future care for the son or daughter with autism.

A CALL TO ACTION – BEING AN EFFECTIVE FAMILY HELPER

The professional needs to go beyond a mere recognition of the needs of families and understanding of the systems that influence families. The professional must exhibit a number of key characteristics that enhance family function. Although not an exhaustive list, we believe the following characteristics are germane to the professional who wishes to help families who have children with autism.

Respect. Professionals must first and foremost respect the family as a unique system, and respect and recognize the individuals who comprise that system. The professional must demonstrate a positive respect via words, gestures, and direct assistance provided.

Trust. Jones, Lepley, and Baker (1984) countered that trust is the basis of effective communication. Professionals must be individuals who can be trusted by family members. Likewise, the professional must be trusting of others (Stewart, 1986). The professional must exhibit confidence in family members.

No Presumption of Pathology. Effective helpers will not presume that the family is sick, but rather accept a posture that the family has unique needs because of the family member with autism. They must recognize that those needs will vary from family to family. Effective professionals reject the pathogenic notion of autism.

Praise. All too often, family members never hear words of praise or encouragement. They hear the reports of the child's problems. They hear blame. They hear words of despair. Effective professionals have an understanding and appreciation for the many demands placed on family members and recognize accomplishments within that context. They seize every opportunity to recognize the accomplishments of the family members.

Empathy. A key characteristic of effective professionals is an ability to understand families. The professional who demonstrates empathy and an ability to understand the needs and feelings of others will be effective with the families they wish to help. An understanding of the family, its interactions, needs, joys, feelings, and attitudes will help the professional provide the necessary support within a context that can be utilized and understood.

Ethics. The title "professional" implies strict adherence to a set of ethical principles of the profession. Family members have a right to expect professionals to behave in accordance with the highest standards expected in the profession. Chief among these high standards are:

- *Maintaining Confidentiality.* The family must know that the professional will never breach a family's confidence. Information about the family must be shared only with permission and then only with other professionals who have a clear need to know.
- *Staying Current.* Professionals must keep their skills and knowledge up-to-date. Professionals who provide erroneous information or lack current skills do a severe disservice to the family. Professionals must ensure that their knowledge and skills are continually developed.
- *Promoting the Interest of the Family.* Professionals must always put the needs and interest of the family before any personal self-interest. Similarly, the professional cannot permit bureaucratic or agency interests to diminish efforts to support families.

Gentleness. Families who face harsh realities do not need harsh professionals. Families need sensitive professionals who practice gentle intervention. Gentle intervention does *not* imply a less-than-aggressive approach to family support. It does imply intervention that is sensitive to family needs and the demands faced by the family. Gentle intervention means using and strengthening natural supports, using sensitive language, listening, and, when possible, working behind-the-scenes to help families. Gentle intervention also implies arranging meetings that are sensitive to the needs of the family.

Limited Demands. Professionals who understand the pressure experienced by families will work to limit extra demands. Effective, empathetic professionals seek ways to support families without adding to their burdens.

Orientation Toward the Future. Families need professionals who are focused on the future, not those who continually look at the past. The effective helper will use the present to prepare the family and individual with autism for the future while helping to shape that future.

Optimism. Families often find themselves surrounded by professionals and friends who convey a pessimistic attitude. They receive sympathy and hear words like "Too bad," "I'm so sorry," "How do you ever do it." Although well-meaning, these statements do little to support the family and can engender despair. Such pessimism is commonly compounded by negative evaluations that focus on the family member's deficiencies. Effective professionals are optimistic about the future. They convey hopeful, optimistic messages that are matched with energy, skill, zeal, and commitment to work for positive futures. Effective professionals focus on the positive attributes of the individual with autism and build upon the person's strengths.

FUTURE DIRECTIONS IN SUPPORTING FAMILIES

We have come a long way in the last 20 years in the support of families who have children with autism. No longer are parents held responsible for the cause of the autism, and there is a common acceptance of the family's right to be supported. However, we also have a long way to go before all families with children with autism are afforded positive futures. In the immediate future, specific attention should be given to the following areas:

1. Support to extended family members. Grandparents, aunts, uncles, cousins, nieces, and nephews all are affected in one way or another by the presence of autism. Extended family members can be a major source of longitudinal and natural support to the immediate family. To facilitate this, we need to find better ways to understand and address the needs of extended family members and provide them with necessary support.
2. Support to single parents. A growing phenomenon in our society is the single-parent household. Although there is a greater recognition of the special needs of the single-parent household, much of the research and demonstration work has concentrated on the traditional, two-parent family. Much more attention needs to be given to support strategies to help single parents of children with autism. Likewise, special attention must be given to the divorced parent who no longer lives with the child with autism. The parenting responsibilities of the divorced father or mother take on new dimensions when the parent may only see the child for short intervals. We need to recognize the importance of these parents and seek strategies to meet their needs.
3. Natural supports. The best support seems to be that which comes from natural sources, like family and friends, as well as generic community services. If we are to capitalize on these, we need to formulate better ways to help families access this support. We need to investigate barriers to developing natural support and discover the types of natural support that are best suited to different families and different times.
4. Assessment of needs. Now that we recognize that families are indeed different and thus have different needs, we need to develop systematic ways to assess those needs. Such strategies will be helpful in the development of new support services and public policy aimed at strengthening families.

5. Rural families. Much of the present work with families has been done with those residing in either large metropolitan settings or suburban communities. It is the family with a child with autism living on an isolated ranch, or in a small rural community, that is often neglected. How can we better develop support services and policies to allow families to choose a rural life style if they have a child with autism and need support?

6. Families whose children cannot live at home. Whereas the vast majority of families do not place their child out of the home, especially during the younger years (Ashbaugh, Spence, Lubin, Houlihan, & Langer, 1985; Perlman, 1985), some families, because of extreme circumstances, may find this their only option. Some families also find in the later years of dealing with a family member with disabilities that they can no longer care for the individual. We need to find ways to understand these families' needs and provide support to them if such a decision is the best alternative. Professionals need to support these families rather than adding to the guilt they already may feel by making such a decision.

7. Quality indicators. As family support services are further developed, we need to begin to establish a set of quality indicators that will guide the service delivery system. What does quality imply? How do we recognize a quality program? Do we all agree on the indicators for quality family services? Although many may purport to provide family support services to those with autism, families and professionals should monitor and control the quality of those services. We need a mechanism that will help families and those who provide funding to recognize quality family services.

HELPING FAMILIES BUILD A POSITIVE FUTURE

Autism is one disability that has been plagued with an overwhelming negative attitude toward parents and a general disregard for family members. The predominant assumption that parents are to blame for autism has yielded to a more enlightened and helpful attitude that parents and family members need to be aggressively supported. Family support needs to be provided in a manner sensitive to the family system, taking into consideration the family's beliefs, values, development, needs, membership, and major functions. Proactive family support uses the natural networks and resources and supplements these as needed. Proactive family support is focused toward the future and is implemented by caring and competent professionals who appreciate the value of the unique relationship we call the parent–professional partnership. We now take a quick look into the future to see what it could hold for Nick, Timmy, Sarah, and their respective families.

Given creative supports from flexible systems and effective professionals, for Nick and his family the future looks bright. Nick lives in his own home and has a real job that pays him just about enough to make ends meet. That's good because he doesn't need to use all of his earnings to pay bills. Nick also gets some financial support that permits him both the freedom to pay for necessities and also things like recreation and a vacation. Two evenings a week Nick takes classes at the community college. He is particularly fond of the classes that he has taken there—after all, that is where he met his fiancée.

Timmy and his family are doing quite well also. Timmy is going to the same neighborhood school that the other children his age are attending. All the members of Timmy's family think that the extended day and extended school year services have been the strongest factor in Timmy's having mastered so many of the skills that even they were reluctant to guess that he would have mastered just a few years ago. Although school has been great, the real key for Timmy and his family has been the live-in assistance that has been provided for them through a coordinated effort of several state and local agencies and their church. Not only has the live-in help relieved a great deal of anxiety that Timmy's parents had about being able to meet the whole family's needs, but the tie-in with the school program has meant wonders for Timmy's learning.

For Sarah and her family, the good things that started for them when she was very young continue to get better. Sarah and her family are fully included in all the community's school and recreation opportunities. Everyone knows her and accepts her. One of the especially nice things that has happened is that Sarah's outgoing family has been instrumental in the development of several mutual support groups in town. Sarah's parents helped start an information and referral system for professionals and families in the region. Sarah's brothers and sisters regularly get together with other children their own age who happen to have siblings who have a variety of disabilities to share information and support each other. Even Sarah's grandparents have gotten in the act and meet at the community center with other grandparents who have grandchildren with disabilities. Sarah's extended family has networked at many levels.

We have hinted at some of the dreamed-of possibilities for three families. But what about Christopher and his family? What will their future hold? We won't pretend to know. The challenge for professionals will be to support all families in flexible, creative ways. It is safe to say that in the future families will be supported in ways we cannot begin to imagine. Let this be a CALL TO ACTION to all who come in contact with Christopher and his family. LET THEM DREAM! DREAM WITH THEM!

REFERENCES

Ackerman, A. L., Lyons, J. S., Hammer, J. S. & Larsen, D. B. (1988). The impact of coexisting depression and timing of consultation on medical patient's length of stay. *Hospital Community Psychiatry, 39*(2), 173–176.

Agosta, J. (1989). Using cash assistance to support family efforts. In G. H. S. Singer & L. K. Irvin (Eds.), *Support for caregiving families: Enabling positive adaptation to disability* (pp. 189–204). Baltimore: Paul Brookes.

Agosta, J., & Bradley, V. J. (Eds.). (1985). *Family care for persons with developmental disabilities: A growing commitment.* Cambridge, MA: Human Services Research Institute.

Anderson, K. (1971). The shopping behavior of parents of mentally retarded children: The professional person's role. *Mental Retardation, 9*(4), 3–5.

Antonovsky, A. (1987). *Unraveling the mystery of health: How people manage stress and stay well.* San Francisco: Jossey Bass.

Apolloni, T. (1989). Guardianship, trusts, and protective services. In G. Singer & L. Irvin (Eds.), *Support for caregiving families* (pp. 283–294). Baltimore: Paul Brookes.

Apolloni, T., & Triest, G. (1983). Respite services in California: Status and recommendations for improvement. *Mental Retardation, 21,* 240–243.

Ashbaugh, J., Spence, R., Lubin, R., Houlihan, J., & Langer, M. (1985). *Summary of data of handicapped children and youth.* Cambridge, MA: Human Services Research Institute.

Avant, R. F. (1988). Psychiatric consultation and referral. *Medical Clinics of NA, 72*(4), 929–935.

Baker, B. (1976). Parent involvement in programming for developmentally disabled children. In L. Lloyd (Ed.), *Communication assessment and intervention strategies* (pp. 691–733). Baltimore: University Park Press.

Bank, S. P., & Kahn, M. P. (1982). *The sibling bond.* New York: Basic Books.

Bebko, J. M., Konstantareas, M. M., & Springer, J. (1987). Parent and professional evaluations of family stress associated with characteristics of autism. *Journal of Autism and Developmental Disorders, 17,* 565–576.

Berlin, I. N. (1973). Simultaneous psychotherapy with a psychotic child and both parents: The reversal of mutism. In S. A. Szurek & I. N. Berlin (Eds.), *Clinical studies in childhood psychoses* (pp. 626–653). New York: Brunner/Mazel.

Bettelheim, B. (1967). *The empty fortress—Infantile autism and the birth of the self.* New York: Free Press.

Bicknell, J. (1983). The psychopathology of handicap. *British Journal of Medical Psychology, 56*(2).

Bodenheimer, C. (1979). For the sake of others. *Journal of Autism and Developmental Disorders, 9*(3), 291–293.

Braddock, D., Hemp, R., Fujiura, G., Bachelder, L., & Mitchell, D. (1989). *Public expenditures for mental retardation and developmental disabilities in the United States: State profiles* (working paper, 3rd ed.). Chicago: University Affiliated Program in Developmental Disabilities, University of Illinois at Chicago.

Bristol, M. M., Gallagher, J. J., & Schopler, E. (1988). Mothers and fathers of young developmentally disabled and nondisabled boys: Adaptation and spousal support. *Developmental Psychology, 24,* 441–451.

Cantwell, D. P., Baker, L., & Rutter, M. (1979). Family factors. In M. Rutter & E. Schopler (Eds.), *Autism: A reappraisal of concepts and treatment* (pp. 269–296). New York: Plenum Press.

Center on Human Policy. (1987). *Statement in support of families and their children.* Syracuse, NY: Author.

Cohen, S., Agosta, J., Cohen, J., & Warren, R. (1989). Supporting families of children with severe disabilities. *The Journal of the Association for Persons with Severe Handicaps, 14,* 155–162.

Cohen, S., & Syme, S. L. (1985). *Social support and health.* New York: Academic Press.

Crnic, K. A., Friedrich, W. N., & Guenberg, M. T. (1983). Adaptation of families with mentally retarded children: A model of stress, coping, and family ecology. *American Journal of Mental Deficiency, 88,* 125–138.

Cutler, B. (1981). *Unraveling the special education maze.* Champaign, IL: Research Press.

Darling, R. B. (1983). Parent-professional interaction: The roots of misunderstanding. In M. Seligman (Ed.), *The family with a handicapped child: Understanding and treatment* (pp. 95-124). Orlando, FL: Grune & Stratton.

Davidson, P. O., Schrag, A. R. (1968). Prognostic indicators for effective child psychiatric consultation. *Canadian Psychiatric Association Journal, 13,* 533.

DeMyer, M. K., Hingtgen, J. N., & Jackson, R. K. (1981). Infantile autism reviewed: A decade of research. *Schizophrenia Bulletin, 7*(3), 49-66.

Donnellan, A. M., & Mirenda, P. L. (1984). Issues related to professional involvement with families of individuals with autism and other severe handicaps. *Journal of the Association for Persons with Severe Handicaps,* 9(1), 16-25.

Dunst, C. & Trivette, C. (1989). An enablement and empowerment perspective of case management. *Topics in Early Childhood Special Education, 8*(4), 87-102.

Featherstone, H. (1980). *A difference in the family: Living with a disabled child.* New York: Basic Books.

Fee, R. W. (1990, Fall). The life planning approach. *New Ways,* 18-19.

Ferguson, P. M., & Asch, A. (1989). Lessons from life: Personal and parental perspective on school, childhood, and disability. In D. Biklen, D. Ferguson, & A. Ford (Eds.), *Schooling and disability; NSSE 88th Yearbook* (pp. 108-140). Chicago: University of Chicago Press.

Friedrich, W. N., & Friedrich, W. L. (1981). Psychosocial assets of parents of handicapped and non-handicapped children. *American Journal of Mental Deficiency, 85,* 551-553.

Gallagher, P. A., & Powell, T. H. (1989). Brothers and sisters: Meeting special needs. *Topics in Early Childhood Special Education, 8,* 24-37.

Gartner, A., Lipsky, D. K., & Turnbull, A. (1991). *Supporting families with a child with a disability: An international outlook.* Baltimore: Paul Brookes.

Gordon, S. B., & Davidson, N. (1981). Behavioral parent training. In A. S. Gurman & D. P. Kniskern (Eds.), *Handbook of family therapy* (pp. 515-575). New York: Brunner/Mazel.

Hamre-Nietupski, S., Krajewski, L., Nietupski, J., Otercamp, D., Sensor, K., & Opheim, B. (1988). Parent-professional partnerships in advocacy: Developing integrated options within restrictive systems. *The Journal of the Association for Persons with Severe Handicaps, 13,* 251-259.

Harris, S. L. (1983). *Families of the developmentally disabled: A guide to behavioral intervention.* New York: Plenum Press.

Harris, S. L, Wolchick, S. A., & Weitz, S. (1981). The acquisition of language skills by autistic children. Can parents do the job? *Journal of Autism and Developmental Disorders, 11,* 373-384.

Hobbs, N., Perrin, A., & Ireys, S. (1986). *Chronically ill children and their families.* San Francisco: Jossey Bass.

Jones, D. A., Lepley, M. K., & Baker, B. A. (1984). *Health assessment across the lifespan.* New York: McGraw Hill.

Kaiser, A. P., & Fox, J. J. (1986). Behavioral parent training research. Contributions to an ecological analysis of families of handicapped children. In J. J. Gallagher & P. M. Vietze (Eds.), *Families of handicapped persons* (pp. 219-235). Baltimore: Paul Brookes.

Kanner, L. (1949). Problems of nosology and psychodynamics of early infantile autism. *American Journal of Orthopsychiatry, 19,* 416-426.

Kazak, A. E., & Marvin, R. S. (1984). Differences, difficulties, and adaptation: Stress and social networks in families with a handicapped child. *Family Relations, 33,* 67-77.

Knoll, J., & Bedford, S. (1989, May/June). Respite services: A national survey of parents' experience. *Exceptional Parent,* pp. 34-37.

Koegel, R. L., Schreibman, L., Britten, K. R., Burke, J. C., & O'Neill, R. E. (1982). A comparison of parent training to direct child treatment. In R. L. Koegel, A. Rincover, & A. L. Egel (Eds.), *Education and understanding autistic children* (pp. 260-281). San Diego, CA: College-Hill Press.

Kolko, D. J. (1984). Parents as behavior therapists for their autistic children: Clinical and empirical considerations. In E. Schopler & G. Mesibov (Eds.), *The effects of autism on the family*. New York: Plenum.

Kozloff, M. A. (1984). A training program for families of children with autism: Responding to family needs. In E. Schopler & G. Mesibov (Eds.), *The effects of autism on the family*. New York: Plenum.

Lamb, M. E. (1983). Fathers of exceptional children. In M. Seligman (Ed)., *The family with a handicapped child*. New York: Grune & Stratton.

Laureys, K., (1982, November). *Autism*. Speech given at the National Society for Children and Adults with Autism, Washington, D.C.

Lettick, S. (1979). Ben. *Journal of Autism and Developmental Disorders, 9*(3), 293–294.

Lilly, D. L. (1974). Dimensions in parent programs: An overview. In J. Grim (Ed.), *Training parents to teach-four models. First chance for children* (Vol. 3, pp. 1–9). Chapel Hill, NC: Technical Assistance Development Systems.

Lyon, S., & Preis, A. (1983). Working with families of severely handicapped persons. In M. Seligman (Ed.), *The family with a handicapped child*. New York: Grune & Stratton.

Meyer, D. J. (1986). Fathers of children with handicaps: Developmental trends in fathers' experiences over the family life cycle. In R. R. Fewell & P. F. Vadasy (Eds.), *Families of handicapped children: Needs and supports across the lifespan* (pp. 35–73) Austin, TX: Pro-Ed.

Miezo, P. M. (1983). *Parenting children with disabilities*. New York: Marcel Bekker.

Milgram, N. A., & Atzil, M. (1988). Parenting stress in raising autistic children. *Journal of Autism and Developmental Disorders, 18*, 415–424.

Minuchin, S. (1974). *Families and family therapy*. Cambridge, MA: Harvard University Press.

Moore, J. A., Hamerlynck, L. A., Barsh, E. T., Spicker, S., & Jones, R. (1982). *Extending family resources* (2nd ed.). Seattle: Childrens' Clinic and Preschool, University of Washington.

Myers, R. (1978). *Like normal people*. New York: McGraw Hill.

National Society for Children and Adults with Autism. (1981). *How they grow: A handbook for parents of young children with autism* (2nd ed.). Washington, DC: Author.

Neugarten, B. (1976). Adaptations and the life cycle. *The Counseling Psychologist, 6*, 16–20.

Noh, S., Dumas, J. E., Wolf, L. C., & Fisman, S. N. (1989). Delineating sources of stress in parents of exceptional children. *Family Relations, 38*, 456–461.

Notarios, C. I., Benson, P. R., & Sloane, P. (1989). Exploring the interface between perception and behavior: An analysis of marital interaction in distressed and nondistressed couples. *Behavioral Assessment, 11*, 39–64.

Nye, F. (1976). *Role structure and analysis of the family*. Beverly Hills: Sage.

O'Dell, S. L. (1985). Program in parent training. In R. M. Eisler, M. Hersen, & P. M. Miller (Eds.), *Progress in behavior modification* (Vol. 19, pp. 57–108). New York: Academic Press.

Ornitz, E. M. (1978). The moderation of sensory input and motor output in autistic children. In E. Schopler & R. J. Reichler (Eds.), *Psychopathology and child development* (pp. 115–133). New York: Plenum Press.

Pahl, J., & Quine, L. (1987). Families with mentally handicapped children. In J. Orford (Ed.), *Treating the disorder, treating the family* (pp. 39–61). Baltimore: Johns Hopkins University Press.

Patton, J. R., Payne, J. S., & Beirne-Smith, M. (1986). *Mental retardation*. Columbus, OH: Merrill.

Perlman, R. H. (1985). *Family home care: Critical issues for services and policies*. New York: Hawthorne Press.

Plienis, A. J., Robbins, F. R., & Dunlap, G. (1988). Parents' adjustment and family stress as factors in behavioral parent training for young autistic children. *Journal of the Multihandicapped Person, 1*(1), 31–52.

Powell, T. H., & Ogle, P. (1985). *Brothers and sisters: A special part of exceptional families.* Baltimore: Paul Brookes.

Rabkin, J. G., & Struening, E. L. (1976). Life events, stress, and illness. *Science, 194,* 1013–1020.

Ritvo, E. R., & Freeman, B. J. (1984). A medical model of autism: Etiology, pathology, and treatment. *Pediatric Annals, 13,* 298–305.

Russell, M. (1990, Fall). Writing the letter of intent. *New Ways,* pp. 20–25.

Salisbury, C. L., & Intagliata, J. (Eds.). (1986). *Respite care: Support for persons with developmental disabilities and their families.* Baltimore, MD: Paul Brookes.

Sample, B. M. (1991). *Shopping behavior: A comparative study.* Unpublished master's thesis, Eastern Montana College, Billings, MT.

Schopler, E. (1976). Toward reducing behavior problems in autistic children. In L. C. Wing (Ed.), *Early childhood autism* (pp. 84–107). Oxford: Pergamon Press.

Schopler, E., & Reichler, R. (1971). Parents as co-therapists in the treatment of psychotic children. *Journal of Autism and Childhood Schizophrenia, 1,* 87–102.

Schreibman, L., Koegel, R. L., Mills, D. L., & Burke J. C. (1984). Training parent–child interactions. In E. Schopler & G. B. Mesibov (Eds.), *The effects of autism on the family* (pp. 187–205). New York: Plenum Press.

Schvaneveldt, J. D., & Ihinger, M. (1979). Sibling relationships in the family. In W. R. Burr, R. Hill, F. I. Nye, & I. L. Reiss (Eds.), *Contemporary theories about the family* (Vol. 1, pp. 453–467). New York: Free Press.

Seligman, M. (1979). *Strategies for helping parents of exceptional children.* New York: Free Press.

Seligman, M., & Darling, R. B. (1989). *Ordinary families and special children: A systems approach to childhood disability.* New York: Guilford Press.

Singer, G. H. S., & Irvin, L. K. (1991). Supporting families of persons with severe disabilities: Emerging findings, practices, and questions. In L. H. Meyer, C. A. Peck, & L. Brown (Eds.), *Critical issues in the lives of people with severe disabilities* (pp. 271–312). Baltimore: Paul Brookes.

Singer, G. H. S., Irvine, A. B., & Irvin, L. K. (1989). Expanding the focus of behavioral parent training: A contextual approach. In G. H. S. Singer & L. K. Irvin (Eds.), *Support for caregiving families: Enabling positive adaptation to disability* (pp. 85–102). Baltimore: Paul Brookes.

Snell, M. E., & Beckman-Brindley, S. (1984). Family involvement in intervention with children having severe handicaps. *Journal of the Association for Persons with Severe Handicaps, 9*(3), 213–230.

Sonnek, I. M. (1986). Grandparents and extended family of handicapped children. In R. R. Fewell & P. F. Vadasy (Eds.), *Families of handicapped children: Needs and supports across the lifespan* (pp. 99–120) Austin, TX: Pro-Ed.

Stewart, C. J. (1986). *Counseling parents of exceptional children.* Columbus, OH: Merrill.

Summers, J. A., Behr, S. K., & Turnbull, A. P. (1989). Positive adaptations and coping strengths of families who have children with disabilities. In G. H. S. Singer & L. K. Irvin (Eds.), *Support for caregiving families: Enabling positive adaptation to disability* (pp. 27–40). Baltimore: Paul Brookes.

Summers, J. A., Turnbull, A. P., & Brotherson, M. J. (1985). *Coping strategies for families with disabled children.* Baltimore: Paul Brookes.

Thoits, P. A. (1986). Social support as coping assistance. *Journal of Consulting and Clinical Psychology, 54,* 416–423.

Tinbergen, E. A., & Tinbergen, N. (1972). *Early childhood autism: An ethological approach.* Berlin: Paul Parey.

Turnbull, A. P., & Turnbull, H. R. (1986). *Families, professionals and exceptionality.* Columbus, OH: Merrill.

Turnbull, H. R., Guess, D., & Turnbull, A. P. (1988). Vox populi and baby doe. *Mental Retardation, 26,* 127–132.

Turnbull, A. P., Summers, J. A., & Brotherson, M. J. (1984). *Working with families with disabled members: A family systems approach.* Lawrence, KS: Kansas University.

Turnbull, A. P., Summers, J., & Brotherson, M. (1986). Family life cycle: Theoretical and empirical implications and future directions for families with mentally retarded members. In J. Gallagher & P. Vietze (Eds.), *Research on families with retarded children* (pp. 45–66). Baltimore: University Park Press.

Vincent, L. J., Laten, S., Salisbury, C., Brown, P., & Baumgart, D. (1981). Family involvement in the educational processes of severely handicapped students: State of the art and directions for the future. In B. Wilcox & R. York (Eds.), *Quality educational services for the severely handicapped: The federal perspective* (pp. 164–179). Washington, DC: Division of Innovation and Development, Department of Education.

Vitaliano, P. P., Maiuro, R. D., Russo, J. J., & Becker, J. (1987). Raw versus relative scores in the assessment of coping strategies. *Journal of Behavioral Medicine, 10,* 1–18.

Waisbren, S. E. (1980). Parent's reactions after birth of a developmentally disabled child. *American Journal of Mental Deficiency, 84,* 345–351.

Wolf, L. C., Noh, S., Fisman, S. N., & Speechley, M. (1989). Brief report: Psychological effects of parenting stress in parents of autistic children. *Journal of Autism and Developmental Disorders, 19,* 157–166.

Zatlow, G. (1982). A sister's lament. *Sibling Information Network Newsletter, 1*(5), 2. (Reprinted from Citizen's Future, 1981).

10 Early Intervention for Children with Autism

Michael D. Powers
Newington Children's Hospital, Newington, CT

Few issues in autism in recent years have generated the intense discussion and debate as has the delivery of early intervention to preschoolers with autism. At the heart of these discussions lies a public policy directive, some data, many assumptions, and the stark reality of the impact of a diagnosis of autism on a young family. The public policy directive, in the form of PL99-457, provided funds for all U. S. states, the District of Columbia, Puerto Rico, and territories to design comprehensive and coordinated interdisciplinary services for infants and toddlers with disabilities and their families. The potential impact and scope of PL99-457 cannot be underestimated; it represents a tremendous step forward in the fight to insure better futures for all children with disabilities.

The data fueling the debate are best embodied in the published work of Lovaas (1987) and Strain and his colleagues (Strain & Hoyson, 1988; Strain, Hoyson, & Jamieson, 1985). These authors, working at UCLA and the University of Pittsburgh/Project LEAP, reported extraordinary successes with preschoolers with autism receiving intensive early intervention services prior to age 5. Indeed, both authors reported that approximately one half of those children previously enrolled in their programs were full mainstreamed in typical first grades (Lovaas, 1987: 47%; Strain & Hoyson, 1988: 52%) and required no special services. Although many other programs for preschoolers with autism have reported important gains and many successes (see Olley, Robbins, & Morelli-Robbins, in press), nowhere else has the success been so dramatic, nor so much in the public eye.

Not surprisingly, data such as these have captured the imaginations of many researchers and clinicians, with considerable debate concerning the empirical, programmatic, and policy implications of the findings. In this debate, several assumptions have been proffered, not all of which enjoy a firm empirical base. These include:

1. All children with autism and pervasive developmental disorder, regardless of severity, will respond well to the same type of early intervention (e.g., integrated, 40 hours per week).
2. Fully integrated programs are more effective than partially integrated or segregated programs.
3. One particular instructional technology (e.g., discrete trial teaching, incidental teaching) is more effective than another.
4. The components of successful early intervention programs have an established empirical base warranting their inclusion as "best practice." That is, thorough component analysis has already been accomplished.

To these assumptions, add the harsh reality confronted by young families still reeling from the initial diagnosis of autism in their son or daughter (Harris & Handleman, 1986; Tommasone & Tommasone, 1989). It comes as no surprise to learn that upon reading reports of the successes of the UCLA or LEAP programs, many young parents considered the viability of relocating their families for the sake of their child with autism's future.

The road for families of a child with autism has never been an easy one. If the advent of early intervention has been a bright ray of hope for their child's future, it has also led to confusion over conflicting reports of effectiveness of particular programs. Coupled with a family's fervent wish to do what is best for their child, we may have made the future brighter, but the present more confusing—at least initially.

This chapter attempts to define some of these issues, present the data, and clarify some of the assumptions parents and professionals must confront in selecting or providing early intervention services to prekindergarten age children with autism. After providing an overview of the characteristics of young children with autism, components considered essential to effective early intervention are described. The chapter concludes with a discussion of early intervention issues requiring additional investigation.

CHARACTERISTICS OF YOUNG CHILDREN WITH AUTISM

Early intervention for children with autism is dependent on early diagnosis. Only recently, however, have researchers begun to address developmental considerations in a manner that facilitates differential diagnosis in children under age five. Despite the lack of clear-cut diagnostic parameters, there is ample clinical and empirical evidence to guide the diagnostic and differential diagnostic process.

"Autism" or the "Autistic Syndromes"?

For as long as autism has been described there has been debate on what constitutes "true" autism. Given an early reliance on the medical model (still prevalent today in many quarters) this is not surprising. Over the past 15 years, however, it has become clearer that autism is a syndrome, not a "disease" in the traditional sense of that word. As a syndrome, symptom manifestation in autism varies on the continuum of severity. Core features must always be observed (i.e., deficits in reciprocal social interactions and deficits of language and communication), but the range of associated features is wide (included here is self-injury, stereotypy, etc.). Thus, degree of impairment, not qualitative distinctions, differentiate preschoolers with autism (Dahl, Cohen, & Provence, 1986). In trying to represent the most up-to-date empirical evidence on nosology, framers of diagnostic criteria have generally concurred on the full syndrome of autism, but have had considerable difficulty diagnosing children clearly affected but to less severe (or to varying) degrees. Terms like Childhood Onset Pervasive Developmental Disorder (COPDD; American Psychiatric Association, 1980), Pervasive Developmental Disorder Not Otherwise Specified (PDDNOS; American Psychiatric Association, 1987), Autistic Spectrum Disorder (Rapin, 1988), and Atypical Pervasive Developmental Disorder (Levine & Demb, 1987), are evident in the clinical literature and in practice. Although the development of syndromal diagnostic frameworks is essential work (see Powers, 1984), for the present, they are less-than-optimal for treatment planning purposes.

Powers and Handleman (1984) have detailed the use of behavioral assessment procedures for purposes of treatment planning and evaluation as an adjunct to syndromal diagnosis. With its attention to individual behavioral repertoires and careful description of behavioral and learning strengths, needs, excesses, and deficits, behavioral assessment offers a comprehensive approach to treatment planning once a diagnosis has been established.

Preschoolers presenting for an evaluation for possible autism present special challenges related to developmental factors such as age or cognitive ability, severity of symptoms, and the changing, highly plastic presentation of autism with infants and toddlers. It is beyond the scope of this chapter to describe the assessment and diagnostic process in detail (see Schopler & Mesibov, 1988, for a comprehensive review), however, it may be useful to describe the range of symptoms observed with children with autism from birth through age five. Table 10.1 presents symptoms in a developmental

TABLE 10.1
Characteristics of Preschoolers with Autism

Ages	*Sensorimotor*	*Language & Communication*	*Social Interaction*	*Imaginative Abilities*
Birth–6 months	Persistent rocking Startled and/or nonresponsive to simuli especially auditory Unusual sleep cycles Less active or demanding than nonhandicapped infant (torpor) Minority are extremely irritable	Failure to vocalize Crying not related to needs	No anticipatory social responses (absent or delayed smiling response and anticipatory reflex) Passive Poor or absent eye contact/gaze avoidant Fails to respond to mother's attention and crib toys	
6–12 months	Sleeping and eating cycles may not develop naturally Motor development is uneven Transition to table foods is difficult Unusual attachment to objects Appears deaf Regarding of hands Hyper- and/or hypo-sensitivity to sensory stimuli Irregular motor development Limp or rigid when held Flicking at objects	Babbling may stop Does not imitate sounds, gestures or expressions Disinterested in communicating	Unaffectionate; difficult to engage in baby games Does not wave bye-bye No interest in toys may be extremely withdrawn and actively reject interaction, or accept some attention but imitate little Difficult to soothe when upset	Repetitive motor behavior in observed play sequence

12–24 months	Sleep problems Previously acquired skills may decline Hypo/hypersensitivity to stimuli Seeks repetitive stimulation Repetitive motor mannerisms appear, e.g., hand-flapping, whirling	No speech or occasional words Talking may stop Ability to use gestures is absent Sounds used noncommunicatively Echolalic sounds may be present (e.g., "eeeee")	Withdrawn Separation anxiety absent Ideosyncratic use of toys, for example, spinning Lining up objects	Little interest in exploring Idiosyncratic use of toys, spinning Lining up objects
24–36 months	Sleep problems continue Appears to be able to do things but refuses Self-care skills delayed Excessive irritability Hypo/hypersensitivity to stimuli and repetitive motor mannerisms continue Hyperactivity and/or hypoactivity	Mute or intermittent talking Echolalia Specific cognitive abilities observed, for example, good rote memory Leads adult by hand to communicate needs Speech tone or rhythm unusual	Does not play with other children Prefers to be left alone Idisyncratic use of toys continues	Object mouthing Symbolic play absent Repetitive motor behavior continues Visual fascination with objects—stares at lights, and so on Visual motor abilities may become evident (e.g., puzzle use)
36–60 months	Some problems continue; sensitivity to stimuli and motor mannerisms may decrease	No speech/odd speech Echolalia Pronoun reversal Unusual tone and rhythm in speech Unusual thoughts	Some problems continue, but may become more social Changes in the child's environment cause distress, sometimes severe	Objects used functionally Perspective-taking with dolls is absent Symbolic play is limited to simple schemes repeated over and over May be unable to pantomime Sociodramatic play absent

sequence from birth through 60 months across the domains of sensorimotor functioning, language and communication, social interaction, and imaginative abilities. Information in the table was adapted from DeMyer (1979), Freeman and Ritvo (1984), Gillberg (1989), Gillberg, Ehlers, Schaumann, Jakobsson, Dahlgren, Lindblom, Bagengholm, Tjuus, and Blinder (1990), Hoshino, Kumashiro, Yashima, Tachibana, Watanabe, and Furukawa (1982), Ornitz, Guthrie, and Farley (1977), Percy, Gillberg, Hagberg, and Witt-Engerstrom (1990), Sugiyama and Abe (1989), and Watson and Marcus (1988).

In reviewing this table, it is essential to recognize that individual variation is the norm with children with autism. Thus, some children will manifest these symptoms earlier or later. The information will be most useful if it serves as a framework for identifying children with autism, specifying their individual symptom profiles, and subsequently lead to behavioral or educational assessment for program planning.

ESSENTIAL COMPONENTS OF EARLY INTERVENTION FOR CHILDREN WITH AUTISM

Long before the advent of PL99-457, researchers were considering the unique educational needs of young children with autism. Although the empirical base that is evolving is by no means complete, it is possible to identify characteristics of early intervention programs for children with autism currently considered to represent "best practice." Several existing programs conform to these best practices (e.g., Anderson, Avery, Dipietro, Edwards, & Christian, 1987; Egel & Powers, 1988; Harris & Handleman, 1989; Lovaas, 1987; McGee, 1991; Strain & Hoyson, 1988). It is noteworthy, however, that these programs are not identical. Differences exist in terms of intensity, location (e.g., public school, private school, research program), instructional technologies relied on, and degree of involvement of families. All programs report significant changes with the majority of children over time, with the most dramatic outcomes reported by Strain and Lovaas. At present, it is not clear which program components contribute most to optimal outcomes among these various programs. "Best practice," then, should be viewed as a dynamic, evolving enterprise that provides a framework for program development while also providing the structure for formative and summative program evaluation, and subsequent change. Eight components are described, based on the work of Anderson et al. (1987); Dunlap, Robbins, Morelli, and Dollman (1988); Egel and Powers (1988); Farran (in press); Harris (1991); Harris and Handleman (1989); Lovaas (1987); McGee (1991); Olley, Robbins, and Morelli-Robbins (in press); Powers (1989); Powers and Olley (1989); Simeonsson, Olley, and

Rosenthal, (1987); and Strain and Hoyson (1988). This section describes the rationale and implications for each component.

Component 1: Structured Treatment Utilizing the Principles of Applied Behavior Analysis

Behavior analysis has long been the mainstay of applied research with children with autism (see Schreibman, Koegel, Charlop, & Egel, 1990, for a comprehensive review). Unfortunately, developmental considerations largely have been underaddressed in work with school-age children. As children grow older, a reliance on developmental indices for program planning increases the risk that learning objectives will not be functional. To many program planners, such risks and the established superiority of functional approaches to educating learners with severe handicaps (see Falvey, 1989) have led to the demise of developmental curricula as a foundation of best practice. For preschoolers, however, issues of developmental versus functional curricula are not so clear-cut. For example, Olley and Stevenson (1989) argue that a combination of both approaches may be best because curricula scope and sequence are well-defined. Because curriculum content is in many ways separate from the technology of behavior analysis, early childhood education may well find new challenges in addressing developmental skills to be taught in a systematic fashion. The emphasis on well-sequenced, structured teaching and evaluation methods characteristic of applied behavior analysis make it uniquely well-suited to the goal of effective instruction.

Structured treatment is characterized by several features:

1. The *scope and sequence* of lessons is structured clearly within and across objectives. While reciprocal social interactions and communication deficits are endemic to autism, numerous other instructional domains present learning challenges. Romanczyk (1990) identified 16 domains, including maladaptive behavior, attentive skills, speech, receptive language, expressive language, concept formation, motor skills, self-help skills, social skills, reading skills, writing skills, arithmetic skills, cultural skills, general information, school-related skills, and life-relevant skills. Each of these areas must be evaluated for behavioral/pre-academic strengths and needs to establish the scope of the preschoolers' individualized educational plan (IEP). Once the scope has been established, an instructional sequence can be determined. Prioritization *across* domains can be based on skill deficits, next-environment considerations (cf. Vincent, Salisbury, Walter, Brown, Gruenewald, & Powers, 1980), or critical need (i.e., skills critical to participation/survival, for example, the elimination of severe aggression).

To address within-domain learning sequences, specific skills to be taught must be task analyzed into their component parts. The pervasive nature of autism demands that skills not only be broken down by topography (what the learner must physically do to demonstrate the skill), but also by social and communicative behavior necessary to prevent the skill from being performed outside of a social–communicative context. For example, in addition to determining the skill sequence for using the toilet independently, preschoolers must learn to solicit their teacher's attention and make eye contact concurrent with a request to use the toilet. The actual form of the attention signal and the proximity to the teacher are dimensions that will vary across classrooms. Failure to include such features in the teaching plan, however, may lead to functional performance that has difficulty generalizing and maintaining across adults and environments.

2. *Specificity in target behavior selection* is a hallmark of applied behavior analysis. Academic, social, and communication skills to be taught must be defined operationally, and their topography, duration/frequency, magnitude, and pervasiveness clearly described (see Powers & Handleman, 1984).

3. Programming should be *databased,* using behavioral assessment technology for predictive, formative, and summative evaluation. Ecological contexts must be considered, including physical, social, and communicative environments. Teaching programs to accelerate or decelerate behavior (including academic skills) should be outlined in detail in a written program plan. Target behaviors should be defined operationally. Performance rates should be documented before (baseline), during, and following treatment, as well as across relevant environments. These data should be recorded regularly (no less than once weekly for skills not yet acquired; more periodically after acquisition to assess maintenance and generalization), and should be presented in a "public" (i.e., available to everyone) form, preferably graphically. Taken together, these documentation dimensions enhance the procedural fidelity, social validity, and empirical integrity of instructional efforts.

4. *Instructional methods* should be based on the characteristics of the skill to be taught and the learner's style, and may include task analysis, incidental teaching, group and individual instruction, discrete trial teaching, and prompting, fading, and correction procedures characteristic of systematic instruction technologies (see Snell, 1987).

5. Intervention must occur within the context of *individualized motivational systems.* Prior to teaching, a reinforcer inventory must be developed for each student. Dyer (1987) recommended that information on reinforcer preferences be obtained through systematic observation of a child's material and activity choices, followed by a test of the salience of the hypothesized reinforcers.

6. It is also important to determine the sensory stimulus preferences of children with autism due to sensory hyper- or hypo-reactivity common with these children. By observing the child and classifying preferred activities/choices by sensory input provided (e.g., tactile, kinesthetic, olfactory, visual), the teacher can identify new *potentially* reinforcing events providing the same sensory feedback. By moving beyond a description of the reinforcer (e.g., a toy car) to a description of the functional sensory feedback the reinforcer provides (e.g., things that roll when pushed), the task of expanding a list of potential reinforcers is made easier.

7. For behavior targeted for deceleration, the variables maintaining inappropriate behavior must be identified. Iwata, Dorsey, Slifer, Bauman, and Richman (1982) have identified several potential maintaining (motivating) variables including access to social attention, sensory feedback, reinforcer loss, escape/avoidance of a demand or a task, and organic causes. Durand and Crimmins (1988) have developed the Motivation Assessment Scale (MAS) to screen for particular variables maintaining specific target behaviors. MAS results, when subjected to post hoc functional analysis with the child, are extremely useful in establishing the individual conditions of behavioral performance/nonperformance.

Component 2: Parent Involvement at Home, in School, and in the Community

During the past 10 years there has been an important shift in understanding families of children with autism. Whereas earlier researchers tried to describe the impact of autism on individual family members (see DeMyer, 1979), recent research and clinical practice has emphasized the family as a system (Powers, 1991) and has described the effect of raising a child with autism on family stress, cohesion, and adaptability (Harris, 1983, 1991; Powers & Egel, 1989a). The recognition of the interdependence in families who have a child with autism permits a broader and better integrated approach to working with families. Whereas the clinical utility of a systems approach has been well-articulated (see Egel & Powers, 1989; Harris, 1983; Powers, 1991), the empirical foundation lags behind (Powers, 1989). The diverse needs of families of preschoolers with autism calls for a highly individualized approach to parent training. Egel and Powers (1989) provide a comprehensive review of approaches, outcomes, and problems in training parents to teach their children at home. In addressing the issue of treatment failures, these authors point out that skill training and behavior management alone may be insufficient objectives for some families. Even when the technical adequacy of behavioral interventions is exemplary, families may fail to maintain learned skills over time because of other impediments within the family (e.g., marital discord) or within the community (e.g., isolation or insularity).

Olley et al. (in press) note that each of the 11 programs providing early intervention to children with autism surveyed included extensive parent involvement as a core component of service delivery. Parent involvement emphasized teaching parents the skills necessary to teach adaptive skills at home and in the community, teaching parents and other family members a technology of generalization (cf. Stokes & Osnes, 1988) so they could expand the environments in which their children could perform competently, and teaching behavioral assessment and treatment strategies to decelerate behavior problems. While not specifically noted, these parent-training activities also promoted a positive, collaborative relationship between the program and families, as well as increased self-efficacy and a "culture of optimism." Parent empowerment and ownership was supported through their inclusion as key participants in their childrens' education. To the extent that parents learned to distinguish effective treatment from ineffective treatment, advocacy skills for use later in their child's life were also developed.

Component 3: Earliest Intervention

The signing into law of PL99-457 (Part H of the Education of the Handicapped Act) on October 8, 1986, heralded a new era of opportunity and responsibility for families of children with autism and for professionals serving them. For the past decade, researchers have documented the effectiveness of early intervention for children with autism using various dependent measures including full integration with special education support into typical classrooms (Lovaas, 1987), attainment of age-appropriate scores on developmental indices (Strain & Hoyson, 1988), and changes in learning rate (Powers & Egel, 1989b; Robbins, Dunlap, & Plienis, 1991). Olley et al. (in press) note that although all programs surveyed report successful outcomes as measured by child progress and parent effectiveness, there are no standard outcome criteria by which cross-program comparisons can be made.

It is noteworthy that many programs adopt an "earlier is better" philosophy despite the lack of clear-cut empirical support for such a position. Such a position has substantial face validity and critical public policy implications and deserves consideration on these grounds alone. However, although the data document the effectiveness of *early* intervention, they are not instructive as to age cut-offs, critical ages, or points below which one type of intervention will be more effective than another. For example, Fenske, Zalenski, Krantz, and McClannahan (1985) reported superior outcomes for children enrolled prior to 60 months compared to those enrolled later. In the Lovaas study (1987), the average age of children in both experimental groups was under 36 months. The children in the LEAP program (Strain, Hoyson, & Jamison 1985) ranged in age from 30 to 53 months. Strain and Hoyson (1988) reported that children who began treatment prior to age 3 fared better on some outcome measures than those beginning after age 3.

The paucity of empirical support for earliest intervention should not forestall incorporation of this policy, however. Several factors support the initiation of educational services as soon as the child is identified. These include:

- The opportunity to intervene prior to the development of nonproductive/interfering behavioral repertoires.
- The opportunity to begin teaching functional communication strategies prior to the development of aberrant communication strategies.
- The opportunity to support the healthy adjustment of the family to their child's autism, and to facilitate the maintenance of social networks.
- The opportunity to teach parents to be their child's teachers at home and in the community when their perceived need is greatest and most acutely felt.

PL99-457 provides for the earliest intervention of children with disabilities, including autism. The manner in which these services are delivered varies widely across the United States. It can safely be said that for nearly all early intervention programs serving children with autism, the eight components of best practice remain under-addressed. As such, personnel preparation issues, in-service staff training needs, and the dissemination of best practices from exemplary programs to the public schools must be goals to which we devote substantial resources in coming years.

Component 4: Intensive Treatment

From the earliest laboratory-type teaching settings for children with autism of the 1960s (cf. Wolf, Risley, & Mees, 1964), treatment intensity has been a hallmark of a behavioral approach to educating these children. Intensity must be considered on several levels including duration of treatment (e.g., number of hours per day or per week; the number of weeks of intervention per year); the number of environments in which teaching occurs (e.g., school, home, community); and the educational validity (cf. Voeltz & Evans, 1983) of interventions provided. Each of these levels is discussed as follows.

The most carefully controlled analysis of treatment duration has been reported by Lovaas (1987, 1989). Substantially more positive outcomes (e.g., successful completion of first grade, IQ scores within the normal range) were observed for children receiving at least 40 hours per week of treatment compared to those children receiving less than 10 hours per week (treatment included teaching time provided by parents and therapists working in home, then community, then school settings). Some methodological concerns have been raised concerning this work (see Schopler, Short, & Mesibov, 1989, and the reply by Lovaas, 1989), yet the implications of such a finding cannot be ignored. While not specifically investigating duration of treatment, other researchers have described their positive results within the context of programs providing at least 30 hours of treatment per week (see Olley et al., in press, for a review). Given the empirical evidence and the heterogeneity of the populations of youngsters studied (particularly with respect to cognitive level at intake), it would be premature to assign a fixed minimum amount of hours per week of teaching required for maximum benefit. For purposes of public policy development it is entirely consistent with the available data to argue for programs not less than 5 hours per day (including home programming), over the entire year.

Early intervention must occur across all relevant environments to which the child is exposed. Beyond home teaching for parents and other family members, this would include school and community settings. At present we know very little as to which environments represent "keystone settings." Current early intervention policy appears to stress a center-based educational program as essential to a more adjunctive home teaching component. The data, however, neither support nor disconfirm this position with regard to autism. Several early intervention programs reporting positive outcomes provide the bulk of their services at home to parents (e.g., Anderson et al., 1987; Lovaas, 1987). Others provide a center-based program supplemented by home teaching (e.g., Dunlap et al., 1988; Egel & Powers, 1988; Harris & Handleman, 1989; McGee, 1988, 1991; Strain et al., 1985). While all address community teaching needs as requested by families, there is no specific formula for the amount of time determined to be optimal. This latter point poses little problem when considered in light of the substantial empirical basis supporting functional, community-based teaching for students with severe disabilities (see Falvey, 1989, for a comprehensive review). Coupled with the difficulties in stimulus control, generalization, and maintenance endemic to persons with autism, there can be little serious disagreement over the importance of teaching skills to preschoolers with autism in the environments where those skills typically occur.

For early intervention to be maximally effective, the many hours of teaching provided across several environments must be high-quality instructional interactions. Allegiance to a behavior analytic approach in and of itself does not guarantee that the skills targeted will be functional, socially valid, or age-appropriate. Implementation of well-written instructional programs may be procedurally unreliable (i.e., there may be systematic or unsystematic errors across staff when teaching with the program), or staff may allot insufficient time or opportunity for the child to learn the skill. Finally, the manner in which teaching decisions are made may bear little resemblance to databased, empirical decision making. Voeltz and Evans (1983) use the term *educational validity* to describe the importance of these issues. Demonstrating the educational validity of targeted skills, teaching procedures, and outcomes must be a component of both intensive and effective treatment.

Component 5: Programming for Generalization

The powerful instructional technologies that have been developed over the years will be of little long-term value to children with autism if skills acquired fail to generalize to untrained environments or fail to maintain over long periods of time (Koegel, Koegel, & O'Neill, 1989). In the absence of an equally powerful technology of generalization and maintenance, the long-term promise of early intervention will remain largely unfulfilled.

Nearly 20 years of research have documented the importance of programming for generalization for students with autism (Harris, 1975; Koegel et al., 1989). To be maximally effective, early intervention for preschoolers with autism must incorporate the emerging technology of generalization into intervention at home, in school, and in community setting. Stokes and Osnes (1988) have described three principles for programming for generalization and several strategies to increase the likelihood that generalization will occur.

1. Principle 1: *Use natural communities of reinforcement.* The home, school, and community environments frequented by a preschooler with autism all contain naturally occurring contingencies of reinforcement that strengthen behavioral repertoires. The key is to use them wittingly. For some children these reinforcers may be immediately evident, as when a child is able to initiate and sustain a social interaction to obtain a desired object or event. For others, reinforcing events may be more subtle and require a specific effort to uncover them by conducting a stimulus preference assessment (see Dyer, 1987). In either case, identification of reinforcing events that occur without training but are available and functional to the child should be considered.

2. Principle 2: *Train diversely*. Selective attention to one part of a stimulus array, known as *stimulus overselectivity*, is an important learning problem affecting children with autism (Schreibman, 1988). This problem

manifests as the learners' behavioral response remaining under the control of irrelevant stimuli, with his or her subsequent difficulty producing the response under more typical conditions. To address this problem Stokes and Osnes (1988) recommend maintaining sufficient instructional control to bring about behavioral change, but incorporating diverse settings into the training sequence to forestall selective attention to stimuli that are environment-specific but irrelevant.

3. Principle 3: *Incorporate functional mediators into untrained (generalization) settings.* Stokes and Osnes (1988) recommended that discriminative stimuli used in training environments be incorporated into novel settings. By using these stimuli as facilitators, the functional equivalence of the trained and untrained settings is enhanced. For example, the generalization of high rates of appropriate requests for social attention (and low rates of tantrums previously maintained by attention) from the classroom to the supermarket might be enhanced if a series of pictures specific to the supermarket were added to the same communication board used successfully in the classroom. Specific training might never take place in the supermarket, but the communication board and the reinforcement history associated with it could serve as functional mediators for appropriate requests for attention.

Several strategies to promote generalization have been described by Stokes and Osnes (1988). Each has practical implications for educating preschoolers with autism.

1. *Teach relevant behaviors.* Relevant behaviors in preschool settings include sustained engagement with a toy or individual, hugging/kissing parents and smiling at peers, turn-taking, and so on. Relevant behavior is more likely to engage the naturally occurring contingencies of reinforcement in the environment, thereby increasing the likelihood of future occurrence.

2. *Modify environments that support maladaptive behavior.* Maladaptive behavior exhibited by very young children with autism typically does not reach the level of severity or intensity found in some older children. To the extent that unscheduled reinforcing consequences follow aberrant behavior in the classroom, or particular environments serve as discriminative stimuli for aberrant behavior, these environments should be modified. For preschoolers, environmental contingencies such as physical space, crowding, and intrusions by other children or adults may occasion behavior not functional in less restrictive environments. Attention from typical peers in an integrated classroom may reinforce whining or tantrums. Horner and

Billingsley (1988) provide assessment and treatment strategies to address these issues.

3. *Identify and recruit natural communities of reinforcers.* Preschoolers with autism can be taught to solicit positive feedback and attention that will then function as a reinforcer. For example, children can be taught exclamations for use with other students (e.g., "All right," "way to go," "give me five") that will serve as reinforcers to typical peers, and will have a high probability of soliciting reciprocal positive social attention.

4. *Teaching must incorporate sufficient stimulus exemplars.* Training situations must be expanded to include a range of stimulus materials and stimulus settings so that the child learns that a particular response *is not* specific to a restricted set of stimulus conditions. For example, teaching a greeting to the teacher would best be accomplished through training at typically occuring greeting times (e.g., upon entering school, at morning circle group, after returning from outside recess, at various times when the teacher enters the child's environment), rather than in a restricted training setting devoid of the natural cues of entering an environment and recognizing a familiar person.

5. *Teaching must incorporate sufficient response exemplars.* If a series of related behaviors is the desired teaching outcome, then various examples of each behavior should be incorporated into the teaching program. For example, if the targeted outcome is a social initiation around play materials by a preschooler with autism toward a typical peer, then the teaching program should include training various verbal initiations with various play materials.

6. *Train loosely.* Simply put, this strategy suggests the incorporation of diversity into training situations. By incorporating periodic distractors into the training environment, the child learns to discriminate essential from nonessential conditions for the delivery of reinforcement.

7. *Contingencies should be indiscriminable.* Instructional control is the goal of systematic instruction for preschoolers with autism, yet efficient generalization may be impeded by the child's ability to discriminate the precise conditions under which reinforcement occurs. Thus, in order to increase the generalizability of the child's responding, the discriminative stimuli should be made less discriminable over time. The importance of differential reinforcement procedures for skill training (e.g., building alternative communicative responses through Differential Reinforcement of Communicative Behavior) and behavior management procedures such as Differential Reinforcement of Incompatible Behavior (DRI) used to build functionally equivalent responses with young children with autism cannot be overstated given the goal of inclusion into typical next environments for these students. At present, it is not clear when discriminative features of

training should be altered for optimal training *and* generalization effects. This remains an important area for future research.

8. *Spontaneous generalizations should be reinforced.* Consistent with the philosophy of training diversely, the reinforcement of unprompted generalizations of a previously taught behavior will enhance the generalization of that behavior.

9. *Use physical stimuli that are common to training and generalization settings.* To the extent that physical stimuli such as materials, apparatus, and toys are common to both settings, they will serve as discriminative stimuli in the untrained (generalization) settings, increasing the likelihood of target behavior performance.

10. *Incorporate common social stimuli.* Deficits in reciprocal social interaction are fundamental to children with autism, increasing the likelihood that they will be inefficient learners in situations where social stimuli have discriminative functions. Given the emphasis on promoting integration between preschoolers with and without autism, it becomes especially important to include same-age peers when training specific target behaviors. The presence of these peers in nontraining situations then increases the likelihood of generalization.

11. *Incorporate self-mediated stimuli.* Self-mediated stimuli refer to those which the child uses to guide (mediate) appropriate behavior. Examples in preschool settings include self-talk (covert or overt self-instructions) self-reinforcement, and self-monitoring (see Koegel & Koegel, 1988, for a comprehensive review). Incorporation of self-mediated stimuli into the training paradigm increases the likelihood of generalization because relevant controlling stimuli will be under the child's control. Use of self-mediated stimuli also enhances the utility of remote or delayed contingencies in treatment (cf. Dunlap, Koegel, Johnson, & O'Neill, 1987).

Component 6: Curricula Must Emphasize the Development of Reciprocal Social Interaction and Communication Skills

Impairments of social interaction and language/communication are core deficits in autism. While the form and severity of these deficits vary between and within children, successful early intervention literally hinges on the child's ability to acquire meaningful and functional social and communicative repertoires. Wing (1988) has divided impairment of social interaction into three related but separate dimensions. These include impairment of social recognition, impairment of social communication, and impairment of social imagination and understanding. Taken together, this triad of deficits of social interaction have special relevance for curriculum design for preschoolers with autism.

Impairment of social recognition refers to the child with autism's difficulty recognizing that other people are the potentially rewarding aspects of the environment. Social communication refers to initiating and responding to nonvocal and vocal social cues, interest and pleasure in communicating, as well as interest in and recognition of others' feelings. The lack of interest in communicating, use of communication for instrumental (i.e., means–end) purposes, and verbalizations outside the social context of the moment all are examples of deficits of social communication. Impairments in social imagination and understanding interfere with learning meaningful imitations, pretend or imaginative play, the development of empathetic behavior, and role or perspective taking (Wing, 1988). For a comprehensive framework for social skill curriculum development the reader is referred to Olley and Stevenson (1989).

Impairment of language and communication refers to the pragmatics, mechanics (e.g., syntax), and comprehension of communication, as well as the language peculiarities demonstrated by many children with autism, including echolalia, neologisms, and pronominal reversals (Wing, 1988). These deficits and excesses interfere with the functionality of communication, that is, the understanding that "communication makes the world happen." Educational interventions must enhance the form, function, and functionality of communication for preschoolers with autism. Schopler and Mesibov (1985) provide an excellent review of issues in communication programming for students with autism. Not surprisingly, the heterogeneity of strengths and needs of individual preschoolers with autism and the multiplicity of settings used to educate them argue against standard curricula. The development of curricula should be based instead on several factors: (a) characteristics of the current, typical (integrated) environment; (b) characteristics of the next, least restrictive educational environment and competencies necessary to maintain there; (c) instructional components to include play, social routines, transitions, school-readiness skills, and survival skills; (d) integration of developmental and functional approaches; and (e) the particular behavioral and academic strengths, needs, and excesses in the preschooler's repertoire. It is beyond the scope of this chapter to discuss each of these in detail, however, key components for consideration are provided.

Characteristics of the Current, Typical Environment. In a very practical sense, autism is a disorder of "goodness of fit." The preschool environments created for typical children often contain elements of design and instruction that challenge the preschooler with autism substantially. Examples might include an emphasis on a looser structure, turn-taking, and picking up toys after use. The attending, social, and communicative prerequisites for these behaviors often are absent from the behavioral repertoires of children with autism. Consideration of behavioral, social, and communication prerequisites and survival skills for the identified integrated preschool classroom is thus the first step in curriculum development. Moreover, as Strain and Hoyson (1988) note, there is no substitute for "in vivo" observation of the current, typical environment as a method for obtaining these curriculum objectives.

Characteristics of the Next Environment. Vincent et al. (1980) argue persuasively that if less restrictive placement is our goal for a child, then that child's curriculum must explicitly teach the skills necessary for success in those next environments. The academic, social, and communication behaviors required for participation in the next, less restrictive placement thus become objectives for an individualized curriculum.

Table 10.2 provides examples of ecological factors to be assessed in the next environment. Skill training needs of the preschooler with autism must be taught within the context of the ecological constraints of the classroom to insure the functionality of the skill to the child.

Instructional Objectives Must Address Play, Social Routines, Transitions, School-Readiness Skills, and Survival Skills. In addition to targeting social interaction and communication, curricula should include objectives designed to address skills that promote inclusion of the preschooler with autism into the moment-to-moment activities of the classroom. Play skills such as block-building, painting, and using a sand or water table, are skills that are valued in most preschools. Activities that promote child–child interactions such as using a seesaw, pulling others in a

TABLE 10.2
Ecological Considerations in Next Environment Assessment

Ecological Considerations
daily schedule
instructional settings/activities used (e.g., work stateions, learning centers, circle group)
behavior management strategies used
implicit and explicit classroom rules
degree of deviance from these rules that is tolerated
type of frequency of teacher–child interactins for each instructional setting
type of frequency of child–child interactions for each instructional setting
reinforcers used (and those implicitly or explicitly forbidden)
punishers used (and those implicitly or explicitly forbidden)
degree/frequency with which staff intervene (teach) language and social interactions incidentally
transitions throughout the day (number, type, how they are managed, how difficulties during transitions are overcome)

wagon, or playing Simon Says should also be considered. Social routines common in preschool settings include greeting adults and other children, sharing, cleaning up toys after use, and the like. Specific instruction in these and other similar skills should be considered.

Children with autism typically experience difficulties with transitions across activities, people, and places. In addition to programming for transitions through use of the technology for generalization described earlier, the curriculum should "teach transitions" as instructional objectives. This is most effectively accomplished using task-analytic teaching methods. In this way a sequential, orderly instructional sequence can be designed and taught using systematic instruction procedures.

Preschools exist to prepare children for the academic programs to follow in elementary school and beyond. For children with autism to integrate more successfully, it would appear important for them to acquire certain basic school readiness skills. These include skills such as color and shape recognition, number and letter recognition, and use of a pencil and scissors. One need only consult a curriculum for typically developing children to identify other examples. Where curriculum modification is necessary, it is wise to begin with efforts to augment the objective rather than replace it entirely. For example, the child who cannot identify colors will be more likely included in the group teaching lesson if she can be allowed to identify the object depicting the color (e.g., a red apple) instead of the color itself. Of course, this does not mean that color identification be discontinued as an instructional objective. Rather, it suggests that inclusion in integrated settings is a goal that may necessitate some modification of the typical curriculum.

Preschool teachers each have their own set of "bottom line behaviors" that constitute essential skills a child must learn in order to remain in their classroom. These survival skills are highly individualized across preschool environments, and must be assessed in order to insure successful integration. Some of the more common survival skills are listed in Table 10.3. As appropriate, these should be part of a child's formal educational program and should be taught systematically.

Integration of Functional and Developmental Approaches. The emphasis on functional, chronologically age-appropriate curriculum objectives is no less important for preschoolers with autism than for older students. However, many of the problems associated with use of developmental models are less troublesome for young children with autism. The issue of discontinuity of skill development may be less prominent with preschoolers. In addition, most typical preschool curricula emphasize developmental sequelae across skill domains of importance to children with autism (e.g.,

TABLE 10.3
Survival Skill Considerations for Curriculum Development

compliance to adult requests
turn-taking
listening to directions from afar or near
sitting quietly during activities
volunteering
raising one's hand to colicit attention
walking in a line
using toilets in classroom versus in the hallway
picking up toys after use
communication of basic needs/wants

gross fine-motor and self-help skills, and cognitive, social, and communication skills). The availability of a developmental scope and sequence thus provides a useful starting point for curriculum development.

For curriculum objectives to be truly useful, however, they must be functional for the child (Sailor et al., 1989; White, 1980). Objectives can be tested for functionality by subjecting them to three questions (Egel, 1989):

1. Is the skill to be taught useful immediately to the child (or a prerequisite to a behavior/skill that will be immediately useful)?
2. Are the materials used to teach the skill common to the child's everyday environment?
3. If this skill is acquired, will it decrease the probability that someone else will have to do it for the child in the future?

If the answers to these three questions are yes, the objective is probably functional and appropriate. Armed with objectives that are functional, chronologically, and developmentally age-appropriate, curriculum development proceeds individually for each child.

Consideration of Individual Behavioral and Academic Strengths, Needs, and Excesses. Children with autism demonstrate highly individualized learning styles both across and within students (Schreibman, Koegel, Charlop, & Egel, 1990). Factors such as stimulus overselectivity, idiosyncratic motivational systems, sequential learning style, and difficulties with symbolic learning all contribute to the classroom experiences of preschoolers with autism. In addition, individual patterns of stereotypy, the presence of self-injurious behavior, communication, and social responsiveness all must be assessed and accounted for in developing teaching programs that will optimize educational outcomes.

Component 7: All Personnel Must be Specifically Trained and Continuously Evaluated

Regular and special education teachers and aides must be specially trained to teach preschoolers with autism. Further, their teaching efforts and child outcomes must be continuously monitored to maintain procedural fidelity. McClannahan and Krantz (1985) argued that failure to provide adequate training and supervision of program staff violates the child with autism's right to effective treatment. Staff must demonstrate competencies in the technologies of systematic instruction, generalization and behavior management, as well as parent training, behavioral assessment, and curriculum design. Reid, McCarn, and Green (1988) and McClannahan (1991) provide comprehensive overviews of staff training issues in autism.

Component 8: Integration with Typical Peers

The empirical evidence clearly supports the integration of children with autism into educational environments with nondisabled peers. Strain (1983) evaluated the effect of integrated versus segregated settings on social interactions with preschoolers with autism. His results indicate that higher rates of social interactions occurred in the integrated settings. Sasso, Simpson, and Novak (1985) demonstrated that typical students were more likely to initiate interactions with students with autism following a training procedure emphasizing structured interactions with, and information about, children with autism. Finally, in a comparison of integrated and segregated programs, Strain (1986) demonstrated significant improvements in expressive language, on-task behavior, cognitive functioning, and significant reductions in maladaptive behavior for preschoolers with autism enrolled in integrated settings.

In their evaluation of the effectiveness of social integration for children with autism, Egel and Gradel (1988) identified 30 logistical and training strategies associated with successful integration. These are presented in Tables 10.4 and 10.5. Egel and Gradel further noted that the empirical literature converges on several themes insofar as effective integration is concerned:

1. Physical integration alone is insufficient.
2. The use of multiple strategies in training programs is typical.
3. Administrative support is essential.
4. Attitude change of staff and children is implicit.
5. Ongoing communication across all program participants (e.g., parents, teachers, administrators) is essential if optimal educa-

TABLE 10.4
Logistical Strategies

Disperse classrooms around building, in proximity to chronological-age peers.
Concurrent use of common student-use areas (e.g., cafeteria, halls, playground).
Incorporate into nonacademic special subjects.
Involve in episodic school functions (e.g., assemblies, graduation, fund-raisers).
Cooperative work projects for regular and special student/for regular and special staff.
Classroom exchanges for staff/students in nonacademic activities.
Common faculty use areas (e.g., lounges/workspace).
Assign special students to school jobs (e.g., monitors, cafeteria/office helpers); use buddy system with peers already in these roles.
Designate selected special education staff to plan, conduct, and monitor integration activities, provide technical assistance and preintegration orientation, "trouble-shoot," and so on.
Set up advocacy/tutoring "special friends" organizations of peers.
Include parents, regular and special staff, and administration in planning and monitoring "task force."
"Open-door" visitatio policy for regular education staff and students in special classes.
Ensure extra special education assistance when students are in specials, exchanges, common use areas, and so on.
Incorporate information and sensitization modules into regular education content areas (e.g., health, social studies).
Special education faculty share total school responsibilities (e.g., extracurricular activities, lunch/bus supervision).
Specialized, "on-call" technical assistance to regular education faculty.
Minimize paperwork for involved regular education staff.
Training/information for faculty/student/parents/ancillary staff (bus drivers, etc.), (a) specific to their roles/types of interaction, or (b) on an ongoing basis.

Note: From Egel and Gradel (1988. Copyright © 1988 by the Association for Advancement of Behavior Therapy. Reprinted by permission).

tional outcomes are to become the norm for preschoolers with autism, use of these logistical and training strategies must become commonplace.

CHALLENGES FOR THE FUTURE

At the present time it is possible to identify best practices based on our current level of knowledge. At once the most satisfying and most disquieting fact, however, is that we know much more about what we don't know. Based on our current understanding, several unresolved issues stand out.

1. We have not yet determined "keystone" social interaction or communication skills. The identification of skill clusters that will enhance stimulus and response generalization for the core deficits of autism continue to elude us.

TABLE 10.5
Training Strategies

Recruit peers for varied, specific roles (e.g., as "buddies," tutors, or friends).
Arrange peer-mediated training formats, with specific plans to decrease adult assistance over time.
Train peers specific to (a) their roles (e.g., as buddies, tutors, etc.), (b) the social skill repertoires/characteristics of target students, and (c) the targeted social interaction skills. Include practice.
Plan and conduct training in the context of activities that have the poetntial for frequent opportunities for interaction.
Select social interaction skills that will likely (a) result in reciprocal interaction chains, (b) be useful across settings, and (c) represent a range of social–communicative functions.
Training should focus on naturally occurring cues, in the context of tasks in which a social component is either critical or highly typical/desirable.
Train student to discrimate both when and when not to use target social skills.
Provide assistance to peers after they have been trained, during ongoing interactions.
Train special education students in relevant, timely, age-appropriate activities that are likely to parallel interests of age peers (e.g., videogames, pinball).
Use systematic training procedures.
Check to see if (a) target skills of special students and 9b) reciprocal interactions of peers occur in nontraining conditions.
Vary peers used in training contexts.

Note: From Egel and Gradel (1988. Copyright © 1988 by the Association for Advancement of Behavior Therapy. Reprinted by permission).

2. Various programs reporting successful outcomes employ different strategies to teach social interaction and communication skills. While these skills typically are taught using multiple methods, we have no information on the effectiveness of particular components of the intervention packages. Knowledge of essential and nonessential components would facilitate comparisons of training methods across settings and between children with varying degrees of severity of autism.

3. Some effective program models emphasize home-based intervention, others emphasize classroom-based teaching with a home component, and others have varying degrees of home–school involvement. It is clearly the case that home-based teaching must accompany classroom instruction for optimal effects. What is not clear is how much home or school programming is necessary to maximize progress. Lovaas' (1987) study compared children exposed to over 40 hours of intensive home and community training with children exposed to less than 10 hours per week. Would those exposed to 25 hours per week have had substantially different outcomes than those receiving 10 hours? Which other variables beside exposure to effective instruction account for the variance? What is the role of degree of cognitive impairment, presence of functional communication strategies, ability to imitate other children spontaneously, or the extent of competing stereotypy vis-à-vis educational outcome? Given the fiscal constraints faced

by many school systems, questions of treatment efficacy are not academic ones. Issues around child variables and their relationship to treatment outcome will be decided by others if empirical investigations ignore these concerns.

4. Many children with autism are identified somewhere between 18–30 months of age. Infants and toddlers with other severe developmental disabilities often receive a combination of home- and center-based intervention services. As these children turn 3, they typically enter a center-based program for 3, 4, or 5 half-days per week. The distinction between service delivery models for preschoolers aged 0–3 and those aged 3–5 are more a function of philosophy than science. Thus, the question of whether one model is more effective than another for preschoolers with autism less than or older than 36 months is unresolved. To the extent that program models contribute to effective outcomes, this issue merits investigation.

5. Many researchers have been concerned with the effect of autism on the family (Schopler & Mesibov, 1984). Of more recent interest is the relationship between family functioning and early intervention outcomes. Powers and Egel (1989b) investigated 12 families of preschoolers with autism where all children were enrolled in an integrated early intervention program. A significant inverse relationship was found between child progress after 1 year in the program and stress attributable to parent or family dysfunction obtained at intake. Findings such as these suggest that treatment efficacy and treatment planning must consider a multiplicity of child and family variables when planning an individualized program for a preschooler with autism. Further research relating treatment outcomes to family functioning is sorely needed if we are to optimize both the child's and family's experience in early intervention.

The development of effective early intervention for preschoolers with autism is a dynamic, fluid process. The methods of inquiry used to document treatment efficacy in the past decade have established many fundamental tenets of early intervention within a constantly expanding database. As behavioral scientists we seem to have answered affirmatively the question "Does it work?" reasonably well, but substantial gaps in our knowledge still exist. The future for preschoolers with autism who participated in the programs of the 1980s is surely brighter than those of the 1960s and 1970s. We have every reason to believe that the explosion in interest by researchers, public policymakers, and parents will make the experience of the preschoolers of the 1990s better still.

ACKNOWLEDGMENTS

Thanks to Liz Garcia and Holly Tetreault for their invaluable help in the preparation of this chapter.

REFERENCES

American Psychiatric Association. (1987). *Diagnostic and statistical manual of mental disorders* (3rd ed. rev., DSM-III-R). Washington, DC: Author.

American Psychiatric Association. (1980). *Diagnostic and statistical manual of mental disorders* (3rd ed., DSM-III). Washington, DC: Author.

Anderson, S. R., Avery, D. L., Dipietro, E. K., Edwards, G. L., & Christian, W. P. (1987). Intensive home-based early intervention with autistic children. *Education and Treatment of Children, 10,* 352–366.

Dahl, E. K., Cohen, D. J., & Provence, S. (1986). Clinical and multivariate approaches to the nosology of pervasive developmental disorders. *Journal of the American Academy of Child Psychiatry, 25,* 170–180.

DeMyer, M. K. (1979). *Parents and children in autism.* New York: Wiley.

Dunlap, G., Koegel, R. L., Johnson, J., & O'Neill, R. E. (1987). Maintaining performance of autistic clients in community settings with delayed contingencies. *Journal of Applied Behavior Analysis, 20,* 185–191.

Dunlap, G., Robbins, F. R., Morelli, M. A., & Dollman, C. (1988). Team training for young children with autism: A regional model for service delivery. *Journal of the Division of Early Childhood, 12,* 147–160.

Durand, V. M., & Crimmins, D. (1988). Identifying the variables maintaining self-injurious behavior. *Journal of Autism and Developmental Disorders, 18,* 99–117.

Dyer, K. (1987). The competition of autistic stereotyped behavior with usual and specifically assessed reinforcers. *Research in Developmental Disabilities, 8,* 607–626.

Egel, A. L. (1989). Finding the right educational program. In M. D. Powers (Ed.), *Children with autism: A parents' guide* (pp. 169–202). Rockville, MD: Woodbine.

Egel, A. L., & Powers, M. D. (1988, July). *Preschoolers with autism in the public schools: Some impediments and solutions.* Paper presented at the annual convention of the Autism Society of America, New Orleans.

Egel, A. L., & Powers, M. D. (1989). Behavioral parent training. In E. Cipani (Ed.), *The treatment of severe behavior disorders* (pp. 153–173). Washington, DC: American Association on Mental Retardation.

Falvey, M. A. (1989). *Community-based curriculum: Instructional strategies for students with severe handicaps.* Baltimore: Paul H. Brookes.

Farren, D. C. (in press). Effects of intervention with disadvantaged and disabled children: A decade review. In S. Meisels & J. Schonkoff (Eds.), *Handbook of intervention.* Cambridge, England: Cambridge University Press.

Fenske, E. C., Zalenski, S., Krantz, P. J., & McClannahan, L. E. (1985). Age at intervention and treatment outcome for autistic children in a comprehensive intervention program. *Analysis and Intervention in Developmental Disabilities, 5,* 49–58.

Freeman, B. J., & Ritvo, E. R. (1984). The syndrome of autism: Establishing the diagnosis and principles of management. *Pediatric Annals, 13,* 281–289.

Gillberg, C. (1989). Early symptoms in autism. In C. Gillberg (Ed.), *Diagnosis and treatment of autism* (pp. 23–32). New York: Plenum.

Gillberg, C., Ehlers, S., Schaumann, H., Jakobsson, G., Dahlgren, S. O., Lindblom, R., Bagenholm, A., Tjuus, T., & Blinder, E. (1990). Autism under age 3 years: A clinical study of 28 cases referred for autistic symptoms in infancy. *Journal of Child Psychology and Psychiatry, 31,* 921–934.

Harris, S. L. (1975). Teaching language to nonverbal children—with emphasis on problems of generalization. *Psychological Bulletin, 82,* 565–580.

Harris, S. L. (1983). *Families of the developmentally disabled.* Elmsford, NY: Pergamon.

Harris, S. L. (1984). Intervention planning for the family of the autistic child: A multilevel assessment of the family system. *Journal of Marital and Family Therapy, 10,* 157–166.

Harris, S. L. (1991, July). *Working with families.* Invited address presented at the annual convention of the Autism Society of America, Indianapolis, IN.

Harris, S. L., & Handleman, J. S. (1986). *Educating the developmentally disabled: Meeting the needs of children and families.* San Diego: College-Hill.

Harris, S. L., & Handleman, J. S. (1989, May). *Assessing changes in preschool children with autism and their normally developing peers.* Paper presented at the annual conference of the Association for Behavior Analysis, Milwaukee, WI.

Horner, R. H., & Billingsley, F. F. (1988). The effect of competing behavior on the generalization and maintenance of adaptive behavior in applied settings. In R. H. Horner, G. Dunlap, & R. L. Koegel (Eds.), *Generalization and maintenance* (pp. 197–220). Baltimore: Paul H. Brookes.

Hoshino, Y., Kumashiro, H., Yashima, Y., Tachibana, R., Watanabe, M., & Furukawa, H. (1982). Early symptoms of autistic children and its diagnostic significance. *Folia Psychiatrica et Neurologica Japonica, 36,* 367–374.

Iwata, B. A., Dorsey, M. F., Slifer, K. J., Bauman, K. E., & Richman, G. S. (1982). Toward a functional analysis of self-injury. *Analysis and Intervention in Developmental Disabilities, 2,* 3–20.

Koegel, R. L., & Koegel, L. K. (1988). Generalized responsivity and pivotal behaviors. In R. H. Horner, G., Dunlap, & R. L. Koegel (Eds.), *Generalization and maintenance* (pp. 41–66). Baltimore: Paul H. Brookes.

Koegel, R. L., Koegel, L. K., & O'Neill, R. (1989). Generalization in the treatment of autism. In L. V. McReynolds & J. E. Spradlin (Eds.), *Generalization strategies in the treatment of communication disorders* (pp. 116–131). Toronto: B. C. Decker.

Levine, J. M., & Demb, H. B. (1987). Characteristics of preschool children diagnosed as having atypical pervasive developmental disorder. *Developmental and Behavioral Pediatrics, 8,* 77–82.

Lovaas, O. I. (1987). Behavioral treatment and normal educational and intellectual functioning in young autistic children. *Journal of Consulting and Clinical Psychology, 55,* 3–4.

Lovaas, O. I. (1989, August). *Behavioral treatment of young autistic children.* Invited address presented at the annual convention of the American Psychological Association, New Orleans.

Lovaas, O. I., Smith, T., & McEachin, J. J. (1989). Clarifying comments on the Young Autism Study: A Reply to Schopler, Short, and Mesibov. *Journal of Consulting and Clinical Psychology, 57,* 165–167.

McClannahan, L. E. (1991, May). *Key issues in staff training.* Invited address presented at the annual conference of the Association for Behavior Analysis, Atlanta.

McClannahan, L. E., & Krantz, P. (1985). Some next steps in rights protection for the developmentally disabled. *School Psychology Review, 14,* 143–149.

McGee, G. G. (1988, July). *The Walden learning center.* Paper presented at the annual convention of the Autism Society of America, New Orleans.

McGee, G. G. (1991, February). *The Walden learning center.* Paper presented at the conference on Innovation in Early Intervention, Amherst, MA.

McGee, G. G., Daly, T., & Risley, T. (1988, May). *In context teaching of social talk.* Paper presented at the annual convention of the Association for Behavior Analysis, Philadelphia.

Olley, J. G., Robbins, F. R., & Morelli-Robbins, M. (in press). Current practices in early intervention with autism. In E. Schopler, M. E. Van Borgondien, & M. Bristol (Eds.), *Preschool issues in autism and related developmental handicaps.* New York: Plenum.

Olley, J. G., & Stevenson, S. E. (1989). Preschool curriculum for children with autism: Addressing early social skills. In G. Dawson (Ed.), *Autism: Nature, diagnosis and treatment* (pp. 346–366). New York: Guilford.

Ornitz, E. M., Guthrie, D., & Farley, A. H. (1977). Early development of autistic children. *Journal of Autism and Childhood Schizophrenia, 7,* 207–229.

Percy, A., Gillberg, C., Hagberg, B., & Witt-Engerstrom, I. (1990). Rett Syndrome and the autistic disorders. *Neurologic Clinics, 8,* 659–676.

Powers, M. D. (1984). Syndromal diagnosis and the behavioral assessment of childhood disorders. *Child and Family Behavior Therapy, 6,* 1–15.

Powers, M. D. (1989, November). *Social integration of children with autism: Facilitating second-order change.* Invited address at the annual convention of the Association for Advancement of Behavior Therapy, Washington, DC.

Powers, M. D. (1991). Intervening with families of young children with severe handicaps: Contributions of a family systems approach. *School Psychology Quarterly, 6,* 131–146.

Powers, M. D., & Egel, A. L. (1989a, May). *Stress, coping, and conflict in families of young autistic children.* Paper presented at the meeting of the Association for Behavior Analysis, Milwaukee, WI.

Powers, M. D., & Egel, A. L. (1989b, August). *Stress and coping in families of young autistic children: Initial findings and the effect on child outcomes.* Paper presented at the annual conference of the American Psychological Association, New Orleans.

Powers, M. D., & Handleman, J. S. (1984). *Behavioral assessment of severe developmental disabilities.* Rockville, MD: Aspen.

Powers, M. D., & Olley, J. G. (1989, May) (co-chairs). *Issues in transitions. Young children with autism into next environments.* Symposium presented at the annual conference of the Association for Behavior Analysis, Milwaukee, WI.

Rapin, I. (1988). Disorders of higher cerebral function preschool children. *American Journal of Diseases in Childhood, 142,* 1178–1186.

Reid, D. H., McCarn, J. E., & Green, C. W. (1988). Staff training and management in school programs for severely developmentally disabled students. In M. D. Powers (Ed.), *Expanding systems of service delivery for persons with developmental disabilities* (pp. 199–215). Baltimore: Paul H. Brookes.

Robbins, F. R., Dunlap, G., & Pleinis, A. J. (1991). Family characteristics, family training, and the progress of young children with autism. *Journal of Early Intervention, 15,* 172–184.

Romanczyk, R. G. (1990, March). *Issues in the treatment of autism: Early intervention through transition.* Invited address at the annual New Jersey COSAC conference, New Brunswick, NJ.

Sailor, W., Anderson, J. L., Halvorsen, A. T., Doering, K., Filler, J., & Goetz, L. (1989). *The comprehensive local school.* Baltimore: Paul H. Brookes.

Sasso, G. M., Simpson, R. L., & Novak, C. G. (1985). Procedures for facilitating integration of autistic children in public school settings. *Analysis and Intervention in Developmental Disabilities, 5,* 233–246.

Schopler, E., & Mesibov, G. B. (Eds.). (1984). *The effect of autism on the family.* New York: Plenum.

Schopler, E., & Mesibov, G. B. (Eds.). (1985). *Communication problems in autism.* New York: Plenum.

Schopler, E., & Mesibov, G. B. (1988). *Diagnosis and assessment in autism.* New York: Plenum.

Schopler, E., Short, A., & Mesibov, G. B. (1989). Relation of behavioral treatment to "normal functioning": Comment on Lovaas. *Journal of Consulting and Clinical Psychology, 57,* 162–164.

Schreibman, L. (1988). *Autism.* Newberry Park, CA: Sage.

Schreibman, L., Koegel, R. L., Charlop, M. H., & Egel, A. L. (1990). Infantile autism. In A. S. Bellack, M. Hersen, & A. E. Kazdin (Eds.), *International handbook of behavior modification and therapy* (pp. 763–789). New York: Plenum.

Simeonsson, R. J., Olley, J. G., & Rosenthal, S. L. (1987). Early intervention for children with autism. In M. J. Guralnick & F. C. Bennett (Eds.), *The effectiveness of early intervention for at-risk and handicapped children* (pp. 275–296). New York: Academic Press.

Snell, M. (1987). *Systematic instruction of persons with severe handicaps.* Colombus, OH: Merrill.

Stokes, T. F., & Osnes, P. G. (1988). The developing applied technology of generalization and maintenance. In R. Horner, G. Dunlap, & R. L. Koegel (Eds.), *Generalization and maintenance* (pp. 5–19). Baltimore: Paul H. Brookes.

Strain, P. S. (1983). Generalization of autistic childrens' social behavior change: Effects of developmentally integrated and segregated settings. *Analysis and Intervention in Developmental Disabilities, 3,* 23–34.

Strain, P. S. (1986). *National Institute of Mental Health Renewal Grant.*

Strain, P. S., & Hoyson, M. (1988, July). *Follow-up of children in LEAP.* Paper presented at the meeting of the Autism Society of America, New Orleans.

Strain, P. S., Hoyson, M., & Jamieson, B. J. (1985). Normally developing preschoolers as intervention agents for autistic-like children. Effects on class deportment and social interactions. *Journal of the Division for Early Childhood, 9,* 105–115.

Sugiyama, T., & Abe, T. (1989). The prevalence of autism in Nagoya, Japan: A total population study. *Journal of Autism and Developmental Disorders, 19,* 87–96.

Tommasone, L., & Tommasone, J. (1989). Adjusting to your child's diagnosis. In M. D. Powers (Ed.), *Children with autism: A parents' guide* (pp. 31–54). Rockville, MD: Woodbine House.

Vincent, L. J., Salisbury, C., Walter, G., Brown, P., Gruenewald, L. J., & Powers, M. (1980). Program evaluation and curriculum development in early childhood special education: Criteria of the next environment. In W. Sailor, B. Wilcox, & L. Brown (Eds.), *Methods of instruction for severely handicapped students* (pp. 303–328). Baltimore: Paul H. Brookes.

Voeltz, L. M., & Evans, I. (1983). Educational validity: Procedures to evaluate outcomes in programs for severely handicapped learners. *Journal of the Association for the Severely Handicapped, 8,* 3–15.

Watson, L., & Marcus, L. M. (1988). Diagnosis and assessment of preschool children. In E. Schopler & G. B. Mesibov (Eds.), *Diagnosis and assessment in autism* (pp. 271–302). New York: Plenum.

White, O. (1980). Adaptive objective performance: Form versus function. In W. Sailor, B. Wilcox, & L. Brown (Eds.), *Methods of instruction for severely handicapped students.* Baltimore: Paul H. Brookes.

Wing, L. (1988). The continuum of autistic characteristics. In E. Schopler & G. B. Mesibov (Eds.), *Diagnosis and assessment in autism* (pp. 91–110). New York: Plenum.

Wolf, M. M., Risley, T., & Mees, H. (1964). Application of operant conditioning procedures to the behavior problems of an autistic child. *Behavior Research and Therapy, 1,* 305–312.

11 Community Integration and Supported Employment

Marcia Datlow Smith
Community Services for Autistic Adults and Children

David Markham awakens each weekday at 7 a.m. He washes, dresses, prepares, and eats breakfast. At 8 a.m. his ride comes, and he leaves for work. Mr. Markham works for a company that prepares snack food trays for vending machines. He sorts the items and places them in their designated bins in the trays.

Mr. Markham has a high level of productivity. In fact, he works faster than most of his coworkers. He earns minimum wage, and is slated for a raise soon. Mr. Markham seems to enjoy his work. He is a quiet worker who keeps to himself and is not given to leaving his work station to exchange idle gossip with coworkers.

In most respects, Mr. Markham does not differ from many other American workers. However, in one respect Mr. Markham is quite different from his coworkers. Mr. Markham is severely disabled by autism. He has no verbal language. His intelligence is considered to be in the profound range of mental retardation. He also has a history of severe self-abuse, including high intensity headbanging.

The circumstances of Mr. Markham's life probably more closely resemble those of his nonhandicapped coworkers than those of other individuals who bear his diagnosis. Unlike most individuals with autism, Mr. Markham enjoys full community integration. His neighbors are nonhandicapped, as are his coworkers. He dines, shops, vacations, and enjoys his free time alongside other nonhandicapped citizens in his community. And, he has been able to work for all of his adult life with the assistance of a job coach provided by a supported employment program.

Community integration has not eliminated Mr. Markham's autism. But neither has autism eliminated integrated work and living experiences from Mr. Markham's life options.

This chapter explores community integration and supported employment for individuals with autism. Traditionally, individuals with autism were considered unemployable. Now, the issue is not whether they are employable, but simply how much support is necessary in order to achieve employment. The purpose of this chapter is to explore the issues and options involved in full integration for people with autism.

INTEGRATED COMMUNITY LIVING

Integrated community living can be an option for all individuals with autism. Autism need not dictate the neighborhood within which the individual can settle. Autism simply dictates the amount of support services necessary to achieve community adjustment. There are several models for integrated community living that can be utilized by people with autism.

Living with Family

In many cultures, and across many periods of history, extended family units were not the exception, but the rule. Several generations lived under one roof, and as the family enlarged, so did the size of the dwelling. During periods of economic or domestic stress in our current culture, adult children may move back in with parents. Certainly, remaining in the family unit is a viable option for some adults with autism and their families.

Living with Foster Family

If circumstances preclude the individual from living within the biological family unit, a foster family situation can be an option. Lakin, Hill, and Bruininks (1988) reported that many states sponsor specialized foster care programs for persons with developmental disabilities. These are typically specially licensed homes, with caregivers receiving training in developmental disabilities.

The behavior management issues that can be associated with autism can make foster care placement difficult. Family foster care is usually provided for persons with mental retardation who do not have serious behavior problems (Eyman, Borthwick-Duffy, & Sheehy, 1987). The provision of support services and specialized training to the foster family provider can make this a viable option for some adults with autism.

Living Independently

Some adults with autism, particularly residual autism, can live independently in the community, with little or no support from family or other agencies. Approximately 25% of people with autism do not have mental retardation, and if social skills and communication deficits are relatively mild, and destructive behaviors are not present, independent living can be a reality. The presence of property destruction, self-injury, or aggression preclude independent living until sufficient gains are made so that there is no risk of injury when the individual is left alone.

Partially Supported Living

Some individuals with autism, because of communication, social, or skill deficits cannot live independently. However, the effects of the disorder might be mild enough so that individuals can live in supported living situations in which partial assistance is available.

One option is to have individuals with autism living with one or two roommates without disabilities, who can provide some assistance with the activities of daily living, as necessary. These individuals may or may not receive compensation for their assistance.

Another option is to have a living arrangement in which assistance is provided for some, but not all, of the hours of the week. Assistance might be provided at critical times, such as in the mornings before work, and in the evenings around dinner time. This arrangement of partial supervision is viable for individuals who do not have severe behavior problems, and who do not require assistance on an around-the-clock basis.

Fully Supported Living

Fully supported living arrangements, when not provided by family or foster families, can be provided through small group residences. One or several individuals in need of assistance live together in a house or apartment, under the supervision of paid staff. Staff provide ongoing assistance with the activities of daily living. Ideally, training in those activities, as well as in social skills and behavior management are included, because these can be critical weaknesses for people with autism.

CRITICAL COMPONENTS FOR COMMUNITY LIVING

Autism is a disorder of behavior and communication, and the nature of this disorder dictates necessary components for a successful community living arrangement that merit further special attention. Summers and Reese (1986) described the components of an ideal residential situation for adults with developmental disabilities. They include adequate physical care, personal and social relationships, leisure and recreational activities, habilitation programming, and respect for human rights.

Supervision

Autism is a disorder of behavior, and as such may be accompanied by challenging behaviors that can be destructive in nature, including property destruction, aggression, self-injury, and pica. Failure to provide adequate supervision can result in significant property destruction, injuries ranging from bruises to head injury to the individual, the ingestion of inedible objects that can include glass or metal and as such are life-threatening, and harm to others. These outcomes not only jeopardize community placement, they also jeopardize the life of the individual.

The amount of supervision can be critical for successful community integration. An individual with mental retardation who does not have challenging behaviors might suffer from lack of supervision by evidencing poor grooming and hygiene and other disquieting but not necessarily devastating signs of neglect. An individual severely disabled by autism, even with above average intelligence, can suffer devastating consequences from inadequate supervision.

Increased supervision can be provided in a group home setting by the assignment of additional staff. In a family or foster care situation, the provision of additional supervision in the form of part-time aides can be effected to maintain the integrity of the placement.

Participatory Living Situation

The provision of full participation opportunities in the home environment is seen as critical to community adjustment, in that, in itself, it is a substantial deterrent to the destructive behaviors that can be so threatening to an integrated community lifestyle. Even those individuals who are most severely disabled by autism can participate at some level in their activities of daily living, home-care, and self-care. Many of the challenging behaviors that can be associated with autism, including self-stimulation, aggression, self-injury, and property destruction can be significantly ameliorated through an enriched environment, which provides ample opportunity for full participation in meaningful tasks.

Living situations of persons with autism should include active daily scheduling, in which individuals participate fully in self-care, home-care, food planning, food preparation, and all activities that are necessary for the maintenance of the home, and the individual. Individuals who are less disabled, and more independent, can participate in these activities independently or with minimal assistance. Individuals who are severely disabled by autism, who may have profound mental retardation and no verbal skills, may need ongoing assistance and supervision. However, such needs should not preclude participation.

Recreation and Leisure

Recreation and leisure activities can be crucial for good mental health of persons with developmental disabilities (Brotherson, Backus, Summers, & Turnbull, 1986). For individuals with autism, such opportunities can be crucial for not only mental health, but for successful community integration. Participation in recreation and leisure activities, such as full participation in home and self-care, can be critical to the management of behavior and communication problems that can be associated with autism.

There is a growing body of research that suggests that self-simulation and even self-injury can be prevented by the provision of alternate sensory stimuli (Favell, McGimsey, & Schell, 1982; Smith, 1986b). Recreation and leisure activities can be seen as the ultimate in alternate sensory stimuli. Such activities are incompatible with the withdrawal and self-stimulation that might be associated with autism. Additionally, these activities, when provided within the context of choice and supervision, can be incompatible with more destructive behaviors such as self-injury and aggression.

For example, a young man with autism might enjoy playing in the toilet. The local swimming pool provides a natural source of alternate, and more acceptable, sensory stimuli. A young boy with autism has life-threatening darting behavior. Unless a staff person holds his elbow or his backpack, he is likely to dart away, unmindful of oncoming vehicles. Frequent excursions to the park, where this boy can freely run and bolt, provide an alternate and more acceptable form of stimulation.

Ideally, recreation and leisure events should be integrated, normalized experiences that persons with autism attend with assistance, if necessary, and participate in with nonhandicapped peers. Such experiences not only provide the stimulation of the activity, but have the advantage of normal role models. Swimming, movie-going, horseback riding, fishing, boating, hiking, and even participation in aerobics classes (i.e., nonhandicapped) are only a few examples of activities that can be enjoyed by individuals with autism.

For persons with developmental disabilities, such as autism, recreation and leisure experiences can enhance the quality of life in the community residential setting (Hawkins, 1988). Further, for individuals who also have challenging behaviors, recreation and leisure activities can play a unique role in the management of these behaviors. As such, these experiences are not simply enhancing, they can be critical for maintaining community adjustment.

Behavior Management

Many individuals with autism can enjoy productive home lives if supervised by caring people, and if provided with full participation in home-care, self-care, and recreation and leisure activities. However, for some, challenging behaviors can be so debilitating that they appear to preclude full participation. Self-injury becomes a deterrent to task presentation, aggression becomes a deterrent to trips to the restaurant, and property destruction appears to preclude shopping. In fact, protecting the society from the menaces of the disabled individual was a justification for the institutionalization of these individuals (Wolfsenberger, 1975). Behavior management has had demonstrated effectiveness in each setting in which it has been applied, since its inception in the laboratory, through segregated settings, and more recently, in integrated community placements.

Behavior management has been successfully applied in home settings to manage self-injury (Berkman & Meyer, 1988; Donnellan, LaVigna, Zambito, & Thvedt, 1985; Smith, 1986a, 1990; Willis & LaVigna, 1988), aggression (Donnellan et al., 1985; Smith, 1986; Woods, 1982), pica (Mace & Knight, 1986; Smith, 1987), and property destruction (Smith, 1990).

Because the most devastating impact of autism can be the associated behavior problems, careful environmental design done under the auspices of a behavioral approach can be a critical element in residential success. Lack of good behavior management procedures can result in well-meant caregivers actually promoting the very behaviors they wish to eliminate. And, if this is the case, even the best supervisory ratios will not overcome the behavioral effects of the disorder. Well-planned behavior management can make efficient use of caregiver time by preventing or minimizing the effects of behavioral crises through promoting a positive, nonaversive but properly structured environment. Behavior management at its most effective typically includes an environmental analysis, a functional analysis of the behavior, and interventions that teach or reward more functional responses, remove or mitigate setting events, and enrich the environment.

Support Services

Individuals with autism living in integrated community settings require many of the same supports that their neighbors without handicaps need. Medical, dental, counseling, and psychiatric services may all be needed. However, they need these supports tailored to their needs.

Although many individuals with autism do well without medication (a survey of a facility serving 70 adults severely disabled by autism revealed that 10% were receiving psychotropic medication), some individuals might benefit from this course of treatment. Treatment can be facilitated by a psychiatrist who has expertise in autism and who is willing to work closely with the family or group home staff to carefully evaluate data each month on those behaviors that are targeted by the medication.

Behavioral support services can be critical, particularly in cases in which individuals exhibit self-injury, aggression, or property destruction. Behavioral support services, typically provided by psychologists or other professionals who have expertise in behavior management and autism, work with the caregiver to design a structured and enriched environment with specific behavior management strategies as dictated by a functional analysis to meet the behavioral challenges of the individual. Support services might need to be long term or ongoing, so that behavior plan implementation and progress can be carefully monitored, and adjustments can be made as necessary.

Donnellan et al. (1985) reported on a time-limited intervention program model to support community placement for persons with severe behavior problems. Specialists provided behavior intervention within the home settings, and were able to achieve significant behavior changes in those settings.

Speech and language services, occupational therapy, physical therapy, and nutritional consultation might all be useful adjuncts to an integrated community lifestyle. Dunn (1991) discussed three models for providing related services, all of which can be applicable to supporting individuals with autism. The direct therapy model involves specialists who provide therapy, such as speech and language therapy, or occupational therapy, directly to the individual. The monitoring model involves a specialist who monitors the implementation of strategies within the home setting, but remains primarily responsible for outcomes. The consultation model utilizes a therapist who serves as consultant to the caregiver who bears the primary responsibility for outcome.

Support services should be directly applicable to problems within the individual's daily life. Individuals with autism have difficulty generalizing, and this difficulty places limitations on the usefulness of therapy that is not directly integrated into and applicable to the individual's daily routine. Research on naturalistic language therapy is illustrative of this point, with several studies pointing to the superiority of language activities within the natural environment (Haring, Neetz, Lovinger, Peck, & Semmel, 1987; Hart & Risley, 1975).

Parents or foster parents often need additional support services, such as part-time assistants within the home, or substitute care that allows the primary caregiver some independent time. For individuals with destructive behaviors, or chronic sleep problems, in-home support in the form of an aide or relief staff can make remaining in the community a reasonable alternative to moving the individual out of the home to a more segregated setting. Families of individuals with developmental disabilities can also benefit from additional support services, including stress management, parenting skills training, support groups, and community-based respite care (Singer, Irvin, Irvine, Hawkins, & Cooley, 1989).

SUPPORTED EMPLOYMENT

Behavior problems associated with autism have typically been considered incompatible with employment. Kanner, Rodrigues, and Ashendan (1972) found that only 10% of a sample of 96 children diagnosed with autism at Johns Hopkins Hospital prior to 1953 were "sufficiently integrated into the texture of our society to be employable . . ." (p. 10).

Supported employment, which has enabled the integrated employment of thousands of persons with mild to moderate handicaps, appears more elusive for those with severe handicaps. Kregel and Wehman (1990) report that a survey spanning eight states revealed that persons with severe or profound handicaps were only minimally represented in supported employment programs. Of the 1,411 consumers of supported employment services surveyed, only 10% displayed challenging behaviors such as physical aggression, self-injury, or self-stimulation.

Despite these initially dismal data, adults with autism have been able to achieve and maintain employment through supported employment programs. Juhrs and Smith (1989) reported on 7 years of supported employment with adults disabled by autism, and found that approximately 70% of those individuals with aggression, self-injury, and property destruction were employed over half of the time that they were served by a supported employment program. Of all of the adults with autism served for at least 3 years in the supported employment program, approximately 75% were employed over 90% of the time.

Many people with autism have been able to work at competitive, nonsheltered employment with the help of specialized support on the job. Workers with autism have been employed in a variety of settings, including manufacturing firms, warehouses, retail stores, libraries, recycling centers, vending machine suppliers, solar energy development, electronic firms, laboratories, and county and federal government agencies.

Models of Supported Employment

Supported employment is provided to individuals with disabilities by habilitation agencies that provide support in the following five ways:

finding appropriate jobs, placing the individual in a job, training on the job, ongoing assessment of performance, and implementing procedures to ensure long-term job retention (Wehman, Parent, Wood, Kregel, & Inge, 1989). The support may also be in noninstructional areas, such as developing relationships with supervisors and coworkers, providing information and training to supervisors and coworkers, and encouraging socialization between the worker and coworkers (Moon, Goodall, Barcus, & Brooke, 1985). The degree of support that may be necessary is dictated by the needs of the individual. Similarly, the manner in which the support is given is also individually determined.

There are several models of support for the worker with autism. The most common is the job coach model. The job coach is typically an employee of a human services organization and is responsible for teaching the individual the job, and managing any instructional, behavioral, or interpersonal issues that may arise at work.

Nisbet and Hagner (1988) propose alternatives to the job coach model, which rely primarily on supports that are naturally occurring in the work environment. These authors propose consideration of a mentor model, in which the job coach does the initial training, and a coworker assumes the role of mentor and subsequent responsibility for the worker; the job sharing model, in which the worker shares a job with a nondisabled person who also assumes some of the responsibility of providing support; and the training consultant option, in which a consultant from a human services agency provides training to coworkers at the site who in turn support the worker with the disability.

The model used may be dictated by the amount of support the worker with autism needs, and the nature of that support. Degrees of support and the length of time such support is needed are reviewed in this section.

Full-Time, Long-Term Support

Some individuals with autism require full-time, long-term support. These are most likely individuals with severe autism, no verbal language, mental retardation, and a history of destructive behaviors, such as property destruction, aggression, pica, or self-injury, and a great deal of difficulty remaining in the work area and on task. These individuals may need continual supervision to ensure their safety and that of those around them, and to manage their behavior through the implementation of intensive behavioral programming.

Certain behavior problems, despite proactive behavior management, may present some ongoing level of danger to the workers and others if not expertly managed. Because of the behavioral needs, and risk of behaviors such as property destruction, aggression, and self-injury, some workers with autism will require constant long-term supervision despite higher levels of intellectual and language functioning. For these individuals, the use of mentor model or trainer–consultation models are not realistic because of the intensive amount of supervision required. The mentor would have little or no time left to attend to other job duties, therefore, the traditional job coach model is preferable for these individuals.

Partial Support

Some individuals with autism may succeed with less than full-time support. Although individuals with sporadic behavior problems (e.g., every few months), or with social skill deficits that require daily or weekly training, may need some level of support monitoring indefinitely, part-time monitoring might suffice.

Persons with autism who need only partial support are promising prospects for the use of supports within the natural environment. The mentor model or trainer–consultation model (Nisbet & Hagner, 1988) provides an efficient and natural way to serve these individuals. Individuals who only need occasional assistance, or sporadic social skills, or instructional training, can obtain such training from coworkers.

Temporary Supports

Some individuals with autism may need help only in finding a suitable job match. Once the job is found, the worker may be able to go to work independently and benefit from the same on-the-job training as nondisabled workers receive. Other workers with autism may have special learning needs that require temporary support in the form of initial instruction and assistance with integration into the worksite. For these workers, temporary support might be sufficient. Once they have learned the routine and tasks, and become familiar with the coworkers and social expectations of the site, supports that were once full time can be gradually withdrawn.

Even persons with challenging behaviors can look forward to some degree of independence on the job. Often specific social skill deficits exist that can be minimized by the type of job held. For example, a lack of social skills is not too detrimental in a stock room where minimal social interactions are required. If persons are placed in jobs in which their deficits are not job threatening, then support can be quickly and possibly permanently faded.

Once the individual has learned the requirements of the job, and performs satisfactorily and reliably, the job coach or mentor can fade back to occasional drop-in visits or interventions. When behavior problems are not destructive in nature, or when such behaviors have been reliably eliminated, the fading of supports can be a realistic option.

CRITICAL ELEMENTS OF SUPPORTED EMPLOYMENT

There are several elements that are critical to successful employment of workers with autism. The intensity of support and length of time that support is available are both critical to job adjustment.

Supervision

Provision of sufficient supervision is necessary for achieving and attaining employment. Failure to provide sufficient supervision from the outset, or withdrawal of supervision, would not only be job threatening for a number of individuals with autism, it would be tantamount to neglect. Without proper and continuous supervision, some of these individuals are at risk from self-injury, pica, or darting. Ongoing provision of support can minimize the frequency of these behaviors, mitigate their effects, and ensure continued employment. Individuals with autism who do not have severe behavior problems might still require high levels of supervision due to the severity of their communication and learning problems, in order to maintain employment.

Job-Worker Match

Although autism does not preclude employment, the characteristics of autism can indeed be incompatible with certain types of employment. Failure to find a suitable job match can be synonymous with failure of the employment experience. Job development, therefore, remains a primary concern among providers of supported employment services (Barcus, 1988). Because the job match can be critical to success (McDonnell, Nofs, & Hardman, 1989), providers must be concerned with this issue.

A primary consideration in job development is interaction of the disability with the demands of the job. Characteristics that might appear to be job threatening in one setting could be advantageous in another. Characteristics often associated with autism and that can be advantageous in job matching include well-developed visual–motor skills, fine motor dexterity, nonverbal reasoning skills, and attention to detail.

Several social–behavioral characteristics that might appear to be problematic can also be advantageous. Dependence on routines and difficulty with change are assets in jobs that have well-established routines. Perseveration on minute details is sometimes advantageous in jobs that require attention to small detail. Even the social withdrawal associated with autism can be an advantage to an employer, as "social loafing" on the job is not usually a problem attributed to employees with autism.

The job match must take into account behavioral or social deficits that might, in fact, prove job threatening in certain settings. Certain types of jobs are best avoided. For example, individuals with problems maintaining moderate voice volume should not seek employment at the public library. Persons with a history of smashing glass might best avoid china shops. However, the former individual could be successful in an industrial site, which has a high level of background noise, and the latter might do fine at a recycling center.

Appropriate job matches can be found by canvassing the local labor market and seeking job openings consistent with worker strengths and deficits. An alternative approach is to assist companies in creating jobs that can be handled well by workers with autism, and that meet specific needs of the employer (Moon, Inge, Wehman, Brooke, & Barcus, 1990). Both of these job development procedures have served to successfully place individuals with severe autism in jobs.

Establishing and Maintaining a Worksite

Job support extends beyond simply placing workers in a job. Job support also consists of work orientation, assessment of training needs, on-the-job training of the worker, stabilization of performance (Moon et al., 1990), and for many workers with autism, intensive, ongoing support in the form of close supervision and implementation of behavior management plans to insure continued success on the job (Smith, 1990).

Job orientation and assessment of training needs typically begin prior to the worker starting. Support staff determine the worker's job duties, learn those job duties, determine the routine of the work place, identify supports within the worksite, design instructional strategies, and become familiar with the role of the worker within both the social and vocational context of the worksite (Moon et al., 1990).

Precise identification of job duties and routines is especially critical. If a routine is to be varied, it is best to teach variation as part of the routine. Otherwise, if the worker adapts to one routine, later it may be difficult to change to another. Resistance to change can be a characteristic of autism, and this characteristic needs to be taken into account when orienting the worker to the new job.

Initial worksite analysis has another important dimension. This initial assessment highlights the potential interaction between behavioral challenges and the work environment, providing valuable information for minimizing the effects of behavior problems at the worksite.

The assessment can lead to adaptations of settings that are helpful in promoting success at the job despite the presence of challenging behaviors. For example, individuals with darting behavior may need to be situated away from exits. Workers with high-volume vocalizations may need to be situated some distance from customer contact. Workers with problems with pica might need to have the area cleaned thoroughly several times per day by the support staff. Workers with aggression or self-injury might need to work some distance from coworkers.

Instructional Procedures

Many workers with autism require specialized assistance to learn the job tasks and routines. The importance of systematically designing and implementing employment training for individuals with disabilities has previously been identified (Bellamy, Horner, & Inman, 1979). Workers with autism may have special learning styles to which untrained employers or coworkers might have difficulty adapting. A precise task analysis and instructional strategies have been demonstrated to be effective in teaching very complex technical and vocational skills to persons with severe handicaps (Bellamy et al., 1979; Bellamy, Peterson, & Close, 1975; Gold, 1972; Gold & Barclay, 1973; Wehman & McLaughlin, 1980).

Relationships with CoWorkers

Development and maintenance of good relationships with employers and coworkers are of major importance. This is especially true for workers with behavioral challenges. Behavior problems associated with autism (e.g., aggression, self-injury, screaming, and property destruction) do sometimes occur at work. If employees without autism displayed such behavior, job termination would likely result. Good relationships with employers lead to cooperation and understanding, and can help save jobs should such behavior problems occur.

Behavior Management

Workers with autism may lose their job due to problems in productivity or accuracy. However, a more overriding concern is the significant social skills deficits and behavior problems that can accompany the disorder. Salzberg, Lignugaris-Kraft, and McCuller (1988) reviewed reasons for job loss among workers with mental retardation, and cited personal–social inadequacies, such as bizarre and aggressive behavior, a factor in failure to retain jobs.

Careful implementation of behavior management plans, which include specific training in necessary social skills, can help workers with autism maintain their jobs despite histories of serious social skills deficits.

Behavior management plans help workers with autism meet the social demands of the worksite, and minimize the likelihood that behavioral challenges will threaten employment. Behavioral assessment can be done at the work site (Moon et al., 1990). Necessary social skills can be targeted and trained. Behavior plans can be developed that can prevent problems from occurring, and that provide for efficient, nonobtrusive management of problems once they do occur. A screaming fit, property destruction, or even aggression or self-injury need not signal the end of employment.

Behavior problems might occur after some time on the job. Functional analyses must then be done onsite to determine the function of the problem behavior (Lennox & Miltenberger, 1989). The behavior change process at work does not vary in form from the process in the home setting. Behavior management plans might be necessary that alter or mitigate setting events or antecedents, teach alternate behaviors, provide motivation to cooperate at work, and provide the structure needed in order to succeed at the job. Behavior management has been successfully used with employees with autism to manage aggression, self-injury, property destruction, and pica (Berkman & Meyer, 1988; Smith, 1986, 1987; Smith & Coleman, 1986).

On-the-job instruction in social skills can be invaluable for workers with autism. Workers with autism might need very specific social skills, such as asking for assistance, offering assistance, greeting coworkers and customers, and answering questions of coworkers and customers. Social skills can be taught in short, structured training sessions directly in job settings. Park and Gaylord-Ross (1989) used a problem-solving approach to social skills training at work for three workers with mental retardation with some success. Standard social skills training packages have been used successfully to improve specific social skills of adults with autism in integrated job settings (Smith, 1985; Smith & Coleman, 1986).

Support Services

Support services for facilitating work adjustment for workers with autism do not differ substantially from what might be necessary to support these individuals in their home environments. Behavior support, and support from specialists in occupational therapy and speech and language therapy can be instrumental in achieving success. As with residential support services, to be most effective, these services need to be integrated within the job setting, and possibly provided through the job coach or other support person. The actual implementation of the specialist's recommendations can be done directly in the job setting under several models, including direct therapy by the specialist, or through the job supporter (such as the job coach) with supervision or consultation from the specialist (Dunn, 1991).

CURRENT STATUS, OBSTACLES, FUTURE DIRECTIONS

Individuals with autism are best served vocationally in supported employment through an individual placement model. The individual placement model allows for individualized job match and job adaptation procedures that take into account the potentially devastating effects of any behavior problems associated with the autism. Additionally, full integration with full exposure to nonhandicapped coworkers, and limited exposure to other individuals with behavioral or learning disabilities, maximizes the benefits of learning through modeling. And, conversely, it minimizes the drawbacks of learning from the misbehavior of others with social or behavioral deficits.

Nationwide, greater numbers of individuals with autism are being exposed to supported employment. Persons with autism have achieved and maintained employment despite serious problems with destructive behavior, and have earned meaningful wages (Juhrs & Smith, 1989) through supported employment services.

State systems change projects have realized impressive success in developing local supported employment programs and including individuals with severe disabilities (Kregel, 1989). Supported employment sites for individuals with autism have been established throughout the country under the auspices of federal grants supporting model program replication (Juhrs, 1990).

The development of jobs in nontraditional areas that are well-suited to the needs of persons with autism have allowed these individuals to achieve employment. The provision of sufficient support, including implementation of behavior management plans tailored to the needs of both the employer and the worker, have enabled workers with autism to maintain employment.

However, as Kregel and Wehman (1989) note, for the most part, the promise of supported employment for persons with severe disabilities remains just that—a promise still deferred. Several obstacles to the expansion of integrated job opportunities exist. One important obstacle is the failure to provide sufficient support for sufficiently long periods of time.

Rusch, Chadsey-Rusch, and Johnson (1991) note that failure to provide sufficient support is an historical problem. These authors suggest that individuals with borderline to mild retardation may now be receiving too much support. However, for the worker with severe autism, no verbal language, profound mental retardation, and a history of self-injury, aggression, or property destruction, providing sufficient support remains the challenge, and for many, the obstacle.

Even so-called high functioning individuals with autism can be vulnerable to this obstacle. Sometimes, the support needs are not as obvious, because the behavioral and communication challenges are more sporadic and less noticeable. However, when they do occur, they can be job threatening in the short term, and lead to a sporadic history of job success over the long term.

Failure to provide adequate support in integrated community settings can result in institutionalization or reinstitutionalization. Some of the behavior problems often associated with autism place individuals at risk for health problems and injuries, and also can put neighbors and support staff at risk.

Failure to provide effective behavior management support is also an obstacle to successful community integration for this population. Individuals with challenging behaviors have been maintained in supported employment for up to 10 years with the support of job coaches who were intensively trained in behavior management. However, an underestimation of the effectiveness of behavior management with severe behavior problems has contributed to many professionals and service providers continuing to view this population as unemployable.

Full integration for people with autism, both at work and at home, has been realized and is currently a reality for a small segment of this population. Allocation of expertise, manpower, and funds needs to be directed towards application and practice of full community integration, so that many can benefit from the experience of the few. Training, replication, and dissemination activities should be an overriding priority if full integration is to become a reality.

Mr. Markham, the individual described at the beginning of this chapter, has a history of severe behavior problems. He has severe autism, and is nonverbal. He has difficulty with pica as well as severe self-injury in the form of intensive headbanging. Nonetheless, he has maintained competitive, integrated living and employment for 10 years with the help of specialized support. The procedures to support and help individuals like Mr. Markham achieve successful integration have been established and proven effective, and Mr. Markham has benefited. His peers with autism are waiting to benefit as well.

ACKNOWLEDGMENTS

Work on this chapter was in part funded by grant #G008730428–89 from the U. S. Department of Education. However, the opinions expressed herein do not necessarily reflect the position or policy of the U. S. Department of Education.

REFERENCES

Barcus, M., Wehman, P., Moon, S., Brooke, V., Goodall, P., & Everson, J. (1988). Design and implementation of a short-term in-service training program for supported employment service providers. *Rehabilitation Education, 2,* 17–33.

Bellamy, T., Horner, R., & Inman, D. (1979). *Vocational rehabilitation of severely retarded adults: A direct service technology.* Baltimore: University Park Press.

Bellamy, T., Peterson, L., & Close D. (1975). Rehabilitation of severely and profoundly retarded: Illustrations of competence. *Education and Training of Mentally Retarded, 10,* 174–186.

Berkman, K. A., & Meyer, L. H. (1988). Alternative strategies and multiple outcomes in the remediation of severe self-injury: Going "all out" nonaversively. *The Journal of the Association for Persons with Severe Handicaps, 13,* 76–88.

Brotherson, J., Backus, L., Summers, J., & Turnbull, A. (1986). Transition to adulthood. In J. Summers (Ed.), *The right to grow up* (pp. 17–44). Baltimore: Brookes.

Donnellan, A. M., LaVigna, G. W., Zambito, J., & Thvedt, J. (1985). A time-limited intensive intervention program model to support community placement for persons with severe behavior problems. *The Journal of the Association for Persons with Severe Handicaps, 10,* 123–131.

Dunn, W. (1991). Integrated related services. In L. H. Meyer, C. A. Peck, & L. Brown (Eds.), *Critical issues in the lives of people with severe disabilities* (pp. 353–378). Baltimore: Brookes.

Eyman, R., Borthwick-Duffy, S., & Sheehy, N. (1987). A longitudinal study of small family care placements. In S. Landesman & P. Vietze (Eds.), *Living environments and mental retardation* (pp. 449–476). Washington, DC: American Association on Mental Retardation.

Favell, J. E., McGimsey, J. F., & Schell, R. M. (1982). Treatment of self-injury by providing alternative sensory activities. *Analysis and Intervention in Developmental Disabilities, 2,* 83–104.

Gold, M. (1972). Stimulus factors in skill training of the retarded on a complex assembly task: Acquisition, transfer, and retention. *The American Journal of Mental Deficiency, 76,* 517–526.

Gold, M., & Barclay, C. (1973). The learning of difficult visual discriminations by the moderately and severely retarded. *Mental Retardation, 11*(2), 9–11.

Haring, T. G., Neetz, J. A., Lovinger, L., Peck, C., & Semmel, M. I. (1987). Effects of four modified incidental teaching procedures to create opportunities for communication. *Journal of the Association for Persons with Severe Handicaps, 12,* 218–226.

Hart, B., & Risley, T. (1975). Incidental teaching of language in the preschool. *Journal of Applied Behavior Analysis, 8,* 411–420.

Hawkins, B. (1988). Leisure and recreational programming. In M. Janicki, M. Krauss, & M. Seltzer (Eds.), *Community residences for persons with developmental disabilities* (pp. 217–230). Baltimore: Brookes.

Juhrs, P. (1990, December). *101 jobs for people with autism.* Paper presented at the meeting of the Association for Persons with Severe Handicaps, Chicago, IL.

Juhrs, P., & Smith, M. (1989). Community based employment for persons with autism. In P. Wehman & J. Kregel (Eds.), *Supported employment and transition: Focus on excellence* (pp. 163–176). New York: Human Sciences Press.

Kanner, L., Rodrigues, A., & Ashenden, B. (1972). How far can autistic children go in matters of social adaptation? *Journal of Autism and Childhood Schizophrenia, 2,* 9–33.

Kregel, J. (1989). Opportunities and challenges: Recommendations for the future of the national supported employment initiative. In P. Wehman, J. Kregel, & M. Shafer (Eds.), *Emerging trends in the national supported employment initiative: A preliminary analysis of*

27 states (pp. 128–137). Virginia: VCU RRTC Supported Employment.

Kregel, J., & Wehman, P. (1989). Supported employment: Promises deferred for persons with severe disabilities. *Journal of the Association for Persons with Severe Handicaps, 14,* 293–303.

Kregel, J., & Wehman, P. (1990). Promises deferred for persons with severe handicaps. In J. Kregel, P. Wehman, & M. Shafer (Eds.), *Supported employment for persons with severe disabilities: From research to practice.* Virginia: VCU RRTC on Supported Employment.

Lakin, K., Hill, B., & Bruininks, R. (1988). Trends and issues in the growth of community residential services. In M. Janicki, M. Krauss, & M. Seltzer (Eds.), *Community residences for persons with developmental disabilities* (pp. 25–42). Baltimore: Brookes.

Lennox, D., & Miltenberger, R. (1989). Conducting a functional assessment in applied settings. *The Journal of the Association for Persons with Severe Handicaps, 14,* 304–311.

Mace, F., & Knight, D. (1986). Functional analysis and treatment of pica. *Journal of Applied Behavior Analysis, 19,* 411–416.

McDonnell, J., Nofs, D., & Hardman, M. (1989). An analysis of the procedural components of supported employment programs associated with employment outcomes. *Journal of Applied Behavior Analysis, 22,* 417–428.

Moon, S., Goodall, D., Barcus M., & Brooke, V. (1985). *The supported work model of competitive employment for citizens with severe handicaps: A guide for job trainers.* Richmond: Virginia Commonwealth University.

Moon, M., Inge, K., Wehman, P., Brooke, V., & Barcus, J. (1990). *Helping persons with severe mental retardation get and keep employment.* Baltimore: Brookes.

Nisbet, J., & Hagner, D. (1988). Natural supports in the workplace: A reexamination of supported employment. *The Journal of the Association for Persons with Severe Handicaps, 13,* 260–267.

Park, H., & Gaylord-Ross, R. (1989). A problem-solving approach to social skills training in employment settings with mentally retarded youth. *Journal of Applied Behavior Analysis, 22,* 373–380.

Rusch, F. R., Chadsey-Rusch, J., & Johnson, J. R. (1991). Supported employment: Emerging opportunities for employment integration. In L. H. Meyer, C. A. Peck, & L. Brown (Eds.), *Critical issues in the lives of people with severe disabilities* (pp. 145–169). Baltimore: Brookes.

Salzberg, C., Lignugaris-Kraft, B., & McCuller, G. (1988). Reasons for job loss: A review of employment termination studies of mentally retarded workers. *Research in Developmental Disabilities, 9,* 153–170.

Singer, G. H., Irvin, L. K., Irvine, B., Hawkins, N., & Cooley, E. (1989). Evaluation of community-based support services for families of persons with developmental disabilities. *The Journal of the Association for Persons with Severe Handicaps, 14,* 312–323.

Smith, M. (1985). Working with autism: Social skills training in the workplace. *The Maryland Psychologist.*

Smith, M. (1986a). Managing the aggressive and self-injurious behavior of adults disabled by autism in the community. *The Journal of Association for Persons with Severe Handicaps, 10,* 228–232.

Smith, M. (1986b). The use of alternate sensory stimuli in the community-based treatment of the self-stimulatory behavior of an adult disabled by autism. *Journal of Behavior Therapy and Experimental Psychiatry, 17,* 121–125.

Smith, M. (1987). Treatment of pica in an adult disabled by autism by differential reinforcement of incompatible behavior. *Journal of Behavior Therapy and Experimental Psychiatry, 10,* 285–288.

Smith, M. (1990). *Autism and life in the community: Successful interventions for behavioral challenges.* Baltimore: Brookes.

Smith, M., & Coleman, D. (1986). Managing the behavior of adults with autism in the job setting. *Journal of Autism and Developmental Disorders, 16,* 145–153.

Summers, J., & Reese, R. (1986). Residential services. In J. Summers (Ed.), *The right to grow up* (pp. 119–148). Baltimore: Brookes.

Wehman, P., & McLaughlin, P. (1980). *Vocational curriculum for developmentally disabled persons.* Baltimore: University Park Press.

Wehman, P., Parent, W., Wood, W., Kregel, J., & Inge, K. (1989). The supported work model of competitive employment: Illustrations of competence in workers with severe and profound handicaps. In P. Wehman & J. Kregel (Eds), *Supported employment and transition: Focus on excellence* (pp. 19–52). New York: Human Sciences Press.

Willis, T., & LaVigna, G. (May, 1988). *Nonaversive treatment of severe self-injury.* Paper presented at the annual meeting of the Association for Behavior Analysis, Philadelphia.

Wolfensberger, W. (1975). *The origin and nature of our institutional models.* New York: Human Policy Press.

Woods, T. (1982). Reducing severe aggressive and self-injurious behaviors: A nonintrusive home-based approach. *Behavioral Disorders, 7,* 180–188.

12 New Directions in Educational Programming for Students with Autism

V. Mark Durand
State University of New York at Albany

It has been approximately 50 years since Leo Kanner first described children with autism. This book portrays some of the accomplishments made in the intervening years that have led to increased understanding and assistance for these individuals and their families. As the reader can see, we have come a long way from the initial descriptions made by Dr. Kanner in 1943. In this chapter, I outline some of those areas that appear to hold promise for moving the field of autism ahead in the years to come.

There is always danger in trying to identify what is *new* in a field. Any attempt to label an idea or procedure as new is typically met with a great deal of skepticism as well as an example of how that approach was used years ago. This cynicism is obviously not unique to the field of autism. Any field that is scientifically based is (and should be) wary of efforts to reintroduce previously tested ideas. At the same time, it is essential that we recognize and embrace new trends in the field that have the potential for improving our educational efforts.

This chapter profiles some of the trends in the field that may prove to be valuable in improving educational programming for students with autism. Incorporated throughout the chapter is the assumption that we have reason to be optimistic at this point in the development of the discipline. These are indeed exciting times. Debates continue over the appropriate place for educating children with autism (e.g., neighborhood schools vs. special residential schools) as well as the content of such teaching (e.g., whether to use "aversives"). Although as early as 5 years ago some of these questions were clouded by polemics, the results from scientific groups as well as from classrooms throughout the country indicate that positive efforts in integrated settings can and do work.

THE ROLE OF VALUES OR, WHEN IS A ROSE NOT A ROSE?

The role of specific values in education and research with persons with autism has been discussed and debated of late (Peck, 1990). One argument has been that the outcomes of our research *alone* should lead to specific educational practices. A different view is that it is impossible to separate out values from research, and therefore we should be explicit about what those values are. The following description from a recent best-selling book metaphorically illustrates how the field of autism has dealt with these conflicts. Oliver Sacks (1987) discussed a particular individual (Dr. P.) who had an unusual neurological disorder in the book *The Man Who Mistook His Wife for a Hat*. Dr. P. is described as originally complaining of visual problems, but it quickly becomes clear that his trouble involves something more puzzling. During his examination, Dr. Sacks wrote of his interaction with this man concerning a rose.

> He took it like a botanist or morphologist given a specimen, not like a person given a flower. "About six inches in length," he commented. "A convoluted red form with a linear green attachment." "Yes," I said encouragingly, "and what do you think it *is*, Dr. P.?" "Not easy to say." He seemed perplexed. "It lacks the simple symmetry of the Platonic solids, although it may have a higher symmetry of its own. . . . I think this could be an inflorescence or flower." (pp. 13–14)

The particular brain disorder experienced by Dr. P. (a form of agnosia) made it difficult for him to make judgments. He had trouble integrating his personal experiences with the information coming into him from his senses. In a way, our field has for many years acted in a manner similar to Dr. P. In an effort to eschew nonproductive theorizing, our science (and those who interpret our science) has sometimes missed important human considerations. For example, one prominent colleague was recently quoted as saying "Whether someone is in an institution with 14 other people or 94 other people is relatively unimportant to me." This statement was based on his interpretation of the literature on deinstitutionalization. Would he have made the same declaration if this were *his* residential option?

A "purely scientific view" of these issues implies that science and research (and ultimately, practice) can be value-free endeavors—clearly, this is not possible. Science as a method for answering questions (e.g., using a multiple baseline design to observe change) can be relatively value-free, but the questions being asked are steeped in the values of the person framing the question (Guess & Siegel-Causey, 1985; Skrtic, 1987; Staats, 1975). For example, in the 1950s, some individuals posed the scientific question, "Would integration of the races in school lead to harm?" At the time I'm sure that some social scientists saw this as a purely scientific question. However, asking the question in this way today would undoubtedly lead to accusations of racism. Contemporary researchers in this area would instead pose the question, "How do we best integrate students of different races?" The value is that integration of the races in school is important, and the issue should be how to facilitate this movement.

In a like manner, the field of autism and developmental disabilities is beginning to recognize that the questions we have asked in the past may need to be changed. For example, instead of asking "Which children should be mainstreamed into the regular school?" the question becomes, "How do we maximize the benefits and minimize the problems of integrating all children in regular schools?" Rather than studying, "Which intervention approach is better, 'aversives' or 'nonaversives'?" we ask, "How do we most effectively reduce challenging behavior without pain or humiliation?" Posing the question, "How do I get her to comply with all my requests?" becomes "How do I teach her to become more independent and make choices?" There is an increasing recognition of values such as inclusion, choice, and freedom from harm, and these are now being incorporated into our programs.

Again, these questions, and many similar questions, are now being asked in the research literature. With these questions comes a realization that the basic values of human dignity and worth that we apply to ourselves and our families are equally important for persons with autism. Let us return to the subtitle of this section—when is a rose not a rose? The answer is when it is a "convoluted red form with a linear green attachment, about six inches in length, that lacks the simple symmetry of the Platonic solids." When is a child with autism not a child? When he or she is a subject or an autistic. Fortunately, there has been a change in our language regarding these children, and a change in the way we view the integration of values and science. Hopefully, readers of this book have observed this important change in the work already presented, and will continue to see this trend in the field.

ASSESSMENT

Elsewhere we have categorized assessment procedures into three areas: medical, traditional psychological, and behavioral assessment (Durand &

Carr, 1988). Medical assessment includes techniques that are designed to measure biological aspects of individuals (e.g., serotonin levels, presence of rubella). Traditional psychological assessment assumes that certain patterns in the way people behave (e.g., cognitive, social, academic) are stable, and individual measures of these behaviors can be compared to group norms. Behavioral assessment seeks to measure overt behaviors (e.g., rocking, echolalia) and their environmental determinants. These approaches are substantially different methodologically and conceptually and are therefore discussed separately.

Assessing individuals with autism is important for a variety of reasons (Bailey & Wolery, 1989). For example, making placement decisions for appropriate special education programs is usually the first reason why children with autism are exposed to assessment procedures. Treatment monitoring and selection are additional goals for assessment. Because of the importance of placement and treatment in the education of individuals with autism, these functions of assessment procedures are highlighted in the discussion to follow. The three assessment procedures (i.e., medical, traditional psychological, and behavioral) are evaluated with respect to how they contribute to these activities. Emerging trends in these areas are discussed in this context.

Medical Assessment

Medical assessment research includes investigations of biochemical abnormalities (Ritvo, Rabin, Yuwiler, Freeman, & Geller, 1978), neurophysiological disorders (Rosenbloom et al., 1984), and disease conditions as they relate to infantile autism. A majority of the medical research has assumed that autism is a disorder with a single cause (Rutter, 1978). Yet, numerous medical conditions have been associated with autism, including congenital rubella (Chess, Korn, & Fernandez, 1971), hypsarrhythmia (Taft & Cohen, 1971), tuberosesclerosis (Lotter, 1974), and cytomegalovirus (Stubbs, Ash, & Williams, 1984). Similarly, a number of biochemical and structural deficits have been identified with children with autism (e.g., Ritvo et al., 1978). However, the general consensus from medical assessment research is that although these children do differ from children without autism on a variety of dimensions, there is significant variability within the group with autism (Ornitz, 1978). No single medical sign or signs have, to date, been useful in differentiating children with autism from others. It is unlikely that one *cause* for autism exists. It appears that there may be many causes for the collection of symptoms referred to as autism.

An important question to ask here is, "What is the value of medical assessment for educators?" Medical information is useful for communicating possible limiting conditions in some children (e.g., presence of seizures). At times, this information has aided educational programming by identifying conditions that restrict efforts to teach. Identifying the presence of certain illnesses can be quite useful when designing intervention programs. One example of recent work in this area is the research being conducted on "biobehavioral states." These efforts involve observations of students in order to assess their level of alertness and/or agitation. For example, Guess et al. (1988) observed students across six biobehavioral states: asleep inactive, asleep active, drowsy, awake inactive–alert, awake active–alert, and crying/agitated. They found tremendous variation both within each student's day, and across students. The implication is that a student's level of alertness must be taken into consideration when presenting educational demands. It is anticipated that pre-task levels of attention will play an important role in the way lesson plans are introduced.

It is important to point out that the utility of medical assessment for placement and/or treatment decisions has not been demonstrated. Although children are sometimes placed together because of medical conditions, there is no evidence that this practice is beneficial. In fact, the trend to integrate all students into regular education programs clearly illustrates the relative unimportance of diagnosing medical conditions in placement or educational decisions. For these types of information we must turn to traditional psychological and behavioral assessment.

Traditional Psychological Assessment

The assessment of children with autism with traditional psychological tests has been carried out routinely for only a relatively short time (Evans, 1990). Up to about 20 years ago, these children were generally considered untestable (Alpern, 1967). However, with the introduction of standardized modifications of traditional tests (Sattler, 1982), along with a behavioral technology for improving compliance, more children with autism have been introduced to psychological assessment.

Traditional psychological tests are instruments that rely on norms to measure differences between individuals (Anastasi, 1968). Specifically, they include measures of academic achievement (e.g., Peabody Individual Achievement Test), IQ (e.g., Wechsler Intelligence Scale for Children—Revised), and social development (e.g., Vineland Adaptive Behavior Scales). Using these tests, global comparisons can be made between children with autism and children without handicaps.

Estimates of IQ from standardized tests yield the following generalizations about these children. Children with autism receive scores at both ends of the continuum. However, the majority fall in the below average range of IQ (IQ below 70), with only a very small percentage scoring average or above average on these tests (DeMyer et al., 1974; Gillberg, 1984). These measures of IQ have been used to determine prognosis. Greater increases in IQ scores have been observed among children with more skills rather than children with fewer skills following intensive training efforts (DeMyer, 1976). IQ scores for these children predict academic achievement and later adjustment as an adult (DeMyer et al., 1973; Rutter & Lockyer, 1967). This research suggests that a child with a low IQ score has a poor prognosis for improvement.

The findings described should be viewed cautiously, however. The follow-up studies cited were conducted on individuals who did not receive the type of intensive behavioral interventions in use today. For example, research with young children with autism suggests that early intervention may be particularly successful (Nordquist & Wahler, 1973; Wolf, Risley, & Mees, 1964), and their prognosis may be more optimistic than previously suggested (Lovaas, 1987). The trend toward early intervention (see Powers, chapter 10, this volume) may change this pessimistic outlook for children scoring low on IQ tests. Because of these encouraging developments, conclusions about current predictions of prognosis should be made carefully.

Perhaps the two most prevalent uses of traditional assessment devices are for research and placement. Special education placements are based primarily on the results of standardized tests (Powers & Handleman, 1984). Information about academic, cognitive, and social functioning is used to place children in settings based on their mental age. What is lacking, however, is evidence that these procedures in fact result in useful placement decisions. For example, would placing children in educational environments based on their chronological age be more or less beneficial to these children? The validity of using these devices to make placement decisions has not been systematically addressed.

Again, it is here where the values of the parent, teacher, and school come into play. Almost all special education services are portable. Any type of teaching that is currently carried out in a special education classroom can be implemented in a regular education classroom. Because of this, decisions about placement become more political and administrative than clinical or educational. Whether or not a child is taught in a private school, a special classroom in a public school, or in an integrated classroom, is based less on the results of IQ or achievement tests, and more on the availability of services. The trend in this area appears to be away from reliance on traditional psychological assessment for placement decisions.

Traditional psychological tests have also had limited impact on the treatment process (Keogh, 1972). Global measures of academic, cognitive, and social functioning may be useful for long-term monitoring of treatment outcome. However, these tests have not been demonstrated to have "treatment utility" (Nelson & Hayes, 1979); in other words, they have not contributed to the process of deciding among specific treatments (e.g., Hoy & Retish, 1984). Behavioral assessment has been suggested as an alternative or adjunct to traditional psychological assessment specifically directed to treatment design.

Behavioral Assessment

Behavioral assessment involves the identification of target behaviors and their controlling variables. The techniques that fall under the general rubric of behavioral assessment include behavioral observations (Johnson & Bolstad, 1973), checklists (e.g., the Autism Screening Instrument for Educational Planning; Krug, Arick, & Almond, 1980), and task analysis (Gold, 1976).

The potential for applying behavioral assessment to placement decisions is promising. The question here is not whether a student should be mainstreamed. Rather, of concern here is the issue of teacher–student "fit." Which teachers work best with which students? This question is answered every year on an informal basis. Principals and building administrators make these decisions based on their own intuition about the teachers, their strengths and weaknesses, and the students in their program. Could assessment procedures be worked out to best match teacher and student? In addition, which mix of peers is best? As we have discussed, formal psychological testing is typically used to make placement decisions in traditional special education settings. However, behavioral assessment has not formally addressed the issue of appropriate placement of children. Although behavioral assessment as an approach (identification of behavioral excesses and deficits and their controlling variables) may be valuable in making these decisions, specific procedures for this purpose do not exist. A new direction for this work should involve the development of assessment methods that are useful for the appropriate placement of children with autism.

Behavioral assessment should play a major role in treatment. And, without a doubt, it is the *sine qua non* of treatment monitoring. Most clinical outcome studies rely on behavioral assessment procedures (e.g., observational data). Moreover, these procedures are ideal for the constant monitoring of programming needed for the successful treatment of individuals with autism. However, treatment utility is lacking. Few behavioral techniques exist for guiding treatment decisions. With respect to providing guidelines for selecting specific treatments, behavioral assessment is a promise that has not been kept.

Future Directions in Assessment

I have been particularly critical of all three types of assessment procedures, and for good reason. Adequate psychometrics alone, for example, do not guarantee useful assessment techniques. Placing students in classrooms on the basis of their IQ scores assumes that this grouping is most beneficial for the children. There is no evidence that this is true. Assessment techniques are needed to point to placement decisions that, in turn, have been demonstrated to result in the acquisition of the greatest number of skills for students, as well as the greatest number of opportunities to socialize with same-age peers. Similarly, reinforcement surveys must point to specific reinforcers for children that have been demonstrated to result in more efficient learning for these children. Finally, procedures that have been demonstrated to help educators pick successful interventions for problem behaviors are necessary. The validity of assessment techniques for persons with autism needs to be assessed on the basis of the outcomes these techniques produce.

Over the past several years, the model and process of assessing persons with autism have begun to shift in emphasis in a number of ways. Historically, the predominant approach has been to "teach the weakness." Using developmentally based tests, specific skill limitations are identified (e.g., verbal information) and instructional objectives are developed to remediate these deficits. More recently, a "functional assessment model" has been put forward. In this approach, skills are targeted that are most likely to lead to the student becoming more independent. According to Gaylord-Ross and Browder (1990), functional assessment has the following characteristics:

1. It focuses on practical, *independent living skills* that enable the person to survive and succeed in the real world.
2. It has an *ecological* emphasis that looks at the individual functioning in his or her surrounding environment.
3. It examines the *process* of learning and performance.
4. It suggests *intervention* techniques that may be successful.
5. It specifies ongoing monitoring procedures that can *evaluate* treatment progress (p. 45).

Related to several of these points, contemporary work in functional assessment of problem behavior (e.g., self-injurious behavior, aggression) has begun to address the issue of outcome-based validation. For example, the Motivation Assessment Scale (MAS) has been designed to assess the role of social (e.g., adult attention) and nonsocial (e.g., sensory feedback) factors in the maintenance of such behaviors (Durand & Crimmins, 1988). Preliminary data have shown the MAS to be capable of reliably predicting how children will behave in a variety of settings. For example, the MAS can predict if a particular child will engage in substantially more self-injury when presented with a difficult task. This information has been shown to be useful in selecting nonaversive interventions (Durand, 1990; Durand & Carr, 1991).

An additional trend in the area of assessment concerns the role of *dynamic* assessment models. Traditionally, assessment is conducted on a yearly basis, with this one-time process guiding decisions throughout the year. However, there has been a recent move to see assessment as an ongoing process. Information obtained about a student can be used to guide decisions on a monthly, weekly, and even a daily basis. What follows is a description of a recent case that illustrates this issue.

I recently helped construct an Individualized Education Plan (IEP) for a 15-year-old student. Based on formal and informal assessment, goals and objectives were developed for his communication training program for the year. However, several weeks following the beginning of our new program it became clear that several objectives were no longer necessary. In addition, it was obvious that some objectives were inappropriate and others were right on target. When recommendations were made for changes, there was some reluctance on the part of both the teachers and the parent. How could the plans we made only 3 weeks ago—and on which we worked so hard—be inappropriate? Were we "giving up" already?

In the past, changes were made on a yearly basis as part of the annual review. Changes in the interim were usually seen as efforts to abandon the goals agreed on previously. What we need is to reinforce the idea that assessment is an ongoing process. Without constant revision, students will invariably stagnate at certain points when they outgrow the task or when previous estimates are unrealistic. Continued progress depends on constant monitoring and updating of the program. There is a movement toward this more dynamic approach to assessment, and it is a trend that will be most beneficial for our students.

INTEGRATION

Perhaps no other trend in education will have more far-reaching effects on daily practice than the full integration of children with autism into regular classrooms. This effort should rival the widespread effects on education observed after the passage of Public Law 94-142. The move to integrate these children into regular classrooms has proceeded slowly but steadily over the past decade. Writers in the early 1980s called for moving children with disabilities out of segregated "special" schools into special classes in the regular school (e.g., Brown et al., 1983). More recently, this movement has followed its logical progression by recommending that all students, regardless of disability, be placed with same age peers in regular schools (e.g., Brown, Long, Udvari-Solner, Davis et al. 1989; Brown, Long, Udvari-

Solner, Schwartz et al., 1989). Although support for integration predates the 1980s, it has only been recently that this idea has been embraced by large numbers of parents and professionals (for a more complete discussion of the history of integration, readers should refer to Meyer & Putnam, 1989, and Scheerenberger, 1983).

As was previously discussed, integration of children with autism will provoke a fundamental change in the process of assessment. For example, the emphasis will change from using assessment as essentially a placement activity because placement will be based primarily on chronological age. In addition, assessing most skills will benefit from the availability of direct comparisons with nonhandicapped peers. For example, determining what is appropriate social behavior will be easier with more accessible, socially competent models.

An additional trend motivated by the increased integration of children will be a change in the content of educational plans. The *how* and *what* of teaching should be influenced directly by the students sharing their classroom. For instance, using restrictive procedures for modifying challenging behavior looks inappropriate given most community standards. Teachers will be even more reticent to use procedures such as contingent electric shock or water sprays in integrated settings. Also, the move away from teaching readiness skills that is already apparent should be helped by integration efforts. Teaching nonfunctional skills should contrast most clearly compared to the activities of their peers.

Finally, one of the most obvious changes that should take place with full integration is a change in expectations. It is inevitable that educators who teach in classrooms with only students who have disabilities will have expectations for them that differ from the norm. Changes in expectations in integrated settings will range from issues of appearance (e.g., finding it unacceptable for a student to come to school with an unbuttoned shirt or with dirty hair) to expectations about interacting with peers (e.g., not allowing students to spend long periods of time alone). Clearly, just placing students in integrated settings without support will not result in meaningful results. However, model programs are being developed throughout the country that successfully integrate students with a broad range of abilities (e.g., Thompson et al., in press).

CURRICULUM CONTENT

Intervention research with students displaying autism has traditionally focused on *how* students are taught, sometimes at the expense of information about *what* these students should be taught. For example, we know a great deal about how to break skills down into individual components (task analysis) and how to shape successive approximations. However, what are the best skills to teach using this technology? Should we teach students the prerequisites to important tasks (e.g., prevocational, preacademic tasks), or should we begin to teach approximations to useful skills right away? Do we need to get students ready to learn language, or should we use augmentative communication strategies to allow them to interact with others more quickly?

These questions are at the forefront of education for children with autism and other developmental disabilities. And to date, there is not an empirical answer to these questions. No one has yet answered the question as to whether or not children need to be "readied" for meaningful education. In the absence of this information, the current trend is to assume that students can learn meaningful skills *while they are being taught meaningful skills*. In other words, rather than teaching isolated skills to prepare a student for an activity, teachers are introducing the real activity in real settings, and teaching necessary approximations. A recent example illustrates these two contrasting approaches.

A teacher in one school was describing to me a program to teach a student how to independently get on and off the school bus. She told me that they had stairs made up that were like the steps in the bus, and that each day they would practice walking up and down the stairs. I commented that the bus had the hand railing on the right side, but their stairs had the railing on the left side. I also noticed that the first step on the bus was much higher than the one in school and that the small opening in the bus appeared to be anxiety-provoking for the student. All of these differences could make the transition from the school stairs to the real bus more difficult. The teacher said that they could get the stairs modified to more closely approximate those of the bus. I then pointed out that they already had stairs that would be perfect—those on the bus. Why not teach the student to climb the bus steps in the minutes that were available at the end of the day while students were waiting to be picked up? Not only were the stairs exactly like those that the teacher wanted the student to master, but as a reward, the student could go home! One solution to problems of generalization and maintenance is to teach useful skills in the setting where you want the student to use the skill (e.g., on the bus), and with the people who will be present there (e.g., the bus driver).

Keeping the "Fun" in Functional

There is a clear and obvious trend away from teaching prerequisite skills in analogue-type settings to teaching useful or functional skills in real settings. As this emphasis continues, a new problem will emerge in our curricula. It is appropriate that we spend a great deal of time teaching our students skills that will assist them in becoming more independent. Yet, at the same time, we must balance these efforts with activities that are not only functional but also fun. Although this is not a concern that is specific to teaching functional skills, it is one that will require attention. Another example will illustrate this point.

This morning it was my turn to awaken our 6-year-old son at 6:30 a.m. Not being a "morning person," I would rather walk over hot coals than wake up that early in the morning. My son must sense this attitude in me, because my mornings with him are usually disastrous. He typically fights getting out of bed, fights getting dressed, fights washing, and so on. . . . In contrast, my wife's mornings with our son are usually quite pleasant. One clue to the differences in our early wake-up routine came one morning when I heard my wife telling my son knock-knock jokes. They teased each other for about 5 minutes before she announced, "Ok, time to get dressed," in a cheery tone of voice. With that vignette in mind, this morning I went into my son's room saying in a soft sing-song voice, "Who's the sleepiest person in the house—I am." A little smirk came across his face, and after a few repetitions, he was answering, "No, I am" with a big smile. The rest of the morning was both productive (he got off to school on time) and fun.

Too often, many good teachers are pressured into teaching so many useful skills in such a short amount of time that they forget that the *process* should be enjoyable. Parents, too, complain that efforts to make them better parent trainers sometimes interfere with the more enjoyable aspects of being a family. The challenge for our field will be to design environments that teach functional skills within a context that encourages play, humor, and friendship. It will be important to keep the *fun* in functional.

Language/Communication Instruction

One area of education that is extremely important for students with autism is the domain of language and communication. A gross deficit in language development is a defining characteristic of individuals with autism. Approximately half of the persons labeled with autism are mute (Lovaas, 1977) and never acquire useful speech (Rutter, 1978). Of those with some speech, much of their communication is unusual in nature (Lovaas, Ackerman, & Taubman, 1983). Language deficits can be seen as pivotal to the problems experienced by persons with autism because they are correlated with an unfavorable prognosis (Lotter, 1978; Rutter, 1968) and may contribute to problems in socialization. The remediation of language deficits therefore has received much attention.

There is voluminous literature on language training for students with autism (e.g., Baer & Guess, 1971; Garcia, Guess, & Byrnes, 1973; Guess,

Sailor, & Baer, 1978; Guess, Sailor, Rutherford, & Baer, 1968; Lovaas, Freitas, Nelson, & Whalen, 1967; Stevens-Long & Rasmussen, 1974). Unfortunately, this apparent success in teaching language has not been achieved in all children. Some children make limited progress despite intensive behavioral intervention (Mack, Webster, & Gokcen, 1980). For them, recent work has focused on alternatives to vocal speech (Guess, 1980; Sailor et al., 1980). Although most of the controlled research on these alternatives has been with the use of sign language (Carr, 1982), there are problems of generalization. Specifically, community members are often unfamiliar with sign language and therefore cannot successfully interact with these students. In addition, the signs made by many students are frequently idiosyncratic, and are difficult to understand by even experienced teachers (Durand, 1990).

One alternative to both spoken and signed speech is the use of augmentative communication systems (Baumgart, Johnson, & Helmstetter, 1990). These systems are formal or informal strategies that assist communication efforts instead of or in addition to spoken speech. These strategies have included using communication boards that require students to point to pictures (Rotholz, Berkowitz, & Burberry, 1989; Mirenda, 1985), vocal output devices that use synthesized speech (Mirenda & Beukelman, 1987), and a variety of other adaptations (Mathy-Laikko et al., 1989).

As alluded to previously, a limitation of previous work is that even though we have demonstrated the ability to teach signs and symbolic forms of communication to persons with severe communicative disabilities, it is not clear that individuals in the community will be able to understand these forms of communication. For example, few individuals in most communities are familiar enough with sign language to understand even basic requests. In addition, many symbolic communication systems are not easily recognized by those in the community (Calculator & Dollaghan, 1982). And, if individuals do not respond to the requests of these students, the applicability of such an intervention approach for community settings is limited.

Vocal output systems have several advantages. Most importantly, others may be more likely to respond to vocal output devices over communication boards. Calculator and Dollaghan (1982), for example, have noted that less than two thirds of the initiations made by students with communication boards are responded to by adults. A variety of vocal output devices have been used recently to promote effective communication among persons with profound or multiple handicaps. For example, Wacker, Wiggins, Fowler, and Berg (1988) recently demonstrated the ability to teach students with profound handicaps to use assistive devices to request toys, social attention, and specific requests. Although research with children having autism is limited, the application of augmentative communication systems to communication training should prove to be a valuable new trend for this group (Reichle & Karlan, 1985; Reichle, Sigafoos, & Piche, 1989).

In addition to occasionally failing to teach speech to children, behavioral procedures have been criticized for not producing language that is used by children to communicate spontaneously with others. For example, a child might be taught to respond to the phrase "What do you want?" with the word, sign, or by pointing to a picture of "soda." However, he or she would probably not spontaneously and appropriately request soda without the prompt. A recent trend in language training research addresses this issue of language use. Hart and Risley (1980) developed a set of "incidental teaching" procedures that have helped language-delayed children to communicate with others more spontaneously. Incidental teaching occurs in the natural context (e.g., in the kitchen, at a shopping mall) and with a variety of relevant persons (e.g., teacher, parents, peers). Teaching episodes are initiated by the child and are encouraged through reinforcers related to the topic of discussion (i.e., "natural" reinforcers). Recent work has begun to apply these procedures with children with autism, with encouraging results (Carr & Kologinsky, 1983; Koegel, O'Dell, & Koegel, 1987). As with other areas of instruction, efforts to teach communication will tend to move away from using simulated settings, tasks, and consequences toward using those aspects of the prevailing environment that are relevant to the skills being taught.

Socialization

Disruption in the development of social relationships is a distinctive feature of autism (Kanner, 1943). In fact, what is most striking to a first-time observer is that some persons with autism appear to treat other people with no more deference than, say, a piece of furniture. Several trends are evident in the teaching of social skills. Recent studies have used nonhandicapped peers as treatment agents. Ragland, Kerr, and Strain (1978) used an age-matched peer to increase social interactions among three children with autism. The peer trainer was successful in increasing the frequency of a variety of rudimentary social behaviors in these children (e.g., touching, hugs, sharing toys). However, both this and a subsequent study (Strain, Kerr, & Ragland, 1979) were unsuccessful in producing social responses that were produced in settings other than the training setting, or with persons other than the trainer.

The previous work describes one approach to increasing social skills—peer initiation training (Strain, 1977). A different approach has been recently explored, one that teaches students with disabilities to initiate interactions themselves. For example, Gaylord-Ross, Haring, Breen, and

Pitts-Conway (1984) employed a variation of multiple exemplar training (i.e., using a number of peer trainers) and found that their subjects generalized trained social responses to other nonhandicapped peers. Haring and Lovinger (1989) taught students with disabilities to initiate interactions and to play appropriately, and observed increases in appropriate social interactions. These studies suggest that a number of social behaviors can be taught to persons with autism and that training may be carried out with the use of peers. However, effective training may have to involve *both* the nonhandicapped peer and the student with autism. Future work in this area may focus on training of both members of the dyad.

Choice

Recent research in the area of choice should have a profound and widespread effect on the way students with autism are treated. It is recognized that not all students have the skills to make meaningful choices, and some workers have explored ways to teach choice making (Datillo, 1986; Green et al., 1988; Parsons & Reid, 1990). Although only in its infancy, this research has explored the effects of providing choice to these students in a number of areas. For example, providing choices has been observed to improve social behavior (e.g., Koegel, Dyer, & Bell, 1987; Peck, 1985) and challenging behavior (e.g., Dyer, Dunlap, & Winterling, 1990). Despite these positive early findings, there are institutional obstacles in many programs that interfere with efforts to increase choice (Bannerman, Sheldon, Sherman, & Harchik, 1990; Guess & Siegel-Causey, 1985). The following description illustrates some of these obstacles.

Several weeks ago, a director of a program for students with autism was discussing problems some of his pupils were having at lunchtime. Students had to constantly be prompted to eat and many times they would become extremely disruptive if teachers kept persisting. Lunchtime had become quite unpleasant and the disruption seemed to negatively affect the rest of the day. The program director was discussing the possibility of letting the students choose—on their own—what they wanted to eat and how much they should eat. Although he felt that it couldn't be worse than what was going on now, he reported that the staff felt this was just "giving in" and resisted his efforts. They had been well-trained in how to control almost every aspect of the students' day, and this suggestion ran counter to their training. I told him that giving the children more choices in this situation would probably solve many of the lunchtime problems and at the same time would encourage more independence. One month after the change, mealtime was no longer a major problem, and the students were eating adequate lunches.

The move to provide students with more choice will be a difficult one.

Research in this area suggests that many settings do not currently allow even the most basic choices to be made by those most affected (Kishi, Teelucksingh, Zollers, Park-Lee, & Meyer, 1988). Turning more control over to students will require a "leap of faith" on the part of some, and will need to be planned into curricula and daily activities. The results of making these efforts, however, appear to be significant.

MEANINGFUL OUTCOMES

A great deal of progress has been made in the education of students with autism. Again, the chapters in this book highlight the tremendous strides made in the last few decades. Yet, despite our accomplishments, it may be useful to reflect on these accomplishments and their impact on the lives of our students. Here the question becomes, "Have these advances resulted in *meaningful* changes in our students?" Finding solutions to this question will prove to be the most difficult challenge facing educators in the next decade.

As described previously, investigators have succeeded in teaching children to engage in a variety of communicative/social behaviors. Yet, interpretation of these results should be viewed with caution. What has yet to be demonstrated is that significant others view these behavioral increases as important. In other words, some measure of the social validity (Voeltz & Evans, 1983; Wolf, 1978) of the effects of this training is needed. For example, are nonhandicapped peers more likely to accept children with autism following social skills training? Will they initiate significant contacts outside of the training contexts (e.g., invitations to parties, choosing them on sports teams)? This issue is particularly important in light of recent findings with learning disabled children. Social skills training with these children does not always result in increased acceptance by classmates (Berler, Gross, & Drabman, 1982). Thus, it seems likely that special efforts may be necessary to produce important changes in the social repertoire of children with more severe disabilities, such as those with autism.

One approach to insuring the social acceptability of our outcomes is appropriate selection of responses as targets for training. For example, hugging may not be appropriate as a first response to teach adolescents who interact with other high school students. Selection of appropriate targets should probably involve persons likely to interact with trainees. These "significant others" may be able to identify the behaviors needed to be accepted by a particular social group. Future research in this area should address the issue of social validity of both the effects and targets of skills training. This emphasis is necessary in order to demonstrate clinically significant results from efforts to improve these childrens' skills.

SUMMARY

I have attempted to identify in this chapter new directions in educational programming. Trends were observed in a variety of areas that may have a profound impact on the way students with autism are taught in the future. Most importantly, pervasive change will result from the continued integration efforts in our schools. This move toward total inclusion (with the accompanying emphasis on providing choice and functional skills training) should influence almost every aspect of the educational process. And, it is anticipated that with proper support, these changes will go a long way toward making meaningful changes in the lives of our students. With the many advances being made in almost all aspects of instruction, there is room for great optimism in the future of education for students with autism.

REFERENCES

Alpern, G. D. (1967). Measurement of "untestable" autistic children. *Journal of Abnormal Psychology, 72,* 478–486.

Anastasi, A. (1968). *Psychological testing* (3rd ed.). New York: Macmillan.

Baer, D. M., & Guess, D. (1971). Receptive training of adjectival inflections in mental retardates. *Journal of Applied Behavior Analysis, 4,* 129–139.

Bailey, D. B., & Wolery, M. (1989). *Assessing infants and preschoolers with handicaps.* Columbus: Merrill.

Bannerman, D. J., Sheldon, J. B., Sherman, J. A., & Harchik, A. E. (1990). Balancing the right to habilitation with the right to personal liberties: The rights of people with developmental disabilities to eat too many doughnuts and take a nap. *Journal of Applied Behavior Analysis, 23,* 79–89.

Baumgart, D., Johnson, J., & Helmstetter, E. (1990). *Augmentative and alternative communication systems for persons with moderate and severe disabilities.* Baltimore: Paul H. Brookes.

Berler, E. S., Gross, A. M., & Drabman, R. S. (1982). Social skills training with children: Proceed with caution. *Journal of Behavior Analysis, 15,* 41–53.

Brown, L., Ford, A., Nisbet, J., Sweet, M., Donnellan, A., & Gruenewald, L. (1983). Opportunities available when severely handicapped students attend chronological age appropriate regular schools. *Journal of The Association for Persons with Severe Handicaps, 8,* 16–24.

Brown, L., Long, E., Udvari-Solner, A., Davis, L., VanDeventer, P., Ahlgren, C., Johnson, F., Gruenewald, L., & Jorgensen, J. (1989). The home school: Why students with severe intellectual disabilities must attend the schools of their brothers, sisters, friends, and neighbors. *Journal of The Association for Persons with Severe Handicaps, 14,* 1–7.

Brown, L., Long, E., Udvari-Solner, A., Schwartz, P., VanDeventer, P., Ahlgren, C., Johnson, F., Gruenewald, L., & Jorgensen, J. (1989). Should students with severe intellectual disabilities be based in regular or special education classrooms in home schools. *Journal of The Association for Persons with Severe Handicaps, 14,* 3–12.

Calculator, S., & Dollaghan, C. (1982). The use of communication boards in a residential setting. *Journal of Speech and Hearing Disorders, 14,* 281–287.

Carr, E. G. (1982). Sign language acquisition: Clinical and theoretical aspects. In R. L. Koegel, A. Rincover, & A. L. Egel (Eds.), *Educating and understanding autistic children* (pp. 142–157). San Diego: College-Hill Press.

Carr, E. G., & Kologinsky, E. (1983). Acquisition of sign language by autistic children: II. Spontaneity and generalization effects. *Journal of Applied Behavior Analysis, 16,* 297–314.

Chess, S., Korn, S. J., & Fernandez, P. B. (1971). *Psychiatric disorders of children with congenital rubella.* New York: Brunner/Mazel.

Dattilo, J. (1986). Computerized assessment of preference for severely handicapped individuals. *Journal of Applied Behavior Analysis, 19,* 445–448.

DeMyer, M. K. (1976). Motor, perceptual-motor, and intellectual disabilities of autistic children. In L. Wing (Ed.), *Early childhood autism* (2nd ed., pp. 169–193). Oxford: Pergamon.

DeMyer, M. K., Barton, S., Alpern, G. D., Kimberlin, C., Allen, J., & Steele, R. (1974). The measured intelligence of autistic children. *Journal of Autism and Childhood Schizophrenia, 4,* 42–60.

DeMyer, M. K., Barton, S., DeMeyer, W. E., Norton, J. A., Allen, J., & Steele, R. (1973). Prognosis in autism: A follow-up study. *Journal of Autism and Childhood Schizophrenia, 3,* 199–246.

Durand, V. M. (1990). *Severe behavior problems: A functional communication training approach.* New York: Guilford Press.

Durand, V. M., & Carr, E. G. (1988). Autism. In V. B. VanHasselt, P. S. Strain, & M. Hersen (Eds.), *Handbook of developmental and physical disabilities* (pp. 195–214). New York: Pergamon Press.

Durand, V. M., & Carr, E. G. (1991). Functional communication training to reduce challenging behavior: Maintenance and application in new settings. *Journal of Applied Behavior Analysis, 24,* 251–264.

Durand, V. M., & Crimmins, D. B. (1988). Identifying the variables maintaining self-injurious behavior. *Journal of Autism and Developmental Disorders, 18,* 99–117.

Dyer, K., Dunlap, G., & Winterling, V. (1990). Effects of choice making on the serious problem behaviors of students with severe handicaps. *Journal of Applied Behavior Analysis, 23,* 515–524.

Evans, I. M. (1990). Testing and diagnosis: A review and evaluation. In L. H. Meyer, C. A. Peck, & L. Brown (Eds.), *Critical issues in the lives of people with severe disabilities* (pp. 25–44). Baltimore: Brookes.

Garcia, E., Guess, D., & Byrnes, J. (1973). Development of syntax in a retarded girl using imitation, reinforcement, and modeling. *Journal of Applied Behavior Analysis, 6,* 299–310.

Gaylord-Ross, R., & Browder, D. (1990). Functional assessment: Dynamic and domain properties. In L. H. Meyer, C. A. Peck, & L. Brown (Eds.), *Critical issues in the lives of people with severe disabilities* (pp. 45–66). Baltimore: Brookes.

Gaylord-Ross, R. J., Haring, T. G., Breen, C., & Pitts-Conway, V. (1984). The training and generalization of social interaction skills with autistic youth. *Journal of Applied Behavior Analysis, 17,* 229–247.

Gillberg, C. (1984). Infantile autism and other childhood psychoses in a Swedish urban region: Epidemiological aspects. *Journal of Child Psychology and Psychiatry, 25,* 35–43.

Gold, M. W. (1976). Task analysis of a complex assembly task by the retarded child. *Exceptional Children, 43,* 78–84.

Green, C. W., Reid, D. H., White, L. K., Halford, R. C., Brittain, D. P., & Gardner, S. M. (1988). Identifying reinforcers for persons with profound handicaps: Staff opinion versus systematic assessment of preferences. *Journal of Applied Behavior Analysis, 21,* 31–43.

Guess, D. (1980). Methods in communication instruction for severely handicapped persons. In W. Sailor, B. Wilcox, & L. Brown (Eds.), *Methods of instruction for severely handicapped students* (pp. 195–225). Baltimore: Brookes.

Guess, D., Mulligan-Ault, M., Roberts, S., Struth, J., Siegel-Causey, E., Thompson, B., Bronicki, G. J. B., & Guy, B. (1988). Implications of biobehavioral states for the education and treatment of students with the most profoundly handicapping conditions. *Journal of The Association for Persons with Severe Handicaps, 13,* 163–174.

Guess, D., Sailor, W., & Baer, D. M. (1978). *Functional speech and language training for the severely handicapped.* Lawrence, KS: H & H Enterprises.

Guess, D., Sailor, W., Rutherford, G., & Baer, D. M. (1968). An experimental analysis of linguistic development: The procedure use of the plural morpheme. *Journal of Applied Behavior Analysis,* 1, 297–306.

Guess, D., & Siegel-Causey, E. (1985). Behavioral control and education of severely handicapped students: Who's doing what to whom? and why? In D. Bricker & J. Fier (Eds.), *Severe mental retardation: From theory to practice* (pp. 230–244). Reston, VA: The Council for Exceptional Children.

Haring, T. G., & Lovinger, L. (1989). Promoting social interaction through teaching generalized play initiation responses to preschool children with autism. *Journal of The Association for Persons with Severe Handicaps, 14,* 58–67.

Hart, B., & Risley, T. R. (1980). In vivo language intervention: Unanticipated general effects. *Journal of Applied Behavior Analysis, 13,* 407–432.

Hoy, M. P., & Retish, P. M. (1984). A comparison of two types of assessment reports. *Exceptional Children, 51,* 225–229.

Johnson, S. M., & Bolstad, O. D. (1973). Methodological issues in naturalistic observations: Some problems and solutions for field research. In L. A. Hamerlynck, L. C. Handy, & E. J. Mash (Eds.), *Behavior change: Methodology, concepts, and practice* (pp. 7–67). Champaign, IL: Research Press.

Kanner, L. (1943). Autistic disturbances of affective contact. *Nervous Child, 2,* 217–250.

Keogh, B. K. (1972). Psychological evaluation of exceptional children: Old hangups and new directions. *Journal of School Psychology, 10,* 141–145.

Kishi, G., Teelucksingh, B., Zollers, N., Park-Lee, S., & Meyer, L. (1988). Daily decision-making in community residences: A social comparison of adults with and without mental retardation. *American Journal of Mental Retardation, 92,* 430–435.

Koegel, R. L., Dyer, K., & Bell, L. K. (1987). The influence of child-preferred activities on autistic children's social behavior. *Journal of Applied Behavior Analysis, 20,* 243–252.

Koegel, R. L., O'Dell, M. C., & Koegel, L. K. (1987). A natural language teaching paradigm for nonverbal autistic children. *Journal of Autism and Developmental Disorders, 17,* 187–200.

Krug, D. A., Arick, J. R., & Almond, P. J. (1980). *Autism screening instrument for educational planning* (ASIEP). Portland, OR: ASIEP Education.

Lotter, V. (1974). Factors related to outcome in autistic children. *Journal of Autism and Childhood Schizophrenia, 4,* 263–277.

Lotter, V. (1978). Follow-up studies. In M. Rutter & E. Schopler (Eds.), *Autism: A reappraisal of concepts and treatment* (pp. 475–495). New York: Plenum.

Lovaas, O. I. (1977). *The autistic child: Language development through behavior modification.* New York: Irvington.

Lovaas, O. I. (1987). Behavioral treatment and normal educational and intellectual functioning in young autistic children. *Journal of Consulting and Clinical Psychology, 55,* 3–9.

Lovaas, O. I., Ackerman, A. B., & Taubman, M. T. (1983). An overview of behavioral treatment of autistic persons. In M. Rosenbaum, C. M. Franks, & Y. Jaffe (Eds.), *Perspectives on behavior therapy in the eighties* (pp. 287–308). New York: Springer.

Lovaas, O. I., Freitas, L., Nelson, K., & Whalen, C. (1967). The establishment of imitation and its use for the development of complex behavior schizophrenic children. *Behavior Research and Therapy, 5,* 171–181.

Mack, J. E., Webster, C. D., & Gokcen, I. (1980). Where are they now and how are they faring? Follow-up of 51 severely handicapped speech-deficient children, 4 years after an operant-based program. In C. D. Webster, M. M. Konstantareas, J. Oxman, & J. E. Mack (Eds.), *Autism: New directions in research and education* (pp. 93–106). New York: Pergamon.

Mathy-Laikko, P., Iacono, T., Ratcliff, A., Villarruel, F., Yoder, D., & Vanderheiden, G. (1989). Teaching a child with multiple disabilities to use a tactile augmentative communication device. *Augmentative and Augmentative Communication, 5,* 249–256.

Meyer, L. H., & Putnam, J. (1989). Social integration. In V. B. VanHasselt, P. S. Strain, & M. Hersen (Eds.), *Handbook of developmental and physical disabilities* (pp. 107–133). New York: Pergamon Press.

Mirenda, P. (1985). Designing pictorial communication systems for physically able-bodied students with severe handicaps. *Augmentative and Alternative Communication, 1,* 58–64.

Mirenda, P., & Beukelman, D. R. (1987). A comparison of speech synthesis intelligibility with listeners from three age groups. *Augmentative and Alternative Communication, 3,* 120–128.

Nelson, R. O., & Hayes, S. C. (1979). Some current dimensions of behavioral assessment. *Behavioral Assessment, 1,* 1–16.

Nordquist, V. M., & Wahler, R. G. (1973). Naturalistic treatment of an autistic child. *Journal of Applied Behavior Analysis, 6,* 79–87.

Ornitz, E. M. (1978). Biological homogeneity or heterogeneity? In M. Rutter & E. Schopler (Eds.), *Autism: A reappraisal of concepts and treatment* (pp. 243–250). New York: Plenum.

Parsons, M. B., & Reid, D. H. (1990). Assessing food preferences among persons with profound mental retardation: Providing opportunities to make choices. *Journal of Applied Behavior Analysis, 23,* 183–195.

Peck, C. A. (1985). Increasing opportunities for social control by children with autism and severe handicaps: Effects on student behavior and perceived classroom climate. *Journal of the Association for the Severely Handicapped, 10,* 183–193.

Peck, C. A. (1990). Linking values and science in social policy decisions affecting citizens with severe disabilities. In L. H. Meyer, C. A. Peck, & L. Brown (Eds.), *Critical issues in the lives of people with severe disabilities* (pp. 1–15). Baltimore: Brookes.

Powers, M. D., & Handleman, J. S. (1984). *Behavioral assessment of severe developmental disabilities.* Rockville, MD: Aspen.

Ragland, E. U., Kerr, M. M., & Strain, P. S. (1978). Behavior of withdrawn autistic children: Effects of peer social interactions. *Behavior Modification, 2,* 565–578.

Reichle, J., & Karlan, G. (1985). The selection of an augmentative system in communication intervention: A critique of decision rules. *Journal of the Association for Persons with Severe Handicaps, 10,* 146–156.

Reichle, J., Sigafoos, J., & Piche, L. (1989). Teaching an adolescent with blindness and severe disabilities: A correspondence between requesting and selecting preferred objects. *Journal of The Association for Persons with Severe Handicaps, 14,* 75–80.

Ritvo, E. R., Rabin, K., Yuwiler, A., Freeman, B. J., & Geller, E. (1978). Biochemical and hematologic studies: A critical review. In M. Rutter & E. Schopler (Eds.), *Autism: A reappraisal of concepts and treatment* (pp. 163–183). New York: Plenum.

Rosenbloom, S., Campbell, M., George, A. E., Kricheff, I. I., Taleporos, E., Anderson, L., Rueben, R. N., & Korein, J. (1984). High resolution CT scanning in infantile autism: A quantitative approach. *Journal of the American Academy of Child Psychiatry, 23,* 72–77.

Rotholz, D. A., Berkowitz, S. F., & Burberry, J. (1989). Functionality of two modes of communication in the community by students with developmental disabilities: A comparison of signing and communication books. *Journal of The Association for Persons with Severe Handicaps, 14,* 227–233.

Rutter, M. (1968). Concepts of autism: A review of research. *Journal of Child Psychology and Psychiatry, 9,* 1–25.

Rutter, M. (1978). Diagnosis and definition of childhood autism. *Journal of Autism and Childhood Schizophrenia, 8,* 139–161.

Rutter, M., & Lockyer, V. (1967). A 5–15 year follow-up study of infantile psychosis: I. Description of sample. *British Journal of Psychiatry, 113,* 1169–1182.

Sacks, O. (1987). *The man who mistook his wife for a hat.* New York: Harper Perennial.

Sailor, W., Guess, D., Goetz, L., Schuler, A., Utley, B., & Baldwin, M. (1980). Language and severely handicapped persons: Deciding what to teach to whom. In W. Sailor, B. Wilcox, & L. Brown (Eds.), *Methods of instruction for severely handicapped students* (pp. 71–105). Baltimore: Brookes.

Sattler, J. M. (1982). *Assessment of children's intelligence and specific abilities* (2nd ed.). Boston: Allyn Bacon.

Scheerenberger, R. C. (1983). *A history of mental retardation.* Baltimore: Brookes.

Skrtic, T. M. (1987). An organizational analysis of special education reform. *Counterpoint, 8,* 15–19.

Staats, A. W. (1975). *Social behaviorism.* Homewood, IL: The Dorsey Press.

Stevens-Long, L., & Rasmussen, M. (1974). The acquisition of simple and compound sentence structure in an autistic child. *Journal of Applied Behavior Analysis, 7,* 473–479.

Strain, P. S. (1977). An experimental analysis of peer social initiations on the behavior of withdrawn preschool children: Some training and generalization effects. *Journal of Abnormal Child Psychology, 6,* 203–209.

Strain, P. S., Kerr, M. M., & Ragland, E. V. (1979). Effects of peer-mediated social initiations and prompting/reinforcement procedures on the social behavior of autistic children. *Journal of Autism and Developmental Disorders, 9,* 41–54.

Stubbs, E. G., Ash, E., & Williams, C. P. S. (1984). Autism and congenital cytomegalovirus. *Journal of Autism and Developmental Disorders, 14,* 183–189.

Taft, L. T., & Cohen, H. J. (1971). Hypsarrhythmia and infantile autism: A clinical report. *Journal of Autism and Childhood Schizophrenia, 1,* 327–336.

Thompson, B., Wickham, D., Shanks, P., Wegner, J., Ault, M. M., Reinertson, B., & Guess, D. (in press). Expanding the circle of inclusion: Integrating young children with severe multiple disabilities into Montessori classrooms. *Montessori Life.*

Voeltz, L. M., & Evans, I. M. (1983). Educational validity: Procedures to evaluate outcomes in programs for severely handicapped learners. *Journal of The Association for Persons with Severe Handicaps, 8,* 3–15.

Wacker, D. P., Wiggins, B., Fowler, M., & Berg, W. K. (1988). Training students with profound or multiple handicaps to make requests via microswitches. *Journal of Applied Behavior Analysis, 21,* 331–343.

Wolf, M. M. (1978). Social validity: The case for subjective measurement or how applied behavior analysis is finding its heart. *Journal of Applied Behavior Analysis, 11,* 203–214.

Wolf, M. M., Risley, T. R., & Mees, H. (1964). Application of operant conditioning procedures to the behavior problems of an autistic child. *Behavior Research and Therapy, 1,* 305–312.

Author Index

D

E

L

M

P

Q

R

S

Y

Z

Subject Index

A